Globalization and the American Century

ALFRED E. ECKES, JR.
Ohio University

THOMAS W. ZEILER
University of Colorado at Boulder

CAMBRIDGE
UNIVERSITY PRESS

PUBLISHED BY THE PRESS SYNDICATE OF THE UNIVERSITY OF CAMBRIDGE
The Pitt Building, Trumpington Street, Cambridge, United Kingdom

CAMBRIDGE UNIVERSITY PRESS
The Edinburgh Building, Cambridge CB2 2RU, UK
40 West 20th Street, New York, NY 10011-4211, USA
477 Williamstown Road, Port Melbourne, VIC 3207, Australia
Ruiz de Alarcón 13, 28014 Madrid, Spain
Dock House, The Waterfront, Cape Town 8001, South Africa

http:// www.cambridge.org

First published 2003

Printed in the United States of America

Typeface Sabon 10/13 pt.   *System* LATEX 2$_\varepsilon$ [TB]

A catalog record for this book is available from the British Library.

Library of Congress Cataloging in Publication Data
Eckes, Alfred E., 1942–
Globalization and the American century / Alfred E. Eckes, Jr., Thomas W. Zeiler.
p.   cm.
Includes bibliographical references and index.
Contents: Toward a new paradigm – Americanizing Britain's world, 1898–1913 –
Globalization in war and peace, 1914–1920 – Exporting the American dream,
1921–1929 – Business busted, diplomacy destroyed, 1929–1939 – Defending allies,
developing frontiers, 1939–1946 – Containing and consuming, 1947–1957 – Transforming
the world, 1958–1973 – Enduring the crises, 1973–1986 – Freedom and free trade,
1986–1995 – Folding the flag : globalization and the new millennium.
ISBN 0-521-80409-4 – ISBN 0-521-00906-5 (pb.)
1. United States – Foreign relations – 20th century.
2. Globalization – History – 20th century.   I. Zeiler, Thomas W.   II. Title.
E744 .E25   2003
327.73′009′04–dc21   2002031353

ISBN 0 521 80409 4 hardback
ISBN 0 521 00906 5 paperback

Contents

Introduction: Toward a New Paradigm

In the years since the end of the Cold War, globalization has emerged as both a buzzword and a defining theme of the new era. The term is new. Professor Theodore Levitt, a marketing professor at the Harvard Business School, apparently first employed it in a 1983 article in the *Harvard Business Review*.[1] But the underlying process has shaped the evolution of the "American Century," and the content and conduct of U.S. diplomacy, subjects of this book, for more than a hundred years.

Indeed, it is arguable that the basic concept has historical roots, extending back to the first explorers and traders, the predecessors of Christopher Columbus and Marco Polo. Defined broadly, globalization is the *process* of integrating nations and peoples – politically, economically, and culturally – into larger communities. In this broad sense, it is little different from internationalization. But we believe that globalization is much more than an incremental process that, over the centuries, has brought people and nations closer together as technological innovations dissolved barriers of time and distance, enhanced flows of information, and promoted greater awareness and understanding.

Globalization is also dynamic, transformational, and synergistic. The focus, as the term suggests, is not on nations but on the entire globe. Consequently, a more sophisticated definition might emphasize that contemporary globalization is a complex, controversial, and synergistic process in which improvements in technology (especially in communications and transportation) combine with the deregulation of markets and open borders to bring about vastly expanded flows of people, money, goods, services, and information. This process integrates people, businesses, nongovernmental organizations, and nations into larger

I

networks. Globalization promotes convergence, harmonization, efficiency, growth, and, perhaps, democratization and homogenization.
These all touch on U.S. diplomacy and have done so over the American
Century, which actually began in the late nineteenth century and extends
to the present.

Regarding diplomacy, globalization has had an impact on it in man-
ifold ways. Improvements in communications have accelerated flows of
information and images about America, its people, their life-styles, and
their values around the world. This was, incidentally, a major factor in
ending the Cold War. Advances in transportation have much expanded the
movements of government officials to and from Washington and given the
State Department some of the functions of a travel agency. The growing
importance of economic issues – involving flows of food, goods, services,
money, and information and the regulation of communications, aviation,
and corporate competition – has forced American foreign policy makers
to engage complex new issues. More and more specialized government
agencies, such as the Securities and Exchange Commission, the Federal
Communications Commission, the Federal Reserve, the Federal Bureau of
Investigation, the Department of Labor, and the Surgeon General, have
been compelled to address aspects of globalization and to become active participants in the diplomatic process. This book will touch on those
matters as well.

To its many modern critics, globalization has a dark side. It produces
economic and social dislocations and arouses public concerns over job
security, the distribution of economic gains, and the impact of volatility on families, investments, cultures, communities, and nations. Many
also worry about growing concentration of economic power, harm to
the environment, danger to public health and safety, the disintegration
of indigenous cultures, and the loss of sovereignty, accountability, and
transparency in government. These, too, are issues that have engaged
U.S. diplomats and officials involved with many functional dimensions of
foreign policy throughout the American Century.

The globalization process has several drivers – technological innovation, business competition, and evolving ideas about optimal public policy. Rapidly changing technologies for transportation and communications continue to dissolve the barriers of time, distance, and ignorance
that once complicated long-range relationships. In the twentieth century,
some of the most important technological innovations were aviation,
wireless radio, satellite communications, fiber-optic cables, personal computers, and, of course, the Internet. The private sector, oriented as it is to

making profits and acquiring market share, is another driving force. In a marketplace integrated by technology, big business takes the view that it has no choice but to think globally about sourcing its products and serving customers. Ideas also shape globalization – particularly the widespread belief among economists that free trade, private enterprise, and competitive markets promote efficiency and economic growth. Another set of ideas also influences the globalization process – the belief among international lawyers that harmonization of standards, rules, and legal systems, including the establishment of dispute-settlement mechanisms, is the most appropriate way to resolve conflicts among governments and private parties. The essence of this study, then, is how markets, technology, and ideas, the building blocks of globalization, have had an impact on American power, policy, and diplomatic conduct.

It is, of course, arguable that the globalization process has other independent drivers – such as demographics, natural resources and the environment, international political and economic instability, and national leadership.[2] In the history of the modern world, a rising population in less-developed areas frequently has triggered emigration to areas of economic opportunity, and this in turn has frequently produced a stream of remittances to family members who remained behind. Famine and malnourishment, as well as the need for energy and industrial raw materials to support advanced economies, also affect the globalization process, promoting greater flows of materials, food, and goods, thus enhancing the interdependence of people and economies. And, it is arguable that two world wars, the Cold War, and the Great Depression disrupted in significant ways the ongoing globalization process through much of the twentieth century. Finally, leadership is an important element of all human activity. Had the United States, as the world's leading economic and military power in the twentieth century, not committed its public policy to promoting an open, and nondiscriminatory, international economic system, it is quite possible that the globalization process would have taken a different course – perhaps one that gave priority to regional blocs centered in Washington, London, Berlin, or Brussels, and perhaps Tokyo or Beijing.

In this book, we begin with the premise that the history of America's foreign relations can productively be viewed within the context of globalization. In this endeavor, our work builds on the efforts of many other scholars, within as well as beyond the historical profession. Scholars based in a variety of disciplines – including the social sciences, humanities, arts, business, and law – have made important contributions to the conceptualizations of globalization. Among historians the famous Wisconsin school of diplomatic historians advanced important insights.[3] To the extent that globalization means the expansion of trade and investments, it includes "economic expansion," a phrase historian David Pletcher employs to describe the transition from territorial expansion to the increasing internationalization of markets.[4] Commercial expansion has limited variants, which capture trade but not investments. In the aftermath of World War II, many writers proposed the phrase "economic internationalism" to suggest the growing interdependence of nations and the development of international institutions, such as the International Monetary Fund, the World Bank, and the General Agreement on Tariffs and Trade, the forerunner of the World Trade Organization.

In our judgment, none of these phrases adequately captures the full extent of what is called globalization. Along with flows of goods, services, and money, it is important to take into account the increasing international mobility of people, especially business professionals and skilled workers, and the emergence of large corporations that choose to view the world not as a series of interlinked national markets but as a single global market in which they can allocate resources, shift production, and market products. Declared Alfred Zein, the CEO of Gillette, "We treat the world as a single nation."[5] Some executives of transnational corporations view themselves as independent of national authority. Carl Gerstacker, the former chairman of Dow Chemicals, once confessed that he had "long dreamed of buying an island owned by no nation and of establishing the Dow's world headquarters on its truly neutral ground, beholden to no nation or society." The president of NCR, Gilbert Williamson, once said: "We at NCR think of ourselves as a globally competitive company that happens to be headquartered in the United States." "The United States does not have an automatic call on our resources. There is no mindset that puts this country first," Cyrill Siewert, chief financial officer of Colgate-Palmolive – which receives at least 30 percent of its total revenues from overseas sales – told the *New York Times*.[6]

Before the September 11, 2001, terrorist attacks on the New York World Trade Center and the Pentagon, it was fashionable to believe that the nation-state was disappearing. "Nation states," Kenichi Ohmae wrote, "are dinosaurs waiting to die." Some saw the multinational, or transnational, corporation as the agent of change.[7] Aurelio Peccei, a director of Fiat, asserted that the multinational corporation was "the most powerful agent for the internationalization of society." *Time* magazine columnist Strobe Talbott, a close friend of President Clinton and then a deputy U.S. secretary of state, effused: "I'll bet that within the next hundred years, nationhood as we know it will be obsolete; all states will recognize a single, global authority. A phrase briefly fashionable in the mid-20th century – 'citizen of the world' – will have assumed real meaning by the end of the 21st century."[8]

In explaining the emergence of globalization, it seems almost trite to observe that underlying forces of technology and economics have transformed the traditional nation-state system and compressed the once formidable barriers of time and space. The result, as business publications emphasize, is a single global market in which money, capital, and skilled workers move rapidly across national borders in response to impersonal decisions made by large global corporations and financiers. According to those who celebrate the new international economic order, globalization is inevitable and irreversible – something as revolutionary to world politics as was the breakdown of feudalism and the rise of the nation-state in the seventeenth century.

The authors of this work embrace a definition of globalization that takes into account not only the elements of economic expansion – including the mobility of labor, goods, and money – but also scientific and technological developments, popular culture, the Information Revolution, and concomitant political and institutional changes. Even though this book emphasizes the power of markets and technology, the authors reject narrow economic or technological determinism.[9] Also central to our interpretation is the spread of information, via mail, telegraph, telephones, satellites, computers, and the Internet. Alfred Chandler, Jr., and James Cortada have written a stimulating book about how Americans entered the "information highway" in colonial times and gradually developed technologies that expanded the reach of information across a continent and to the whole world.[10] This is an important, and less-well-understood, dimension of the globalization process.

Our study will follow the U.S. rise to world preeminence through the lens of globalization, and thereby offer a new interpretation of American diplomatic history. The interpretation both complements and criticizes economic determinism and challenges mainstream realists to consider economics as a driving force in diplomacy. We appreciate that U.S. foreign relations reflect a variety of concerns at various times, such as advancing national security, promoting national ideals, pursuing humanitarianism, and expanding markets. Our argument is that globalization encompasses all these priorities; it is an umbrella under which they can be grouped and explained in a coherent way. For too long, historians have neglected underlying economic and technological forces. We hope that our account moves the discussion of diplomacy and an understanding of American history forward to another level, one that considers business and technological influences, as well as an overarching framework that considers the phenomenon of globalization.

Next, we must say a few words about terminology. The term "globalization" apparently was first used in 1983, but it is apparent that the globalization process has a long history, dating back at least to the travels of Marco Polo and perhaps much farther back. From the first contacts and trade among human beings in different locations, the incremental globalization process – involving flows of money, goods, ideas, and people – began to integrate peoples and villages into larger communities, networks, and nations. Thus, we do not hesitate to use the term "globalization" to describe the process of integration from early in this century.

Interestingly, in the mid nineteenth century, Karl Marx and Frederick Engels wrote about this dynamic globalization process in the *Communist Manifesto* and sensed the potential for global turmoil and revolution. They credited the bourgeoisie for creating a

world market, given a cosmopolitan character to production and consumption in every country.... All old-established national industries have been destroyed or are daily being destroyed. They are dislodged by new industries,... whose products are consumed, not only at home, but in every quarter of the globe. In the place of the old wants, satisfied by the production of the country, we find new wants, requiring for their satisfaction the products of distant lands and climes. In place of the old local and national seclusion and self-sufficiency, we have intercourse in every direction, universal inter-dependence of nations.[11]

Marx and Engels also noted that "improved means of communication ... created by Modern Industry" was unifying the proletariat into a revolutionary class and preparing the way for the eventual overthrow of capitalism.

Except for the communists, few business and political leaders had a truly global outlook, one of a world without significant borders, until the 1980s. Few understood the synergies resulting from dramatic improvements in transportation and communications and the power of markets. Few understood how treating the world as a single marketplace both for sourcing and producing goods and for serving customers was transforming the marketplace. Like Marx and Engels, political leaders like William McKinley recognized that technological innovations in transportation and communications were transforming their environment and had the potential for changing the world. Alfred T. Mahan and Theodore Roosevelt also thought broadly and deeply about world events, and about the struggle for power among nations. But, their world was one of competing states and empires, in which governments communicated still through foreign ministries and diplomats. Ambassadors wore gloves, high hats, and long-tailed coats. This was not a wired world of long-haired geeks and instantaneous interactive communications. It was not the global village in which governments, businesses, and people communicated quickly with each other, using faxes, satellite communications, and e-mail. In this book, we do not hesitate to use the term "globalization" to describe the ongoing process and to identify individuals who began to think in global, as opposed to, international terms. Occasionally, we use other terms such as "cosmopolitan," "international," and "world" to avoid unnecessary use of "global" and confusion with the concept of "globalization." The globalization process has deep roots, but we believe strongly that the modern age of globalization did not arrive until the last quarter of the twentieth century. Parallel developments in technology, business, and public policy, as well as the end of the Cold War, permitted phenomenal synergies in the marketplace and weakened the hold of states on cross-border contacts.

Finally, we need to say a word about our division of labor. In the best sense of the phrase, this is a joint undertaking in which both authors drafted, commented on, and revised each other's work. We occasionally differed on interpretations, but the striking thing was the degree of consensus and our success in resolving minor disputes. Because of his work in the federal government with trade issues and his current teaching in the Ohio University Executive MBA program, Alfred Eckes initially focused on matters relating to the economic, business, and technological dimensions of globalization. Thomas Zeiler, whose teaching and research have been more oriented to diplomacy and foreign relations, and who is currently executive editor of the journal *Diplomatic History*, took the lead on issues of foreign policy and drafted many of the short personal profiles of key figures interspersed in the text. Both of us found the joint writing project extraordinarily stimulating, and the final product is like globalization, truly synergistic.

The authors wish to recognize the valuable contributions of many colleagues and students who interacted with the themes of this book. Tom Zeiler offers his appreciation to the Department of History and graduate students in his American Empire seminar at the University of Colorado and to the working group on globalization at the University of Toronto. Alfred Eckes thanks faculty and students in the Department of History and the Contemporary History Institute at Ohio University, as well as graduate students in his Executive MBA International Business seminar. James Waite, a history graduate student, provided invaluable assistance, commenting on the manuscipt and helping to prepare it for publication.

Both authors would also like to thank Sara Black, who carefully, and professionally, edited copy for Cambridge University Press.

I

Americanizing Britain's World, 1898–1913

As the American Century opened, a lean and ambitious Uncle Sam challenged a rotund John Bull for titular leadership of the world economy. The second phase of globalization had begun. American technology, trade, money, power, and ideas gradually transformed the international order. During World War I, the dynamic United States formally supplanted Great Britain as the principal proponent and guardian of globalization.

During the century of relative peace, from the defeat of Napoleon to the outbreak of World War I, the British dominated a loosely structured but dynamic Atlantic economy. Colonial areas in Africa and Asia supplied important raw materials and played a subordinate role in this first global system, which London managed. Britain's economic hegemony rested on its adherence to free trade, its open capital markets, and the international gold standard, as well as its dominance of sea lanes, merchant shipping, and communications. This extraordinary era of British economic leadership came to a close in the summer of 1914.

Uncle Sam's paradigm was somewhat different. It germinated before World War I and flowered in the 1920s and after World War II, evolving over the course of a turbulent century in response to shifting international conditions. Two world wars, a depression, and the Cold War distorted relationships. Like Britain, the United States sought to expand and liberalize international trade, open capital markets, and promote convertible currencies. It pursued a variety of business-friendly policies, including access to foreign markets for American goods, farm products, and services – such as films and television programs, protection for inventions and intellectual property, support for strategic technologies, and a rules-based international economic system. In such an open, and structured, environment,

1. "Free Trade England Wants the Earth," *Judge*, October 27, 1888. (Special Collections, Alden Library, Ohio University)

it was believed that entrepreneurs and inventors could thrive. Private enterprise could export, and produce abroad, the fruits of America's leadership in technology and intellectual property. People and ideas could move easily, facilitating the outward diffusion of America's political ideals and cultural values. Underlying this model was the belief in mutually beneficial interdependence. Proponents stated that America would gain, as would the rest of the world, from a more efficient utilization of resources, vigorous competition, and dynamic growth. At the turn of the century, America had little experience with leadership. The United States had erratically attempted to assert its influence abroad after the Civil War, mostly by commercial means rather than territorial conquest. This was the era of informal imperialism. U.S. investment and trade accompanied missionaries and, on occasion, military might into the Caribbean, Asia, and elsewhere. Fueled by nationalism, and a growing feeling of Darwinist superiority, the Americans expanded past their natural frontiers to markets abroad. During the period from 1870 to 1913, the United States grew at about twice the rate of Britain. By the 1890s, the United States had surpassed Britain as the world's leading industrial power, and its producers increasingly looked abroad to sell surplus production of manufactures, as well as surplus agriculture. In 1913, as Tables A.1 and A.2 in the appendix show, the United States had a per-capita gross domestic product of $5,307 compared to $5,032 for Britain.

To the poor of southern and eastern Europe, America was the land of opportunity, and about one million people on the average immigrated during the years from 1900 to 1914. Improvements in transportation helped explain the surge of people moving from Europe to the New World. Fast steamships dramatically reduced the cost and time of crossing the North Atlantic from a month in the early nineteenth century to about a week in 1900. Travel had become easier and cheaper for people as well as goods.[1]

Technological innovation was thus important to America's growth and to its strategy for penetrating world markets. The steamship, and engineering marvels like the Suez Canal, accelerated the flows of American goods around the world. Trans-Atlantic cables, the direct telegraph links to Latin America and connections through British cable to Asia, allowed U.S. investors and merchants to communicate faster abroad, thus expanding their markets. The great expositions of the age – in Chicago in 1893, Omaha in 1898, Buffalo three years later, and St. Louis in 1904, as well as later gatherings in West Coast cities – publicized American achievements and the promise of empire, which were based on progress in technology.[2]

Global networks shrunk the world itself by the 1890s, and the United States was poised to benefit as the American Century dawned.

Roots of the American Century

Business enthusiasm for American overseas expansion came from various industrial, agricultural, and service providers. Some such as the Singer Sewing Machine Company and the Otis Elevator Company introduced new products that satisfied consumer needs; others merely wanted to find markets for periodic gluts of commodities, like steel, cotton, tobacco, and wheat. Railroad builders, oilmen, agricultural machinery makers, and others moved into markets around the world – in Asia, Latin America, Europe, and Russia. The Americans went "over there" well before the First World War, and their business activities ranged from manufactures to agriculture and services such as insurance. Initially, the lack of federal support for international business was an impediment to expansion, but by the turn of the century the U.S. government had taken steps to become more supportive. It sponsored trade fairs to exhibit American wares and practices and finally began cleaning up the corrupt patronage system of the consular service. It is true that U.S. tariffs remained high, but more government officials stressed the need to export and urged Congress to reduce tariffs so as to gain improved access to foreign markets.[3]

Several other factors contributed to the emergence of more cosmopolitan thinking in America. These included the movement for a modern navy, the Spanish-American War, the open-door ideology, the rise of large corporations, and a changing domestic mood. At the outset of the American Century, the U.S. military expanded significantly; Americans let go of their cherished belief that a large, permanent standing army was a danger to the republic. Notably, the navy expanded and modernized, moving from defending the coastline to duty overseas, particularly in the Pacific and Caribbean. American shores were safe by this time; American commerce and territorial interests abroad were not. A coterie of politicians, shipbuilders, armaments manufacturers, merchants, and young naval officers determined to correct these weaknesses by modernizing the navy and thus allowing the United States to compete in the international game: imperialism. Captain Alfred T. Mahan, a most formidable military thinker on a global scale and an instructor at the Naval War College with truly world fame and influence (the Japanese, British, and Germans, among others, lauded his theories), argued that national power depended on sea power. America must build its navy to protect international economic interests, which would expand and thus require a larger fleet of warships. Sea power, he concluded, "is the center around which other events move, not it around them."[4]

By the early 1890s, the U.S. navy ranked seventh in the world, transformed from wooden boats to steel-plated, steam-driven hulls of an offshore battle fleet. Increasingly, the United States projected the use of its new naval muscle in support of its overseas interests. Naval vessels appeared off the coasts of Korea, Japan, and China; they carried troops ashore in Latin America; and they even raised America's credibility in European eyes regarding African affairs. The navy also gave the president, for the first time in U.S. history, the freedom to determine the pace of its quest for empire. This new navy was instrumental in America's first great international victory, against Spain.[5]

A product of the modernized navy, the battleship *Maine*, a second-class category ship with a new, off-center turret, was destroyed in Havana harbor in February 1898. This event quickened the momentum for a war to liberate Cuba and, as the U.S. imperialists of the day hoped, to acquire Caribbean possessions, a hemispheric canal route, and a strong presence in the Pacific. The new navy triumphed, its technological advantages apparent. The first-line battleship *Oregon*, at 10,288 tons and equipped with four 13-inch guns, steamed 14,700 miles from Puget Sound on the Pacific through the Straits of Magellan to Key West in sixty-eight days, arriving tardily in Cuba when war broke out. World responsibilities – in the Caribbean and the Philippines – steadily enlarged the Navy; by 1913, America had thirty-nine battleships either commissioned or authorized for construction. In comparison to the *Oregon*, the new *Pennsylvania* was three times its weight and carried twelve 14-inch guns. Military strategy hinged on defending America's Atlantic and Pacific flanks.

Naval power led to the annexation of Hawaii and to the conversion of the Caribbean into an American lake. These takings were not without their dissenters – it was not until World War II that Americans of various political stripes, backgrounds, and interests came to a consensus on expansion. Pursuit of these ambitions pointed to the need for more technological advances, such as the building of an isthmian canal that would speed transport and naval movement in the hemisphere.[6]

The Spanish-American War placed the United States at the fore of imperial powers, with a twist. America preferred to use economic power – backed by its navy and army – rather than formal military and bureaucratic mechanisms of colonial government to assert its dominance. President William McKinley's decision to annex Hawaii, for example, was supported by a host of outward-looking interests. Merchants and investors prospered from the sugar trade and eyed the islands as a stepping-stone to the Philippines and the dream of China market beyond. Missionaries hoped Hawaii could become "a base of operations for the enterprise of universal evangelization." And military strategists did not want it to fall into the hands of rival Germany. Likewise, the Philippines were important in military and economic senses, with China being the major focus as a target of investment and a buyer of surplus American production. However bitter the expansionist versus anti-imperialist debate, the facts were clear: holdings in the Pacific were profitable as exports soared. Above all, the United States increasingly looked outward, as economic expansion compelled a search for bases to renew fuel for the navy and merchant ships plying the oceans.[7]

The war with Spain catalyzed thinking about American commercial expansion. The government devised the Open Door doctrine to ensure nondiscriminatory access to markets abroad. Enunciated by President William McKinley's secretary of state, John Hay, the Open Door focused on preserving for U.S. business a piece of the commercial action in China, an empire that had been carved up into exclusive concessions by rapacious European and Japanese imperialists. To Hay, a former aide to Abraham Lincoln, the doctrine expressed faith in the workings of the market. That faith proved more important than the specific issue of rescuing China, which it was designed to address. The Americans went on record upholding certain fundamental principles that later became cornerstones of efforts to structure the global trading system for transnational business. These involved nondiscrimination at the border (most-favored-nation treatment, but not necessarily free trade), market access and national treatment within the host nation under certain conditions, and protection for intellectual property. These basic principles undergirded the American Century ahead. In effect, Hay's Open Door policy, and particularly the 1903 bilateral commercial treaty, foreshadowed later multilateral efforts to establish rules for the conduct of international business. The World Trade Organization is thus a lineal heir to the Open Door.[8]

The United States developed policies and institutions to support business expansion, but it also became better equipped internally to pursue big power status in the world economy. At the most basic level, the United States changed in the early twentieth century from a nation of villages and farmers guided by a faith in individualism and laissez-faire to one driven increasingly by the needs of large corporations and the concerns of individuals – particularly workers, farmers, and consumers.

2. "New Year's 1901: Century Race of Nations," *Judge*, January 5, 1901. (Special Collections, Alden Library, Ohio University)

The modern corporation arrived in the form of tremendous combinations. Mergers joined over 1,800 manufacturing firms into 157 consolidated entities and created unprecedentedly huge economies of "scale and scope." In 1903, these combinations were worth $7 billion, up from $1 billion six years before. Businessmen perfected management techniques that sought stabilization of the economy rather than exploitation. A culture of consumption – spurred by advertising that built a large middle class – nationalized the economy, instilled market ethics in economic relations, and irritated social critics who decried rampant materialism.

With modernization splintering society and alienating many workers, farmers, and consumers, the emerging middle class offered leadership to bring stability and order out of the chaos of economic and social change. The government bureaucracy expanded as progressives sought to use the powers of the federal government to regulate the marketplace. Progressives reshaped the public ethos into one of pragmatic reform combined with a faith in efficiently operated democracy. While some social critics disdained the predatory nature of a corporate America, most accepted the inevitability of economies of scale and professional management. The progressives generally looked for ways to reform big business, not return to the earlier agrarian era. The world had changed because of the second industrial revolution. Indeed, as an economist noted, "if the carboniferous age returned and the earth repeopled itself with dinosaurs, the change would scarcely seem greater than that made in the business world by these monster corporations."[9]

Liberal progressives railed, but corporate growth continued, both at home and abroad. Companies sent goods and investments, as well as trained personnel, into markets abroad, for profit and for self-preservation for, as John D. Rockefeller noted in 1899, by depending on local business, "we should have failed long ago."[10] Workers fought this juggernaut but more often compromised with the unstoppable force of corporate America. As they did so, America became ever more productive, and thus an even greater presence overseas. Incorporated into the workforce were immigrants from Europe, Asia, and elsewhere, who poured into factories and cities by the millions in search of wealth, opportunity, and freedom, and who manifested the growth of globalization.

McKinley and the American Century

Ironically, President William McKinley (1897–1901), a protectionist Republican from Ohio, presided over the transformation of America from a continental to an international power and charted the course for the American Century. He was the last U.S. president to fight in the Civil War and a public official who cut his political teeth on the prestigious House Ways and Means Committee, raising the tariff and protecting the American market. But like other successful leaders, McKinley was sensitive to change and adapted with the times. Speaking at the Pan American exposition in Buffalo on September 5, 1901, McKinley explained how technology and economics were transforming the world. In 1815, it had taken a government messenger nineteen days to carry news of the peace treaty with Britain from Washington, D.C., to General Andrew Jackson in New Orleans. In 1901, news about events and markets events traveled to the remotest parts of the earth in minutes. Improvements in transportation and communications – particularly the steam engine and the telegraph – had conquered the barriers of time and distance. "God and man have linked the nations together," he exclaimed, "No nation can longer be indifferent to any other."[11]

Perceiving that the period of national exclusiveness was past, McKinley sought to lay the foundation for business expansion under American leadership. Commercial wars were "unprofitable," McKinley said. He called for nations to adjust disputes in courts of arbitration and for the United States to take the lead in negotiating reciprocity treaties to expand trade. Trained as a lawyer, he gave presidential support to the international lawyers, who favored binding dispute resolution to resolve economic differences, long before nations established a mechanism to attain this end in the World Trade Organization (1995). He exhorted American support for an isthmian canal, a Pacific cable, and merchant marine. In effect, William McKinley, once considered the Hercules of protectionism, proposed that America take the lead in building the infrastructure and institutions to support the international expansion of business.[12]

McKinley, who was assassinated after his Buffalo speech, personified the optimism of a new era, one energized by technological change and business leadership. The year 1901 was one of such marvels. A 389-foot illuminated Electric Tower at the Pan American Exposition symbolized the age of electricity. In December, Italian inventor Guglielmo Marconi completed the first transatlantic radio transmission. Newspapers wrote optimistically about robotic factories and 150-mile-per-hour trains of the future. Wall Street financier J. P. Morgan merged several competing steel companies into the first billion-dollar corporation, U.S. Steel. McKinley's presidency, thus, marked several important milestones: a small step in chronology from one century to another; a significant transition in world leadership as Uncle Sam joined John Bull in pursuit of empire; and strong presidential support for expanding U.S. international business and finance.

During the McKinley administration, America, and the world, awoke to the emergence of a powerful new competitor in markets for manufactures. In 1900, Secretary of State John Hay chortled that "the United States is approaching, even more swiftly than was expected, a position of eminence in the world's markets."[13] Nonetheless, before World War I, America was not the leading trading power. The values of British and German exports both exceeded those of the United States. Nor, was America so tightly integrated into the evolving world economy as its European competitors. Viewed as a share of gross domestic product (GDP), U.S. exports in 1913 amounted to only 3.7 percent, compared with 17.7 percent for Britain, 15.6 percent in Germany, and 8.2 percent in France. Japan, incidentally, was less dependent on world markets; exports amounted to 2.4 percent of GDP.[14] Nonetheless, other data show that U.S. trade (exports plus imports) made up a higher share of national product in 1913 than during the half century from 1921 to 1970.[15] And, while European competitors generally imported raw materials and exported manufactures, the United States had become a diversified trader of primary products, semiprocessed goods, and manufactures by 1910. Cotton, tobacco, oil, and other raw materials and food accounted for 55 percent of U.S. exports. Nonetheless, there was a growing interdependence among nations in the North Atlantic region. British textile and footwear factories, for instance, relied on American cotton, leather, and machinery. As the auto age dawned, Europe was also heavily reliant on oil imports, and America was the world's leading petroleum exporter. See Table A.5 for U.S. trade patterns in the century from 1900 to 2000.

Made in America

One reason that the surge of American trade aroused so much comment was that, during the 1890s, European consumers fell in love with "ingenious American inventions" – including typewriters, sewing machines, phonographs, automobiles, telephones, elevators, and incandescent electric lights. These "admirably perfected machines" gave the United States a new reputation as an exporter of mass-produced consumer goods. Abroad, residents looked to the emerging colossus of the western hemisphere for state-of-the-art technology and quality products. Everywhere the trademark "Made in America" identified products of superior quality at affordable prices. The *English Daily Mail* reportedly observed that "there is hardly a work shop now of any importance in the world of the United Kingdom which does not use American tools and labor-saving devices."[16] Exports of these finished manufactures – particularly electrical products – nearly doubled in twenty years after 1890 – rising from 15.7 percent to 29.2 percent of all U.S. exports.[17]

One of the most successful exporters was a capital goods firm, the Baldwin Locomotive Works of Philadelphia, whose engines came to symbolize power, speed, and the march of civilization. In 1900, Baldwin exported an average of one engine a day. It shipped locomotives to South America, Africa, Asia, Australia, and Europe. Exports soared after its engines gained recognition for their speed and hauling weight up steep grades. At the turn of the twentieth century, Baldwins climbed Pikes Peak, hauled the Trans-Siberian Express, roamed the Argentine Pampas, and whistled past the Egyptian pyramids. In the British Empire, American firms won contracts for building railroad bridges in Uganda and supplying rails for construction of Cecil Rhodes's Cape to Cairo Railway, a project intended to develop British trade in Africa. Elsewhere, in the world's breadbaskets, Argentine, Australian, and Russian farmers used U.S. machinery to gather grain.[18]

Early in the twentieth century some Europeans worried about the American "invasion" and the "Americanization of the world." They complained that the North American "newcomers have acquired control of almost every new industry created during the past fifteen years." Fred Mackenzie, a British journalist, grumbled in 1900 about how dependent the typical Britisher had become on American products.

The average man rises in the morning from his New England sheets, he shaves with "Williams" soap and a Yankee safety razor, pulls on his Boston boots over his socks from North Carolina, fastens his Connecticut braces, slips his Waltham or Waterbury watch in his pocket, and sits down to breakfast. There he congratulates his wife on the way her Illinois straight-front corset sets off her Massachusetts blouse, and he tackles his breakfast, where he eats bread made from prairie flour (possibly doctored at the special establishments on the lakes), tinned oysters from Baltimore, and a little Kansas City bacon, while his wife plays with a slice of Chicago ox-tongue. The children are given "Quaker" oats. At the same time he reads his morning paper printed by American machines, on American paper, with American ink, and, possibly, edited by a smart journalist from New York City. He rushes out, catches the electric tram (New York) to Shepherd's Bush, where he gets in a Yankee elevator to take him on to the American-fitted electric railway to the City. At his office, of course, everything is American. He sits on a Nebraskan swivel chair, before a Michigan roll-top desk, writes his letters on a Syracuse typewriter, signing them with a New York fountain pen, and drying them with a blotting-sheet from New England. The letter copies are put away in files manufactured in Grand Rapids. At lunch-time he hastily swallows some cold roast beef that comes from the Mid-West cow, and flavors it with Pittsburgh pickles, followed by a few Delaware tinned peaches, and then soothes his mind with a couple of Virginia cigarettes. To follow his course all day would be wearisome. But when evening comes he seeks relaxation at the latest American musical comedy, drinks a cocktail or some Californian wine, and finishes up with a couple of "little liver pills" "made in America."[19]

Patent Protection

What accounted for the success of American manufactures in export markets? Several factors stand out. One was the extraordinary protection that the American government gave to patents and to intellectual property. "[T]he inventive faculty of Americans is the most dangerous weapon of this formidable competition," wrote Benjamin Thwaite, a British engineer. "Whilst our [British] soldiers and sailors are opening up new highways of commerce, the American by his ingenuity is producing machinery that will enable him to undersell the Briton in every market of the world." Thwaite called attention to the testimony of Patent Commissioner C. H. Duell to Congress: "I assert, without fear of contradiction, that we mainly owe to our patent system such foothold as we have gained (during the past fifty years) in foreign lands for our manufactured goods."[20]

The U.S. patent system did spur invention. Article I, Paragraph 8, of the Constitution gave Congress the power "to promote the progress of science and the useful arts by securing for limited times to authors and inventors the exclusive rights to their respective writings and discoveries." President George Washington recognized the need to build up a diversified economic base, and he urged Congress in 1790 to move speedily to reward inventors. As a result, Congress enacted a statute granting letter patents to inventors for fourteen-year terms. It was amended in 1861 to provide a nonrenewable seventeen-year term. The United States thus became one of the first countries to grant inventors a monopoly as a reward for their inventions. Many of the products that transformed the international workplace and the lives of people in the early twentieth century were developed with American patent protection. These included the telephone (Alexander Graham Bell, 1876), the phonograph (Thomas Edison, 1878), incandescent lamp (Edison, 1880), aluminum (Charles Hall, 1889), and linotype (Ottmar Mergenthaler, 1890), as well as the

typewriter (multiple inventors, 1870) and pyroxyline, the basis of the celluloid industry (multiple inventors, 1870). Wilbur and Orville Wright,
bicycle mechanics from Dayton, Ohio, obtained a patent for their "flying
machine" in May 1906. The number of U.S. patents doubled from 1870 to
1900 – rising from 13,313 to 26,499. Approval of the 1883 Paris Convention on Industrial Property permitted citizens of the signatory countries
to file for protection within twelve months and the effective date of application was the date of the original application. However, until 1907,
British law contained a loophole. It allowed a foreigner, like Edison, to
take out a patent but not work it in the United Kingdom.[21]

The U.S. patent system also facilitated accumulation of great fortunes
for individual inventors. For America as a nation, this form of protectionism produced the labor-saving inventions that enabled it to conquer world
markets, despite higher wages. Technological leadership fueled overseas
expansion of U.S. business. Mira Wilkins, a leading scholar of multinational enterprises, observed that before 1914, "the U.S. companies
with novel products and farsighted leadership came to make the most
far-ranging entries into foreign lands."[22] These included General Electric, National Cash Register, Otis Elevator, Eastman Kodak, United Shoe
Machinery, and Ford, among others. Their expansion in the first years
of the twentieth century also coincided with business restructuring and
the emergence of large cartels. A good example involved electrical motors, which contained many parts and depended on a plethora of patents
covering generating, transmitting, and switching equipment. An understandable desire to simplify access to the relevant patents seems to have
been the major reason for Edison General Electric and Thomson-Houston
combining in 1892 to become General Electric. In 1896, General Electric
and its rival Westinghouse signing an industry-wide cross-licensing agreement for patents.[23]

Strategy and Structures

Another important reason for the American invasion of Europe related to
management practices and business structures. In Britain, small family-
based manufacturing firms predominated at the turn of the century, and
many lacked professional managers, the capital, and other resources for
international expansion. Indeed, some economic historians argue that the
city of London, run by "gentlemanly capitalists," was more interested in
exporting capital than in supporting domestic industry. This was not the
case in the United States, where the growth of a vast continental market

transformed the structures and strategies of firms. Large corporations with complex vertically and horizontally integrated structures responded to improvements in transportation, communications, and production technologies by dominating major industries in the national market. But by the 1890s, as the frontier closed, they began looking outward for growth opportunities in Europe, Asia, and the Americas. In particular, they chose first to export, and then to manufacture abroad, the products of American invention.[24]

Overseas Investments

Almost every prominent tycoon of the era had some interest in foreign businesses. The list included railroad builders Cornelius Vanderbilt and E. H. Harriman as well as banker J. P. Morgan. Companies like Standard Oil of New Jersey, Singer Sewing Machine, International Harvester, and New York Life had established significant positions abroad – and profits from these operations were important to overall corporate earnings.[25] By the outbreak of World War I, the data show that U.S. direct investment abroad amounted to $2.65 billion, about 7 percent of GDP. Another $900 million represented U.S. portfolio investment. By comparison, the book value of British foreign investments was $18.3 billion (including $6.5 billion of direct and $11.8 billion of portfolio). Much of U.S. direct investment went to neighboring Canada ($618 million) and Mexico ($587 million), but there was also a significant stake in the Caribbean and Central America ($371 million) and South America ($323 million). Much investment in developing countries was in oil, mining, and railroads as well as agriculture. U.S. direct investment in Europe ($573 million) was concentrated in sales, assembly, distribution, and manufacturing for higher-income markets, which took advantage of technological leadership. The Asian market, although promising, had attracted only $120 million. Investments in Oceania and Africa were minuscule.[26]

Anglo-American Competition

If America had the competitive edge in product development and manufacturing, Britain in the years before World War I retained strong competitive advantages in transportation, banking, and finance, which helped to sustain a widening merchandise trade deficit. Britain continued to operate half of the world's ocean-going steam tonnage and to monopolize the carrying trade. Before 1914, U.K. ships carried 58 percent of American foreign trade, while U.S. flag ships carried only 8 percent of America's net foreign trade tonnage.[27] U.S. goods bound for Latin America frequently traveled first to Liverpool and then were transshipped because there was no adequate direct shipping. The benefits of British dominance in shipping extended to international banking, insurance, and finance. Until World War I, no American banks existed in South America to serve U.S. trading interests.[28]

Britain held another competitive advantage derived from its control of submarine cables and business communications. It controlled the flow of information. In 1866, when the trans-Atlantic cable opened, the New York-to-London rate was $100 for ten words. Twenty years later, as a consequence of increased competition, rates fell as low as twelve cents a word before the cable companies agreed to fix the price at twenty-five cents a word. While the entire business world benefited from the dramatic improvements in communications and the fall of costs, Britain was the major national beneficiary. It had developed the machinery to produce, and the ships to lay, long submarine cables. Also, British investors saw opportunities to create global networks spreading out from London, which left the British government uniquely positioned to monitor communications and to access information. British hegemony in international communications involved a close working relationship between private investors and the government. The Foreign Office assisted the cable companies, and in return the owners placed former officials and aristocrats on the boards of the various companies, thus protecting the symbiotic relationship.[29]

The cable revolution accelerated the integration of markets and communications. Soon, the London and New York Stock Exchanges operated only two to three minutes apart. With more than half of the world's commercial information and diplomatic dispatches moving through the Eastern system, the British government and the city of London gained an invaluable two- to three-hour lead on information relating to important events.[30]

Until World War I, Britain enjoyed a third advantage as well – the financial power of the city of London and the world's leading capital market. During the late nineteenth century, London and its various stock, bond, and commodity markets became an international distributor of financial resources. Thousands of Britons invested their savings in overseas ventures – so much that by 1913 overseas assets were 1.8 times larger than Britain's gross domestic product. U.S. railroad securities were listed on the London Stock Exchange. London also became the center of the world's metals trade.[31]

British investment in the United States was primarily portfolio investment, meaning purchases of securities, rather than direct investments involving management responsibilities. Of the $7.1 billion invested long
term in the United States, $4.17 billion was in railroads. Britain was the
leading investor in America, with an amount estimated at $4.25 billion in
1914. That was about 60 percent of total foreign investment in America.
Germany was second with about 15 percent. While much of the portfolio
investment involved railroads and local government bonds, foreign investors poured money into Western cattle ranches, mines, and timber. The
West became a region connected to the dynamic flow of capital and capitalist expansion, which swept the international system after the American
Civil War. In manufacturing, U.S. breweries were favored. In the open
international capital markets of the pre–World War I period foreigners
bought and sold American securities easily, and the liquidity of these instruments also produced some volatility. In 1893, for instance, a British
House of Commons committee recommended that the mint stop coining
silver rupees in India, causing, within hours, a drop in silver prices by
20 percent worldwide, including in the U.S. West. Periodic alarm about
rising risks – associated with the politics of populism and bimetallism as
well as concerns about currency depreciation and interest-rate changes –
prompted investors to divest. Fears of losses led to heavy withdrawals
during the mid 1870s and the mid 1890s.[32]

Until World War I, America's exporters and overseas investors chafed
at Britain's restrictions and demanded more vigorous representation and
support from the U.S. government. They wanted nondiscriminatory access
to foreign markets, protection for intellectual property, secure communications, interoceanic canals, and banking and shipping services independent of British influence. President McKinley and his successors, Theodore
Roosevelt and William Howard Taft, were sensitive to these concerns.[33]

In the early years of the twentieth century, American business leaders saw the responsibilities of government in a more positive light. The
National Association of Manufacturers wanted government assistance in
trade expansion – particularly, in improving transportation and credit facilities, building an isthmian canal, and reforming the consular service
to improve overseas reporting. This represented a shift in thinking from
the traditional view that government should merely protect the safety of
persons and property and leave the conduct of trade to private enterprise.
Business continued to grumble about British control of information and
shipping.[34]

When President Teddy Roosevelt sent the fleet around the world
in 1908 to show the flag and demonstrate America's commitment to

international leadership, he revealed this country's weakness in merchant shipping. Foreign-owned supply ships accompanied the fleet, carrying its fuel and supplies. To be sure, Mahan had argued that a shipping fleet was unneeded, for any nation could carry American goods while U.S. capital should be focused on a navy. Yet this was more a professional naval officer's contempt for what he looked on as narrow-minded businessmen of his day than opposition to efforts to boost his country's strength. For the 430,000 tons of coal consumed on this round-the-world trip, the United States relied on British goodwill to purchase coal and access shore facilities.[35]

With world commerce and business opportunities flourishing, private developers proposed a series of interoceanic canals to facilitate internationalization. The Suez Canal, which opened in 1869, shortened the distance between Europe and the Far East. Ferdinand DeLesseps, the French engineer and developer, had a romantic vision of such construction projects "drawing peoples together, and thereby bringing about an era in which men, by knowing one another, will finally cease fighting."[36] American President McKinley expressed similar sentiments the day before he was assassinated in September 1901. He committed the United States to construction of a transoceanic canal through Central America, a long-time goal of U.S. business leaders.

McKinley's Republican successors worked to satisfy business concerns. No president was more supportive of American economic expansion than Theodore Roosevelt, who took steps to build an isthmian canal and who established protectorates designed not only to secure America's position in Panama but also to educate and teach the principles of good government to developing nations. Among those principles was debt repayment. Roosevelt's support for commerce included his decision to send the Navy around the world, demonstrating the power of American commerce, and his efforts to obtain from Congress shipping subsidies for the merchant marine. Yet, however pedestrian, these were the elements of international power. The president, from the very inception of his administration, was an unabashed proponent of the American Century. The nation, he proclaimed in 1901, "has only just begun to assume that commanding position in the international business world which we believe will more and more be hers."[37]

This was also McKinleyism. Teddy Roosevelt's bite often matched his bark, but he largely followed McKinley's lead in assuming a more dominating influence over the western hemisphere and cautiously probing in Asia and elsewhere. He also understood that corporations and trusts were permanent elements of the American economy. Roosevelt thought more

systematically about his nation's new world position than did his predecessor and two successors. He reasoned that military and economic power,
joined by social order, comprised a country's strength. His fear was that
rival nations, namely Russia, Japan, and Germany, had designs on areas of
importance to American security and prosperity. Teddy Roosevelt was a
strategist; he promoted and used power in world affairs, and so he pushed
policies to protect U.S. interests from these threatening nations.[38]

In many ways, Roosevelt led America into the twentieth century. His
strengthening of the presidency was one example. Not only did he elevate
the office above the stature of Congress, which he deemed too unwieldy
and partisan to run the nation, but he also used the White House as the
"bully pulpit" to effect change. Teddy Roosevelt installed the first press
room in the White House in 1902 and, from it, publicized himself, progressive reforms, muscular cultural values, and presidential leadership in
foreign policy. Roosevelt was the first manager in the office, centraliz-
ing foreign-policy decisions, manipulating Congress, and avoiding public
discourse when he could. He fashioned the imperial presidency, which
boosted American power in the world. For instance, stomping on international law and congressional demands, he rammed through the Senate
in 1903 a treaty that secured the Panama Canal Zone for the United States
in perpetuity. He also visited the Canal Zone, in 1906, becoming the first
sitting American president to leave the country – and thereby establishing another precedent for future presidents who, too, traveled abroad to
exhibit American leadership in international affairs.[39]

The Panama Canal episode also indicated other influences on the
globalization process, such as technological advances in both engineering and medicine and the close relationship of diplomacy and finance.
American know-how built the canal with an amazing combination of
digging and locks, aided by 61,000,000 pounds of dynamite (which was
more explosives than America had used in all of its wars up to that time).
Scientific advance epitomized the American Century; medical discovery
and practices eradicated the perilous yellow fever and malaria. And, of
course, the Panama Canal dramatically sped up maritime freight service
between large east coast ports (such as New York) and the west coast of
the Americas.

Big Power Diplomacy

The Panama Canal elevated U.S. power in the western hemisphere for the
entire century. Bolstering the Monroe Doctrine, Roosevelt determined that

the United States would police the region, stabilizing regional economies oftentimes by direct military intervention, pushing an open door for American investment and trade, and ensuring that Europeans got a return on their sizable outlays in Latin America. His intentions were clear during the Dominican crisis of 1904–5, when he orchestrated a deal through an executive agreement, thereby bypassing a reluctant Senate, that gave the United States (or, rather, New York banking houses J. P. Morgan and Kuhn, Loeb and Company) authority to assume the Dominican debt and thus effectively control the Caribbean nation. This was the sort of informal empire that contrasted with Britain's more institutionally based colonialism. American marines entered Central America over a dozen more times during the succeeding decade or so, bringing capital and trade with them.[40]

In regard to the pivotal relationship with Europe, Teddy Roosevelt insinuated himself into such key issues as the Russo-Japanese War of 1905 and Franco-German imperial rivalry in North Africa. Most importantly, the British reached a rapprochement that signaled the latter's relative decline in comparison to the raw military and economic power of the United States. Roosevelt welcomed Anglo-American cooperation, but he pushed the United States, with its youth and vigor and technological prowess, to take the lead in international affairs. The British, who faced competition in Europe as well as an embarrassingly difficult war against the Boers in Africa, understood the enormity of U.S. power. Many banked on the Anglo-American relationship solidifying into a tight community. Preacher and reformer William Stead, however, went further in extolling the "Americanization of the World," the title of his 1901 book. His was an extreme and sensational view that addressed the arrival of the American Century. "Is there no Morgan who will undertake to bring about the greatest combination of all – a combination of the whole English-speaking race?" he asked, alluding to the financial foundation of U.S. economic power. Stead took his hopes with him to his watery grave, a victim on the mighty *Titanic*. Its very resting place, between Europe and the United States, symbolized the dream for some of the new international political and economic structure based on the Anglo-American rapprochement.[41]

Roosevelt's chosen successor, William Howard Taft, continued many of these policies but also pushed for true integration and legal solutions to conflicts that marked the globalization era of the late twentieth century. For instance, Taft promoted reciprocity with Canada in an effort to create a vast North American continental market. That Canada later rejected

3. "United We Stand for Civilization and Peace," *Puck*, June 8, 1898. (Special Collections, Alden Library, Ohio University)

this design – protective of its national sovereignty – is evidence of the tensions that globalization and market integration aroused. But the much-maligned Taft actually promoted an approach to the international arena that was nearly a century ahead of its time. It was legalist in its conceptualization, preferring courts and compromise to the marines, and economically driven in its orientation. Criticized by a hostile reporter as "dollar diplomacy," Taft foreign policy found its way in a world of revolution and big-power brinkmanship. Joined by Secretary of State Philander Knox, one of America's top corporate lawyers, Taft set out to help corporations prosper as a way of ensuring international peace – the essence of dollar diplomacy, or, the substitution of dollars for bullets in international affairs. Like Teddy Roosevelt, Taft militarily intervened in the Caribbean, Mexico, and Asia, but he was more sensitive to corporate interests.

Taft was modern in the sense that he recognized that economic and other foreign policies shaped the destiny of the nation. His reciprocity try with Canada notwithstanding, he envisioned a North American continental market that presaged the North American Free Trade Agreement (NAFTA). The high Payne-Aldrich Tariff of 1909 infuriated exporters and worried a president who knew that the explosion in trade and investment since the turn of the century was a dynamic element of the U.S. economy. As a means of settling disputes according to the rule of law – yet another post–Cold War objective – Knox developed a system of arbitration treaties that, though never ratified by Congress, established international commissions to ponder issues under dispute. Indeed, these treaties were the "great jewel" of Taft's tenure as president, for such a system recognized that the advanced nations had to devise a different way than war to settle their grievances. In essence, he realized that "nations could no longer afford war"; their very nationalism was archaic in an interdependent world economy. Thus, arbitration treaties, like dollar diplomacy, addressed the changes of the new century, even though, as Taft wrote to Knox after the president's failed reelection bid in 1913, "you and I seemed to be a little in advance."[42] And finally, although Taft was a staunch supporter of Wall Street and mergers, he was also a noted trust-buster who disliked unnecessary economic centralization (unlike Roosevelt but similar to Bill Clinton).[43]

Abroad, Taft confronted instability resulting from poverty, ignorance, and bad government. This at times jeopardized the interests of American investors, who had staked out Latin America business opportunities. A good example involved the United Fruit Company (UFCO) of Boston, founded in 1899. Improvements in transportation – refrigerated shipping and the Panama Canal – and radio communications enabled this company, nicknamed the "Octopus," to prosper from a growing trade in perishable products. UFCO invested heavily in Central American plantations and became involved in every aspect of society. In effect, it helped create banana republics that became the fertile playgrounds of entrepreneurial adventurers, such as Sam "the Banana Man" Zemurray. Within seven years, UFCO had erected three radio stations; owned more than one hundred square miles of banana lands in Colombia, Cuba, Jamaica, the Dominican Republic, Honduras, Nicaragua, Guatemala, and Costa Rica; employed 15,000 people; and operated railroad lines, steamships, and chartered vessels. As the UFCO example suggests, separating the interests of multinational companies from political intrigue and larger national interests was often difficult.[44]

In Mexico, the sheer enormity of U.S. investments in mining (oil and silver) and real estate created dependence on America. Businessmen rushed to compete with the British and others in oil, but Mexico soon dissolved into revolution. Not surprisingly, American business supported Mexican leaders who were likely to favor their business over British, and who could bring stability to the nation. The Mexican situation deteriorated after Taft left office and during World War I.

Farther afield, across the globe, President Taft, and his subordinates in the State Department, shared a grander vision of seizing the vast China market, the prize of merchants the world over. Japan and Russia had divided up the lucrative Manchurian railways, Japan had taken over Korea, and the U.S. open door seemed to be closing. Taft and Knox believed that America could safeguard Chinese integrity from the imperial Europeans and Japan with the help of railroad baron E. H. Harriman. This kingpin of the railroads and steamship lines had issued a bold plan in 1905 to join his railroads to a shipping-railroad route that would encircle the globe and link the four most populous nations (America, Russia, China, and Japan) on earth. Doing so would bring him riches, but the ambitious Harriman, fearful of Japanese and Russian power, also sought, as he wrote then-Secretary of War Taft, "to save the commercial interests of the United States from being entirely wiped from the Pacific Ocean in the future."[45]

A key element of the Harriman scheme was to buy the Manchurian railways from Russia and Japan and then to use Harriman's money and influence with other U.S. financiers to form a Manchurian bank to float American enterprise in China. Much hinged on Japanese acceptance, although Harriman, while welcoming Japan's cooperation, derided the nation's people for "lacking the quality of working together" as well as its small-scale business practices. In light of the Japanese economic miracle that began a half century later, such a view reveals that the Master Builder's accuracy as a prophet sometimes did not match his vision. Harriman's timing was also inopportune: the Russo-Japanese War of 1905, outrage in Tokyo at U.S. diplomatic intervention, and a bank panic in the United States in 1907 delayed an agreement with Japan. Willard Straight, the consul general in the area, organized the banker combination in 1908, headed by J. P. Morgan, but the following year Harriman died.[46]

Still, the idea of consolidating U.S. interests in China, whether by the grand around-the-world transport system or simply by building new lines, lived on. The U.S. minister in Beijing, William Rockhill, got the bankers into a European financial consortium, which also included Russia and Japan, that was raising a huge loan to build the Huguang Railway joining Beijing and Canton in 1910. Straight then resigned from the State Department to work for Morgan, but the Chinese Revolution intervened to delay construction of the Huguang project until 1913. By then, Taft's successor, Woodrow Wilson, aimed to erase the taint of dollar diplomacy and to recognize the Chinese Republic as an entity independent from foreigners, by withdrawing U.S. participation in the six-power banking consortium.[47] Yet Taft's dollar diplomacy established a precedent; economic means could achieve larger ends. Indeed, a leading newspaper of the day called the bankers' group "the most striking diplomatic achievement and international financing event of the 20th century."[48]

There is another fascinating aspect to this story. Placing Harriman's world transportation network in the context of World War I, future diplomat George Kennan pondered that if an international transportation structure had existed, Russia might have received enough heavy loads of war materiel from Japan and the United States to fend off the Germans in Poland and western Russia, thus changing the course of the war and very possibly the fortunes of Lenin's Bolsheviks, and subsequent Russo-American relations with them.[49]

Despite some frictions, American business, financial, and government leaders perceived during the first years of the twentieth century that positive underlying trends were reshaping the world economy in ways favorable to U.S. interests. Europeans even began to sell bonds and raise money in the United States. Wall Street bankers began to dream of the day when New York would become the money center for the entire world. Secretary of State Hay voiced the confidence of this era when he told Congress in

1902 that "the financial center of the world, which required thousands of years to journey from the Euphrates to the Thames and Seine, seems passing to the Hudson between daybreak and dark."[50]

American Cultural Influences

The outward spread of American influence was also evident in religion, popular culture, entertainment, and sports. In the mid nineteenth century, American evangelists like Dwight L. Moody brought revivalism to Britain. By the turn of the century, thousands of young Americans were going abroad on missions, believing that millions of the world's people lived in ignorance, superstition, idolatry, and corruption. Many believed that the times they lived in promised a sweeping transformation in the destiny of mankind – perhaps the most important development since the birth of Jesus. John R. Mott, a Cornell graduate and YMCA leader wrote a pamphlet, *Evangelization of the World in this Generation* (1900), which college students in the Student Volunteers for Foreign Missions took as their motto in the 1890s. Inspired by this, the YMCA launched a crusade to promote American-style Christianity around the world and, by 1915, had nearly 170,000 Chinese enrolled in mission schools. There were perhaps 2,000 to 2,500 Protestant missionaries in China at the time.[51]

The fervor of this Christian mission was intense, particularly in guiding Americans on their imperial mission. Imperialists were confident that God was on their side, and that the United States was the providential source of spreading Christian values worldwide. Thus, Senate Republican Orville Platt rationalized annexing territories by asserting that "the next great world wave of civilization is to overspread China," and that it was up to Britain and the United States, "first in the family of nations," to unite as English-speaking nations and confront "the institutions of despotism and irreligion" in Asia. Hence, John Mott visited twenty-two nations and arranged two dozen conferences and conventions in just over a year and a half at the end of the 1890s, convinced that the masses in China, India, and elsewhere could be converted to Christianity. And missionaries, moreover, in promoting Western values, provided another impetus to commercial expansion. Indeed, magazines ran articles with such titles as "Do Foreign Missions Pay?"[52]

Working closely with the YMCA to spread American cultural values was the world's Woman's Christian Temperance Union (WCTU). Led by Frances Willard, the WCTU set out to promote woman's suffrage and to banish alcohol. During this era, it was said that the sun never set on the British Empire, or the WCTU. In 1910, the organization claimed two million followers in forty countries, with the largest numbers in the United States, Great Britain, and other English-speaking nations. International work became a vehicle during the period from 1880 to the 1920s to disseminate American temperance principles around the world. The WCTU movement worked closely with missionaries, taking a strong stand against forcing alcohol and other narcotics upon "savages and uncivilized communities." The movement also spread American thinking about housework and home technology. Temperance women frequently boasted about the superiority of American home methods and prized American cook stoves, sewing machines, and books.[53]

With the flow of migrants to the United States having quickened early in the century, American women, as the key consumers, benefited from the ongoing globalization process. From roughly the 1890s well into the 1920s, women were the leading investors, manufacturers, and distributors of beauty products. The competition was stiff and international. Helena Rubinstein went from London in 1908 to a salon in Paris four years later. When world war started, she fled for New York City and an illustrious career on Fifth Avenue. Along with others from across the Atlantic, she made America's beauty culture into a profitable business that took style and marketing cues from foreign lands.[54]

Improvements in transportation also facilitated the export of American-style entertainment. After the Civil War, Buffalo Bill took the frontier to London with his famous Wild West Show. With the arrival of the celluloid age – early in the twentieth century – came a flood American films perpetuating familiar stereotypes of cowboys, Indians, desperate lovers, and desperadoes. Before World War I, an estimated 60 percent to 75 percent of the films shown in Britain were American. And in 1906, for the first time, only American authors appeared on the U.S. best-seller list, when a decade before the compilation was dominated by Brits.[55]

Internationalization also took place in society and marriage. In 1900, it was estimated that about 15,000 Americans resided in London. Tourism grew impressively; 100,000 Americans visited Britain in 1913, while 29,000 Englishman came across the Atlantic. American writers and artists gained increasing acceptance. In 1902, Edwin Abbey, an American artist, was invited to paint the crowning of Edward VII.[56] When a large number of European aristocrats and diplomats returned home with American heiresses as their wives, some in the European press worried about the Americanization of society. One who did was Jennie Jerome, the daughter of a prominent New York speculator, who married Randolph Churchill.

Their son was Winston Churchill. Jerome's father, Leonard, known as the "King of Wall Street," made a fortune selling stocks short in the Panic of 1857. Still, the pattern also played out the other way; in 1906, six British heads of diplomatic missions in the American capital had U.S. wives.[57]

One of the founders of the National Association of Manufacturers interpreted this trend in marriages as additional evidence of a flawed trade policy. "Are they [the British] not able to come over here every day, and trade us a second-class duke or a third-class earl for a first-class American girl, and get several million dollars to boot? And the next day the entire outfit goes back to Europe on a British vessel. We don't even get the freight back to Liverpool on the earl, the girl, or the money."[58] The costs of international marriages could be exceedingly dear. When Consuelo Vanderbilt and the Duke of Marlborough finally divorced in 1906 after twelve years of marriage, the Vanderbilt's expenses were roughly $10 million, which prompted peals of laughter in Parliament about the British aristocracy selling out for American dollars.[59]

Another manifestation of the Americanization of Britain's world involved magnates like Andrew Carnegie and John D. Rockefeller who turned to foreign philanthropy to protect their names and to advance their social concerns. Critics charged they were buying insulation from public censure, but Carnegie stated his reasons for philanthropy pithily: "The man who dies rich dies disgraced." Carnegie bequeathed millions to build public libraries in the United States and throughout the British dominions. By 1919, his Scottish Trust, aimed at saving his homeland's universities from bankruptcy, had piled up $15 million in its coffers, much of it from U.S. Steel Company bonds. For his part, Rockefeller established a huge foundation with a global mission – "to promote the well being of mankind throughout the world." Rockefeller personally contributed some $530 million to foundations and his son added another $537 million. These millions went for medical and scientific research as well as public health, education, and international exchange programs. The foundation combated yellow fever and tropical African diseases. In China, it established Peking Union Medical College to spread knowledge of medicine and sanitation, conduct research, and support the medical activities of Western missionaries. These two business barons were not the only ones to transfer substantial portions of their personal wealth to aid humanity. Summarizing these philanthropic activities between the Spanish-American War and the First World War, historian Merle Curti concluded that voluntary donations and government aid "saved the lives of ten thousands in all quarters of the globe."[60]

4. "The International Siamese Twins," *Judge*, June 21, 1902. (Special Collections, Alden Library, Ohio University)

In sports, London coverage of the Boer War was subordinated to reporting on the America's Cup yacht competition. The United States won the first match in 1851 and dominated successive tests for 130 years until 1983. In horse racing, Britain was stunned in 1901 when Americans won both the Derby and the Oak, the two most prestigious horse races. In boxing, the Americans also reigned supreme, as they did in the Olympics. The modern summer games began in Athens, Greece, in 1896. American athletes dominated the quest for gold medals, although at the London Games of 1908, the British repeatedly fudged rules to the advantage of Englishmen athletes over their American counterparts. In the years before World War I, Americans won 167 gold medals, compared to 96 for second-place Britain. This pattern continued until 1956 when the Soviet Union finally broke the American hold.[61]

Sustaining Globalization

Early in the twentieth century, there were persuasive reasons to think that the world would continue to globalize, as technology advanced and America's influence spread outward. Further improvements in transportation and communications promised to hasten the integration of nations and to facilitate expanded flows of people, goods, and capital. That potential was demonstrated on December 17, 1903, when two bicycle mechanics from Dayton, Ohio, soared for twelve seconds and traveled 120 feet in a "flying machine" at Kitty Hawk, North Carolina. After initial skepticism, Wilbur and Orville Wright received a U.S. patent and soon gained world recognition in 1908 for showing how aviation might dramatically compress the barriers of time and distance.

The growing popularity of international marriages, sports competition, cultural diffusion, and the emergence of private philanthropy all pointed in the same direction. In the world of business and finance, many saw the trend toward economic internationalism as a grand panacea for the world's power rivalries – one likely to promote both peace and prosperity. In effect, there was a revival of Cobdenism, the free-trade ideology associated with Richard Cobden, a mid-nineteenth-century English textile manufacturer and leader of the English anti-Corn Law forces. He claimed that "commerce is the grand panacea, which, like a beneficent medical discovery, will serve to inoculate with the healthy and saving taste for civilization all the nations of the world." After more than a half century of free trade without a major international war, commerce did seem to be suppressing international rivalries and creating a climate for benign economic forces to promote prosperity and peace. This liberal vision had support in Germany as well as the English-speaking nations. In his book *The American "Commercial Invasion" of Europe*, published in 1902, New York banker Frank Vanderlip quoted approvingly a German economist about how "the perfect and instant communication between distant parts of the world, the cheapening of transportation, the wider knowledge of every country, its products and its needs, have brought about an interdependence of nations that is now almost as great as the dependence of one class of industrial workers on another." Perhaps, the most Utopian statement of the Cobdenite vision appeared in *The Great Illusion* by Norman Angell, a British peace activist. He noted how closely related financial markets had become, making the dangers of war more unrealistic.

International finance has become so interdependent and so interwoven with trade and industry that ... political and military power can in reality do nothing.... These little recognized facts, mainly the outcome of purely modern conditions (rapidity of communication creating a greater complexity and delicacy of the credit system), have rendered the problems of modern international politics profoundly and essentially different from the ancient.[62]

Not all observers saw trends through such rose-colored glasses. There was growing concern about German militarism. But it did seem that the United States was rapidly assuming a leadership role in a world once run from London. Had World War I not interrupted Utopian dreams and terminated the era of British economic hegemony, a peaceful transfer of economic and diplomatic leadership between the English-speaking cousins – John Bull and Uncle Sam – might have occurred routinely a decade or two later. The outbreak of a major European war in August 1914 accelerated that transition and altered the course of globalization.[63]

2

Globalization in War and Peace, 1914–1920

World War I disrupted the first international economy and set back the globalization process for two generations. For Europe, it was the first catastrophe of the twentieth century. The war inflicted 13 million casualties and dislocated European economies and politics. One 1920 estimate placed the *direct* costs of the war at $200 billion, perhaps $1.5 trillion in contemporary prices. For the United States, the conflict presented unique opportunities to gain leadership experience, to acquire new markets for American products and cultural influences, and to prepare for an era of American-led globalization after the war.[1]

The Great War, as it was known, had multiple causes, the most immediate being the assassination of the Austrian archduke on June 28, 1914, in the Balkans. This event activated the tangled web of European alliances and defense pacts. Behind the government decisions for war, however, were a number of underlying political and military stimuli, such as an arms races, national rivalries, calculations of the balance of power, rigid military mobilization plans, and, in the case of Germany, an aggressive mentality. The war also had an economic dimension, which was arguably the most significant, as historian Paul Kennedy concluded. There were trade rivalries, competition for raw materials and colonies, and a fierce competition for overseas markets. Insofar "as the British and German governments were concerned," he wrote, "the 1914–18 conflict was essentially entered into because the former power wished to preserve the existing *status quo* whereas the latter, for a mixture of offensive and defensive motives, was taking steps to alter it."[2]

War and Interdependence

In revisiting this conflict, it is important to observe how forces promoting globalization influenced the war. During the century of relative peace before 1914, both Britain and Germany had become dependent on imports. Britain relied heavily on overseas suppliers for food and industrial raw materials. Imports amounted to more than 25 percent of gross domestic product and provided an estimated 58 percent of the calories consumed in Britain. Other critical materials – including iron ore, timber, wheat, cotton, and petroleum – came from distant locations requiring sea transport. To pay for these imports of raw materials and foodstuffs, England relied on its earnings from shipping and financial services to offset the resulting merchandise trade deficit. This pattern of international specialization was efficient, and Britain as a nation was undoubtedly much wealthier than it would have been under the protectionist alternative. But, free trade and cheap imports came with a price. Sustaining the system required naval supremacy and a strong merchant marine.[3]

Germany had a similar economic predicament. Lacking a diversified resource base, it relied on trade. In 1913, imports amounted to 20 percent of net national product; exports, 17.5 percent. Like Britain, Germany had a large merchant fleet and looked outward for markets, exchanging its manufactures for foodstuffs and raw materials. In peacetime, about 19 percent of the calories consumed in Germany were imported. Germany also depended on foreign supplies of petroleum and certain strategic materials – copper, tin, chromium, manganese.[4]

Before the war, a triangular relationship of mutual dependence had developed among Britain, Germany, and America. Britain and Germany both relied on American foodstuffs and raw materials. One commodity (cotton) accounted for $547 million (22.5 percent) of America's total exports ($2,429 million) in 1913, and 41 percent of all U.S. cotton went to markets in Britain and Germany. At the outbreak of war, the United States was the world's largest economy, a diversified exporter of state-of-the-art manufactures, food, and raw materials. Its two principal trading partners were Britain and Germany. U.S. exports to Britain amount to $597 million in 1913 – and of this 37 percent was raw cotton ($221 million). Cotton (valued at $144.2 million) accounted for 43.5 percent of U.S. exports to Germany ($331.7 million). To complete this circle of commercial interdependence, Britain and Germany were each other's second leading trading partner. This intricate web of interdependence underscores the negative side of globalization in time of general war, and it demonstrates that commercial entanglements do not necessarily assure peace.[5]

Paradoxically, the very economic specialization that benefited British and German producers and consumers in peacetime enhanced their vulnerability in wartime. The long sea lanes invited the attention of British and German naval planners determined to take advantage of their adversary's economic dependence. Not surprisingly, Britain and Germany both pursued similar economic war objectives. For two-and-one-half years, they both sought to expand trade with America, to ensure that country's neutrality and to deny its products to the other side.[6]

To these ends, both sides engaged in extensive propaganda and deceit. Britain enjoyed several inherent advantages – a common English language, greater familiarity with the American culture, and, significantly, control of the only operating cable facilities. Using these assets of the globalization process, London attempted to manipulate and persuade influential Americans, such as business leaders, financiers, government officials, journalists, academics, and teachers, among others, that Germans were cruel tyrants bent on world domination. Britain shut off from the submarine cable network any bank or business doing business with the Germans, using cable censorship to reinforce its program of restrictions on commercial shipments. Most famously, British intelligence intercepted the Zimmermann cable from Berlin, which promised Mexico territorial compensation from the American southwest if it would join Germany in a war on the United States.[7] The release of the note resulted in public outrage that helped mobilize American public opinion in favor of U.S. intervention in 1917.

Perhaps the most effective British weapon was the economic blockade, which was gradually expanded to include food and nonmunitions. In the summer of 1916, the British intercepted an average of 135 merchant ships per month bound for the continent. Accustomed to substantial quantities of imported foodstuffs from the United States, the Germans were reduced to a bread-and-potatoes diet and, after the 1916 potato crop failed, to an austere turnip diet during the next winter. German officials in the United States looked for ways to obtain funds in America and to restore the Atlantic supply line with exports of wheat and fats. To counter the British blockade, they even chartered American-flag vessels, but these efforts had little impact. President Wilson, who was privately sympathetic to Britain's position, was not disposed to challenge London's expansive definition of contraband or to use naval power to break the blockade so that neutral America could trade with Germany or with other neutrals.[8]

Of course, America was hardly neutral in thought and deed, and the new technology made this goal doubly difficult. In this world war, being situated on the other side of the Atlantic no longer brought immunity from the fighting. Merchants and tourists traveled in the war zone, and several fell victim to German submarines. The shocking sinking of the magnificent *Lusitania* in May 1915 by a German U-20 sub, with a loss of 1,198 lives, was all the more tragic because passengers, like the public, had been told that the huge liner was safer than a trolley car. The vessel was fast, having set a new trans-Atlantic speed record during its maiden voyage, and big – it carried hundreds of voyagers as well as a tremendous cargo that included contraband war materiel for the British. Thus, the spread of new transportation technology bred false confidence. Of course, the rapidly changing technology of war gave both sides devastating new weapons, such as long-range cannons and machine guns. The resulting carnage was staggering – in 1915 alone, France suffered 1.3 million casualties; Germany, 848,000; and Britain, 313,000.[9]

Given the magnitude of the casualties, and the divisions in American public opinion, President Woodrow Wilson looked for ways to end the conflict and promote permanent peace. He sought to use American neutrality to push the belligerents to the negotiating table, where America could press for international acceptance of the open door and a peaceful settlement of global problems. In essence, the New World – the progressive United States – would use its influence to redress the grievances of the "old order." Wilson and his closest foreign policy advisors – trusted emissary Edward House and his two secretaries of state, William Jennings Bryan and Robert Lansing – all believed firmly in international mediation of disputes. But, they recognized that America could arbitrate an end to war only if both sides agreed to attend a peace conference chaperoned by the United States. By 1916, when House broached this issue with the British, U.S. arbitration was not as unrealistic as it was before the American Century. But, Wilson's rigid and legalistic approach to neutral rights did not take account of the new realities of war or the shortcomings of traditional international law. Submarines, for example, could not be expected to surface and then seize and search a freighter or a passenger liner for contraband of war. In practice, Wilson's policy of maintaining close economic ties with Britain became decidedly unneutral. But it was compatible with the cultural affinity of the English-speaking peoples and the leadership elites.[10]

Secure in their control of the surface sea lanes, London expanded imports of U.S. supplies. The British government organized a major North American supply mission, and by November 1916, 40 percent of Britain's war expenditures were for American goods. When the United States formally entered the war in April 1917, Britain had a massive supply base in the neutral United States. This mission, which grew to 10,000 people by the end of the year, purchased munitions, food and clothing, and raw materials; supervised transportation; and even made "propaganda forays into the wilds of deepest America," historian Kathleen Burk noted. During the last two years of the war, America supplied Britain with half of its bread and flour, and some 80 percent of meat and fats.[11]

Philanthropy also helped the Allied cause and represented another manifestation of the patterns of people-to-people linkages that the globalization process strengthened. The effort directed at Britain and France was most striking. Prominent New York financiers and industrialists organized the War Relief Clearing House for France and her allies when the war was under way. This organization – led by Charles Coffin, the president of General Electric Company; A. Barton Hepburn of Chase National Bank; and Cornelius Vanderbilt, among others – received contributions ranging from cash to shovels to toys and sugar and then shipped the contributions across the Atlantic on the French Line. When America entered the war in April 1917, the clearing house was absorbed into the Red Cross as part of the governmental war effort.

The Commission on Belgian Relief was perhaps the most famous initiative and a good example of private and public international linkages. When Belgium was invaded and occupied by the Germans in 1914, the commission emerged from a small committee with multinational membership, including three Americans, the Spanish ambassador, and Belgium's richest person, M. Ernest Solvay. Abandoning his well-paid job, and his dream of becoming president of Stanford University, Herbert Hoover joined the commission to take charge and paid for expenses out of his own pocket. Americans rushed to support the relief mission, creating committees all over the nation. The Philadelphia Belgian Relief Committee cooperated with the *Ladies Home Journal* to send 2,900 tons of cereal to the occupied nation. Money and gifts from the United States to Belgium totaled $28,469,167 by 1917, or ten cents given by every American, and drew German suspicion. Serbia, Rumania, Russia, Turkey, Persia, and Palestinian Jews were also beneficiaries of U.S. largesse; the Germans and Austro-Hungarians only got about $2 million, sent through the Red Cross, for their war victims. The trans-Atlantic flows of migrants retained ties to families and communities in war-devastated Europe. When America formally entered the war, this overseas philanthropy expanded as large-scale business-run enterprises became integrated into government operations.[12]

Eager to offset Britain's naval dominance of sea lanes, Germany freely experimented with new military technologies, such as the submarine. Berlin hoped to starve Britain into submission before America's overwhelming economic power translated into comparable military force. Its move to unrestricted submarine warfare against neutral shipping in February 1917, however, inevitably took the lives of Americans and led the United States to war against Germany. Still, Germany's bold strategy was nearly successful. Submarine attacks disrupted trade between overseas suppliers of raw materials and British consumers. German submarines destroyed 536,000 tons of shipping in February 1917 and 603,000 tons in March. During those two months, only 300 ships entered British ports, compared to 1,149 ships in 1916. Between May and September 1917, the Standard Oil Company lost six tankers, and Britain's oil supply dropped to less than a three-months supply. Short on fuel, the Royal Navy was in jeopardy.[13] Britain succeeded in reducing these shipping losses with government-enforced pooling systems to control and coordinate oil shipments and with the use of the convoy system to protect tankers and supply ships.

America's Financial and Maritime Ascendancy

Britain survived the submarine campaign, but World War I proved an insuperable financial burden. To pay for American supplies, the British were forced to sell overseas investments. To handle these transactions, raise additional loans, and organize the flow of materiel, London relied on experienced private bankers. The house of J. P. Morgan, which gained prominence in the nineteenth century helping to underwrite railroad investments in the United States, assumed a critical role in financing London's purchases during the period of U.S. neutrality. At a time when President Wilson urged Americans to be impartial in thought as well as action, the bankers zealously pressed the interests of their British clients. Morgan official Thomas Lamont later admitted, "We wanted the Allies to win, from the outset of the war. We were pro-Ally by inheritance, by instinct, by opinion." Members of the Morgan firm also sought to sway American public opinion. Lamont bought the *New York Post*, a newspaper

critical of the Allied effort, and turned it into a mouthpiece for closer relations with Britain.[14]

After the United States formally entered the war in 1917, Britain,
having exhausted credit from private sources, sought aid from the U.S.
Treasury and support for the pound-sterling. But Treasury Secretary
William G. McAdoo stood firm insisting that Britain liquidate its remaining assets and assume the responsibility of servicing its debts. Reluctantly,
Britain did so. From 1914 to 1919, the value of foreign investments in the
United States declined from $7.2 billion to $3.3 billion. The reduction in
long-term portfolio holdings was especially significant – declining from
$5.4 billion in 1914 to $1.6 billion in 1919. Meanwhile, Britain's debt
to the U.S. government soared to nearly $5 billion. A decade after the
war, some 40 percent of Britain's budget was earmarked for war-debt
payments.[15]

Both victorious Britain and defeated Germany thus emerged from
the war as debtors. Like the British, the Germans had hoped to obtain
American supplies, but they failed. Certainly, the Wall Street banking firm
of Kuhn-Loeb had German sympathies and wanted to provide some assistance. The basic problem was the blockade. Germany lacked control of the
sea lanes. And the Wilson administration acceded to heavy-handed British
interference with neutral shipments. As a result, the American economy
produced few benefits for Germany and ultimately led to its defeat and
to the burden of paying war reparations to the victors.[16]

As world war drained the financial and material resources of Europe
and shattered the British-led system of economic interdependence, it accelerated America's rise to world leadership. In 1914, America was the
world's leading debtor, having borrowed European capital to construct
railroads and develop the vast continental market. Five years later, at
the end of the war, America had become the world's leading creditor.
There were $2.5 billion in foreign long-term investments in the United
States (36 percent direct, 64 percent portfolio), while the United States
had $6.5 billion in long-term investments abroad (60 percent direct,
40 percent portfolio).[17]

America emerged from the war as a financial leader. Before the war,
London had managed the gold standard, and governments had permitted private individuals to import and export gold. But once war began, governments regulated gold flows and issued fiat money, unbacked
by gold, to mobilize resources. As a result, inflation soared, and exchange rates fluctuated wildly. Much gold flowed to America to finance
the purchase of war materials. As a result, in 1918, circumstances had

changed so that old currency relationships had no relevance, and only the United States stood ready to convert gold for its currency. America was the only power to emerge from the war with the financial resources to restore the gold standard and provide international monetary leadership.[18]

World War I turned the United States into a major maritime power. In 1914, the United States had virtually no merchant marine, and only 9.7 percent of U.S. exports traveled on American ships. More than half of prewar U.S. commerce typically traveled on British vessels, and another 15 percent, on German and Austrian ships. Encountering unprecedented demand from the belligerents for American manufactures and raw materials, the United States had to rely heavily on foreign bottoms for sea transportation. This vulnerability, and dependence on British shipping and naval protection, inspired those in commercial and naval circles to build merchant and naval vessels. President Woodrow Wilson was sympathetic. His world view contemplated vigorous commercial expansion. During the 1912 campaign, he asserted: "Without a great merchant marine we cannot take our rightful place in the commerce of the world."[19]

After the outbreak of World War I, Wilson's aides advanced ideas for a government-owned and -operated merchant marine. Their ship construction plan encountered resistance from private shippers but was finally enacted in September 1916. Under Edward Hurley, an Illinois businessman interested in export expansion, the United States Shipping Board (USSB) initiated a major shipbuilding program. In 1918, USSB launched three million tons of ships, an amount equal to total world output during any prewar year. The Merchant Marine Act of 1920 (Jones Act) marked the conclusion of Wilson's nationalistic merchant marine program. It authorized preferential rail rates for U.S. shippers and discrimination in favor of U.S. shipping.[20]

The massive wartime building program temporarily transformed world shipping patterns. The share of American commerce transported on American ships rose significantly, reaching 42.7 percent in 1920. This change mirrored broader patterns as Japan, and other emerging competitors, built up their merchant marines. Britain, once the dominant carrying nation, lost its position in shipping during this period. (See Table A.10.) The United States had more tonnage, as a result of an unprecedented buildup, and Japan became a formidable competitor in Asia. The relative growth of merchant shipping tonnage in America and Asia offered another measure of Britain's economic decline.[21]

U.S. Business Expansion

World War I accelerated the expansion of U.S. business overseas. American firms were especially successful in replacing dominant British firms in western hemisphere and Asian markets. In addition, war requirements created a soaring U.S. demand for raw materials, especially copper, iron, and other key mineral products. Soon American firms began scouring the world for essential raw materials and setting up operations overseas in European colonies. Rubber companies acquired plantations in Sumatra, sugar producers expanded operations in Cuba, and meatpackers enlarged operations in South America. Paper companies opened pulp and paper mills in Canada, while mining companies purchased nitrate, iron, and copper mines in Chile. Oil companies explored China, the Dutch Indies, and other remote regions and invested heavily in unstable Mexico. Except for supply-oriented investments in minerals and rubber in remote areas of the Americas or the Dutch East Indies, most United States-owned foreign investments during the World War I period went into nearby areas. U.S. direct foreign investment grew from $2.7 billion in 1914 to $3.9 billion in 1919. Some of the greatest growth occurred in Caribbean agriculture and Canadian manufacturing. There was little to attract U.S. firms to Mexico, except oil. Oil investments in Mexico climbed from $85 million in 1914 to $200 million in 1919.[22]

War needs drove much of this overseas expansion, but American business leaders were not oblivious to long-term opportunities. An important symbolic act occurred in 1915, when Frank Vanderlip of National City Bank created the American International Corporation (AIC), owned 50 percent by the bank and 50 percent by other "interests." The establishment of AIC illustrated the emerging determination of big American businesses to play an active role in world business affairs. AIC's board included top officials of Armour & Company (meatpacking), General Electric, Great Northern Railway, W. R. Grace (diversified businesses on the west coast of South America), International Nickel, Standard Oil, Anaconda, Westinghouse Electric, and American Telephone and Telegraph. During the war, AIC entered a variety of undertakings, including shipping, rubber plantations, and meat canning. Afterward when prices slumped, AIC cut back, withdrawing from direct investment and acting as a holding company for portfolio investments. But, during the war, it sought to address many of the bottlenecks caused by the withdrawal of British finance and the disruption of international trade and finance.[23]

Another significant change involved financial services. With London unable to provide trade credit – as well as shipping services – big American traders like U.S. Steel, DuPont, W. R. Grace, International Harvester, Armour, and Standard Oil pressed for American banks to expand abroad. The National City Bank, forerunner of powerful Citibank, responded.[24] In only three years after the Federal Reserve Act opened the way for overseas banking, Frank Vanderlip's National City Bank became a major force, using foreign branches to provide a range of services – including financing for domestic corporations, banking for foreign correspondents and foreign exchange trading. Opening its first branch in Buenos Aires in November 1914, National City Bank had fifty-seven foreign branches abroad by 1920. These included an extensive network of banks in the Pacific after it purchased International Bank Corporation with seventeen branches, including locations in Japan, China, the Philippines, India, and Malaya.[25]

The film industry was another beneficiary of war. The conflict curtailed film production in France, the principal rival; as a result, Hollywood producers recovered the domestic market and expanded overseas, achieving a dominant position in silent films. In December 1913, U.S. films held a 57 percent share of the British market and expanded that to a peak of 82 percent in December 1917. Interestingly, these gains came with considerable government assistance. The Wilson administration saw the film industry as a propaganda instrument and insisted on close cooperation. George Creel, who directed the Committee on Public Information, with the support of the War Industries Board, expedited film shipments that included both comedies and dramas of interest to war-weary foreigners. Disseminated with these films were "educational material" sponsored by Creel's organization, along with the requirement that American films not be rented to theaters showing German films. According to one of Creel's aides, "the government has gone into partnership with the moving-picture industry to the end that the unique and tremendous power of the moving picture as an instrument of propaganda may be utilized to the fullest possible extent for the nation's needs." War dislocations and government support gave American film producers access not just to the European market but also to once-closed film markets in South American, Australasia, and Southeast Asia. But basic economics underlay American dominance of the new entertainment medium. By the early 1920s, there were about 18,000 theaters in the United States, compared to 4,000 in Britain, 3,700 in Germany, and 2,500 in France. This meant that Hollywood could afford to spend more on film production, assured of a large domestic market, and then sell big films cheaply abroad. Soon Europeans would complain about American cultural colonization.[26]

Business and Government Linkages

In 1912, presidential candidate Woodrow Wilson had waged an antibusiness campaign. Conditions of war compelled the administration to work closely with his private-sector antagonists. Indeed, the war produced some peculiar linkages, including global supply chains and the beginnings of the national-security state. Gradually, Wilson emerged as a strong backer of business expansion. The British government outsourced much of its arms production to the United States and to its dominions. J. P. Morgan and Company's massive procurement policies on behalf of Britain and France (in the aggregate, Morgan's purchasing and financing ran to an astonishing $48 billion), coupled with its direct investments in U.S. arms manufacturing, demonstrated the complex international linkages forged among international bankers, industry, and national governments. The relationships were so controversial that in the 1930s, arms makers and their financiers came under the scrutiny of Congress for encroaching on the nation's sovereignty and independence. The tangled relationships between business and foreign governments benefited the Morgan bankers and the United States. The transactions helped expand the U.S. industrial base and transform this country from the world's largest debtor to its largest creditor in three short years.[27]

World War I also saw the emergence of the national-security state. Under the War Industries Board, established in July 1917, government encouraged regulated business contributions to the war. Munitions makers had operated on such a cooperative basis for years; since its creation in 1883, the Navy's Gun-Foundry Board blended government contracts with federal assembly factories to build U.S. armaments supplies. Technological advances, the international naval race, and reorganization in military command – all occurring in the first decade of the century – had further stimulated the private-public nexus. The sinking of the *Lusitania* brought the further realization that the world war was a mechanized affair that required the coordination of inventors, entrepreneurs, and manufacturers. Thus, Congress began appropriating larger sums for armaments; in 1916, it voted for a $12 million expenditure to develop machine guns and additional sums to create an Army Aviation Section. The General Board of the Navy added in a $285 million military package. In the final two years of the conflict, the advent of the military airplane, self-propelled tanks, and automotive transport beyond railheads necessitated even more funding.

And all this was stimulated further by the preparedness campaign of 1916 that expanded the American army and navy, replete with a national guard of reserves, to nearly a million and a half men in arms in 1917. By the summer of 1918, America was landing seven soldiers and their equipment in Europe every minute twenty-four hours a day. The effort was a total one that targeted the economy. As President Wilson wrote in May 1917, "[t]he idea of the draft is not only the drawing of men into the military service of the Government but the virtual assigning of men to the necessary labor of the country. Its central idea was to disturb the industrial and social structure of the country just as little as possible."[28] By the end of the war, the U.S. economy had become far more dependent on the national security state. Thousands of businesses – large and small – relied on government contracts for a significant share of their revenues.[29]

But government during the war continued to have poor relations with one key industry – the oil industry. President Wilson and his aides blamed instability in neighboring Mexico on English and American oil companies. Before the war, Wilson was hostile to business expansion in Mexico, and his State Department expressed opposition to "monopolistic" oil concessions in Colombia. Estrangement between the president and the oil giant continued in the aftermath of the Supreme Court decision to break up Standard Oil of New Jersey (the forerunner of mighty Exxon), which viewed the administration with considerable suspicion. The company also faced difficulties abroad. It confronted expropriation and confiscation in several foreign producing ventures (Peru, Mexico, and the Dutch Indies) and lacked the oil reserves needed to serve its refining capacity and satisfy customer needs. Fearful that Wilson would pursue an anti-oil-company agenda, Standard Oil contemplated moving its headquarters to Canada to escape the reach of Washington.[30]

In light of Wilson's antibusiness campaign rhetoric in 1912, it might seem surprising to learn that his administration gradually warmed to big-business expansionism. Initially, for political reasons, Wilson sought to keep the New York bankers and oil monopolists at arms length. But problems of wartime financing and the need for talented, experienced individuals available in the New York financial community forced Wilson to relent. Edward Stettinius, the father of a future secretary of state, coordinated Allied purchasing. Thomas Lamont, a Wilson favorite, took a leading role in postwar peacemaking. This move was not entirely unexpected, as conservative internationalists – such as Taft, Roosevelt, and a host of diplomats, lawyers, and businessmen – supported Wilson's intervention and peace plans, though not for the same reasons as progressives. At the Paris Peace Conference of 1919, J. P. Morgan's men were everywhere; Democratic financier Bernard Baruch grumbled that the financiers were running the show.[31]

As the European war ended, the Wilson administration became increasingly apprehensive of European aspirations and supportive of American business and financial expansion. In March 1920, the president wrote: "It is evident to me that we are on the eve of a commercial war of the severest sort, and I am afraid that Great Britain will prove capable of as great commercial savagery as Germany has displayed for so many years in her competitive methods." To assist reconstruction efforts, the executive branch approved banking legislation, setting up Edge corporations to finance foreign trade. The Wilson administration also approved modifications to existing antitrust laws permitting combinations of U.S. manufacturers in export trade. The Webb-Pomerene Act facilitated cooperation against European cartels determined to recover lost market share in the Americas and other export markets.[32]

One important exception to this trend of closer cooperation between Washington and Wall Street occurred when the U.S. Treasury under Wilson resisted proposals for a banking consortium, appointed by and backed by the governments of the United States and other important nations exporting to Europe. The individual who blocked the Wall Street plan was Assistant Secretary of the Treasury Russell Leffingwell. Later he went to Wall Street, became the lead partner at J. P. Morgan, and chaired the Council on Foreign Relations. Leffingwell claimed the controversial Morgan-inspired plan was for a "private monopoly of international trade and finance." This episode shows that the close working relationship between Washington and Wall Street during the war frayed as the two sides contemplated expensive and entangling postwar relationships.[33]

From discussions with his advisors at the Paris Peace Conference, Wilson came to believe that three sectors – transportation, communications, and energy – were critical to America's leadership in international relations. In each sector, his administration vigorously supported American interests. Regarding merchant shipping, it is significant that the Wilson administration chose to continue the emergency shipbuilding program after the war ended in 1918. Wilson himself seems to have supported this decision. According to Navy Secretary Josephus Daniels, Wilson said in 1920 that "he favored freedom of the seas but wished the American flag to float there [and] . . . was strong for merchant shipping."

Altogether 1,234 ships were completed in the years 1919 to 1922, giving the United States a large government-owned merchant fleet competitive with the British.[34]

In communications, the administration embarked on a nationalistic course that helped break British monopolies. Britain had wired the world in the twenty years after 1866, circling the globe with submarine cables and maintaining tight controls over equipment and knowledge. Ordinary Americans may have turned isolationist at the end of World War I, but leaders of the American establishment aspired to expand U.S. influence and commerce and resented British obstructions. In effect, they determined to leap-frog over British control of cables to establish American dominance in radio telegraphy. Unwilling to allow the Marconi interests with ties to Britain to dominate long-distance radio transmissions, Navy officials persuaded the Wilson administration to block a proposed sale of leading-edge alternator technology from General Electric to British Marconi. Instead, the U.S. government forced the sale of American Marconi to a newly created GE subsidiary, Radio Corporation of America (RCA). Its charter restricted foreign ownership to 20 percent and provided for a American government representative to sit on the RCA board. In this undertaking, Wilson authorized W. H. G. Bullard, the Director of Naval Communications, to represent the government.

Owen Young, the politically connected GE lawyer, who chaired the RCA board, wanted to make "America the center of the world" in radio communications.[35] RCA succeeded. Charging eighteen cents a word as compared with the submarine cable rate of twenty-five cents, RCA, the U.S. champion, quickly captured 30 percent of the Atlantic traffic and 50 percent of the Pacific by 1923. The growth of wireless had great significance. This success facilitated commercial and financial expansion, but it also fulfilled a national political need for "independence from British interference." Interestingly, in November 1929, shortly after the stock-market crash, a seismic upheaval on the bed of the Atlantic broke thirteen of twenty-one transatlantic cables. But few noticed this upheaval. The traffic simply moved to radio.[36]

Another area where the Wilson administration reversed course and embraced business expansion involved oil. The war had demonstrated the importance of oil. Petroleum was essential for many civilian uses and for much war production – and was vital for sea and land transportation. Naval ships and motor vehicles ran on oil. With Russia engulfed in war, America became the principal source for oil needed to fuel and lubricate the new technologies of warfare – the tank, the submarine, and motor vehicles. In 1914, the United States produced 65 percent of the world's petroleum and, after the war, shut off Allied access to Russian oil; America had to supply 80 percent of the Allies wartime oil requirements. When petroleum demand began outstripping supply, U.S. leaders began to worry that the nation would deplete its energy base and experience a "gasoline famine." In August 1919, the U.S. Geological Survey stated that domestic petroleum resources were inadequate to provide the estimated 100 million barrels needed by 1922 to operate the navy and the merchant marine. The United States would have to compete with other nations for imports of crude oil.[37]

British and French leaders also understood that oil was the blood of victory. Lord Curzon commented how Britain "floated to victory on a sea of American oil," and from this perceived vulnerability came British and French determination to acquire adequate oil supplies to support future military and diplomatic strategies. In 1919, American oil companies awakened to the realization that British companies had acquired more than half of the world's estimated oil reserves. Britain and France looked to new fields among remnants of the Turkish Empire. In May 1920, the two governments approved the infamous San Remo accord, carving up the Mesopotamian (Iraqi) oil fields for Anglo-Persian, the British champion, and a French competitor. America's former allies seemed to be moving swiftly to gain a monopoly of critical Middle East oil fields and to exclude American oilmen from the Dutch East Indies. Meanwhile, British oil executives told the press that the United States would soon be dependent on British oil resources.

The challenge aroused Washington and produced a rapprochement between Wilson and the oil industry. A series of State Department reports to Congress demonstrated that British and Dutch oil interests were engaged in a worldwide campaign to establish themselves in promising oil fields and to exclude American competitors. The specter of a domestic oil shortage, a 50 percent increase in oil prices at the end of the war, and the fear of British treachery helped produce a rapprochement between the oil industry and the Wilson administration. When the British excluded U.S. oil company geologists from the mandate, Secretary of State Bainbridge Colby protested in November 1919. The industry enjoyed closer relations with the Navy Department. Standard Oil of New Jersey's unofficial ambassador, E. J. Sadler, a graduate of the Naval Academy traveled to Turkey and visited with an academy classmate who commanded the cruiser *Galveston* then in Constantinople. The two then talked with Rear Admiral Mark Bristol, the U.S. commissioner to Turkey. Working together, these three succeeded in turning Washington officials around. Soon Navy Secretary Daniels complained that "Great Britain is getting oil here and buying concessions everywhere and expects to control commerce and merchant marine through control of oil."[38]

They also succeeded in arousing the State Department to challenge the San Remo pact. Wilson's State Department voiced dismay about the secret deal to divide the spoils of war and demanded an American presence in any rewards from the Turkish Empire. In effect, the State Department reiterated the Open Door policy, insisting that American firms not be excluded from the mandate. British diplomats in Washington interpreted the U.S. protest as evidence of the vast influence Standard Oil could bring to bear on officials in Washington, since Secretary of State Colby had previously acted as a legal advisor to Standard Oil. "The American Executive," Ambassador A. Geddes told London in July 1920, "can no more control the oil interests than a young girl can physically hold a charging bull."[39]

Liberal Internationalism

Woodrow Wilson is often remembered for his vision of a League of Nations, providing a permanent guarantee of each member's territorial integrity and political independence. The league's structure also rested on an institutional foundation of economic internationalism, including open trade and freedom of the seas. In effect, the league offered the world economic community rules and institutions to facilitate growing cooperation and interdependence. Looking back, scholars note that Versailles led to the establishment of the first functional international organization (the International Labor Organization) and set in motion plans for cooperation in transit and communications. This work, and related economic conferences, offered an "apprenticeship in international economic cooperation" that led to the establishment of permanent trade and financial institutions after World War II.[40]

The president's path-breaking plan for peace took note of underlying factors driving the globalization process. Wilson recognized the significance of technological innovation in transforming the conduct of warfare and strategic thought about war. In undelivered remarks given to his stenographer in late autumn 1916, just months before America declared war, Wilson expressed his understanding of the most dangerous development in military affairs of the young century: the concept of total war. Before this conflagration, war had been "a sort of national excursion," but it had lost its glory because of the "modern processes" of armed conflict.[41] Because of the devastation wrought by technology, the intense and stubborn national ambitions of the belligerents, and the global nature of the war, Wilson thought of the conflict as an object lesson for the future. Allies and enemies alike had a common interest in eliminating warfare as a means of conducting their foreign relations; his fourteen-point peace plan addressed the interdependence of all nations in a global political and economic system to make war obsolete.

Idealistic in conceptualization, Wilson's plan reformulated America's relationship with the world at a time when the dislocations of war threatened long-term harm to the flows of goods and capital that had integrated financial and commercial markets in the Atlantic region before World War I. Beyond the specific territorial considerations of the Fourteen Points, his liberal scheme undercut the ancien regime in favor of the American legalist-capitalist version, and thus faced rough treatment from the European Allies at the peace conference in Paris in 1919. Several controversial points dealt with empowering colonial and occupied peoples to choose their own forms of government. Wilson wanted to democratize a world, believing that enlightened public opinion would restrain the militaristic elites responsible for World War I. In effect, his Fourteen Points appealed to Germans eager to jettison the kaiser and represented a conscious effort to undercut Bolshevism in Russia. The Bolsheviks promoted their own brand of globalization, one based on the notion of a class struggle pitting the world's workers against capitalists.

Wilson's Fourteen Points and his peace plans proposed to institutionalize the open-door ideology in the structure of the League of Nations. Freedom of the seas, the removal of trade barriers, disposition of colonial issues, an end to secret diplomacy and alliances, and curbs on wasteful arms spending were all part of his grand design. Liberals like Wilson questioned realpolitik and the operation of the balance of power, for they believed that such thinking had produced the horrors of World War I. A liberal settlement, based on open diplomacy and greater democracy, as well as open markets and a mechanism for resolving disputes and assuring collective security, would preserve peace in the American Century.

The League of Nations embodied American progressivism and globalism. It was Wilson's idea that victors and vanquished alike, in full understanding of their intimate linkages to each other, would form a universal alliance under the guidance of the big powers. No longer would alliances or even a balance-of-power structure rule the international arena. Instead, nations would join in collective security, rationally deciding matters in an international version of progressive-era administrative bodies. The league was comprised of a legislative (Assembly), an executive (Council), and an independent judicial (the Permanent Court of International Justice) branches, with its peace, economic, and social missions served by various commissions and an administrative Secretariat. Wilson emphasized that his was not an idealistic structure but one built on modern "scientific" concepts.[42]

Wilson believed (however erroneously, as the next twenty years would show) that interdependence compelled international cooperation. As one historian put it, "wars were now global, because interdependence was more than economic; indeed, the globe was like a dry forest that could easily be set ablaze even by sparks struck from small conflicts." Any conflict involving the major European powers had worldwide implications, as indeed the First World War showed. One reason Wilson had chosen to intervene was because he feared Germany's advance through Central and Eastern Europe, once accomplished, would consolidate Berlin's control over European trade. The kaiser might then strike out for Asia, dominating commercial routes and, hence, the world. This early version of the domino theory, perhaps alarmist, nonetheless spoke volumes about how World War I had globalized conceptions of diplomacy and warfare.[43]

In arousing public expectations of a liberal postwar peace, based on the League of Nations and the Fourteen Points, Wilson made it difficult to compromise differences with the European victors who took a more cynical view of diplomatic relationships. Britain and France wanted Germany to pay the costs of the war, and so the Treaty of Versailles's provisions treated Germany harshly. The treaty handed to Germany in June 1919 took territory and compelled a huge payment of reparations to the Allies. The Germans, who had come to the peace table thinking themselves equals, not the vanquished, felt betrayed. The harsh economic and territorial provisions, as well as the war-guilt clause, played into Adolph Hitler's hands, providing fodder for him to denounce the European democracies and launch Germany on the road to war once again. Meanwhile, the Treaty of Versailles created resentment in Asia. The victors gave Germany's possessions in China to Japan, thus further vitiating the principles of the Open Door. Then Wilson antagonized the Japanese by siding with the European powers to defeat a declaration on racial equality. As a result, the peace settlement that was supposed to heal and provide a structure for peace and prosperity created new controversies. The winds of globalization weakened at Versailles.[44]

Nor were a majority of Americans ready to accept the responsibilities that went with greater international integration. When Wilson returned home with his league and the treaty, he found a country divided. Liberals accused him of selling out his progressive principles when he allowed the Allies to impose selfish demands on Germany. In general, the left and liberals had welcomed his denunciations of imperialism, Teddy Roosevelt's Big Stick diplomacy, and Taft's dollar diplomacy. Pacifists as well as internationalists had rallied to his side, having themselves formulated the original elements of the League of Nations idea. They looked to the league to reunite socialists and liberals, but they were disappointed by his compromises in Paris and disillusioned with the fading possibilities of social justice at home, due to wartime nationalist propaganda that made such internationalist endeavors as collective security more difficult.

Conservatives believed that the league idea was premature. The peace treaty failed to win the support of the Republican majority in the U.S. Senate, who saw the opportunity for political gains in coming elections. Conservative internationalists understood that global interdependence necessitated American commitments to uphold world security and prosperity. But the league went too far for them. Teddy Roosevelt worried that the United States would place too much stock in collective security while giving up its own military preparedness. Some senators had political motives for rejecting Wilson's league, even though the league's charter was indeed utopian in conception. It imposed enormous security responsibilities – relating to the members' territorial integrity and political independence – on an untested international organization. The document also abandoned some 150 years of American foreign policy in which the nation had largely tried to stay aloof from international organizations. Regardless of the changes wrought by globalization, the American people were not prepared for such sweeping commitments in 1919. President Wilson, who suffered a paralyzing stroke during the course of his public campaign to sell the league, failed to educate the public and many of the elite as to why America should assume such far-reaching peacekeeping responsibilities.[45]

As it turned out, Wilson did not succeed in creating conditions for permanent peace, establishing durable institutions for world governance, or transforming the basis of international relations. His undertaking was not a complete failure. In the economic area, Wilson left an enduring mark and established a pattern for his presidential successors. Generally supportive of economic internationalism, as it existed before World War I under British leadership, Wilson and his intellectual heirs determined to provide American public and private leadership for the postwar economic and financial system. In light of Wilson's early antipathy to big business, it is ironic that he must be remembered as an architect of the American

Century. It took World War I and Wilson's presidency to give structure to McKinley's visions.

But if Wilson was the first president to give impetus to institutional internationalism, he was also the first to encounter the intense passions and conflicts aroused in more recent debates over globalization. After World War I, Americans were not disposed to relinquish sovereignty and freedom of action for the benefits of an international agreement. They were not disposed to open their borders to the world's goods, to help the vanquished recover, or to maintain open borders to people who wished to migrate. The defeat of the Treaty of Versailles showed the variations in thinking about globalization. Prevailing sentiment was unprepared to abandon the nationalism so prevalent in society and politics even as the expansive course of global commerce and investment and America's role in the world maintained its momentum. Americans would never fully adopt Wilsonian ideals until the end of the century. During the Cold War they reformulated the balance of power into regional, Free World military and economic pacts that diverged from Wilson's worldwide internationalism.[46]

The conflict between transnational business and revolutionary nationalism – another of the conflicts aroused by globalization – surfaced in the Wilson era during the Mexican and Soviet Revolutions. For a time, the nationalists prevailed. Mexico's postrevolution constitution restricted foreign ownership of land and subsoil resources. This threatened American and British oil properties. In Russia, the Bolshevik government survived a shaky start, including a civil war in which Americans participated and helped to create a decidedly anticapitalist regime. The Soviet Union lashed out at the imperialist nature of capitalist globalization but then retreated to build a socialist state under Communist Party control at home. Many Westerners who had invested in Russia also found their assets nationalized. Together the Mexican and Soviet Revolutions marked a distinct setback for the ideas of nineteenth-century liberalism and a sharp deterioration of the investment climate in developing nations. Thus, ideologically and politically, the world started to split even as Wilson's vision reached its expressive high point.[47]

At the economic level, the belligerents of the First World War had served notice that, although they may support the League of Nations, they would protect their national economic interests. They retained their colonies, constrained commercial freedom, and forced the losers to pay heavy reparations, unmindful or uncaring about the economic consequences of the peace. Nationalism prevailed in the Treaty of Versailles, and thus undercut the globalized vision of Wilson and others. Had Wilson's vision prevailed in Paris and at home, America might have assumed formally the responsibilities of global leadership by 1920. As it turned out, Wilson's defeat signaled a different outcome. In the years ahead, technology, business, personal contacts, and cultural forces continued to draw Europe and the Americas closer together. A divergent pattern emerged in government political and economic policies, however. Responding to renewed nationalism and isolationist sentiment, U.S. officials backpedaled on several proposals that might have established rules and structures for globalization process and hastened America's leadership role in world political and financial institutions.

3

Exporting the American Dream, 1921–1929

Under American financial and business leadership, the globalization process resumed during the 1920s. Despite a resurgence of nationalistic sentiment in the United States, leaders of the private sector took the initiative to expand overseas commercial and cultural relationships. They sought to transfer the "miracles" of American individualism, inventions, and industry to a world weary of military conflicts and searching for direction. Using citizen-to-citizen contacts, they sought to sew the seeds for a durable peace and closer economic cooperation. Although the U.S. government kept its distance from the ill-fated League of Nations, officials were not oblivious to issues of emerging strategic economic significance such as access to vital raw materials (petroleum and rubber) and promotion of American interests in radio and aviation. They also used diplomacy to head off a strategic arms race and to promote the peaceful resolution of conflicts. The Great Depression and World War II disrupted, and partially discredited, many of these efforts. Yet, the decade after World War I is vital to understanding the universal appeal of "Americanization" and the determination of American leaders to succeed in building a mutually beneficial global system after World War II.

In the aftermath of World War II, and for much of the Cold War era, it was fashionable for historians to describe the 1920s as a decade when Americans turned their backs on the League of Nations and European reconstruction. But recent interpretations offer a more robust view of the period, stressing business and cultural involvement in international activities, public and private sector cooperation, and constructive diplomatic efforts. The latter interpretations are more compatible with reality of the ongoing globalization process.[1]

Nationalism and Internationalism

The twin defeats in 1920 of the Treaty of Versailles in the Senate and the internationalist Democrats in the presidential election stalled American diplomatic efforts to establish a high-profile institutional structure to channel the globalization process and to promote international security under the auspices of the League of Nations. But, it did not dampen the executive branch's enthusiasm for diplomatic initiatives and for international cooperation – especially in technical economic areas and in arms control. The United States was now the world's leading creditor and largest exporter. It emerged from World War I with a powerful military force and the world's largest merchant fleet. These realities compelled the country to play a leadership role in world politics. But the postwar recession, the Red Scare and efforts to regulate immigration, and the sharp hike in tariffs under the new Republican administration indicated that many Americans adhered to a more parochial view of national interests. In particular, farmers, who had overexpanded during World War I, and import-competing businesses, fearful of cheap postwar European competition, understandably placed their own short-term needs for protection above the broader concern for international recovery. Thus, Congress raised import barriers and insisted that their former allies in Europe repay their war debts.

Congress was more isolationist and protectionist in outlook, as reflected in the Fordney-McCumber Tariff of 1923, but the State Department necessarily looked outward, pursuing policies and initiatives intended to achieve long-term peace and prosperity. Because Europe had bought three-fifths of American exports before the war, it was in America's interest to help restore good customers to health and to discourage European restrictions on American trade and investments. Signaling American interest in general negotiations to reduce tariff barriers, Secretary of State Charles Evans Hughes in 1923 committed the United States to the unconditional most-favored-nation policy, a bargaining procedure that extended the same benefits to all trading partners. More generally, Washington policy makers embraced elements of internationalism, engaging in world affairs without becoming involved in Wilson's ill-fated League of Nations. One particularly successful initiative involved efforts to regulate arms competition by international treaties. The decade thus witnessed major conferences resulting in limits on warship construction and tonnage, and also an agreement on fortifications in the Pacific to enhance the Open Door doctrine.[2] This effort energized citizens, diplomats, and businesses into even more cooperative, internationalist endeavors during the era.

The spillover of internationalist thought into foreign policy was extensive. Disarmament was one arena; regional stabilization and multilateralism were others. The high point of idealism arrived with the Kellogg-Briand Pact of 1928, when thirty-three countries (the United States included) proclaimed war to be an illegal means of settling disputes. Outlawing war was sheer fantasy, but the pact symbolized faith in an international system of peace. Furthermore, not only did the European powers guarantee their borders, but the Chinese and Japanese also took part in disarmament treaties, and even the United States veered from the unilateralism of the Monroe Doctrine in Latin America and turned toward pan-Americanism. Secretary of State Charles Evans Hughes negotiated a series of conventions providing ways to settle disputes through diplomatic or judicial means, instead of military power. Americans talked of the "sanctity of contract" as the basis for global commercial expansion. The climax was Herbert Hoover's tour of the region in 1928, when the president-elect promised that his nation would be a "good neighbor" by, among other policies, not intervening militarily in Latin America. He made good on his pledge during his presidency.[3]

Rebuilding the World Economy

At a time when Congress reflected the isolationist impulses of grassroots America on tariff and war-debt issues, the New York banking community worked to restore the international economy, and reestablish the conditions for private capital flows and the reintegration of financial markets. They enjoyed considerable success, until the Great Depression shattered their efforts.

Central bankers – like Benjamin Strong of the New York Federal Reserve Bank and Montagu Norman of the Bank of England – operated with considerable autonomy from elected officials, and they assumed broad responsibilities with the backing and support of powerful private bankers like J. P. Morgan and Company. Strong cooperated with his British counterpart to stabilize key currencies on an ad hoc basis and to restore the gold standard. In 1925, Winston Churchill, the chancellor of the exchequer, made the fateful decision for Britain to return to the gold standard at a dollar-exchange rate of $4.86. This decision pleased, and saved, the financial services sector and the city of London.

But, it left the pound overvalued, imposing a heavy burden on British labor and industry – especially coal and textiles – that relied on export sales.[4]

Britain's return to gold followed a private understanding between Norman and Strong. The two central bankers agreed that interest rates in London should be higher than in New York. This would tend to strengthen sterling by diverting short-term balances to London. Strong's decision to subordinate U.S. interest rates to London rates had the effect of contributing to stock-market speculation in the United States and creating the speculative mania that ended in the crash of 1929. President Herbert Hoover subsequently blamed the Federal Reserve for the stock-market boom and for giving higher priority to global responsibilities than to domestic concerns. He wrote that the misguided Federal Reserve cheap-money policies, pursued by governor Strong and the Federal Reserve Board in Washington, "emphasizes the dangers of undue powers in the hands of mere individuals, governmental or private."[5]

Paradoxically, Strong's effort to stabilize the British currency and to establish the basis for international financial stability may have set in motion speculative forces that ultimately had catastrophic consequences for economic internationalism. But in the short run, they seemed successful. Britain's return to gold in 1925 soon led to similar political decisions. By 1926, thirty-nine countries had adopted the gold standard. This stabilization proved unsustainable, however. The pound was overvalued, while the U.S. dollar and French franc were undervalued. This depressed British exports and stimulated imports; in France and America, it had the opposite effect. Running huge trade surpluses, France and the United States soon garnered the lion's share of the world's gold supply. By 1929, they had 60 percent of the world's gold but only about a third of international trade.

Another important architect of international economic reconstruction, who worked closely with the central bankers, was Morgan partner Thomas Lamont, himself a protégé of Woodrow Wilson. Lamont and his banking colleagues advanced a suave, cosmopolitan public image of themselves as "statesmen of finance, engaged in great public service in directing huge flows of capital to bolster the world's economies for the common good." Lamont enjoyed the limelight, but bankers generally shunned the press and politicians and acted in what they perceived to be the broader interests of international civilization.[6] Because of the political conflicts in Washington, the New York Federal Reserve and the treasury could not openly support European stabilization, so the House of Morgan provided stabilization loans to Austria in 1921 and then acted for the State Department in organizing the Dawes Plan to stabilize Germany. The Dawes loan (for $110 million) was something of a charade. It improved the private investment climate in Germany after the hyperinflation of 1923, and U.S. private capital poured in. Ford, General Motors, Dupont, General Electric, Standard Oil of New Jersey, and Dow Chemical all expanded their direct investments – decisions that provided Adolf Hitler with a splendid industrial machine and money to finance massive rearmament. But as Ron Chernow observed: "the world was trapped in a circular charade in which American money paid to Germany was handed over as reparations payments to the Allies, who sent it back to the United States as war debt." Privately, Morgan partners were skeptical about the viability of the Dawes loan.[7]

In a similar fashion, the Morgan interests assisted Italy. Thomas Lamont helped Benito Mussolini negotiate a lenient debt settlement with Italy in 1926. As with the Dawes Plan for Germany, Morgan provided a $100 million loan to Italy and provided a catalyst for further U.S. investment. The bank also lent money to the city of Rome and to two large Italian corporations, Fiat and Pirelli. Assisting Benjamin Strong and the central bankers, the Morgan partners provided a credit to the Banca d'Italia that permitted its return to the gold standard. Thus, at a time when Congress and the executive branch opposed further government loans to Italy and Germany, the State Department seems to have worked quietly with private bankers to stabilize currencies, restore the open international economy, and prepare the way for private capital flows.[8]

During the 1920s, the New York investment banking community achieved its aspiration of becoming a major lending center, and the United States became the world's leading creditor. From 1919 to 1931, total portfolio investment (loans) increased rapidly from $2.2 billion to $7.2 billion, while U.S. direct investments rose steadily from $3.5 billion to $7.996 billion. The peak came in 1927–8 after the Dawes Plan and stabilization of the British pound sterling. But with the increase of the U.S. discount rate from 3.5 percent to 5 percent in 1928 to stem stock-market speculation, U.S. foreign lending halted. Over the period, 40 percent of the foreign dollar loans were issued for Europeans and 22.2 percent, for Latin Americans. Reflecting a complete shift of Canadian borrowing from London to New York, 29 percent involved North America. Germany was the largest borrower, obtaining $1.3 billion in the U.S. market (14 percent of the total), while Argentina was the second largest borrower with $741.2 million (8 percent).[9]

American Elites Become Internationalized

Despite America's nonmembership in the League of Nations, individual Americans actively took part in the activities of its affiliated agencies, especially the International Labor Organization, World Health Organization, World Court, and a committee designed to enhance scholarly and artistic exchanges. The latter activities recognized that economic and social problems could be solved globally only through "cooperation across national boundaries," as historian Akira Iriye noted. Downplaying patriotism, intellectuals took part in league exchange activities. Such cultural internationalism grew stronger as nations created numerous associations designed to facilitate global ties.

In the United States, political scientists began studying the causes of war, and universities offered new courses in various national histories and languages, all a reflection of the need to understand the global context in which America operated. Americans participated in the league's intellectual cooperation committee (Raymond Fosdick of the Rockefeller Foundation was the U.S. delegate) and organized hundreds of scholarly discussion groups, such as the Institute for Pacific Relations, a multinational association of journalists, academics, and businesspeople based in New York. Universities also devised programs to improve public understanding of America's new world responsibilities. President Harry Garfield of Williams College organized the Williamstown Institute of Politics, which every summer brought business leaders, diplomats, and scholars to Massachusetts to discuss international problems. And, Archibald Carey Coolidge, a Harvard history professor, helped found the Council on Foreign Relations and edited its journal *Foreign Affairs* to educate the attentive public about world affairs.[10]

In the 1920s, America increasingly took the view that international exchanges fostered international understanding and promoted world peace. The new Guggenheim Foundation funded artistic projects and scholarly research, focusing on Latin American intellectuals. And the nation supported student exchanges. The Institute of International Education funded and directed foreign students to universities throughout the United States. Asians were the main beneficiaries, but, increasingly, Latin American and European youth traveled to America to study.[11]

A number of nongovernmental service organizations supported international activities during the 1920s. One was Rotary, a service organization founded in Chicago (1905) and composed of businesspeople and professionals. It expanded rapidly after World War I. Rotarians soon changed the organization's name to Rotary International and pledged to advance understanding, goodwill, and international peace through service. The devastating 1923 Tokyo earthquake presented an early opportunity. Rotarians raised $89,000 to assist victims. They also sponsored exchanges between France and Germany to build personal relationships, hoping to avert another war.[12]

Government-Business Partnership

The actions and perspectives of big business are important to understanding how the globalization process continued to build linkages among nations and peoples in the 1920s. After the destruction of World War I, many in the private sector spoke confidently of a "new era" in which the world benefited from business. Their optimism reflected faith that new commercial technologies would transform the world and help overcome political differences. Dramatic improvements in transportation (the airplane and the automobile) and communications (the radio and movies) facilitated the movement of people and ideas while conquering the ignorance associated with isolation. Thomas Lamont, a J. P. Morgan partner, was one of the cosmopolitans who thought America's intellectual power and material resources could "render high service to the world and to herself." Owen Young, a founder of RCA and chairman of General Electric, also held U.S. cultural and "economic integration of the world" vital for world peace and prosperity. Henry Ford, one of the icons of the age, believed that global industrialization would solve problems of poverty and channel revolutionary nationalism toward moderation. According to Ford, by promoting the mass-production techniques of Taylorism, America could export its efficiency and management styles around the world. "[P]olitical boundaries and political opinions don't really make much difference. It is the economic condition which really forces change and compels progress."[13]

One of the leading boosters of business expansionism was Secretary of Commerce Herbert Hoover. Called the nation's "first international citizen," he began his distinguished career as a mining engineer in Australia, and then served as U.S. food administrator during World War I, spearheaded the relief mission to Europe afterward, and acquired a reputation as an expert on Asia and Latin America. As commerce secretary, Hoover brought a pragmatic, nonpolitical approach to government, where he reorganized the Commerce Department and promoted business opportunities abroad. He quintupled the personnel and budget of the Bureau of

Foreign and Domestic Commerce to provide assistance for export promotion. Under Hoover, the Commerce Department, became a hub of activity. The business community was pleased with Hoover's initiatives. His organization provided a wealth of foreign commercial information to producers interested in expanding their international business.[14]

There was especially close cooperation between the public and private sectors in certain strategic industries – communications, transportation, and petroleum. Probusiness Republican administrations vigorously backed the expansion of American corporate champions important to the globalization process and the success of the American Century. As noted previously, the federal government helped create RCA to break British dominance of international communications. RCA, eager to introduce long-distance wireless communications between the United States and Europe, and the United States and Asia, invested in radio stations in Poland, Sweden, China, the Philippines, and Argentina. The State Department supported RCA's expansion – as when it urged a monopoly concession in Poland for a radio station. RCA enjoyed such phenomenal success in only two years that David J. Sarnoff, the head of RCA, could proudly assert in November 1922: "the center of the world's most modern communication system has transferred from London to New York." Noting that trade is often said to follow the flag, Sarnoff observed that "before trade can follow the flag, communications must precede it."[15]

Government support in the 1920s contributed to the emergence of another national champion in the communications area: International Telephone and Telegraph Corporation (ITT). Colonel Sosthenes Behn, considered a zealous and fervent expansionist, created a global telephone empire during the 1920s with money borrowed from J. P. Morgan and National City Bank. He bought British telephone companies in Uruguay, Chile, Brazil, and Argentina and linked them with long-distance lines. He even purchased the entire Spanish telephone system. By 1929, Behn's ITT controlled two-thirds of the telephones and half the cables in Latin America, one-third of the Atlantic cables, and factories and utilities throughout the world. He did "all this on borrowed money!" Nine years after its formation, ITT had a burgeoning communications business entirely outside the United States, and it had a worldwide employment of 95,000 – more than any other U.S. corporation abroad.[16]

Other communications firms and networks expanded, too. AT&T strengthened its international positions during the 1920s, although the extent of U.S. government assistance is unclear. American Telephone and Telegraph (AT&T) opened telephone service from New York to London in January 1927. Initially, the price for a three-minute phone conversation was $75. By 1936, that fell to $21. The growth of business during the 1920s was a boon for Western Union. In 1929, it transmitted 87,372,278 words internationally, compared with 37,972,000 in 1913. In addition, in the late 1920s, United Press International and Associated Press broke European regional monopolies run by Reuters, Havas, and Wolff and created the first worldwide news empire.[17]

Hoover and his subordinates in the Commerce Department vigorously supported efforts to build up the maritime industry and to expand American aviation. The Jones-White Act, or Merchant Marine Act of 1928, established for the first time a national shipping policy. It created a $250 million construction fund to build ships in American yards and authorized the postmaster to make long-term contracts, not to exceed ten years, for the purposes of establishing fast and regular shipping lines to all corners of the world. For the Grace Company, which served the west coast of South America, mail contracts, not the freight or passenger service, determined profitability.[18]

As commercial aviation emerged, the U.S. government made available similar mail subsidies and effectively picked national champions. Aviation appealed to the sense of pan-Americanism, of joining the hemisphere together, as well as to expanding U.S. influence around the world. One major beneficiary was Juan Trippe's Pan American Airways. The son of a New York investment banker and a Yale University graduate, Trippe became interested in air transport after World War I. In 1922, he signed a contract with the United Fruit Company to fly documents over the mountains from the Honduran coast to the capital city of Tegucigalpa, a trip that took three days by land but hours by air. Business soon sagged, but by the middle of the decade, Trippe had formed several air transport companies to break into the shipping business. He had grand dreams of dominating Latin American routes, which had already grabbed the attention of the Germans and an American group led by Henry "Hap" Arnold of the Army Air Corps. He also envisioned an "air bridge" from Alaska across the Bering Strait to Russia and Asia, a dream close to E. H. Harriman's world transportation network of two decades before. In 1925, he eyed the Key West–Havana route. By shrewd investments, which partnered him with rich young and adventurous bankers such as Bill Rockefeller, he formed Pan Am two years later to accomplish this mission. In 1925, the U.S. Post Office was given authority to contract with private parties to send mail by air, and U.S. mail subsidies (authorized under the Foreign Air Mail Act of March 8, 1928) soon offered generous assistance to start-up airlines. Trippe obtained the contract for service between Key West and Havana and successfully began mail service in October 1927. To guard his investment, Trippe wisely christened the plane the *General Machado*, in honor of the Cuban dictator.[19]

Trippe had met Charles Lindbergh in 1926, claiming he had watched the "American Eagle" take off on his historic flight across the Atlantic. Now Trippe enlisted the famous flyer to work for Pan Am. Lindbergh not only flew some of the newly won Foreign Air Mail routes in the hemisphere but signed a contract in 1929 for four years as a technical advisor. Pan Am qualified for several routes to Mexico, the Caribbean, and then Central America; Lindbergh flew the Miami-Panama Canal inaugural leg, with hundreds of fans in attendance at both ends.

Pan Am continued to expand. In 1929, Trippe bought up Campania Mexicana de Aviacion, which dominated Mexican air transport that served the cardinal purpose of flying sacks of gold over the heads of frustrated banditos. This allowed Pan Am to take hold of the mail links for this American neighbor, which also furthered Ambassador Dwight Morrow's efforts to smooth over economic relations between the two nations. Then, Trippe combined with W. R. Grace to establish Panagra (Pan American & Grace Airways) serving the west coast of South America. By 1930, the airline had routes throughout Latin America. Trippe also thought of passenger traffic, too, devising (with Lindbergh) ways that "flying boats" could take people through the region, and even outward across the Pacific. Assisted by the State Department, he negotiated air routes throughout the hemisphere. According to one historian, the U.S. government favored Pan Am. "The U.S. government attempted to use air connections as a tool in diplomacy in order to hold a regional superiority for the United States in Latin America, to encourage U.S. trade, and to serve as a challenge to the air links Europeans were making."[20]

In energy policy, the Republican presidents took a more vigorous approach in support of U.S. industry than had the Wilson administration. After Harding's inauguration in March 1921, American oil producers found a friend in the White House and one of their own, Albert Fall, as secretary of the interior. In announcing the administration's intention to support American oil interests, Secretary of State Charles Evan Hughes made it clear that the State Department would prefer not to choose between American claims. In effect, the Harding administration invited Standard Oil to join with some other producers, and the U.S. government pressed this joint claim with a vigorous oil policy. Along with opposition to the San Remo accord, it resisted expropriation of American interests in Mexico and offered strong diplomatic representations to discrimination in Dutch colonies. The Harding administration also pushed settlement of an outstanding dispute with Colombia over the Panama Canal, thus opening the way for U.S. oilmen in that once unfriendly nation. The British Foreign Office, which had resisted the outgoing Wilson administration and opposed the Harding claims, finally awoke to the advisability of a settlement with the red-line agreement of 1928. It opened the Middle East to American participation, and soon Jersey Standard and four other American firms had a major stake in the Middle East. What produced the shift in British thinking? Historians believe it was the foreign ministry's recognition of the need for a general rapprochement with America.[21]

With Mexico, President Calvin Coolidge finally managed an agreement on oil rights that exhibited the business-led globalization of the era. Plutarco Calles, the president of Mexico, hailed from a development wing of Mexican nationalists willing to trade radicalism for goods, money, and modernization. American oilmen were pleased and, in fact, helped finance his government. In return, they sidestepped the British and soon dominated the Mexican oil business. Coolidge named Wall Street banker Dwight Morrow as his new ambassador to Mexico in 1927, and Morrow and Calles (whom many U.S. entrepreneurs deemed a dangerous socialist) sought to settle the simmering subsoil petroleum issue. A member of J. P. Morgan and Company who was involved in negotiating a U.S.-Mexican debt repayment agreement in 1925, Morrow was a welcome emissary to Mexico, particularly because the ambassador abhorred armed intervention and preferred diplomacy as a means of twisting arms.[22]

Morrow turned his attention to banker diplomacy, establishing contacts with Mexicans, oilmen, and the State Department and encouraging U.S. producers to reach an equitable solution to the subsoil issue. The eventual accord gave foreign oilmen rights to concessions on property on which they had undertaken "positive acts," such as drilling, before May 1917. This episode did not end the conflict between international oilmen, the U.S. government, and revolutionary Mexico. Indeed, Mexico would expropriate those properties in 1938. But it underscored the nature of the continuing conflict between sponsors of globalization, who wished to exploit resources and serve international markets, and the defenders of nationalism, determined to retain control over domestic resources.[23]

Soviet Relations

A somewhat different situation involving foreign business interests and revolutionary governments troubled U.S.-Soviet relations. In this case, the Republican administrations also strove to balance foreign policy and commercial considerations. Disdainful of the Bolsheviks, Washington refused to establish diplomatic relations with the Soviet Union until 1933. There were a number of reasons for this policy. Lenin's government, which was hostile to private property and capitalism, appeared determined to spread its revolutionary ideology around the world. U.S. oil companies attributed disputes in Mexico over American subsoil property rights to Lenin's influence. Soviet ties to factions competing for control in China radicalized nationalism there, which led to attacks on foreign (including American) merchants and missionaries. Deportees and ex-patriots from the United States, including hundreds of Wobblies, and American communists worked in the Soviet Union to build the worker state.

Yet, despite the political problems, private contacts continued. Herbert Hoover's famine relief efforts under the American Relief Administration, which reportedly saved ten million Russians from starvation, represented a visible example of how philanthropic work mimicked the realities of globalization. American business saw Russia as a "New Eldorado" of opportunity, much the way transnational business saw similar opportunities in China at the end of the twentieth century and believed that trade would effect change. Moreover, the U.S. government permitted trade and direct investments, which helped prop up the Bolshevik government and modernize the Soviet economy with new technology. Sinclair Oil Company developed oil fields in northern Sakhalin with a newly won concession, and a number of entrepreneurs rushed into niches in the Soviet nation, including W. Averell Harriman in manganese mining, Henry Ford in tractor factories, and Armand Hammer in pencils. Ford, convinced that a U.S. industrial presence would help destroy communism, controlled 80 percent of the Russian tractor market by 1926. Three years later, he aided construction of a Russian-owned auto plant that turned out 100,000 cars a year. U.S. business thus attempted to teach the Soviets mass-production techniques. Outside influences may have had an impact on Soviet policy. The new Soviet leader, Josef Stalin, soon abandoned Lenin's world revolutionary strategy for one of domestic development. Therefore, in the 1920s, American capitalism – and the technological innovations associated with the automobile and mass production – proved an effective instrument of globalization, bringing people and nations closer together, harmonizing methods of production, creating jobs, and helping to bridge political differences.[24]

Exporting Autos and Images

Henry Ford, despite his quirks and flaws, is one individual who transformed the ways of people and nations. He did it with the automobile and mass production. During World War I, the Ford Motor Company chalked up an impressive record of wartime production, supplying cars, ambulances, trucks, tractors, and boats to the Allied cause. Scholars estimate that the Allies had 125,000 Model Ts, and they proved extraordinarily versatile and durable. In the 1920s, his Model T became known the world over, and foreign sales and assembly facilities soared. Ford understood the importance of technological advances that were globalizing the world and enhancing peace. Indeed, he did not truck with the past, believing that history served little purpose; the future was the key. He envisioned a "United States of the World" in which the airplane (Lindbergh took Ford up for his first flight ever in the *Spirit of St. Louis* just months after the historic solo Atlantic crossing; Ford also started producing planes for commercial purposes beginning in 1926), radio, and cinema "pass over the dotted lines on the map without heed or hindrance. They are binding the world together in a way no other systems can." What the auto did for America, the airplane, radio, and film "may do for the world. A wider circulation of right ideas always breaks down prejudices and helps secure universal understanding," Ford concluded.[25]

Another influential instrument of Americanization in the 1920s was the motion picture. It transmitted visual images of America, its people, and their products to audiences around the world. Along with the spread of radio, cinema was not only an American phenomenon but a global one as well – people around the world listened and watched the new media and thus developed some common cultural markers. Hollywood enjoyed the strong backing of the U.S. government after Will Hays, a former Republican member of Congress from Indiana, became president of the Motion Picture Producers and Distributors. In 1926, Congress appropriated funds to the Commerce Department to assist film exports.

In the period before talking pictures, Charlie Chaplin, Mary Pickford, and Douglas Fairbanks dominated the silent screen, and American films held 75 percent to 90 percent market share in most nations. Foreign markets generated 35 percent of film revenue, enabling Hollywood to produce hundreds of action films with violence, blazing guns, and bank robberies, as well as images of glittery new cities, open ranges, and extravagant consumption. Leaping over cultural barriers and market segmentation, the filmmakers in Los Angeles thus created a global image of life in the fast lane – a life that 99 percent of movie viewers could never expect to achieve. And Hollywood helped sell American products. With American films shaping consumer demand, orders surged for American cars, furniture, clothes, and appliances. In the 1920s, it was said, the sun never set on the British empire or on American films.[26]

Chaplin, Pickford, and Fairbanks became household names throughout the world. In 1914–15, after his meteoric rise to fame from poverty, Chaplin traveled the world, sought out even for his political views (he sympathized with antipoverty and global disarmament campaigns). Some thought he was a Bolshevik. For her part, Pickford – a seasoned European traveler received by an international elite of aristocrats, artists, and, on occasion, dictators such as Italy's Benito Mussolini – had reached the height of her fame in the mid 1920s. In Russia in 1926, she and Fairbanks were idolized by the 35,000 fans who greeted them at the Moscow railroad station, yelling her nickname Marushka. As Douglas Fairbanks, Jr., would remark decades later, Pickford and Fairbanks, Sr., "enjoyed a status in the world's imagination that is ... inconceivable and incomparable by today's standards."[27] American cultural expansion was a key element of globalization in an increasingly nationalistic world.

Yet even these three stars had to adjust to technology. When vacuum tubes were shown to catch waves of sound and release them over radio waves, the movie industry rapidly converted to talkies from the spring of 1928 through 1929. Chaplin resented the new medium because it undercut the skill and artistry of mime. He kept making silent movies, including *City Lights* in the mid 1930s, but gradually the introduction of talkies cut off non-English audiences from his films. Hollywood adapted to the new technology and collaborated with overseas firms to dub films in several languages. By 1931, Americans producers had regained almost all the German market they had lost because of talkies.[28]

The popularity of American films, and the dominance of Hollywood, aroused protests and strong reactions abroad. England's Lord Lee of Fareham, for example, castigated U.S. films as a "positive menace" to the world because they gushed with "cheap sentiment, ... vice, lust, greed, infidelity, murder, depravity, nationalism, non-American villains." France, determined to protect the French language, complained that American films were in "the process of Americanizing the world." This criticism was stepped up by French writers who, in 1930, published *The American*

Cancer. It warned that American industry, banks, and trade were subsuming Europe under their mechanized culture, eliminating national spirit and rights. To preserve their own cultures, and protect national film industries, Europeans soon imposed quotas on American films. Germany, France, and Britain all sought to limit Hollywood's influence.[29]

Trade Linkages

The spread of America's popular culture and its technology was reflected in trade patterns. The demand for popular U.S. products – particularly the automobile – soared during the 1920s. Cotton remained America's single largest export (14.9 percent of total exports) in 1929, but machinery (11.9 percent) and automobiles gained ground rapidly (10.5 percent), both up sharply from early in the decade. In each year of the decade, the United States enjoyed a merchandise trade surplus (exports minus imports). Beneath the data was another important reality: consumers everywhere aspired to own American products. They wanted Ford cars and tractors and American clothing and furnishings. Indeed, 10 percent of all autos produced in the United States entered export trade, and the leading markets were Canada, Australia, and Argentina followed by Belgium, Britain, Germany, and Japan. As Herbert Hoover announced, "Not a single automobile would run; not a dynamo would turn; not a telephone, telegraph, or radio would operate" without trade. International exchange was not "the noisy dickering of merchants and bankers – it is the lifeblood of modern civilization."[30]

After international trade regained prewar levels in the mid 1920s, it was clear that the United States had become the world's leading commercial power. While world trade, for all nations, rose only 13 percent between 1913 and 1929, America's more than doubled, evidence that the United States was the dynamic influence that shaped consumer wants around the world. Europe declined in importance as a trade partner – just before the war, Europeans accounted for nearly half of U.S. imports, but by 1929, they represented less than one-third. Japan and Canada both nearly doubled their share of U.S. imports. On the export side, there was phenomenal growth in sales to Pacific markets. Between 1913 and 1929, exports to Asia rose from 5.7 percent to 12.3 percent of total exports.

The Commerce Department promoted exports to China, and Congress, under prodding from Herbert Hoover, offered tax incentives to U.S. companies. They were not altogether successful, even as they joined the Japanese, for instance, in a multinational banking consortium aimed at facilitating trade expansion in China. Chinese nationalism at the end of the decade, as well as a lack of business interest, undermined the export promotion effort. Still, one positive outcome was increasing American-Japanese cooperation. It was manifest in naval limitation agreements in 1927 and 1930 and in expanded trade. Trade between the two nations at the end of the decade was more than twice the value of American-Chinese commerce. Indeed, in 1926 Japan surpassed Britain as America's second leading supplier of imports, but it remained behind Canada.[31]

Another huge growth area for exports was the western hemisphere. At the end of the 1920s, some 37 percent of U.S. exports went to hemisphere markets, up from 31 percent before the war. Trade expansion ran hand in hand with focused, and successful, U.S. efforts to capture European holdings in the region. Before the decade was out, businessmen, encouraged by the Commerce Department, invested large amounts of capital in natural resources, promoted the construction of a hemispheric transportation system, and advised many nations on improvements in their currency and banking procedures.[32]

Impressive as U.S. trade figures were, what is also striking was how the complex pattern of American trade helped effect recovery from the dislocations of World War I. Not only did the United States develop worldwide economic interests during the 1920s, but its trade was also part of a complex multilateral web, linking together customers in different regions. America ran merchandise deficits with primary producers in Latin America and Asia. They in turn used dollar earnings to buy manufactures from Europe, which used its earnings to buy goods from the United States and make payments on outstanding war debts. Unlike bilateral trade between an imperial power and its colonies, American trade in the 1920s spurred transactions among third parties. Herbert Hoover understood the practical benefits of this approach. America's depressed farms needed European markets, but European recovery required finding buyers for European manufactures. Hoover did not look on commerce as a war. He preferred a "larger vision," in which "our export trade does not grow by supplanting the other fellow but from the increased consuming power of the world."[33]

Expanding Investments

A review of investment data for the 1920s shows that total U.S. direct investment nearly doubled from $3.89 billion to $7.55 billion during the decade. For the most part, business sought opportunities in high-income areas – Canada and Europe – not in unstable developing lands. American investment in South America went into Argentine manufacturing or Venezuelan oil. The latter had long-term significance. Facing government pressures in Mexico after the revolution, oil companies turned to Venezuela where production costs were cheaper and the investment climate more receptive. By the end of the decade, Venezuela ranked second in world oil production to the United States. Oil soon provided 76 percent of its exports and generated half of government revenues.[34]

Other supply-oriented investments occurred in Central American agriculture. During the 1920s, the United Fruit Company expanded from the Caribbean to the Pacific coast of Central America. Soon United Fruit had a budget larger than that of Costa Rica. The export of bananas had become big business. Critics accused United Fruit of intervening in local politics in order to protect existing investments and to maintain political stability. In West Africa, the Firestone Rubber Company invested heavily in Liberian plantations, an action encouraged by local politicians concerned about British and French encroachments on Liberian sovereignty. They reasoned that with Firestone present, the U.S. government would protect the corporation from European incursions, which is indeed what happened.[35]

In Asia, the investments were smaller than in other regions but still represented a substantial $1 billion. American investments in Japan jumped after a 1923 earthquake devastated Tokyo. Taking advantage of Japanese manufacturing opportunities, Ford Motor Company built factories and autos in Japan, and other U.S. companies invested in chemicals and electronics. In China, the pattern was different. The bulk of U.S. investment capital went into Chinese utilities and telephone systems. Stanvac, a joint venture of Standard Oil of New Jersey and Standard Oil of New York, eager to serve expanding Asian markets for gasoline, refined petroleum in the Dutch East Indies and elsewhere in Asia.[36]

A desire to gain market share and take advantage of technological leadership drove many U.S. investments in Canada and Europe. American firms leaped over high tariff walls and established plants near their customers. Canada afforded a convenient base for penetrating the British Commonwealth preferential system of tariffs. In effect, the renewal of protectionism in the postwar period accelerated the outflow of American direct investment capital. During the decade, General Electric was one of the most expansion-minded American multinationals. Led by Gerard Swope and Owen Young, a friend of Woodrow Wilson, GE acquired a 90 percent share of Canada's largest electrical manufacturer and moved rapidly into all major markets. From worldwide investments of $24 million in 1927 (excluding Canada), the company's investments soared to $111.6 million in 1930. Some of the biggest GE gains were in Great Britain where it acquired a significant interest in the leading electrical enterprise and a significant minority share in Germany of Allgemeine Elektrizitats Gesellschaft (AEG). GE embarked on a global strategy to stabilize markets, diversify holdings, enforce its patents, and export products from the United States. A 1926 Supreme Court decision, upholding GE's famous "light-bulb cartel," which licensed its patents to domestic and foreign competitors, facilitated GE's efforts to use restrictive private business agreements to stabilize prices and markets.[37]

On foreign investment issues, Republican leaders in the White House and Congress during the 1920s did not jump at Wall Street's command. Many had strong ties to import-competing industries and even labor unions. With small town constituencies and strong support from labor-intensive industries, Republicans in government worried less about the problems of international financial stability than about the dangers that unfair competition from foreign cartels and nations with cheap currencies posed to American industries and workers. In contrast with a later generation of corporate Republicans, the small-town Republicans of the 1920s had reservations about business firms investing abroad in manufacturing plants that might later compete for sales in the American market. Secretary Hoover and his associates actually criticized the patriotism of firms that dared invest abroad to serve the American market. Said Louis Domeratzky, a Commerce Department official in 1925: "it would be an unpatriotic act ... to promote the sale of foreign products competing with those of the United States, even when such foreign products are the results of investment of American capital."[38]

But for export-competing and strategic industries and for investments supporting U.S. foreign policy interests, the government provided strong support. Presidents Harding and Coolidge issued statements backing overseas investors, and their administrations went out of their way to encourage investments in developing nations – particularly China. Concerned that policy not favor monopolies abroad, officials preferred to offer verbal support for nondiscriminatory approaches, such as the open door for U.S. business enterprises. Enlightened as this principle seemed, official efforts to encourage business expansion led inevitably to appeals that government intervene to protect the lives and properties of American citizens. Such interventions occurred in Nicaragua and China. In May 1928, the United States had 1,500 Marines stationed in China to protect

American citizens, including scholars, missionaries, government officials, and businesspeople, when the Nationalists came to power and tried to revise the Washington treaties that maintained the status quo of imperial domination at the expense of China.[39]

Tourism

Along with increased flows of goods and investments, tourism brought people closer together in the 1920s. Many GIs returned to Europe with their wives to visit the battlefields and friends. Immigrants used the peaceful interlude to visit family members who had remained in the Old World. The number of U.S. travelers departing for Europe and the Mediterranean rose from 196,000 in 1920 to 350,000 in 1929. From 1921 to 1930, an average of 414,000 individuals left the United States to go overseas – about two-thirds of them to Europe. But, travel was largely one way. The number of European visitors rose slightly from 36,000 in 1920 to 45,000 in 1929, and the flow of immigrants to America dropped sharply. In 1924, the United States imposed quotas on immigrants; thereafter European immigration slowed until 1931 when there was a small net emigration. Asians were barred entirely, and people from the Middle East and Africa were severely curtailed.[40] Pressure for immigration restrictions had the effect of slowing a major driver of the globalization process by the mid 1920s.

Pundits commented on spreading U.S. influence during the 1920s. Journalist Edgar Ansel Mowrer compared the "Americanizing of Europe" to the "Romanizing of the Mediterranean world some 2000 years ago" and predicted that America would prove "more powerful, more humane, more educated, more democratic and more glorious" than Rome. Certainly, Europeans complained about American vulgarity and bad taste – such as gum-chewing introduced by the U.S. Army – and grumbled in envy of American wealth. Nonetheless, they imitated the new Romans, acquiring household conveniences – vacuum cleaners, refrigerators, and washing machines – and modifying their attire in accordance with American styles. European males acquired American hats, open shirts, shoes, and hip-length trousers with belts. Previously Europeans had worn trousers close to the arm pits. Paris still dictated ladies' fashions, but even in this area Mowrer perceived the emerging influence of American buyers on trends.[41]

Perhaps nothing captured the attention of Europeans more than the trans-Atlantic flight of Charles Lindbergh in 1927. This was the 1920s

5. Charles Lindbergh and his plane the *Spirit of St. Louis*, which crossed the Atlantic in May 1927, initiating a revolution in travel and compressing the barriers of time and distance. (Denver Public Library)

equivalent of America's moon landing some forty years later. Days after two French pilots disappeared in their attempt to cross the Atlantic, "Lucky Lindy" took off from Roosevelt Field on Long Island, on May 20, and made his historic solo flight to Paris, 3,400 miles away and thirty-three-and-one-half hours later. He became an instant hero who also dramatized elements of techno-globalization. Reports of his journey came by telephone and were followed on the radio. The French Foreign Office raised the American flag, the first time a private citizen had been so saluted, while the British House of Commons gave him a standing ovation, another first for that body. Lindbergh himself understood the technical feat of his flight. Addressing the French Assembly, he told of former diplomat Benjamin Franklin's interest in eighteenth century French balloon trials. Air travel had leapt ahead since then; the voyage of his *Spirit of St. Louis* was the culmination of stunning invention and experimentation.

In addition, the "American Eagle" personified the commercial-diplomatic dynamism of his times. He piloted the first Pan Am flight between Mexico City and Brownsville, Texas (attached to Juan Trippe's new airmail empire) and flew a goodwill mission to Mexico just months after he returned from Europe on behalf of his future father-in-law, Dwight Morrow. Lindbergh lived up to the thousands of poems written about him and his flight, paens that flooded into magazines from every corner of the earth. Like the global business dreamers of the twentieth century, Lindbergh was, in the title of one, the "Last Frontiersman," a young Deadalus who exceeded the bounds of human activity.[42] Unfortunately for him, and for American business, too, the coming decade would cast grand visions of globalization down to earth.

The cosmopolitans of this phase of the American Century – particularly those in government, big industry like Ford and General Electric, and finance like Lamont – failed to establish lasting conditions for globalization. The Great Depression and the resurgence of economic nationalism destroyed their efforts. Also, they failed to convert mass public opinion. Small-town America was more concerned about farm prices and domestic jobs than about mastering markets for the benefit of Wall Street and big business. And, grassroots America had the support of key leaders in Congress.[43]

Reed Smoot, the chairman of the Senate Finance Committee, epitomized the isolationist mind-set of the older generation of leaders who controlled congressional levers of power. The only Mormon to serve in Congress while also sitting on the Latter Day Saint's governing board, Smoot was an apostle of protectionism. A talented legislator, he had a major hand in every tariff bill enacted in the first three decades of the American Century. Free-traders scorned Smoot for his ardent defense of the sugar tariff (where the Mormon Church had a direct business interest). Internationalists despised him for his opposition to the League of Nations, tepid support of disarmament pacts, and ardent backing of war debt repayment based on a rather severe interpretation of the "capacity to pay" principle. Smoot was unbending. A Republican nationalist, Smoot did not "understand why any American should consider the interests of the Iquotenose in the jungles of South America above those of our own people who are in distress because of excessive imports of foreign products." He saw the United States as a vulnerable island surrounded by a sea of world economic instability. To those who urged lower U.S. tariffs to facilitate European war-debts repayments, Smoot offered an alternative. He wanted the Europeans to cut wasteful military spending.[44]

During the 1920s, Republican administrations could not overcome the bedrock resistance to change from seniors members of Congress such as Smoot. As a result, little progress was made on tariffs, war debts, and relations with the league. But, they succeeded in encouraging the new technologies of globalization – particularly radio and aviation – and in advancing new ideas for structuring international relationships, such as the unconditional most-favored-nation policy, and arms control. But, as it turned out, the globalizers were battling against a strong nationalist tide.

4

Business Busted, Diplomacy Destroyed, 1929–1939

The Great Depression was one of the twentieth century's defining events. Following the crash of the New York stock market in 1929, the economic collapse spread globally, disrupting efforts to restore a vibrant international economy and demolishing diplomatic initiatives to establish a durable structure for world peace. To cope with the economic chaos, governments attempted to regulate business and markets. As the public-policy pendulum swung away from laissez-faire solutions, governments attempted to insulate national economies from the global financial contagion. Officials experimented freely, using various tools such as bureaucratic oversight, currency controls, trade barriers, barter payments, and restrictions on capital flows and migration.[1]

The economic disruptions shook the confidence of prominent academic economists who had long extolled the benefits of free trade and economic internationalism. John Maynard Keynes, the brilliant Cambridge University economist, became increasingly nationalistic and skeptical of free trade and capital flows. "I sympathize," he said, "with those who would minimize, rather than with those who would maximize, economic entanglement between nations. Ideas, knowledge, art, hospitality, travel – these are the things which should of their nature be international. But let goods be homespun whenever it is reasonably and conveniently possible; and, above all, let finance be primarily national."[2]

But paradoxically, as governments turned away from efforts to harmonize and integrate the international economy to cope with domestic distresses, advances in technology continued to erode the barriers of time, distance, and information that separated nations and people. Some of the most significant improvements took place in air travel and mass communications, particularly the movies and shortwave radio. At a time when dire economic circumstances compelled most government leaders to think locally, a few leaders in government and business dared to speak up for international economic cooperation. "[W]orld trade is the surest road to world peace," asserted Thomas J. Watson, the head of IBM and the International Chamber of Commerce. If goods did not cross borders, he feared that armies would.[3]

The Great Depression

The Great Depression's timing could not have been worse for America, the world, and the march of globalization. On the eve of the stock-market crash, the United States was a main engine of the global economy, accounting for two-fifths of its industrial production and 16 percent of its commerce. From 1929 to 1932, America's exports plummeted, production fell by half, and unemployment rocketed from 1.5 million to 12 million people. Hopes fell for debt and reparations settlement, monetary stabilization, capital flows, and expanded trade. The strain on gold reserves prompted currency restrictions and forced many nations off the gold standard. Wall Street, the principal source of international investment capital, virtually suspended operations. In place of open capital markets and multilateral trade, which had characterized the last years of the 1920s and reinforced the globalization process, the world turned to protectionist trade barriers, bilateralism, preferences, barter, and other forms of state intervention. The closed autarkic systems of Germany, Japan, and the Soviet Union, far more than the open trade and capital markets of nineteenth-century Britain, appeared to be the wave of the future.[4]

International flows of people, money, and trade declined sharply during the Depression. European emigration and travel was one victim of dire economic circumstances. Only 1.2 million departed during the 1930s. This was far less than the average of 8.1 million people emigrating each decade in the half century beginning in 1881. American tourism and travel also suffered. From 1921 to 1930, an average of 414,000 individuals left the United States to go overseas – about two-thirds of them to Europe. During the next decade, travel fell 19 percent.[5] A series of financial and political dislocations after 1929 severely depressed foreign capital flows until after recovery from World War II. The inflow of foreign long-term investment (calculated in constant dollars) exceeded 1928 levels ($463 million) only once until 1966. Meanwhile, U.S. direct investment abroad, which peaked in 1929 at $602 million, did not surpass that level until 1956.

Not surprisingly, the Depression brought great volatility in currency and capital markets – as speculators sought to shift assets into gold and strong currencies.[6]

Trade was another major casualty. League of Nations data show a severe contraction as the value of world imports fell from $3 billion in April 1929 to $944 million in February 1933. The quantity of U.S. exports dropped an estimated 47 percent from 1929 to 1933, while U.S. imports fell 34 percent. Another important indicator of internationalization is the percentage of a nation's trade as a share of gross domestic product. This measure shows the linkages of imports and exports (goods and services) to foreign customers and suppliers. During the decade from 1929 to 1938, the share of GDP related to American trade declined from 11.1 percent to 7.7 percent. (See Table A.9.) For the United States and other leading powers, dependence on overseas markets and suppliers declined markedly in the years from World War I to about 1970. The extent of the collapse of international trade and finance and the enormous problems of coordinating a response help to explain why policy makers chose to emphasize domestic remedies rather than systemic solutions.[7]

For many years historians tended to blame the Hoover administration and the Federal Reserve for failing to reign in a speculative bubble and banking irregularities. The eighteen-month struggle to write the Smoot-Hawley Tariff of 1930 may also have compounded uncertainty and depressed business investment at a critical time. But the Depression also had causes external to the United States. Winston Churchill, British chancellor of the exchequer, rued the day in 1925 when he returned Britain to the gold standard and overvalued the pound, thereby rendering his nation more susceptible to global financial strains. In the summer of 1931, a banking crisis in Europe quickly led to international currency disruptions and the collapse of world trade.[8]

President Herbert Hoover stepped in, but his call for a one-year moratorium on reparations and war-debt repayments in June 1931 fell flat. Two months into the moratorium, Britain's financial condition worsened, and, in September, the Bank of England abandoned the gold standard. Currency chaos ensued. France welcomed the halt in war-debt payments but still insisted on reparations from Germany. Europeans now demanded gold from American banks, which in turn called in their loans to U.S. business, thereby accelerating bank closings and bankruptcies. German banks had already closed. The conservative belief in honoring debt repayment at all costs persisted. Hoover refused to extend the debt moratorium, and the Roosevelt administration acceded to the Johnson Act of 1934, which prohibited new credits to any nation that had defaulted on its war debts.[9] Never were the vulnerabilities of an interconnected world economy more apparent.

The economic and human tragedy was profound and amply documented – plunging stock prices, joblessness, stagnant production, bank runs as anxious depositors sought to withdraw funds, and even breadlines, hobos, and young drifters. Along with the ensuing social disruptions came a series of demagogic political attacks on big business, Wall Street, and alleged international conspiracies of bankers and moguls. Senator Huey Long of Louisiana advocated sweeping welfare and income redistribution programs. The Reverend Gerald L. K. Smith pursued similar themes. And Catholic radio priest Father Charles Coughlin hammered away at the rich and, eventually, the New Deal. "Get out of Europe! Get out of the Orient!" Coughlin demanded, as he urged "[l]ess care for internationalism and more concern for national prosperity."[10] The specific grievances related to conditions of the Depression; however, the ferocity of the attack on corporate, financial, and international interests underscored another of the perils of globalization: it seemed to be a fair weather system, conceived by corporate and government elites but vulnerable to the attacks of grassroots demagogues in bad times.[11]

During the 1930s, globalization was out of favor with liberals and conservatives. In his book *Open Door at Home*, historian Charles Beard argued that America should focus on its own economy rather than pursue prosperity through international trade agreements. Senator Gerald Nye, a progressive Republican from North Dakota, was one of the more effective opponents of international business during the 1930s. He chaired hearings in 1934, examining the influence of the munitions industry on foreign policy, and on American involvement in World War I. Critical of internationalism in all of its forms, Nye denounced the World Court in 1925 as being imposed on Americans "by men who are makers of war, the international bankers." These financiers had extensive investments that required a "world-wide collection agency" such as the Court. Understanding the global reach of the bankers, Nye accused them of aggregating their wealth in a few hands, and then "seeking new fields to invade and to mass the wealth, not of one lone nation, but the nations of all the world."[12]

Faith in the ability of capitalism and free markets to promote democracy, prosperity, and peace took a pounding during the 1930s. Many business and financial leaders, who a decade earlier trumpeted a new era based on technological innovation and overseas expansion, found their views discredited in the Depression. Meanwhile, economic experiments in Nazi

Germany, Fascist Italy, and Soviet Russia spurned free enterprise in favor of collectivism and fascism, dictatorship and autarky, and class struggle and war. In Western Europe and the United States, many questioned the benefits of economic interdependence promulgated in the American Century and embraced nationalistic alternatives. Even the New Deal – with its corporatist collaboration of government, labor, farmers, and business and efforts to fix prices and the terms of labor – seemed far removed from the laissez-faire values that inspired economic internationalism and global expansion.[13]

From Hoover to Roosevelt

It was ironic that Herbert Hoover – the widely acclaimed leader of European relief after World War I, who saved 100 million lives, and the secretary of commerce, who zealously pushed the overseas expansion of American business in the 1920s – should, as president, oversee the disintegration of the postwar economy. An energetic, experienced executive, Hoover was no match for the magnitude of the economic debacle of the 1930s. He lacked the personal charisma and public relations skills needed to rally domestic public opinion and restore confidence.[14]

Defeated overwhelmingly in the 1932 presidential election, Hoover lost to an individual with personal magnetism and superior communications skills. Franklin Roosevelt, the former governor of New York, exuded confidence but exhibited in his actions uncertainty about how to proceed. At first impression, Roosevelt seemed an internationalist and economic expansionist in the Wilson tradition. As assistant secretary of the Navy during World War I, he championed American efforts to seize control of the new radio technologies.[15] He also loyally supported the League of Nations concept in 1920 but abandoned it and other internationalist causes during the 1932 election in order to win isolationist support at the Democratic convention. His decision as president-elect to appoint Tennessee Senator Cordell Hull, an ardent proponent of tariff liberalization, to the position of secretary of state appeared to reaffirm his affinity with Wilson's laissez-faire globalism. But Roosevelt was a master of contradictions. FDR, who had good friends in the business community, among them Bernard Baruch and Averell Harriman, was no doctrinaire internationalist. During the Depression, he pragmatically reached out to a diverse cast of advisors who included economic nationalists like Raymond Moley, the Columbia University economist, and George Peek, the Illinois plow maker and advocate of managed trade.[16]

If anything, Roosevelt's own inclinations about economic policy leaned heavily toward experimentation. Indeed, big investors familiar with his penchant anticipated dollar devaluation. They shrewdly rushed out to buy gold before he took office. In his inaugural address, the new president hinted that he was prepared to throw traditional remedies to the wind. "Our international trade relations, though vastly important, are in point of time and necessity secondary to the establishment of a sound national economy. I favor as a practical policy the putting of first things first," Roosevelt said.[17]

The address also set the tone for a series of key decisions. Soon, Roosevelt torpedoed the World Economic Conference of June 1933, where major nations meeting in London wanted the United States to agree to currency stabilization and tariff liberalization. This was the largest economic meeting ever assembled up to that time; it involved sixty-six national delegations with millions around the world listening on the radio. Secretary of State Hull, the head of the American delegation, urged the conferees to "rearticulate the scattered family" of nations, focusing on international cooperation in trade. Hull put more emphasis on devising a means to limit trade barriers than on financial arrangements, the latter being outside the State Department's jurisdiction. He warned that focusing on the domestic would curtail acreage for agriculture, production for industry, and opportunity for workers, while it would bring "provincialism, a narrowing of ideas, if not of ideals" for all nations. Without "the knowledge of the customs and manners and learning of the rest of the world, which is one of the benefits of extensive international commerce, nations inevitably tend to decline and to decay," he noted. In effect, Hull, an unwavering Wilsonian internationalist, insisted on restating the case for globalization despite the isolationist mood of the times. The secretary of state hoped he could have as positive an influence on world trade as his predecessor, Charles Evans Hughes, had on naval arms at the Washington Conference of 1921.[18]

It was not to be; the president and the major European powers preferred a more nationalistic outcome. Hull did manage to obtain a tariff truce, but no monetary agreement resulted from the London conference. Decrying the "fetishes of so-called international bankers," Roosevelt issued a bombshell that destroyed the meeting, asserting that "the sound internal economic situation of a nation is a greater factor in its well-being than the price of its currency." He had no intention of tying his hands, subordinating domestic recovery to the requirements of external stability, and so he rejected a currency stabilization agreement worked out at

London. His subsequent decision to devalue the dollar from a gold price of $20.67 per ounce to $35.00 per ounce effectively boosted protection for U.S. industry and subsidized exports.[19]

Roosevelt's dollar devaluation was the type of nationalistic action that defied traditional international economic reason. It ignited a round of competitive devaluations and further unsettled the international economy. Indeed, Great Britain used the American devaluation as the occasion to strengthen its sterling-area clearing system, accelerating the move toward regional trade and currency blocs. In raising the gold price, and over-valuing that commodity, Roosevelt effectively invited the world's gold to American shores. Setting a higher price for gold encouraged capital flight from Europe and forced the remaining gold bloc countries to de-value and to abandon gold. The flight of European gold and capital to America began in 1934 and continued through much of the decade as European political conditions deteriorated. During the seven years 1935 through 1941, over $14.5 billion in gold entered the United States, drain-ing the world of monetary bullion. During World War II, the United States held two-thirds of the world's monetary gold. Federal Reserve officials did not permit the gold inflows to support expansion of the money supply in accordance with classical gold-standard theory. Instead, they sterilized the inflows, fearful that an increased quantity of money in circulation would ignite inflation. In short, the old classical gold-standard adjust-ment mechanism did not work during this period because government intervened in the market to manage currency flows. It is even arguable that this policy of sterilization delayed economic recovery in the United States.[20]

In a series of actions, Roosevelt and his congressional allies took other steps to de-link the domestic from the global economy. To appease the silver bloc in Congress, Roosevelt embarked on a silver purchase pro-gram to drive up prices. This move had the unintended effect of draw-ing silver from Mexico and China, two countries that based their cur-rencies on silver, and creating instability in China. Concluded economic historian Charles F. Kindleberger, "it represented a beggar-thy-neighbor policy where the hurt to the neighbor was wanton, and provided no do-mestic economic and little political benefit."[21] The Agricultural Adjust-ment Act (AAA) sought to control production and to regulate farm prices, and it did so by restricting imports, such as sugar. Both the National Industrial Recovery Act and the AAA gave the executive authority to control imports in order to protect domestic programs. New Deal la-bor legislation aided labor-union organization and mandated fair labor practices such as minimum wages and maximum hours. But these domestic price-fixing programs contradicted Cordell Hull's campaign to open foreign markets to American exporters in exchange for improved foreign access to the U.S. market. Roosevelt's penchant for experimentation may have helped restore public confidence, but it did little to end the Depression.[22]

The Global Swing to Economic Nationalism

It is important to view Depression-era economic disintegration in global perspective. The United States, although the world's largest economy and its de facto leader, was not the only nor indeed the first country to practice economic nationalism. Every major government sought to manage trade and payments during the 1930s, a trend that began incidentally during World War I. To some extent, state intervention reflected the urgency of the war emergency, but afterward the expansion of government regulation drew strength from the spread of universal suffrage and democratic associationalism – particularly the growth of trade unions – as economist Karl Polanyi noted in 1944. In Great Britain, the government intervened actively during World War I, then expanded oversight during the 1920s into new areas – air transportation, broadcasting, and radio communications. Government also moved to amalgamate railways, to encourage mergers among chemical companies and the creation of giant Imperial Chemical Industries (1927), to create monopolies in iron and steel, to establish a coal cartel, and to regulate agricultural prices and output. As Eric Hobsbawm observed, "Between the wars, and especially during the 1930s, Britain ... turned from one of the least into one of the most trustified or controlled economies"[23] Perhaps the most significant casualties were what remained of Britain's commitment to the global economy. In 1931, Britain abandoned both free trade and the gold standard, the last symbols of laissez-faire.[24]

The world economic crisis also pushed Japan along a nationalist-corporatist path. The decline of American demand for imported silk created distress in the Japanese textile industry. Britain's abandonment of the gold standard in September 1931 compounded the crisis. The new Japanese government that took office in late 1931 floated the yen and began a Keynesian-type of reflationary program under Finance Minister Takahashi. Gradually, the export-oriented Japanese business community became discouraged about prospects for gaining access to Western markets, and they turned to collaboration with the bureaucracy and the military. The program of East Asian regionalism and autarky that emerged from these consultations ended in war with the United States and the British Empire.[25]

Japan's regional designs posed a direct threat to America's commercial interests and its traditional commitment to the Open Door, the source of its proposals for nondiscrimination and national treatment to guide global economic relations. Although U.S. investment in China had never been large, the dream of a market of millions of people needing capital and goods for development persisted. Yet by 1938, Japan (after a year of war against China) had replaced America as China's major supplier, and it imported Chinese cotton as a substitute for American cotton. Tokyo had established a tightly managed yen bloc in East Asia and drove for self-sufficiency within this Co-Prosperity Sphere. Japanese regionalism threatened such key U.S. exports as iron, steel, copper, paper products, and machinery. And, Americans feared that the Japanese might shut off vital raw material exports from Southeast Asia and elsewhere in the Pacific region. These included natural rubber, manila fiber, quinine, and tin, as well as a host of metals and other commodities in short supply. An interdependent global economy depended on unrestricted commercial access to the world's resources and raw materials, but Japanese policy jeopardized the open system. Insisted Standard Oil Company of New York, "the strict maintenance of the 'Open Door' policy is the only hope for the protection of American interests in Manchuria."[26]

There was an ironic dimension to American relations with the future Axis powers. Hull and others might detest Japanese expansionism and German autarky, but American business did well in both markets. Japan bought more American goods than the rest of Asia combined and was America's third largest export market (behind Britain and Canada). All but a few officials counseled against a boycott of exports to Japan as too extreme, and the president concurred up until the very brink of war. The China market remained a dream; the reality was that America's global businesspeople had done their work well. In 1938, the United States accounted for about 44 percent of Japan's total imports. Acknowledging the close trade partnership, one of Japan's delegates to the League of Nations assured the New York Council on Foreign Relations that Japan would not close the open door in China out of fear of retaliation. "I think your heads are with us in spite of your prejudice," he said. "I think your hearts are with China in spite of your common sense."[27]

During the 1920s, Germany had been America's third largest export market, but during the 1930s, bilateral trade stagnated, reflecting Nazi efforts to manage trade for national advantage. Yet U.S. direct investments in Germany rose substantially. Many American businesspeople simply ignored Nazi ideology and urged Roosevelt to avoid war against Japan in Asia. They continued to believe that open markets and the binding ties of trade and finance would mitigate political problems. As it turned out, the outbreak of war in Europe, and the attack on Pearl Harbor, exposed the flaws of such unidimensional thinking.[28]

Adolph Hitler and the Nazis who came to power in January 1933 were enthusiastic economic nationalists who favored protective tariffs and trade restrictions to end Germany's debilitating dependence on the world economy. They confronted widespread unemployment – eight million new jobless – falling trade and industrial production, and burdensome war debts. Their long-term solution was to remilitarize and to use military force to acquire living space. Hitler rejected the laissez-faire claim that peaceful competition would promote prosperity. He worried about the international flow of capital. A German firm might benefit from building a shipyard in China, he wrote, but it would come at the expense of German jobs and exports.[29] Hitler also feared competition from efficient American automobile producers with their large-scale operations. Germany, he thought, was vulnerable. It lacked raw materials and foodstuffs. It remained too dependent on other countries. In his opinion, the "ultimate decision as to the outcome of the struggle for the world market will lie in power, and not in economics.... The sword," he said, "had to stand before the plough and an army before economics." And, so the German state tried to manipulate trade for national advantage.[30]

During the mid 1930s, until the threat of German and Japanese aggression brought a shift in the public mood, U.S. foreign policy also took a nationalistic course. On the heels of accusations that business had driven America into World War I, Congress passed the first Neutrality act, in 1935, to prevent future involvement in European conflict. The legislation prohibited the selling of arms to all belligerents; revisions of the act in the ensuing few years discouraged travel, loans, and other international exchanges which might lure America into war. This came at a time, in mid-decade, when the President began to worry about Hitler's militarization and initial territorial advances, denounced Italy's incursion into Ethiopia and Japan's into China, and lamented the outbreak of civil war in Spain. But politics, pacifism, and the Depression compelled FDR to react indecisively to international crises. Moral sanctions and expressions of neutrality, rather than forceful economic embargoes, were America's responses to Hitler's violations of the Versailles Treaty and German Jewry, to the League of Nation's attempt to sanction Mussolini's war in north Africa, and to Japan's seizure of Manchuria and eventual war in China.

Two other seemingly internationalist initiatives during the era actually reflected more the imperative of national economic recovery. In late 1933, Roosevelt resumed formal diplomatic relations with the Soviet Union, ending sixteen years of nonrecognition. He did so to help merchants and producers at home expand markets in the vast developing communist nation. There was little grand strategic design behind recognition, although FDR rationalized the move as a way to hold off Japanese advances in the Far East. For the most part, this was strictly a business deal. In 1935, the two nations signed a trade agreement that promised $30 million in Russian purchases from the United States, a figure that later rose to $86 million. Meanwhile, it was Josef Stalin's government, not Roosevelt's, that pushed its own version of globalization in diplomacy. The Comintern Congress of 1935 called for a worldwide Popular Front against the Fascist powers. Except for some eager American radicals, the United States shunned the movement.[31]

Roosevelt's approach to Latin America also represented a departure from Wilsonian internationalism, which was compatible with globalization and marked a swing back toward Monroe Doctrine-style regionalism. Despite the occurrence of revolutions and border disputes in the region that might have prompted U.S. military involvement, Cordell Hull announced at the seventh conference of American states in Montevideo, Uruguay, in 1933 the policy of U.S. military nonintervention in regional affairs. This was the Good Neighbor policy, and Roosevelt backed up words with deeds, removing troops from Haiti and renouncing the right to intervene unilaterally in Cuba. The only troops left in the region were at Guantanamo Bay naval base and in the Canal Zone. But as historian Akira Iriye noted, this initiative also indicated "an emerging approach to the Western Hemisphere in the framework of regionalism, that is, as part of the global trend toward regional, as opposed to global, arrangements." The Good Neighbor policy encouraged intimacy among the American nations. The reciprocal trade program gave particular emphasis to Latin America. Regional ties helped secure the hemisphere from Nazi, and later Soviet, threats, but they were also products of an isolationist quest by the United States to take care of its own people, and backyard, before concerning itself with the rest of the world.[32]

A closer look at Roosevelt economic policies in Latin America reveals how the United States departed from a truly globalist approach. The reciprocal trade program appeared to require bilateral negotiations with all trading partners, but, as it turned out, politics drove the choice of negotiating partners. Because Argentine agriculture competed with U.S. farmers, Washington was not in any hurry to rush an accord with Argentina until after the outbreak of war in Europe. Concessions were advisable, but the "real question is as to political expediency," wrote Assistant Secretary of State Francis Sayre. Meanwhile, the State Department escalated its efforts to export industrial goods to Latin America, issuing loans through the new Ex-Im Bank linked to purchases in the United States. The State Department masterminded the ouster of two Cuban leaders, in part by manipulating loans and holding out the promise of a commercial treaty. But, after dictator Fulgencio Batista took power, he obtained both credits and a reciprocal trade agreement.

U.S. domination of the region continued, but in the 1930s, Washington made many concessions due to the insecurity generated by the Great Depression and the rise of military aggressors in Europe. Dollar diplomacy did not end; it was transformed into a tool of government that pressed more zealously than during the fabled days of dollar diplomacy, under President Taft. During the 1930s, the image of the Good Neighbor replaced the gunboat, but the United States still prevailed as regional leader. Thus, when the Mexican government nationalized foreign oil holdings in 1938, an angry Cordell Hull attempted to cut off Mexico from valuable foreign-exchange sources by refusing to buy silver, but the treasury under Henry Morgenthau undercut Hull's policy. The U.S. Treasury believed such bellicosity unwarranted and damaging to currency markets. The policy divisions in Washington contrasted with Great Britain's abrupt decision to impose sanctions. British nationals owned 70 percent of the Mexican oil industry. Roosevelt was more cautious, for he feared that the Cardenas government would embrace fascist powers if so punished. In the end, the United States acquiesced to the expropriations in exchange for wartime supplies and assistance. During World War II, 450,000 braceros entered the United States to supply agricultural labor and harvest vegetables so that Americans could serve in the armed forces.[33]

Economic Internationalism and Appeasement

Even in the darkest hours of the Depression, a few officials in the U.S. administration never lost faith in the verities of economic internationalism. Cordell Hull was their leader. He believed that a liberal trade policy could appease international discontents. During his nearly three decades in Congress, this Tennessean had staked his political power on attacking the Republican tariff. Hull was justifiably known as a one-issue politician, having followed tariff bills since his teenage years in the 1880s. As a congressman for most of his legislative career, and during his short stint in the early 1930s as a senator, Hull pushed for freer trade not only to help farmers (a traditional stance for southern Democrats) but also as a means of preventing armed conflict. This stance was not unusual, for Hull was an ardent supporter of Woodrow Wilson. Viewed from the perspective of the new millennium, Hull's position was "a modern approach to trade issues . . . one that was well ahead of its time." Since the carnage of World War I, Hull had shifted his criticism of the domestic tariff to the international level. He argued in Cobdenite terms that "unhampered trade dovetailed with peace; high tariffs, trade barriers and unfair economic competition with war." At the London Conference in June 1933, Hull insisted that "the power and influence of a nation are judged more by the extent and character of its commerce than by any other standard."[34]

Franklin Roosevelt's nationalistic advisors initially held the upper hand, but Hull gradually won FDR's endorsement of an initiative to lower trade barriers through reciprocal negotiations. Congress approved Hull's reciprocal trade program in 1934 as an emergency measure. The bill emphasized the administration's hope that bilateral negotiations would succeed in opening foreign markets; little was said about increased imports. FDR endorsed freer trade once his first New Deal coalition fell apart, appealing to multinational industrialists and bankers who then supported his reelection in 1936. Democrats backed freer trade for the next several decades, but the reciprocal trade program also had a dramatic impact over time. It succeeded in sharply lowering U.S. tariffs and stimulating imports of manufactures. Historians debate whether the trade program, as administered by the State Department, achieved meaningful or sham reciprocity. For a generation after World War II, exporters continued to face protectionist barriers in foreign markets, where nontariff and structural barriers hampered U.S. access, especially for farm products. Still, at a time when economic nationalism reigned, the reciprocal trade program (regardless of its regional and nationalist uses) offered some support for the globalization process. A State Department official in 1935 exaggeratedly claimed that Americans were "meshing our domestic economy into the world economy" to a greater degree than ever before, but it was true that Roosevelt signed more legislation and agreements to expand trade than ever before in U.S. history.[35]

After devaluation of the dollar in 1934, parallel efforts in the Treasury Department of Henry Morgenthau promoted currency stabilization and international financial cooperation. By 1936, the Treasury had worked out tripartite stabilization arrangements with Britain and France intended to restore some order to international finance. While the pre–World War I and postwar international economies enjoyed free capital movements, the presence of disruptive hot-money surges and exchange rate instability during the Great Depression forced officials to restrict money flows. The rise of the regulatory state marked a major transition in government policies. Blaming private bankers for currency problems and speculators for capital flights, the New Dealers insisted on greater public accountability and responsibility. Treasury Secretary Morgenthau put the idea vividly. It was the task of officials, he said, to drive the "usurious money lenders from the temple of international finance." In effect, he wanted to extend New Deal style-government regulation to international finance.[36]

Given the breakdown of private lending, it is not surprising that the administration also took an active role in financing trade. The Roosevelt administration revived and expanded the responsibilities of Hoover's Reconstruction Finance Corporation to include international activities. In 1934, Roosevelt persuaded Congress to create the Export-Import Bank. Both institutions took an active role in extending credits and loans to foreign purchasers of U.S. goods, previously the responsibility of banks. Although public financing of trade contributed to the overall expansion of trade and appeared compatible with the aims of Hull's program, it actually was another example of Roosevelt's trade nationalism. Government financing at noncommercial rates represented a transfer of wealth from taxpayers to large corporations and exporters. It was defensible in the context of the 1930s because many other governments used subsidies to export their unemployment.[37]

As the Ex-Im Bank example suggests, Roosevelt's policies were mired in contradictions, as his administration improvised and experimented to get out of the Depression. His first two terms generally represented a retreat from internationalism. Roosevelt was a Wilsonian in the abstract. The immediate realities of the Great Depression at home and militarism abroad compelled him to set aside planning for global peace and prosperity and deal with isolationist sentiment; build the New Deal liberal bloc; and confront Mussolini, Hitler, and Tojo. Hence, he backed not just the Johnson Debt Default Act but also the Reciprocal Trade program. He scuttled the World Economic Conference but announced the Good Neighbor policy. FDR's withdrawing the military from Latin America, as well as his signing legislation in 1934 for the independence of the Philippines after a ten-year transition, confirmed to potential foreign aggressors that

America was vacillating. The sight of thousands of veterans and students marching for peace in the mid 1930s, the accusations of the Nye Committee against business sponsorship of World War I, and five versions of the neutrality laws beginning in 1935 compelled the president to be cautious and sensitive to isolationist public opinion.

This was globalization's darkest hour. America turned its back on the victims of Nazi persecution. As a result of the National Origins Act of 1924, the United States built a paper wall of quotas and bureaucratic obstacles that effectively brought the massive flow of migrants, which had proven important to building the American Century, to a sputtering halt. European Jews, facing Nazi persecution, became unfortunate world travelers, desperately seeking entry into the United States and Latin America.

There were successes on the human rights front, however, that exposed the flickering flame of globalization. One involved the Berlin Olympic Games of 1936. The U.S. Olympic Committee decided to attend the summer event despite Hitler's ruling barring German Jews from participating (the track coach pulled the only two American Jewish team members from the 400-meter relay). But it was African-American runners who gave Hitler fits. Jesse Owens won four gold medals – three running and one jumping – and three other black athletes also took the highest honors. African Americans won every track event from the 100 to the 800 meters; Owens himself set four Olympic records and one world mark. The German chancellor was told he must either shake every victorious athlete's hand, or none at all. He left his box after Owens won the long jump, never meeting the champion.[38] But nationalism and racial prejudice could not extinguish world cultural linkages.

The Games were also replete with the type of innovations that spurred globalization. The massive Olympic stadium was a spectacle. With the great *Hindenburg* dirigible hovering overhead, 110,000 spectators watched the athletes parade past Hitler and Olympic dignitaries. The Fuhrer consigned the director Leni Riefenstahl to film the Berlin Games, the first time an Olympics had a movie record. Riefenstahl directed cameras from the field, from the stands, and from a dirigible, rolling 1.3 million feet of footage that went into the making of the movie *Olympian*. Another novelty was televised sport. Bulky cameras relayed fuzzy electronic images to the Olympic Village and eighteen halls around the city, where viewers tried to discern the athletes, who looked "like human beings floating in a milk bath."

Of course, these games also reflected the turbulent international politics of the time. Hitler had remilitarized the Rhineland, Franco had begun the

Spanish Civil War as the games opened, and Mussolini was fresh from victory the year before in Africa. Within four years, the Berlin Olympic Village was converted into an infantry training center, and a restaurant and music hall on the grounds had been made into a military hospital.[39]

Fascism would soon take bolder steps to challenge global democracy. When President Roosevelt appealed for nonaggression in April 1939, Hitler leapt at the opportunity to defend Germany as a victim, to brand European democracies as unfair, and to dismiss America as an anti-internationalist nation that had no right to criticize the Nazis. It was the United States that had not joined the League of Nations. And Roosevelt had failed to pull his rich nation, with its global economic prospects, out of the Depression, while Hitler had taken his downtrodden country to new heights.[40] The Germans were just months away from taking the final step – world war – to secure their new international economic order.

Multinational Business in the Great Depression

For international business, the unstable 1930s were extraordinarily difficult years. For one thing, business and finance operated under a dark political cloud. Many historians and public officials blamed bankers and munitions makers for involving the United States in World War I. On Capitol Hill, Nye's committee investigating the munitions industry emphasized how J. P. Morgan and the "munitions makers" – aircraft manufacturers, the chemical industry, ordnance makers – had acquired a stake in Allied victory and sought to protect that stake through intervention. America had been duped by England, or more specifically the Bank of England, and its friends on Wall Street. Sensitive to this unfavorable image, and fearful that another war would have disastrous consequence, the business community also adhered to the conviction that involvement in World War I had been a serious mistake.[41]

During the first two years of the New Deal, U.S. international trade remained sharply depressed. The quantities of exports and imports did not reach 1929 pre-Depression levels again until war year 1941. During the period currencies depreciated, and volatile short-term capital flows proved to be highly destabilizing. In such circumstances, the international business climate turned sharply negative. What is striking in retrospect is how overall foreign investment stagnated during these years of depression and war years. At the end of World War II, U.S. direct foreign investment was $7.2 billion, up only slightly from $7.0 billion in 1940, but down from a $7.55 billion peak in 1929 (see Table A.8).[42] Bilateral data show a few notable exceptions to these trends. While U.S. investments in Cuba and Mexico declined precipitously, reflecting declining commodity prices as well as the unstable investment climate, investment in Canada rose sharply from 1929 to 1940. The increased flow of U.S. investment capital to Canada reflected the dominion's political stability and its special position within the British preferential tariff system. This discriminatory regime effectively offered a green light to American firms eager to serve the vast regional market from within the tariff walls.

Interestingly, Germany was also a lure for American investors during the Depression. After approval of the Dawes Plan, manufacturing investments in Germany climbed, rising from $138.9 million in 1929 to $206.3 million in 1940, an increase of 48.5 percent. Although initially American firms experienced some discrimination, U.S. diplomatic officials pressed the Nazi regime to honor an existing Treaty of Friendship, Commerce and Consular Rights that guaranteed American or American-owned firms the same rights in Germany as German-owned firms. Soon, the business community was trumpeting its new opportunities. A familiar motto in the West, according to business historian Robert Sobel, was "You Can Do Business with Hitler," and more than a hundred American corporations did just that. Some were actively involved in arms production. Ambassador William E. Dodd reported that the DuPonts had three allies, including I. G. Farben, in Germany that were "aiding in the armament business." International Harvester was also linked to arms production. General Motors's Opel plants produced tanks and military vehicles. Opel, benefiting from Hitler's desire to encourage inexpensive automobile transportation, gained a tax-exempt status and expanded market share from 33 percent in 1933 to over 50 percent in 1935. Standard Oil reportedly helped the Germans make ersatz gas for war purposes. Henry Ford authorized increased investments in Germany.[43]

The Ford case is an interesting example. Like other American auto manufacturers, Ford encountered virulent economic nationalism during the Great Depression. In France, Louis Renault, a local automaker, warned: "If Ford and General Motors dominate the French markets, one and a half million Frenchmen will have died in vain in the last war. We shall have escaped German suzerainty only to fall under the sway of America. Idleness will confront several million workers. Our rusting factories can no longer supply war materials." The French government imposed duties and quotas that effectively reserved the domestic market for local car makers. In Italy, Mussolini supported Fiat and effectively excluded Ford. In Germany, Ford maintained an assembly facility in Cologne but resisted Nazi entreaties to expand their operations and standardize parts, making the parts of one German manufacturer interchangeable with another. Finally, the Ford Company agreed to build a truck plant in the Berlin area, which the Nazi leadership dedicated to production for the German army. On his seventy-fifth birthday, Henry Ford was the first recipient of the highest Nazi award given to foreigners: the Grand Cross Order of the Eagle.[44]

The Nazis decorated two other prominent Americans with second-level Orders of the Eagle. One was aviator Charles Lindbergh; the other was IBM president Thomas J. Watson. In 1937, Watson as president of the International Chamber of Commerce (ICC) offered a keynote address to an ICC convention in Berlin focusing on the theme: "World Peace through World Trade." He later regretted his speech, and private talk with Hitler, and returned his medal in 1940.

Watson, one of America's highest paid businessmen and a supporter of the New Deal (IBM reaped huge revenues in helping with the bookkeeping and data recording of social security and industry codes), had long held a great faith in international business's ability to correct the world's ills. Indeed, like others before him, Watson dreamed of a global transportation system, especially when he witnessed the arrival in America of the German airship, the *Graf Zeppelin*. Although he determined to extend IBM's name abroad by tireless travel and promotion, he also tended to ignore the excesses of the dictators. Watson lauded Mussolini as a pioneer, drawing similarities to Il Duce's New Italy and the cooperation and loyalty Watson cultivated at IBM. He also got enmeshed with the Nazis, believing his German industrialist friends that Hitler could be controlled. His receipt of the white and gold Nazi medal decorated with a swastika revealed extraordinary naivete.[45]

In retrospect, business leaders were shockingly unsophisticated about world politics. The Italo-Ethiopian War is a case in point. After the outbreak of war between Italy and Ethiopia in 1935, and passage of neutrality legislation barring shipments of war implements to the belligerents, some in the business and financial communities sought to profit from the situation. Oil exporters, in particular, did not reduce shipments to Italy, taking the view that "there is nothing in the present situation to cause them to curtail their function of supplying petroleum and products to a country that is formally on good terms with the United States." In effect, those doing business with Italy tended to adhere to the traditional view of neutral rights and freedom of the seas, while those without a direct stake seemed more sensitive to public opinion and isolationist sentiment. Meanwhile, others like J. P. Morgan partner Thomas Lamont spoke out against sanctions as unworkable and urged Mussolini to express his support for world peace.[46]

In Japan, a similar pattern of American financial and business activity occurred before World War II but on a much smaller scale. In 1930, American business had $61.4 million of direct investment in Japan, an amount less than 1 percent of total U.S. direct investment abroad. The American stake in Japan was considerably smaller than in China, the Philippines, or the Dutch East Indies. U.S. direct investment in Japan dropped to $47 million in 1936 and fell again to $37.7 million in 1940. Nonetheless, technologically advanced corporations made some direct investments in Japan, and their technology transfers undoubtedly facilitated development of that country's military-industrial base. National Cash Register opened a joint venture for manufacturing in 1934. IBM began manufacturing in Japan in 1937. Some firms such as National Lead participated in Japanese ventures with German firms like I. G. Farben.

Ford and General Motors both had assembled cars and trucks in Japan in the early 1930s but found their expansion plans blocked by the Japanese government. Instead, Nissan and Toyota were licensed as manufacturers. Similarly, Japanese squeezed out B. F. Goodrich, reduced General Electric's position, and crowded out multinationals in oil and office equipment. Historian Mira Wilkins concluded that "U.S. business in Japan had been copied, absorbed, manipulated, and molded to Japanese requirements – by the rules of the Japanese state and by the initiative of Japanese business leaders." In Japan, as in Germany, however, U.S. businessmen had only one common sentiment: "they did not want America to become involved in a Far Eastern war." During times of turmoil they merely sought to survive and profit. Thomas Lamont of J. P. Morgan actively lobbied the U.S. government against employing sanctions against Japan. Like Secretary Hull, Lamont favored "policies of appeasement." As late as April 1940, U.S. investors held hundreds of millions of dollars in Japanese national, municipal, and corporate bonds.[47]

In the Far East, those businesses with no direct stake were disposed to take a storm cellar approach. They noted that America's economic involvement in Asia was small. Trade with Japan was four times that with China, although investments in China, the Philippines, and the Dutch Indies far surpassed investments in Japan. Nonetheless, as a share of total exports, Asia took about 17 percent of total exports, and it had attracted only about 6 percent of U.S. direct investments. Said the *Magazine of Wall Street* in October 1936: "it would take more than the Orient appears to offer us in economic advantages to induce the United States to risk war." But for Japan, war was possible because the Great Depression so ruined its trade that Tokyo felt compelled to take Manchuria in 1931. This "export or die" mentality prompted an industrial policy focused on state and private collaboration, for exporting as well as production (particularly of military goods). Japanese economic experts had looked to the industrial powers, with their systems of tariffs and subsidies, as models of self-sufficiency, and the war against China in 1937 and the advance southward toward the resources of Southeast Asia were integral to their autarkic plans. Japan's regionalism – and the de-linking of globalization – drove the nation to war.[48]

Eventually, Roosevelt ignored the international business community and began to cut back on trade. His loans and military aid to China had been endorsed by missionary groups; exporters, on the other hand, urged him not to excite Japan to the extent that Tokyo cut their lucrative trade. They welcomed his nonbelligerent resolution of the *Panay* incident. American sales to Japan peaked in 1937; thereafter, Roosevelt began licensing exports, which put Japanese industrialization and militarization in jeopardy. Tokyo, by late 1938, had declared its pursuit of a "New Order" in East Asia based on a regional economic network of Japan, Manchukuo, and China. When Japan threatened British holdings in China in mid 1939, Roosevelt asked U.S. businesses to cut back their trade, and many obliged, including U.S. Steel and Alcoa. Cordell Hull followed by abrogating the U.S.-Japan Commercial Treaty of 1911 in January 1940. Tojo's ally, Adolf Hitler, had already invaded Poland to begin the European war.[49] Like Japan, American businesses and globalization itself were engulfed in a military conflict that brought their worldwide activities to a halt.

Technological Advances

One of the ironies of the 1930s is that, in a decade when economic and political nationalism segmented markets, technology continued to facilitate the globalization process. In transportation and communications, there were several important developments that facilitated the integration and harmonization of markets and nations. One was the phenomenal expansion of air travel and commerce. In 1929, U.S. airlines existed primarily to carry mail, and they subsisted on government subsidies allocated by Postmaster General Walter Brown. That year only 11,000 revenue-paying passengers flew on eighty-three aircraft. The number of passengers increased tenfold to 111,000 in 1935 and then quadrupled to 476,000 during World War II. One reason for this rapid expansion was an impromptu partnership between government and industry that resulted in production of cost-efficient long-range passenger planes. The first was the rugged two-engine DC-3, launched in 1936. It carried twenty-one passengers, cruised at 170 miles per hour, and was the first plane to make money carrying passengers. Lowering the cost of travel from 12 cents to 5.1 cents per mile, it appealed to domestic business travelers.

International flight also advanced rapidly during the 1930s. Juan Trippe's Pan American Airways inaugurated passenger service across the Pacific from San Francisco to Manila and Hong Kong in November 1935. By January 1939, Pan Am served forty-seven countries with 127 planes, and had 54,000 route miles. The arrival of the Boeing 314, a new flying boat with double decks, a cruising speed of 180 miles per hour, and space for seventy-four passengers, enabled Pan Am to begin regular trans-Atlantic flights in mid 1939. The growth of civilian aviation, like the emergence of regular steamship service in the late nineteenth century, had an enormous impact on daily life and business. "A man in Pago Pago or Chengtu," wrote one student of commercial aviation, "may order a badly needed radio tube, a portable typewriter, or a new razor, through the great American mail-order houses in Chicago by air mail, and have his order filled by air express within four or five days."[50]

Improvements in business communications were less dramatic than the expansion of commercial aviation but equally significant. The number of overseas telephone calls rose from 30,000 in 1929 to 75,000 in 1936 and 360,000 in 1945. To some extent the telephone competed with the telegraph, and the number of international telegraph messages, which peaked at 21,565,000 in 1929, fell to 10,437,000 in 1932, and did not crack the 20,000,000 barrier again until 1945. Western Union labs developed facsimile transmissions in the 1930s, and Chester Carlson made his first "Xerographic" image with electrophotography.[51]

Some of the most spectacular, and significant, steps to bridge national boundaries occurred in radio and the cinema. Shortwave broadcasting arrived in the 1930s. The United States did not establish the Voice of America for another decade; however, the German and British governments were quick to employ this technology as a propaganda tool. In December 1932, the BBC initiated its international service, distinguished by the strident chimes of Big Ben and the phrase "London calling." By 1938, the Germans were broadcasting twenty-four hours per day in twelve languages, hoping to bond all three million overseas Germans to the homeland.[52]

Hollywood proved to be America's most successful salesperson. As "talkies" arrived in the late 1920s to supplant silent films, Hollywood worried at first about declining revenues (as much as 40 percent of film revenue came from overseas sales) and the revitalization of European competition. But as it turned out, the high cost of sound equipment handicapped foreign producers, and soon Will Hays's Motion Picture Producers and Distributors Association was aggressively pressing sales and soliciting government support. By 1937, American movies played in eighty countries, and averaged over 70 percent of the world's screen time. Hollywood's critics accused Hays of trying to homogenize the world, although he interpreted the record differently. American films succeeded because they offered good entertainment and appealed to the aspirations of other peoples. In this sense, the film industry was an "unofficial ambassador of good will and understanding." *Variety* claimed that American films were the "subtlest and most efficient form of propaganda any nation has ever had at its command. They are still the best machinery for flooding the world with the idea that the American way of living is best, that this Republic with all its shortcoming is a garden spot in a world too full of woe." [53]

Some countries found the emphasis in American films on crime, wealth, and sex troublesome, and censorship grew through the decade. Japan cut out kissing scenes; the British, references to the deity and shots depicting cruelty to animals. The film *Lawless Rider* was banned in Mexico because it depicted a Mexican being kicked around and derided. Chinese censors banned *Ben Hur* on the grounds that it glorified "Christian superstition." Some government even restricted the repatriation of American film dollars. Ultimately, Germany, Italy, and Japan succeeded in squeezing out U.S. filmmakers.

Perhaps the most successful American film exports in the 1930s involved Walt Disney's animated cartoons. Disney's most famous creation, Mickey Mouse, became the most popular international figure of the era. In Japan, he was more popular than anyone but the emperor. In Britain, King George V reportedly refused to attend movies unless Mickey Mouse was playing. And by the mid 1930s the Mouse was being shown in thirty-eight nations, and a wax image was on display in Madame Tussaud's museum in London. The League of Nations presented Disney with a scroll in 1937 proclaiming Mickey Mouse an "international symbol of good will." The secret to Mickey Mouse's success involved the appeal of fantasy, bold colors, and uncomplicated messages. Mickey carried an egalitarian message celebrating the triumph of the little guy. Only Hitler had the temerity to ban Mickey Mouse, claiming that the "wearing of German military helmets by an army of cats which oppose a militia of mice . . . offensive to national dignity."[54]

Hitler, and Japan, had the final say during the 1930s. Increasing sanctions against Germany and Japan by 1938, credits to help Chinese leader Jiang Jeshi fight the Japanese, and even an Anglo-American Trade Agreement to show solidarity among the democracies to the Nazis did not stop the militarists. Hull discouraged exports and credits to Japan and complained that Tokyo violated the Open Door. But the administration's goal of keeping Latin America loyal to the democratic cause was more successful. Roosevelt provided loans to hemisphere governments and stockpiled raw materials, programs that prevented Germany from greatly penetrating Latin America. All these measures were taken to meet a crisis situation, however, and none pretended to promote a renewal of globalization.

The Depression years marked a halt in efforts to create an integrated global market, except among the Nazis, the Japanese, and the Soviets who held differing dreams of world domination. Technology progressed, to be sure. Yet America and its capitalist friends turned inward to solve their economic problems. Even with such allies as Great Britain, there was a certain suspicion about imperial preferences and devaluation, on the American side, and an uneasiness about dependence and Hull's aggressive pursuit of the Open Door on the British end. From 1934 to 1939, Cordell Hull truly tried to reestablish multilateral principles, but, as the president lamented, the "world [was] marching too fast" for economic liberalization to work at the end of the decade. Six of the nine proposals for peace given to the Japanese ambassador on November 26, 1941, focused on commercial expansion.[55] Eleven days later, Tokyo gave its response – at Pearl Harbor. Hull, Roosevelt, and American business would have to wait out several years of conflict before the process of postwar planning enabled American leaders once again to promote a structure of international institutions to regulate and guide the globalization of peoples and nations.

5

Defending Allies, Developing Frontiers, 1939–1946

World War II threatened the survival of the Anglo-American pattern for globalization. The Axis powers – a loose coalition of Germany, Italy, and Japan – resorted to military force to overthrow the post-Versailles world order and to establish closed, regional systems dominated from Berlin, Rome, and Tokyo. The conflict afforded the United States a second chance to provide leadership and to promote its vision of a peaceful, prosperous, and capitalist world. The Roosevelt administration pressed plans for international rules and institutions that would structure the post–World War II global economic and political system. In joining technology with national security, the war forged an enduring partnership among business, government, and science. Afterward, the new military-industrial complex would sustain America as an economic and military superpower, develop "endless frontiers" for scientific discovery, and speed the globalization process.

Axis Challenge and Vulnerabilities

The European phase of the war began in September 1939 when Nazi Germany invaded Poland. Britain and France responded with war declarations. After a quiet winter, Hitler's armies turned westward in the spring of 1940, knocking France out in six weeks. The ensuing air battle for Britain – the Blitz – quickly captured the American public's attention. Radio provided live war coverage with CBS correspondent Edward R. Murrow calmly beginning each report: "This...is London." As he talked, listeners thousands of miles away could hear exploding bombs and screaming air raid sirens. Presenting the British point of view, Murrow's accounts helped sway American public opinion. In the Pacific, the war had begun earlier – in July 1937 – when Japan invaded China. But until December 7, 1941, most Americans exhibited little interest in this remote war between unfamiliar Asian peoples. Japan's surprise attack on Pearl Harbor punctured indifference. Pearl Harbor meant that America was at war and the world in flames.[1]

Axis aggression had roots in the harsh peace settlement imposed at the end of World War I but also in the world economy. The Axis powers envied British and American access to the world's petroleum and raw materials, as well as their dominance of trade and finance. While Secretary of State Cordell Hull and other Western leaders encouraged them to pursue their commercial ambitions in an international economy open to all nations, the Axis dismissed this option as requiring them to submit to Anglo-American dominance. Leaders in Berlin, Rome, and Tokyo experimented with autarkic approaches, hoping to cushion their home economies from periodic disruptions and to acquire by military force the resources (such as oil) needed to sustain modern industry.[2]

Like World War I, the Second World War exposed both the shortcomings and advantages of economic interdependence. Hitler's decision to attack in Europe and Japan's challenge to the imperial powers (especially Britain and America) in Asia were daring acts of desperation. Neither aggressor – or Italy – had the large and diverse industrial base required for a long war of attrition. The major Allies (including the United States) had an 80 percent larger population than the principal Axis powers and a gross domestic product 140 percent greater. It was not surprising that when the full resources of the United States were brought to bear, they enjoyed substantial numerical advantages on both the Eastern, Western, and Pacific fronts. Also, both Germany and Japan lacked sufficient resources – particularly petroleum, ferro alloys, and foodstuffs – to endure economic sanctions in a protracted war. The Axis relied on surprise and quick victories to topple the Anglo-American system of globalization. (See Table A.4.)

As it turned out, the leaders of Germany and Japan made a number of critical mistakes early in the war, but their lack of resources led to their eventual defeat. Simply, they exceeded their supplies and supply lines. Shortages of petroleum and other strategic and critical resources eventually brought Germany to its knees in 1945. The Nazis lacked tungsten and chromium – two ferro alloys required to harden steel. These were obtained in Portugal, Spain, and Turkey. But, the United States and its allies engaged in a variety of economic warfare techniques – including preclusive buying – to shut off supplies of these vital materials. The strategic air offensive against German fuel supplies also had a major impact on the Nazi collapse. The Luftwaffe, for instance, had too little aviation fuel to take advantage of Germany's lead in jet-plane technology and to challenge Allied control of the air.[3]

Similarly, in the Far East, oil was critical to the outcome. Had the Japanese attack on Pearl Harbor in December 1941 succeeded in destroying the U.S. aircraft carriers and the Pacific Fleet's fuel reserves, the aggressors would have obtained time to consolidate a resource-rich empire in Asia. In such circumstances, the Axis might have established self-sufficient regional empires providing markets and raw materials for their manufactures free from British or American interference. Had this occurred, history might have taken a different course. Britain and the United States also relied on international trade to obtain raw materials and foodstuffs, and they recognized that the powers controlling Middle East oil directed the economic destiny of the world economy. Had Hitler's armies succeeded in 1941–2, the Axis might have seized these crucial reserves and dictated oil prices for years to come. The post–World War II era might have been remembered as the Axis Century rather than the American Century.[4]

Accessing American Resources

As in World War I, Britain and France needed America's productive and natural resources to withstand the German assault and repel the aggressors. But once again, the American people yearned to stay out of war. Nonetheless, Prime Minister Winston Churchill remained optimistic that he could woo the United States. Without U.S. aid, he could not defeat the Axis. Roosevelt understood this truth, too, and overcame isolationist sentiment by persuading Congress to modify the neutrality acts designed to keep America out of war by restricting U.S. trade and travel.[5]

In response to the German attack on Poland in September 1939, Congress placed U.S. commerce with the belligerents on a cash-and-carry basis. Although England and France could buy American goods, U.S.-flag ships could not go to their ports or to Germany and neighboring countries. To avoid this restriction, American steamship companies, which were dependent on the Atlantic carrying trade, engaged in subterfuge. They transferred ships to foreign registry, sold them to the British or to neutrals, and redeployed existing vessels. Between September 1939 and June 1941, the U.S. government approved the transfer of sixty-three U.S.-flag vessels to Panamanian registry. Another 126 vessels were transferred or sold to England for operation under the British flag without U.S. crews. In March 1941, Congress approved the Lend-Lease program, essentially a military aid program for the British Empire and the Soviet Union. During the war, the United States provided $50 billion in Lend-Lease aid, of which $27 billion went to Britain and $10 billion went to the Soviet Union. The program reportedly supplied 25 percent of all weapons used in the British Empire. To the Soviet Union, the United States provided food and transportation equipment, including 427,000 trucks and 13,000 combat vehicles to give Soviet forces mobility.[6]

These supplies were made possible, in part, by an American internationalism that was cultivated by the British. Historian Thomas Mahl found evidence that British intelligence mounted a series of covert operations to discredit isolationism and to involve America in the war. These included helping to mobilize a middle- and upper-class power elite of lawyers, bankers, and college professors and working for the nomination of Republican internationalist Wendell Willkie, thus undercutting GOP isolationism, which was a threat to British interests. Whether covert operations actually tipped the scales for intervention is debatable, but the power elite did seek to awaken America to the dangers of a Nazi victory, and during the war they brought business leadership to government. "Dollar a year men" – like Edward Stettinius of U.S. Steel; William Knudson of General Motors; Donald Nelson of Sears, Roebuck; and Will Clayton of Anderson, Clayton cotton brokers – entered the Roosevelt administration to assist in war mobilization and to advance an internationalist postwar agenda. The Council on Foreign Relations, funded by Wall Street and corporate internationalists, sought to become the "think-tank" of postwar internationalism.[7]

Ironically, the British campaign for U.S. involvement threatened to undercut Britain's own power. The State Department insisted on attaching strings to Lend-Lease aid, requiring the British to abandon imperial trade preferences that discriminated against U.S. exports for an open multilateral global economic system after the war. Treasury Secretary Henry Morgenthau and his advisor, Henry Dexter White, had parallel ideas. They sought to use the leverage of aid to crack the sterling/pound bloc in the British Empire and make the dollar supreme. Both plans spelled trouble for Britain. Churchill resisted U.S. demands throughout the war, and FDR did not press hard, fearful of upsetting the wartime alliance. But, London gradually realized the difficulties in resisting the Open Door. Americans proclaimed that after the war, the "oyster shell" of the British Empire would be pried open according to the principles of the Atlantic

Charter of 1941, the statement of Allied war aims, which included freer trade and financial exchanges. It actually took years before Britain abandoned the imperial system of trade and finance; multilateralism remained a visionary goal of postwar planners. But World War II completed the decades-long "changing of the guard" of leadership over the world economy from Britain to America.[8]

Like Germany and Japan, Britain and America relied on the international economy for raw materials and encountered serious supply dislocations as a result of U-boat warfare. Yet scientific advances enabled the Western Allies to neutralize Axis submarines and restore ocean supply lines. Oil was a case in point. Britain had entered World War II with inadequate stockpiles and no crude production of its own. It relied on western hemisphere sources and was vulnerable to both American trade controls and German submarine attacks. To circumvent American neutrality laws barring merchants ships from the war zone, Standard Oil used tankers registered in Canada, Britain, and Panama to serve the North Atlantic route. During this phase, Standard Oil of New Jersey and its affiliates lost twenty-six ocean-going tankers; after Pearl Harbor (from December 1941 to 1945), Jersey and its affiliates lost another fifty-six tankers (twenty-nine of those in 1942), or 42 percent of the tanker fleet under Allied or neutral control at the beginning of the war.

From 1940 to early 1943 German U-boats terrorized Atlantic shipping routes. They feasted on merchant ships as well as tankers, even sinking oil tankers in sight of major east coast cities. The U-boat campaign nearly brought Britain to its knees, sinking 2,000 Allied merchant ships in sixty-eight months. During World War II, Britain lost 11.4 millions tons of merchant shipping or 54 percent of its prewar tonnage. The nadir came in the early months of 1943 when German submarine attacks cut food imports below 75 percent of prewar levels, which was insufficient to meet current civilian requirements and production needs. As it turned out, the British people never lacked adequate nourishment. Britain conserved and sharply boosted domestic production of grains, fruit, and other necessities. Developments in antisubmarine warfare – including new radar; ULTRA code-breaking; long-range aircraft; searchlights; and convoy procedures – helped the Allies recover control of Atlantic shipping routes by 1943. During the war, American shipyards would build large numbers of tankers, and capacity rose from 2.5 million tons in 1941 to 11.4 million tons in 1945.[9]

This massive production had to be organized, and a key element of this mobilization was expansion and coordination of the American bureaucracy. To reduce competition among agencies and increase efficiency, Roosevelt combined the staffs and resources of fourteen bureaucracies in September 1943. Charged with supervising overseas economic operations, the Foreign Economic Administration under Leo Crowley administered Lend-Lease, procured strategic materials, denied raw materials to the enemy, oversaw export controls, directed relief operations, and disseminated information about Axis economies. Although these undertakings had mixed results (Germany, for instance, maintained its levels of iron ore imports from Sweden into 1944 and built a two-year stockpile of wolfram from Spain and Portugal despite American efforts), the overall outcome was a vast enlargement of the federal bureaucracy. The State Department had 974 employees in 1939, as the war in Europe began; when it ended, personnel had expanded to four times that number. Such growth also allowed the United States to provide leadership in all aspects of postwar planning for the world economy.[10]

For the U.S. economy as a whole, World War II defense spending was a boon. It proved the tonic that lifted the nation out of depression. Unemployment declined sharply, as the labor force created 17.3 million jobs (net). Also, 5.2 million women entered the workforce. The economy rapidly geared up to support 12 million soldiers and sailors and to produce aircraft, ships, weapons, and electronic equipment for U.S. and Allied forces. By 1943, mobilization of industrial and military resources began to prove decisive. The domestic economy produced $181 billion worth of munitions and consumed 41 percent of gross national product in the peak war production years of 1943 and 1944. The merchant marine expanded from 11 million to 40 million gross tons as 5,545 vessels were constructed in U.S. shipyards. From seven carriers at the beginning of the war, the United States built thirty-five fleet carriers and sixty-six escort carriers. The Army increased from ten prewar active divisions to ninety-two active divisions in 1945. Army and Naval air forces expanded from 2,200 combat planes to 16,000. Incredibly, the United States, which had produced a total of 13,500 military aircraft in the twenty years preceding World War II, was soon making well over 50,000 planes per year (96,000 in 1944), overwhelming Axis production.[11]

If the sheer numbers were not impressive enough, the "quality" of these weapons shrank the globe. The United States and Japan, along the island-hopping campaign, were roughly 8,000 miles apart, but the tremendous flotilla of aircraft carrier task forces and their naval air power technology bridged the huge space across the Pacific Ocean. The carriers were floating airfields with 3,000-man crews, supplied by a train of fuel, repair, medical, transport, and escort ships and, in the case of the biggest *Essex*-class ships, were able to launch ninety to one hundred planes off their decks. Strategists could think, pragmatically, in global terms. Meanwhile, long-range bombers hit Japan repeatedly from bases in China and the Pacific islands and strategic bombing campaigns increased over Europe. And, of course, the atomic bomb's manufacture and delivery – the product of a large, costly, and secret government-science effort – brought the whole world under the threat of nuclear war from August 6, 1945 through the new millennium. At a cost of over $2 billion, the Manhattan Project employed 150,000 people. The atomic bomb made the worldwide procurement of strategic materials, especially uranium, all the more necessary. And the weapon changed diplomatic calculations in the American Century, heightening the menace of mass destruction and rendering a gruesome reality to warnings and threats.[12]

Science and Technology in Support of the State

Behind the production statistics was another fascinating story, one of close business and government cooperation. The need to cooperate against the Axis menace forced the Roosevelt administration and its business critics to bury the hatchet for the duration of the war. They did not always succeed. World War II added a new dimension to this relationship: the growing involvement of scientists and engineers in defense research. Vannevar Bush, the MIT electrical engineer who served as President Roosevelt's advisor on military technology, had to fight daily the professional military's opposition to new technologies. In particular, Admiral Ernest King, remembering the success of convoy escorts during World War I, resisted Bush's efforts to introduce new microwave radar to help locate Axis submarines during the Battle of the Atlantic. But Secretary of War Henry L. Stimson believed in technology, and the military gradually became more receptive to civilian scientists. The latter introduced a number of decisive new weapons: radar, the proximity fuse, and the atomic bomb, among others.

In effect, with government funding and direction, scientists and their laboratories contributed in a major way to the success of the war effort. In the process, they developed many new products that had commercial applications and would transform the postwar world. Atomic energy, for instance, had many peaceful applications – particularly as a source of electrical power. Radar provided the basis of microwave cooking. And the mass production of penicillin transformed the treatment of disease.

The first computers appeared during World War II to assist the military with code-breaking and long-distance ballistics calculations. Engineering Numerical Integrator and Computer or ENIAC, one of the first computers, was a huge machine, occupying 1,800 square feet and using 18,000 bulky vacuum tubes. Not until the development of the transistor, and the resulting microchips, could cheap and reliable computing power be loaded into desktop and portable units. The transistor, which was developed in 1947–8, grew out of wartime research on silicon and germanium at Bell Telephone Laboratories in New Jersey. "Without the transistor, the personal computer would have been inconceivable, and the Information Age it spawned could never have happened," noted two historians.[13]

No industry benefited more from wartime cooperation and federal contracts than aviation. At the outbreak of war, the Boeing Company of Seattle, renown for its seaplanes and engineering skills, had fewer than 2,000 employees and was on the verge of bankruptcy. From this inauspicious beginning, Boeing flourished on the strength of its bombers (the B-17 *Flying Fortress* and the B-29 *Superfortress*). Employment rose to nearly 45,000. At the end of the war, Boeing, on the strength of its experience and reputation in military aircraft production, turned its attention to the civilian market. The B-29 converted to the luxurious 377 *Stratocruiser* that Pan Am used on Atlantic routes. It contained a spiral staircase and a downstairs bar, but it was soon superceded by the four-engine 707 passenger jet, launched in 1954. The latter also had roots in military work to develop a jet tanker, and from wind tunnel experiments with jet engines during World War II. Thus, with government assistance, American companies like Boeing, Douglas, and Lockheed came to dominate the rapidly expanding world market for civilian aviation.[14]

Another important area of public-private cooperation involved strategic minerals. During the First World War, the United States had largely satisfied its war needs from North American sources, but the changing nature of defense production required far more extensive international sourcing during World War II. The United States imported about sixty different minerals – twenty-seven of these came *exclusively* from foreign sources. "Except for coal, iron, and salt," said geologist Alan Bateman, "some quantity of every mineral needed for our war effort had to be imported." These imported materials came from fifty-three different countries extending from Canada and eleven Latin American nations to Australia, New Caledonia, China, and India in the Pacific. Certain items even arrived from European sources in Spain, Portugal, Cyprus, and Turkey, as well as fourteen African countries.[15]

To obtain critical materials, the U.S. government engaged in preclusive buying activities, involving the Metals Reserve Corporation and the Reconstruction Finance Corporation (RFC). The Metals Reserve Corporation became the leading buyer for Latin American copper and a purchaser of aluminum for stockpile purposes. The United States even sent one thousand troops to Surinam in November 1941 – before Pearl Harbor – to protect Alcoa facilities. While the Metals Reserve Corporation did not buy exclusively from American-owned firms, it worked closely with U.S. private mining interests. The Rubber Reserve Company, another affiliate of the RFC, initially sought to stockpile rubber and then entered a historic information-sharing agreement with private companies, and universities, to produce synthetic rubber for the war effort. By 1944, the program was producing 670,268 tons a year, an amount critical to winning the war.[16]

Often there were international partnerships between units of the U.S. government and private enterprise. To obtain nickel, the Defense Plants Corporation entered into a venture with Freeport Sulphur to build and operate nickel facilities in Cuba. The government worked closely with Anaconda copper, encouraging it to expand production in Chile and Mexico and purchasing its production. The State Department and Metals Reserve Company negotiated directly with the Mexican government over access to that country's reserves. Kennecott and Phelps Dodge also worked closely with the government purchasing agencies. The Metals Reserve Company spent $2.75 billion, acquiring roughly fifty different metals from fifty-one foreign countries and domestic sources. It financed projects at home and in Latin America and Canada.[17]

When energy was concerned, government and business had more difficulty papering over differences and establishing a cooperative relationship. Although the United States was still a net oil exporter during World War II and the principal supplier to Britain, it needed access to supplementary supplies for future needs. In December 1943, Interior Secretary Harold Ickes aroused attention with an article headlined: "We're Running Out of Oil!" He warned that "if there should be a World War III it would have to be fought with someone else's petroleum, because the United States wouldn't have it." In dire wartime circumstances, fear of depleted reserves ignited a new scramble for oil – one that focused on Mexico, Venezuela, and the Middle East.[18]

The situation in neighboring Mexico was complex and had simmered without satisfactory resolution since World War I. In 1938, the populist government of President Lazaro Cardenas, following the example of Bolivia the year before, expropriated foreign (British and America) oil properties. Cardenas, a military man, thought the oil companies arrogant in the way they treated Mexico as "conquered territory." He determined to force a confrontation, at a time when the oil companies had shifted production to Venezuela and Mexico's oil revenues ran low. Although initially insisting that Mexico compensate the owners of expropriated properties, the State Department shifted course as the international situation continued to deteriorate. The State Department and the new Mexican president General Manuel Avila Camacho worked out a settlement in November 1941 that essentially had the U.S. government furnishing – through the Export-Import Bank and other sources – funds for Mexico to pay minimal compensation for the property expropriated. The oil companies – and the British government – had opposed the settlement. They worried that the agreements, considered highly favorable to the two countries involved, would encourage other producers to expropriate oil properties. Said the British ambassador privately: "The State Department apparently considered its relations with its Mexican neighbor to be of far greater importance than the prosperity of the oil companies or the claims of its unfortunate nationals."[19]

As it turned out, the oil companies' fears were warranted. Venezuela, one of the world's largest exporters, was the next domino to fall in the test of power between nationalists and global corporations. With oil revenues down after the outbreak of war in Europe disrupted sales, the Venezuelan government decided to demand a more favorable split of profits. Fearful that Venezuela might follow the Mexican example and expropriate oil properties after General Isaias Medina became president in early 1941, the State Department counseled the oil companies to be flexible. During the first half of 1942, when the tides of war shifted temporarily against the Allies, Venezuelan production dropped sharply, the result of German attacks on oil refineries on Aruba and pressure from the new Venezuelan government determined to increase revenues. The U.S. State Department, which had declined to back the oil companies in their compensation disputes with Mexico, now advised the oil companies to reopen negotiations and to replace their local officials with individuals not tied to the former Gomez regime. The result was an unprecedented agreement with Venezuela to share profits on a 50–50 basis beginning in 1948.[20]

As a result of the agreement, more oil companies entered Venezuela and production rose rapidly, making a vital contribution to the European war effort. Standard Oil of New Jersey, which obtained 30 percent of its crude from Venezuela in 1940, relied on Venezuela for 38 percent in 1945. In World War II, historians of Standard Oil wrote later, "the sea of oil on which the Allies floated to victory came in large part from Venezuela." It is interesting to note that while private investment developed the Venezuelan fields, the U.S. government was an active participant providing substantial economic assistance.[21]

The Middle East was another area of feverish petroleum activity and backstabbing diplomacy. With his oil production curtailed because of wartime transportation disruptions, the King of Saudi Arabia asked Britain for financial support. Jesse Jones, the influential Texas business-man and secretary of commerce, initially persuaded Roosevelt that Saudi Arabia was in the British sphere. As a result, the United States allowed the British government to divert direct Lend-Lease assistance to Saudi Arabia as their support for King Ibn Sa'ud. But the oil companies were not prepared to write off Saudi Arabia to the British. Executives of Texas Oil and Standard Oil of California warned President Roosevelt that "the Middle East oil reserve is without question the world's greatest oil re-serve," and they urged the Roosevelt administration to provide direct U.S. assistance to Saudi Arabia rather than to rely on indirect aid through Britain. On February 16, 1943, FDR issued an executive order making Saudi Arabia eligible for Lend-Lease. Secretary of War Stimson, Secretary of the Navy Frank Knox, and Harold Ickes (the petroleum administrator) urged the government to become a part owner of the California Arabian Standard Oil Company; however, Secretary of State Hull opposed this move. The RFC then established a Petroleum Reserves Corporation that had broad authority to participate in every aspect of the oil business.[22]

When the U.S. government sought to obtain the entire stock holdings of Texaco and Standard Oil of California for a government-owned oil com-pany, it sent a shock through the private community. The oil firms chose not to sell, and ultimately the plan died. Instead, with government assis-tance, the oil companies developed wells and refining capacity in Saudi Arabia. Interior Secretary Ickes next sought U.S. government ownership of a key pipeline connecting the Persian Gulf to the Mediterranean, but this project did not get off the ground until after the war, and then only with private ownership.

Another aspect of the Persian Gulf oil situation stirred particular controversy. As U.S. oil companies pursued stakes in oil-rich Iran, ten-sions rose with the British government. There was a hot exchange be-tween London and Washington, in which Churchill accused America of seeking to deprive the United Kingdom of Iranian oil, and President Roosevelt charged that Britain was "horning in" on U.S. holdings. The two governments reached an Anglo-American Petroleum Agreement in August 1944. It was not a cartel, American negotiators claimed, but rather an intergovernmental commodity agreement, "directed toward assuring the availability of ample supplies of petroleum to meet market demands." The essence of the proposed agreement, however, involved the establishment of an eight-member commission to estimate global demand and to allocate production. The two governments took steps to ensure that their nationals conformed to the agreement. When it was submitted to the Senate for ratification, the oil companies forced its renegotiation. Finally, they killed it; fearing the ramifications of having political appointees (half "limeys" and half Roosevelt appointees) managing world oil production, the major oil firms wanted to take no chances.[23]

Thus, even though the Roosevelt administration failed to establish a basis for formal U.S. government involvement in production or transportation of Middle East oil, government aid during the war undoubtedly kept Saudi Arabia out of the British sphere of influence and open to American firms. As it turned out, Roosevelt's policy proved consistent with earlier Republican policies during the 1920s. They all opposed foreign discrimination against U.S. oil firms and provided diplomatic support to ensure that private energy firms "are amply protected." Nonetheless, the relationship between oil companies and the government was not a comfortable one. New Dealers like Ickes had proven themselves less than reliable supporters of oil companies. The State Department's acquiescence to Mexico's nationalization of U.S. petroleum properties had set off alarm bells in the business community. It suspected that FDR's successors would demonstrate similar vacillation and weakness in coping with future disputes.[24]

The sensitive communications and transportation sectors also saw extensive government involvement during World War II, benefiting national champions like ITT and Pan Am. The government encouraged ITT's ambitions to expand in the hemisphere. The State Department reportedly believed that "it was necessary to assure the predominance of American interests in the communication field as against any European interests." Similarly, the administration provided Lend-Lease funds to build airports for Pan American Airways. During the war Pan Am, which had often operated at cross purposes with the New Deal, functioned as a giant military air transport command – ferrying 540 bombers and transports to North Africa in 1942 and carrying cargo to obscure military destinations. While Pan Am and its president Juan Trippe regarded the airline as the "chosen instrument" of U.S. policy, New Dealers worked to bloc Trippe's postwar ambitions. Washington was not disposed to allow a single airline (Pan Am) to negotiate with foreign governments or to dominate international air travel in the postwar period. The State Department encouraged other American participants and established international government rules for civil aviation. Similarly, in shipping the government took control in February 1942 with the War Shipping Administration, which managed government-owned and -chartered vessels. The huge buildup of *Liberty* vessels left the United States with 60 percent of the world's merchant tonnage in 1945, which the government promptly sold off to U.S. and foreign buyers.[25]

The outbreak of World War II threatened the viability of the American film industry, which depended on exports for 40 percent of its world revenue. Early Axis victories reduced revenues 50 percent because the Axis did not permit the circulation of American films in controlled areas of Europe and Asia. And European Allies like Britain regulated remittances to save foreign exchange. In such circumstances, it was easy for Hollywood and Washington to work together in support of the wartime consensus. Under Will Hays, who retired in 1945 and was succeeded by Chamber of Commerce president Eric Johnston, Washington continued to work hand-in-glove with Hollywood. Even before Pearl Harbor, Hollywood was turning out interventionist films like *Yank in the RAF*, which showed Americans patriotically circumventing the Neutrality Act to aid the British. In American films, the Japanese were quickly stigmatized as "little Jap monkeys" and the Germans as arrogant, black-shirted Nazis. Similar propaganda films portrayed the people of Stalinist Russia as "simple, honest people who love the same things Americans do, home, family, friends, and freedom." *Mission to Moscow*, a 1943 Warner Brothers film, presented the Soviet Union in a positive light.[26]

Despite the dislocations, Hollywood did well during the war. World revenues rose from $390 million to $410 million in 1942 to $480 million in 1944 (about 35 percent from foreign sources). Over one-fifth of revenue came from the United Kingdom. The film industry also earned $50 million from the government for "carefully selected" films distributed in liberated countries. Indeed, the *Wall Street Journal* wrote that American films went into continental battlefields right behind the landing barges and were distributed to foreign populations along with food and DDT louse killer. In return for its support in helping the administration make its case to the public, Hollywood enjoyed strong support in Washington. In 1944, Assistant Secretary of State Adolph Berle argued that U.S. movies had "an important intellectual value" in the postwar world. They could present "a picture of this nation, its culture, its institutions, its method of dealing with social problems, and its people, which can be invaluable from the political, cultural and commercial point of view." With Hays as an effective interlocutor, the State Department pressed for access to foreign markets to aid the sale of American products and the dissemination of American values.[27]

The American Century

World War II and the New Deal had witnessed an extraordinary expansion of U.S. government involvement in economic activities. As the war came to an end, some in business were wary of further federal regulations and regulators and fearful of renewed depression. Twelve years of experience with the Roosevelt administration and its conflicting oversight policies had done little to inspire business enthusiasm about the prospects for mutually beneficial cooperation after the war. Indeed, the strident criticisms of business activity voiced by wartime congressional investigating committees – including one chaired by Senator, and later President, Harry Truman – appeared to confirm the worst suspicions of many in finance and industry. When Roosevelt and Truman talked about a "new deal" for the postwar world – as they did in selling the Bretton Woods accords – the image of a world run by government regulators traumatized the private sector, especially among those with fiduciary responsibilities to weigh relative risks and gains in assessing investment opportunities.

The succession of disruptive events since 1914 – two great wars, a global depression, and the rise of the regulatory state – had dampened business confidence about international business opportunities. Many of the older generation of business statesmen – such as Henry Ford, Thomas Lamont, Thomas Watson, and Owen Young – who had zealously promoted internationalism in the 1920s and then endured the dislocations of the 1930s and 1940s, had retired or grown bitter from unpleasant experiences. Some prominent newcomers were cautious.

Industrialist Henry Kaiser, who became a celebrity as a wartime shipbuilder and mastered the art of entrepreneurship with government contracts, had cold feet about foreign opportunities. A successful high school dropout famous for his "can-do" attitude, Kaiser had little interest in investing abroad immediately after World War II. Negative experiences in the 1920s had dampened his zeal. Building a highway in Cuba, he discovered that government officials expected kickbacks. Exposed to the climate of bribery, he said: "If that's the way it works, we'll never go overseas again." But the postwar world offered attractions that led him to defy his own words. Kaiser sent cement to the Canal Zone; developed hydroelectric plants, highways, and natural gas pipelines in Venezuela; and forged an innovative contract with Argentine leader Juan Peron in 1954 to produce automobiles. His Argentine endeavor yielded 30,000 cars by 1959, employed 9000 people by 1964, and became that nation's largest manufacturing plant. A format in a Jeep factory in Brazil brought similar results, and similar huge profits. He ventured into the auto markets in Holland in 1948 and in Israel and Mexico a few years later by investing in small plants and was responsible for assembling the first American car in Japan since Pearl Harbor, in June 1951, called the "Henry J." Still, Kaiser's dreams of perpetuating his Brazil-Argentine successes did not reach fruition in Mexico and Colombia; he often sold out to other manufacturers in Latin America and left the field, and even his successes were predicated on the disposal of surplus production equipment no longer needed in the United States.[28]

Eric Johnston, president of the Chamber of Commerce of the United States, represented the cautious middle ground of business opinion. While recognizing the end of isolationism, he urged "humility and restraint in an exceedingly complicated world." Commenting on his foreign travels, Johnston said, "I have been less impressed with the 'oneness' of the world than with its dizzy multiplicity. Space has been telescoped by the airplane, but the differences between nations and peoples are as formidable as ever." Johnson concluded that circumstances were sufficiently fluid that "it is not impossible that in the postwar world our country may become an island of free enterprise in a sea of socialized economy."[29]

Socialized or not, the world held great opportunities in the eyes of other business leaders. Robert Woodruff, who had taken over the Coca-Cola Company in 1922, aimed to make his beverage an ordinary, everyday item for Americans and people around the world. He built on his foreign operations during the Second World War, particularly in Europe, by having Coke accompany the military overseas. Soldiers not only identified with Woodruff's product during and after the war, but heroes requested it – as did an American pilot who crashed in Scotland and asked, upon regaining consciousness, for a Coke. The Nazis denigrated the beverage as the only thing America had ever contributed to civilization, and the Japanese claimed that the soda brought germs of diseased American society. Still, a captured jungle city in Western New Britain revealed cases of Coke horded by Japanese soldiers. A clear "white Coke" soda bottled with a red star label allowed the Russians to drink without being tainted by a symbol of U.S. imperialism. By war's end, the company ran sixty-three bottling plants across the globe, on every continent. As one of Woodruff's officers noted, World War II resulted in "the almost universal acceptance of the goodness of Coca-Cola."[30]

Others among the opinion-shaping elite were optimistic about America's capacity to lead a troubled world. Early in the war, New York publisher Henry Luce advanced a vision of an "American Century," in which "we...undertake...to be the Good Samaritan of the entire world." He said that "the vision of America as the principal guarantor of the freedom of the seas, the vision of America as the dynamic leader of world trade, has within it the possibilities of such enormous human progress as to stagger the imagination." Luce urged America to send abroad its engineers, scientists, doctors, filmmakers, makers of entertainment, developers of airlines, builders of roads, teachers, and educators to transform the world.[31] His magazines – *Time, Life, Fortune,* and others – publicized their accomplishments. By 1964, the international editions of *Time* and *Life* hit 13 million, circulating in 200 countries among the educated elites and expatriate Americans. Luce thought of his correspondents as "second only to the American ambassador" in the countries from which they reported. In an emerging information age, his influence came through ideas communicated globally.[32]

Luce's ideas resonated not only because of their reach but because of their timing. His famous "American Century" article projected idealism and confidence about a constructive leadership role for America in the postwar world. Internationalists poured out their gratitude to him, sending him thousands of letters welcoming his views. The isolationists took him to task, as Senator Robert Taft warned that to accomplish such a global reach the United States would have to construct a huge and expensive peacetime military establishment. Taft turned out to be right, though Luce certainly did not mind. Luce was ahead of his times in many respects. In 1946, he urged businessmen to "open that door" abroad to investment. More than tariff cuts were in order; Americans had to be creative and abandon "the 19th-century Trader Horn job of trading beads for ivory tusks." They must "participate in a worldwide capital expansion of a sort that will link our industries, our finances and our markets directly with every other country in the world." This globalization rhetoric smacked of the 1990s, but Luce pushed it in the 1950s. A staunch believer in world trade expansion, he had a key ally in the Eisenhower administration in C. D. Jackson, his vice president at *Time* who became advisor to the president. Luce railed against rising protectionism, envisioning an open door "to an expanding future in which the issues and choices will be all new and not even discernible to us here now."[33]

Luce was not the only booster of the American Century, or of American power. In 1940, Republican presidential candidate Wendell Willkie voiced similar themes in his book *One World*, urging America to "win not only the war, but also the peace." Envisaging a single market for a single world, Willkie called for breaking down barriers to trade. "Not only must people have access to what other peoples produce, but their own products must in turn have some chance of reaching men all over the world." Perhaps the most euphoric voice was Vice President Henry A. Wallace who wrote about a *Century of the Common Man*. A futurist and globalist, Wallace thought that improved transportation was the "key that will unlock the resources of the vast undeveloped regions of the world." He proposed as the first order of postwar business the establishment of a network of "globe-girdling airways," including internationalizing large airports and establishing an international aviation authority.[34]

Scientists also had a futuristic vision of American leadership and technology transforming the world. As World War II came to an end, President Roosevelt asked Vannevar Bush to think about future government involvement in science. In one famous essay, published in 1945, Bush – a mathematician and engineer born into the fertile world of invention just before the American Century began – envisioned a new world of information technology. Bush seized on the opportunities presented by the world war to push technology to the fore in government planning and used his considerable political skills to bring his vision to practical reality. He proposed a desktop machine, the so-called memex, that would display pictures and text from microfilm at the touch of a button. Using this personal information processor, individuals could even pursue storable hypertext links similar to the ones today's web surfers use.

In another famous report, Bush argued that the U.S. government should continue to support independent scientific researchers in order to conquer the "endless frontiers" of science. He envisaged progress in the war against disease and further developments in the basic science from which commercialization grows. He foresaw that the nation's defense would depend on overpowering technological superiority. "Science is a proper concern of government," Bush said. " [I]t has been the basic United States policy that government should foster the opening of new frontiers." Government, he asserted, had opened the seas to clipper ships and provided land to pioneers. "Although these frontiers have more or less disappeared, the frontier of science remains. It is in keeping with the American tradition ... that new frontiers shall be made accessible for development by all American citizens." In effect, Vannevar Bush offered a linear model for the postwar military-industrial complex. Have the government support basic research, and almost automatically the private sector would harvest new technologies creating jobs, improving health, introducing new products, and advancing national security.[35]

Visions (and Illusions) of Convergence

Within the Roosevelt administration officials fashioned plans for a series of supranational institutions and rules to govern the postwar world under American direction. Their efforts grew out of preparations for the United Nations (UN) international security system. But they also reflected the hopes of leaders who had witnessed the disintegration of world order after the last war, and who resolved to do better. Framers of the UN system understood that economic cooperation was imperative to avoid the kind of instability and want that had led to the Second World War. This theme was emphasized when the nations met first in Bretton Woods, New Hampshire, in July 1944 to formulate plans for international monetary and financial cooperation, nine months before the San Francisco meeting to establish the United Nations. The interdependence of security and economics was reinforced when Secretary of State Cordell Hull won the Nobel Peace Prize in 1945. The Nobel Committee commended Hull's "untiring efforts in the field of commercial diplomacy." As it turned out, the UN charter, many of its institutions, and the theme of one-world universalism preceded their times, as the League of Nations had done. The big powers soon divided the world into separate spheres of influence. While this revival of power politics represented another setback for the globalization process, wartime intergovernmental efforts to devise institutions and rules for world governance demonstrated the commitment of public- and private-sector elites in the United States to convergence, integration, and harmonization, the foundation stones of globalization.[36]

Despite deadlocks in the Security Council and conflicts in the General Assembly, a number of the several specialized UN agencies did succeed in linking the postwar world together. The UN Economic, Scientific, and Cultural Organization (UNESCO), the Food and Agriculture Organization (FAO), the World Health Organization (WHO), and the International Labor Organization (ILO) were the four most important because their activities touched all nations. UNESCO had a broad mission to spread and democratize knowledge, education, and culture. There were other more narrowly focused institutions with a broad global reach. The oft-ignored International Standards Organization (ISO) set uniform measurements to facilitate global commercial exchanges. Some existed before World War II (such as the Universal Postal Union and the International Telecommunications Union); some came well after the UN's creation (the World Meteorological Organization in 1951, the International Atomic Energy Agency of 1957, the International Maritime Organization in 1959, and the World Intellectual Property Organization of 1970). Others born with the UN included the International Civil Aviation Organization and the UN International Children's Emergency Fund (UNICEF). All created collaborative networks of information and standards that helped member states cooperate in specialized services and later smoothed the way to globalization.[37]

One of the more successful examples involved health care. A product of decades of international cooperation to disseminate information and prevent the spread of disease, WHO drew on scientific knowledge to make medicine, in Catholic Archbishop (soon Cardinal) Francis Spellman's words, "one of the pillars of peace." World War II had destroyed lives but also saved them; such medical discoveries as penicillin, new antibiotics, and sulfa drugs helped the wounded fend off infection. The advent of DDT reduced the incidence of typhus and malaria, although its indiscriminate use as a miracle dust after the war posed environmental dangers. Health concerns appeared in the UN charter, and led to creation of WHO in 1948. Burgeoning epidemics, including a cholera crisis in Egypt in 1947 that claimed over 20,000 lives, led many nations to join the body. After the UN's interim commission on health launched an historic airlift of 20 million doses of the cholera vaccine to Cairo from the United States, Russia, India, and elsewhere, nations ratifying the WHO constitution doubled.

Unlike most other UN agencies, WHO even proved somewhat resistant to the Cold War. The Soviet Union, China, and the Russian satellite nations withdrew from WHO in the late 1940s and early 1950s, but agreed to adhere to its principles and purposes. The communist nations returned to full membership by the end of the 1950s; by 1957, WHO had eighty-five members and an additional number of associates and had formulated a traveler's bill of rights, quarantine policies, and approaches to other transnational concerns. It took a leading role in helping to exterminate dread diseases such as smallpox and polio.[38]

In recent years, as public attention turned to the relationship between labor standards and trade expansion, one of the oldest specialized institutions in the UN system came under critical scrutiny. The International Labor Organization originated at the Paris Peace Conference of 1919 and was authorized to establish international rules and standards pertaining to workers, employers, and governments. Originally an instrument of the League of Nations, the ILO became a UN specialized agency in 1946. Meeting in Philadelphia in 1944, forty-one ILO members confidently proclaimed their determination to raise postwar standards of living and work. In pursuing this goal, ILO has taken the position that social justice should complement economic development. It has emphasized the social costs of unfettered trade and the negative aspects of austerity programs, administered by the International Monetary Fund (IMF).

The gulf between the ILO's philosophy of social justice and universal peace on one side, and hard national and international realities on the other, remains a yawning one. Members of ILO have obligations to bring domestic laws into conformity with some two hundred conventions on conditions of work, discrimination in employment, and related issues. But members often lack the will and the capacity to implement their commitments. Thus, ILO has relied on noncoercive methods of enforcement, including international monitoring, to promote respect for the labor conventions. Nonetheless, in a world rife with sweatshops, child labor, and lax enforcement of domestic labor laws, many question whether ILO's methods are appropriate to the challenges of a global marketplace.[39]

Another important UN affiliate was established to oversee technical and safety matters pertaining to aviation. The International Civil Aviation Organization (ICAO) emerged from an international conference in Chicago, held in late 1944, that fifty-two nations attended. Initially, the United States urged open skies and equal opportunity in the air so that shippers and passengers could choose the carriers they preferred, and the airlines could utilize as many planes as the traffic warranted. But Britain and other European nations insisted on a more regulated system based on national ownership and designated flag carriers. One result was that ICAO had limited jurisdiction, but the multilateral agreement did provide a framework for the vast expansion of commercial aviation after World War II. By the late 1960s, its 116 member nations had integrated various technical aspects of airplane transport, such as air navigation codes, and established a mechanism to resolve civil disputes, promote simpler procedures at borders, and boost Third World development in civil aviation – all enhancing globalization through air transport. But bilateral air service agreements, negotiated between individual governments, determined which carriers had access to which markets, when, and at what fares. To assist ICAO and individual governments with negotiations, airlines organized the International Air Transport Association (IATA) at a conference in Havana in April 1945. Until 1979, IATA operated as a cartel ensuring that carriers charged the same price on the same route. Its 230-plus members cooperated on technical matters, such as interline arrangements and ticketing procedures, and shared information on a wide variety of aviation-related subjects.[40]

Finally, architects of the United Nations system envisaged three key institutions with responsibilities for currency stabilization, reconstruction and development, and trade liberalization. At Bretton Woods, New Hampshire, in July 1944, nations met to establish the IMF and the International Bank for Reconstruction and Development (commonly referred to as the World Bank). The third agency, the proposed International Trade Organization (ITO), proceeded on a separate, slower track. In these matters, the British and Americans, the principal trading and financial powers, frequently advanced divergent ideas tailored to their own postwar needs and aspirations. They battled over nondiscrimination and preferences (the Open Door versus the closed British Empire), the relative roles of the dollar and the pound in the postwar international monetary system, the importance of government full-employment policies to future prosperity, and America's responsibility to assist European reconstruction and recovery.[41]

Weighing heavily on the minds of the postwar economic planners were the chaotic monetary and trade conditions of the interwar period that disrupted international business. Forced to abandon the gold standard, governments had allowed currencies to fluctuate, or had imposed exchange controls, and they had employed a variety of protectionist devices to manage trade. Postwar planners, like economists Harry Dexter White of the U.S. Treasury and Lord John Maynard Keynes of Britain, wanted to establish predictable exchange rates and restore currency convertibility so as to facilitate the revival of international trade. They did not envisage capital account convertibility. Given the magnitude of past losses and future risks, postwar conditions simply did not favor a resumption of private direct and portfolio investment, which both Keynes and White thought could prove a disruptive force. Thus, the two economists designed the IMF to assist governments in maintaining stable rates of exchange and convertible currencies only for current-account transactions. Technically, the IMF restored a version of the gold standard in which members defined their currencies in terms of gold or the U.S. dollar. Underlying this arrangement was the American commitment to buy and sell gold at $35 per ounce, a pledge that effectively made the dollar the anchor of the system. The IMF, in which the United States and Britain had the leading roles, operated as a currency pool, providing short-term assistance to members to finance payments deficits and ease the pain of adjusting exchange rates. IMF approval was required for any change in exchange rates, which were "fixed but adjustable," and adjustment ensued after a weighted vote, in which the United States had the most clout because of its share of world trade, national income, and large population.[42]

As it turned out, the IMF was unsuited for conditions of the postwar world. It was legalistic and mechanistic. Central bankers, who had traditionally dealt with these matters, were skeptical of U.S. Treasury designs. The plan's universalism rested on the dubious assumption that all countries could participate on an equal footing. Moreover, the IMF lacked sufficient resources to address two fundamental problems of postwar adjustment – the shortage of dollars and gold outside the United States and the accumulation of blocked sterling debts (IOUs), which jeopardized Britain's effort to make the pound sterling convertible. To address these problems, Keynes, Britain's chief monetary planner, proposed a different type of agency (the Clearing Union) empowered to issue an international money (bancor) on which debtors could draw without limits. This approach would better address Britain's postwar predicament. But America's negotiator, Harry Dexter White, rejected that idea as politically unacceptable. White understood that Britain and other deficit nations could easily exploit the situation and effectively force the United States to extend dollar credits as gifts. This might prove highly inflationary.[43]

For a variety of reasons, White, who was the second most important person in the U.S. Treasury, is a fascinating enigma. An abrasive personality, White was a theoretical economist who believed that war could be avoided by rational human beings as long as they understood that conflict was economically rooted. A son of Russian immigrants, White climbed the career ladder by earning a PhD at Harvard in international finance and had experience in retail work, on farms, as a social worker, and even in the military – he served in France during World War II. His globalist vision confirmed to him that domestic economies were subject to world financial fluctuations; the international and home arenas were inseparable. White distrusted Wall Street, Britain, and the State Department – as did his boss, Morgenthau. Thus, it is not surprising that his plan for the currency pool envisaged a leading role for the U.S.

Treasury and effectively cut private lenders and central bankers out of the action. Although Keynes was his idol, White reminded his British negotiating counterpart, in his oftentimes rude, humorless, and arrogant way (he referred to Keynes, with biting irony, as "Your Royal Highness") that America was the preponderant power when it came to the world economy and global planning.[44]

White's influence extended far beyond monetary affairs, although the White Plan was his lasting legacy as the basis of the international monetary system. He was intimately involved with every international aspect of U.S. Treasury policy during the war, including sensitive negotiations to provide gold to Jíang Jeshi Nationalist government in China and the Morgenthau Plan, which called for the pastoralization of Germany after the war. In January 1945, White proposed a $10 billion U.S. loan for the Soviet Union, more than the Kremlin had requested. After the war, he oversaw the inaugural meeting of the IMF and IBRD in Savannah, Georgia, and presided as the first American Executive Director of the IMF until his abrupt resignation in March 1947 under a cloud of accusations that he had passed state secrets to the Soviet communist government. The charges forever tarnished his name. Historians who have examined the supersecret Venona intercepts of Soviet intelligence telegrams confirm that White was intimately involved with Soviet intelligence and used his powerful position "to influence American policy to serve Communist interests." They debate whether White's activity was treasonable or only his own effort to advance FDR's policies and "bolster the cause of world peace."[45]

As it turned out, the IMF was unsuited to the postwar world and would not achieve its promise until the 1950s. In August 1947, after a brief attempt at making the pound convertible, Britain encountered a massive drain of hard currency reserves. Unable to sustain its commitment to open markets, Britain suspended convertibility for the pound sterling and postponed compliance with the commitments undertaken at Bretton Woods. Other war-weakened nations also acted in nationalistic ways, imposing exchange and trade restrictions. And so, in the years immediately following the Second World War, the IMF husbanded its resources and waited for the return of more normal conditions.

Because planners expected the world economy to return to normal about five years after the war, they initially proposed to facilitate recovery with loans from the International Bank for Reconstruction and Development (later called the World Bank). With a capitalization of $10 billion, the bank had authority to underwrite loans and issue securities to raise new funds. Harry Dexter White was instrumental in the bank's genesis, too. Grounding his objective in the universal aspirations of the times, he noted that "it is not an overstatement to say that the greatest contribution that we could make to sustained peace and continually rising worldwide prosperity is to make certain that adequate capital is available for productive uses to capital-poor countries on reasonable terms. With abundant capital, the devastated countries can move steadily toward rehabilitation and a constantly improving standard of living."[46]

But like the IMF, the IBRD lacked adequate resources to play a major role during the reconstruction period. Many European and developing countries looked to the IBRD for assistance, but it turned a deaf ear. It needed the support of Wall Street to sell bonds, and in 1946 and 1947 private bankers were skeptical of the new institution and its New Deal associations. Wall Street wanted the new bank to act in ways that would inspire confidence. And so, the bank management proceeded gingerly. It chose not to dispense money like a relief agency, but rather looked for sound and productive projects that met conventional bank-lending criteria with little risk of default. For example, in making a $15 million loan to Chile in 1948 for power equipment and agricultural machinery, the bank required Chile to reach a settlement with holders of defaulted prewar bonds, a step that sent a positive signal to Wall Street.[47] This example illustrates how in the formative years the Bretton Woods institutions, which were located in Washington, D.C., the capital of the largest contributor, became captive to what scholars would later label the Washington-Wall Street consensus, involving open markets and respect for contractual obligations. By 1947, the IBRD and IMF were subordinate arms of America's power, wrote one historian, operating "no longer in the universal interest but as instruments of United States policy."[48]

British economic weakness and Soviet disengagement contributed to this result. While London and Washington debated the future of globalization in various postwar planning meetings, Stalin's Russia, which had suffered some 20 million war casualties, turned inward. At Chicago in 1944, the Soviets insisted on closed skies for aviation; at Bretton Woods that same year, they refused to release data about gold or financial reserves and later opted not to join the IMF and the IBRD; and at Geneva in 1947, the Soviets opted out of multilateral trade negotiations. With Western Europe reeling under massive economic dislocations, the Soviets apparently awaited a resumption of the Great Depression and the "inevitable" collapse of capitalism. Meanwhile, they pursued a unilateral strategy. Having dominated Eastern Europe and threatened the Near East,

Stalin refused to cooperate in Germany, and left-wing parties gained influence in England, Italy, and France.

As it turned out, the recovery of Western Europe and other devastated areas awaited the American decision to suspend multilateralism and to pursue unilateral leadership. After the war, Europe lacked dollars and had little to export to earn foreign exchange. The United States gave $3 billion in relief funds and a $3.75 billion loan to Britain in late 1946 to help that nation recover and stabilize its currency. Still, America continued to run large payments surpluses while the Europeans piled up larger and larger international debts. With the multilateral Bretton Woods institutions unsuited to a problem of this magnitude, the United States turned to unilateral aid, under auspices of the Marshall Plan, to jump-start the European economies and reduce the dollar shortage.[49]

Nonetheless, open markets and stable, convertible currencies remained a long-term objective of the British and the Americans, as did the goal of freeing and expanding trade. During World War II, planners designed a code of trade principles and laws to be incorporated into and adjudicated by the International Trade Organization. Plans for the ITO included a charter that addressed everything affecting trade – from tariffs and cartels to employment, investment, and development for poor nations. The ITO charter also bowed to the wishes of big government proponents. In light of recovery needs and the socialized economic practices of many European nations, that was understandable, but U.S. business leaders deemed the charter unacceptable. They resisted statist and bureaucratic solutions to world problems. Due to deep-seated American hostility, Congress never approved the charter; instead the General Agreement on Tariffs and Trade (GATT), its stepchild, took its place. GATT had a more limited focus. It served as a tariff-negotiating forum and offered a basic set of rules to guide the world trading system. GATT survived for nearly half a century until the World Trade Organization in 1995. Interestingly, a series of U.S. administrations chose to treat GATT as a "contractual obligation" and never submitted it to Congress for approval. At negotiating "rounds," the first occurring in 1947, GATT members agreed to lower tariffs and adhere to the principles of nondiscrimination and national treatment in trade relations and consensus in GATT decision making. While postwar conditions delayed progress to lower trade barriers, GATT succeeded in reducing industrial tariff barriers to minimal levels by the late 1960s and in establishing a program of trade preferences for developing countries. It was not successful in removing agricultural protectionism or in establishing a workable dispute settlement mechanism.[50]

Toward Cold War Deglobalization

The UN economic institutions aspired to universal membership, but the Soviet Union never joined them. A growing schism between the Russians and the Western nations was readily apparent as World War II came to a close. This arose from the inherent conflict between capitalism and communism, the West and the Bolsheviks, as well as from the assessment of Soviet experts like George Kennan who took a dire view of prospects for Soviet-American cooperation and stirred Washington to action with his famous memorandum. British suspicions also influenced American thinking. The origins of the Cold War were also event- and policy-driven. For instance, the dropping of the American atomic bomb signaled hostility to the Soviets, while Russian leader Josef Stalin's refusal to vacate countries of Eastern Europe occupied by the Red Army validated Western fears of Soviet expansionism.

As the war ended, tension grew as both sides focused on Europe, a continent devastated by war and in need of massive reconstruction. Yet the entire world eventually became the arena of their rivalry. Crisis after crisis ensued: a civil war in Greece and China, Soviet resistance to the United Nations and anger at having been refused an American loan as well as postwar Lend-Lease aid, the U.S.-Soviet argument over sharing atomic technology, the division of Germany, British withdrawal from the Near and Middle East, and the occupation of Japan. Initially, Britain decried Soviet adventurism. The Americans, though wary, were eventually persuaded to seize the mantle of leadership of the Free World by 1947. Tough talk erupted on both sides of the "Iron Curtain." The United States shook loose the cobwebs of confusion, abandoned isolationism (although right-wing Republicans who captured Congress in 1946 would make a last stand) and formed a consensus of internationalism driven by national security and economic concerns, and began to mobilize for a long and dangerous confrontation with the Soviet Union.[51]

America soon clashed with the Soviet Union over spheres of influence and over ideology. The Bretton Woods and trade institutions became one battleground for these disputes and, with Soviet refusal to join them, American tools in the nascent Cold War. This historic conflict soon encompassed the world. Wartime multilateral dreams of a united, stable global economy supervised by international institutions gradually fell by the wayside, under attack by the competition between the two budding superpowers. Until about 1946, nations seemed to be converging toward one world, having learned the hard lessons of nationalism during the

Great Depression and world war.[52] The Cold War shattered those dreams and segmented international politics and economics. National security concerns trumped the open-door vision of an open, nondiscriminatory world. Nonetheless, new technological innovations in aviation, computing, and communications – many of them the offspring of World War II defense research – continued to drive the globalization process forward even as Cold War regionalism displaced wartime universalism.

6

Containing and Consuming, 1947–1957

The protracted Cold War struggle lasted well over four decades, dividing the world into two spheres of influence – one led from Washington, the other from Moscow. During this era, national security considerations, rather than invisible market forces, defined international relationships. Governments continued to regulate trade and payments, despite efforts to lower barriers and promote commerce.

As it turned out, the United States held several trump cards in the evolving Cold War. America's technological advantage, adaptable production processes, and access to resources, so decisive in the struggle against Axis aggressors, helped win the new conflict. Also, a new generation of U.S. political and corporate leaders, familiar with mistakes made at the end of World War I when the United States shunned overseas responsibilities, chose to accept this second opportunity to guide the world. These internationalists proved better salesmen than Josef Stalin and his stodgy heirs, who presided over a decrepit, controlled Soviet economy unable to satisfy basic consumer wants. Aware that a troubled world had an insatiable appetite for American values, goods, and services, U.S. leaders exploited their comparative advantage in communications and marketing to spread the American dream of democracy, prosperity, mass consumption, and individual enterprise. In the long Cold War, that formula proved a winner.

Containing Chaos, Confusion, and Communism

In early 1947, the European and Japanese economies still lay shattered and their people destitute and demoralized. America faced the daunting task of pacifying, feeding, and housing 120 million people in Germany, Austria, and Japan, as well as aiding war-damaged partners on the European continent such as the Netherlands, the Benelux countries, and France. In addition, the United States assisted some 20 million Filipinos in their recovery from the destructive Japanese occupation and helped them move from commonwealth status to full independence in 1946. The military encountered similar problems in Korea and on the Chinese mainland where it assisted with the surrender of Japanese troops. In many areas, the economic devastation was so widespread that industrial production had fallen far below pre–World War I levels. In postwar Japan, with 76 million people, industrial production was at one-fifth of 1913 levels, and in Germany at half that level.[1]

Meanwhile, the emerging Cold War hampered economic reconstruction, dampened the spirit of the wartime United Nations, and dashed the idealistic hopes of internationalists. Facing grave economic problems at home, Stalin soon made clear his desire for autarky in Eastern Europe (although a closed economic system did not emerge for a few more years) and insulation from the capitalist world economy. In early 1946, he expressed his intention of confronting the West, and the Americans and their Western European allies responded in kind with policies to contain Soviet power.[2]

Much preparation went into elaborating the containment doctrine, so much that the Cold War revolutionized American institutions and ideology. The United States organized on a permanent war footing, creating a national security state that involved anticommunism in politics, a forceful military approach in foreign affairs, and an economy at home and abroad geared to Cold War needs. President Harry Truman's last secretary of state, Dean Acheson, exhorted the country to get "itself together." He meant accepting greater business-government cooperation, political bipartisanship, and a strong presidency to carry out policies and "correlating logistics with strategy and of integrating war planning with resource capabilities." Containment divided the world but, ironically, facilitated the spread of American-style globalization.[3]

Containment involved psychological warfare and sophisticated cultural and information programs to exploit nationality problems in the Soviet bloc and to enhance understanding of American values in Western Europe. Indeed, National Security Council Paper No. 68 (NSC 68) the most famous statement of the official U.S. response, envisaged use of "psychological warfare calculated to encourage mass defections from Soviet allegiance." Seeking to foster fundamental change in the Soviet system, it envisaged a war of ideas, emphasizing the economic opportunities and political liberties available in the West. In transmitting such information and encouraging personal contacts among peoples separated by political barriers, the containment policy thus had the effect of advancing the globalization process and ultimately ending the Cold War.[4]

The Voice of America (VOA) had broadcast during World War II to counter Axis propaganda. In February 1947, VOA became accessible to the 1.3 million radio sets in the Soviet Union, in the Russian language. It articulated American ideals, such as those expressed in the writings of Henry Luce. VOA communicated a vision of America as the "good Samaritan," believing that it was more blessed to give than to receive and promoting freedom, justice, and democracy.[5] Concerned that VOA was having some impact, Soviet propagandists denounced the broadcasts as the "voice of Wall Street," and Stalin's government turned to deliberate jamming in February 1948. Using CIA-funded emigre radio stations, Radio Free Europe began broadcasting to Bulgaria, Czechoslovakia, Hungary, Poland, and Romania in the summer of 1950. Radio Liberty followed, broadcasting from Germany to the Soviet Union and adopting a more militant tone against Stalinism. Its first broadcast on March 1, 1953, came seven days before Stalin's death.[6]

Another little-noticed initiative to counter Soviet propaganda was America's cultural diplomacy program, which included the Fulbright program for scholars. Until World War II, the United States had largely been an importer of foreign cultures. American students studied abroad at Oxford and Cambridge in the United Kingdom, or in one of the prestigious French or German universities and returned home with a lifelong commitment to internationalism and European perceptions of America. World War II marked the turning point, as the United States became a net exporter of cultural values. Thousands of foreign students traveled to American shores – far more than the number of Americans going abroad. In 1954, for instance, there were 34,232 foreign students studying in the United States. Of these only 15 percent came from Europe. The largest group (30 percent) came from Asia, followed by Latin America (25 percent). Over time, thousands returned home with a greater appreciation of American political and economic values – determined to promote greater democracy and to achieve individual opportunity.[7]

Behind the containment policy lay a unique policy consensus binding together the nation's internationalist elite in business, finance, and government. Chastened by claims that their disengagement lost the peace after World War I, America's leaders cooperated after World War II to promote a permanent structure for peace, one that advanced American values of democracy and free enterprise and undercut the appeal of communism. Recalling the turbulence of the interwar period and the resulting political and economic instability, American business leaders worried about the spread of communism abroad. Rather than battle the federal government as big business and finance had during the New Deal years, a more enlightened generation of business leaders sought to work closely with the Truman administration to promote peace, prosperity, and the national interest. Trade associations such as the U.S. Chamber of Commerce, the National Association of Manufacturers, agricultural organizations, and even elements of organized labor joined in this Cold War consensus. Vigorous leadership came from big capital-intensive business, such as autos and steel, Wall Street, law firms, and export-oriented agriculture. Paul Hoffman, Averell Harriman, John McCloy, Robert Lovett, Will Clayton, and Dean Acheson numbered among the talented individuals attracted to public service. Despite differences over domestic labor legislation that regulated union organization and strikes, big business and government worked hand-in-glove with big labor to combat leftist politics and Stalinism abroad. Walter Reuther of the Congress of Industrial Organizations (CIO) enthusiastically funneled U.S. government funds to free trade unions in Western Europe and pursued his own ambition of building a world council of all unions bargaining with a single corporation.[8]

Paul Hoffman of Studebaker epitomized the post–World War II business leader. A founding member of the Committee for Economic Development, a public policy-oriented business-academic group eager to find accommodation, Hoffman spoke with enthusiasm about peace and prosperity depending on the expansion of international trade. Needing a Republican businessperson to win congressional approval of the Marshall Plan, President Truman nominated Hoffman to administer the European Recovery Program. In supporting U.S. government aid to bring about European recovery, Hoffman advocated a production-oriented, middle-way strategy. He argued that, with expert administrators and local involvement, the aid plan could achieve its goal of assisting European recovery, halting Soviet expansion, and expanding overseas opportunities for U.S. business.[9]

Soviet moves, combined with America's intention to assert itself in the world and protect its interests, shaped the history of the early Cold War. Stalin's machinations to alter the balance of power in Europe, particularly by trying to drive the Western powers out of Berlin in 1948–9, prompted a consensus in the United States in favor of American intervention in

Europe and elsewhere. Specifically, Washington constructed regional arrangements oriented to recovery and security that departed from the grand multilateral design of World War II planners. President Truman told Congress that nations "must choose between alternate ways of life."[10] The resulting breakdown of the world into two principal blocs, one led from Washington, the other from Moscow, created new opportunities for economic expansion and technological innovation – the long-term forces for globalization. Until the Cold War ended in 1989, U.S. business had only a small stake in the Soviet Union or mainland China.

Initially, containment took the form of economic initiatives – trade, government aid, and technical assistance – placed in the "service of political and strategic ends."[11] Drastic shortages in Western Europe, associated with slow recovery from the war and exacerbated by blizzard conditions during the harsh winter of 1946–7, grabbed the attention of U.S. policy makers and legislators. But it was menacing economic distress – namely the fear carried over from the interwar period that stumbling economies created conditions ripe for political instability – that eventually persuaded America to undertake a massive regional aid program. Political competition from the Left and the specter of electoral victories for communists in such vulnerable nations as France and Italy raised worries about the threat to democracy and the teetering balance of power posed by Kremlin operatives. Officials feared that the industrial complex of Western Europe and Germany would fall into Soviet hands, thus handing Stalin supremacy in a core area of the world, and one critical to U.S. safety and prosperity.

The United States had the economic resources to alleviate the dire conditions and prevent democratic dominoes from tumbling to perceived and real Soviet threats. Policy makers feared that if Western Europe slid into the Soviet system, the internationalist world order would be the victim. America would be left alone in the industrial world, its trade and investment capital deprived of historically important European markets and its open door and democratic ideologies stripped of meaning. America understood that its chronic payments surplus with the region was not healthy, and that global prosperity hinged on a more balanced pattern of trade and payments.

Stop-gap measures aimed at recovery and resistance to communism centered on aid, most notably the Marshall Plan, or European Recovery Program of 1948–52. The $13 billion Marshall Plan (over $100 billion in today's dollars) was designed to get allies back on their feet and to steer them toward more market-driven patterns of trade and production (and away from socialism). It was also fashioned to solidify the anticommunist bloc and to seal off the Soviet satellites in Eastern Europe from Western business and technology transfers. The plight and future of occupied Germany, and the cost of the occupation itself, also weighed heavily on American, British, and French minds. The Marshall Plan provided solutions to all of these concerns, although historians debate its necessity and effects. Suffice it to say that the aid primed the economies of Western Europe to the point that economic confidence returned, bottlenecks in production and distribution abated, and the region's industrial and agricultural output climbed above prewar levels by 1952.[12]

The European Recovery Program underscored the magnitude of the dislocations that doomed idealistic efforts during World War II to create an open world economic and security system. The Soviet Union refused to permit its satellites to participate in the Marshall Plan, instead engaging in autarkic state trading, currency manipulation, and the creation of a closed economic system known as Comecon. But the West had its own form of Cold War mercantilism called CoCom (short for Coordinating Committee), which placed export controls on trade with Eastern Europe ostensibly to deal with the problem of supply shortages. This was gradually expanded to include a broadly defined range of "strategic" goods that included civilian-use items. Reluctant Western European allies, who relied on trade with the East for raw materials, participated in export controls as a requirement for American aid. The Korean War gave the Truman administration even more leverage, particularly over transactions with China. During the 1950s, however, the CoCom system loosened as Europeans found loopholes and insisted on expanding trade with communist nations. Moreover, the Eisenhower administration took a more lenient approach to Poland and Yugoslavia, believing that expanding trade with Eastern Europe would encourage "centrifugal forces" in the Soviet bloc and reduce dependence on Moscow.[13]

Europe's dollar shortage, which impeded the importation of food, raw materials, and industrial equipment, was the specific motivation for the Marshall Plan. But this problem was not confined to one region. Marshall Planners recognized the dollar gap as "a world problem" with a solution lying in "the closest possible economic association with countries outside Europe" from which Western Europe imported. Thus, the Europeans enhanced production and exports from their colonies and territories to reduce the dollar deficits. These Third World possessions then transferred food and raw materials to Europe, allowing the Marshall Plan countries to buy fewer resources from the United States and to reduce the need for dollars. The Americans recognized the utility of such an approach and, as a consequence, sent millions of dollars in aid to the colonies. At the same time, both the American economy and national security depended on securing raw materials. Thus Truman proposed the Point Four program of technical assistance in 1949, although the aid was minimal. Still, while security policy necessitated the division of the world into two camps, the economic initiatives pointed over the long term toward internationalist solutions to problems of growth and recovery.

No Marshall Plan followed for Asia, but the United States did provide aid and trade for the same reason it assisted Europe: recovery in the interest of national security. Washington deemed Japan the linchpin of the future Asian economy. Its economic reconstruction was critical to regional rebuilding and prosperity and for the political stability required to fend off Soviet (and later communist Chinese) ambitions. Until a peace treaty was signed in 1951, the United States directed the occupation of Japan under General Douglas MacArthur. At first, MacArthur focused on democratizing the Japanese political system and decentralizing its economy, a structural overhaul from the inside out. The Americans purged the government of militarists and fascists, granted the vote to women, legalized labor unions, and proposed educational reforms. A new constitution outlawed a Japanese military. Initially, MacArthur targeted for decapitation the monopolistic *zaibatsu*, the large industrial concerns that had combined with huge commercial banks to provide Japan's military production base. The occupation sought to remake Japan into a benign, weak, and parochial entity in Asia. As one historian wrote, the general "disdained the Wilsonian theory of open-markets-openly-arrived-at"; Japan's economy would run through his office and be cut off from foreign investors.[14]

But these initiatives ran into problems. Between 1946 and 1949, Japan suffered from rampant inflation and food shortages. Exports were virtually nonexistent. Conservatives resisted the social and economic changes, nationalism arose as a protest to U.S. policies, and the nation stood at the brink of chaos. To make matters worse, Japan's problems were a symptom of *global* crisis. In early 1947, the Truman administration faced Arab-Jewish conflict in the Middle East, Western European economic disintegration, Stalin's control of Eastern Europe, and, in China, America's ally Jiang Jeshi's retreat from communist offensives, which resulted in the victorious revolution of communist Mao Zedong in October 1949. In this context, the president pledged, on March 12, 1947, to resist communist aggression under his Truman Doctrine, and the same day, the State Department proposed to reverse occupation policies and promote a self-sustaining Japanese economy within three years. This move prevented more losses for capitalism in the region. Thus, purges were reduced, as were deconcentration and democratization policies.

The Cold War necessitated this policy reversal, but regional and even international economic considerations also drove the transformation. The United States decided to link Japan to the Open Door ideology of a market-driven system operating under American tutelage. In order to protect U.S. security, trade, and investment interests, policy makers aimed to integrate Japan, the divided Korean peninsula, the Philippines, and, eventually, such European colonial possessions as French Indochina into a regional anticommunist bloc. Japan served as the hub of this economic network, with American aid, trade, investment, and military presence its engine. General MacArthur complained in 1948 that "the big Wall Street combines" were behind the new approach of revitalizing the Japanese economy, namely by rebuilding the *zaibatsu* and linking it regionwide. He was correct, although Wall Street complained that the national security state circumscribed its opportunities.[15]

America approved of Asian integration as a means of preventing a resurgence of militarism in Japan, but the concept of the Greater East Asian Co-Prosperity Sphere was still valid. Many analysts recognized that Japan's industrial core depended on its "raw materials relationships with Korea, Formosa, Manchuria and North China." Knitting Asia into a whole would support political stability in Asia against communism, facilitate the flow from the region to America and Marshall Plan nations of strategic raw materials, and promote interdependence among the islands of the Western Pacific.[16] Eisenhower's secretary of state, John Foster Dulles, also noted that the future of the free world lay in Japanese recovery and integration into the West. He warned Ike's cabinet in mid 1954 that "we must permit Japan to enter into the open world competitive market with us, the British and Germany," for Stalin had remarked before his death that "the free world would find itself in the position where it could not absorb the industrial capacities of Japan and Germany; that the free world would try to set up trade barriers between Germany and Japan and would fall apart eventually on this question, and all the Reds would have to do then would be [to] pick up the pieces."[17] Global prosperity and peace hinged on the economic-security nexus.

Policies adopted during the occupation years to rebuild Japan and integrate it into the world economy had long-term consequences for that country's competitiveness and culture. They illustrate the transformational power of technology in support of the globalization process even in the most adverse times. For example, in 1946, occupation officials invited

American engineers, scientists, and business officials to provide technical assistance. General McArthur wanted reliable radios to communicate with the Japanese people and invited engineers from Bell Laboratories to provide them. Soon management consultant W. Edwards Deming arrived to lecture Japanese business on the importance of quality in production. His lessons proved invaluable for the revival of Japanese production. Indeed, in May 1960, Emperor Hirohito bestowed on Deming the Second Order Medal of the Sacred Treasure. The citation attributed the rebirth of Japanese industry and the successful marketing of radios, transistors, cameras, binoculars, and sewing machines all over the world to Deming's work. Similarly, American firms like RCA were encouraged to license use of patents to Japanese firms, thus facilitating the transfer of Western technology and aiding the rise of Japanese electronics competition. In 1960, General David Sarnoff, the head of RCA, also received an award from Emperor Hirohito, the Order of the Rising Sun, Third Class, for fostering the Japanese consumer electronics industry.[18]

From 1951 to 1984, it is estimated that Japanese companies entered into 42,000 contracts for the importation of Western technology. This massive flow of technology from America and Western Europe, which cost Japan about $17 billion over a period of twenty years, was the key to rebuilding the technological base for all of Japan's modern industries. For American firms like RCA, the decision to sell technology would of course "create competitive nightmares" as Japanese firms took over the American consumer electronics market in the 1970s. On the cultural side, the occupation used films as a medium for transmitting Western values such as respect for individualism and basic human and civil rights. To avoid controversial subjects such as the emperor, while teaching the tenets of democracy, U.S. film censors promoted universal themes such as sex and sports – particularly baseball.[19]

Restoring the International Economy

In the minds of American strategists, restoration of the international economy was always the long-term key to post–World War II peace and prosperity and to victory in the Cold War. At a time when direct foreign aid was unpopular in Congress, the State Department promoted a "trade, not aid" strategy, proposing to offer trade concessions to expand foreign dollar holdings. Thus, it was no surprise that the U.S. delegation to the 1947 GATT trade conference in Geneva offered lower tariffs to trading partners and abandoned the campaign to abolish the British imperial preferential tariff network that discriminated against American exports – particularly agricultural products. To assist beleaguered foreign economies and demonstrate Free World unity, the Americans concluded GATT talks on terms that had an adverse impact on a number of labor-intensive U.S. industries. Not doing so, warned a State Department official, would permit the Russians to "exploit fully any such differences between the US and U.K. just as they are now trying to capitalize on British weakness by increasing pressure throughout Eastern Europe and the Near East."[20] This security-oriented approach shaped trade policy for several decades.

The next rounds of trade negotiations – in Annecy, France, in 1949 and Torquay, England, in 1951 – conformed to the initial Cold War mold. The British Commonwealth refused to end internal trade preferences; America relented. The United States also pursued the inclusion of former enemies turned Cold War allies (West Germany, Italy, and Japan) into the GATT system. The first two were admitted, but the Europeans rejected Japan because of its prewar reputation as an aggressive trader. The security-trade link arose regularly in policy making. Truman stymied a rebellion by Arizona legislators against the importation of Italian lemons during the Annecy talks, warning that a vulnerable ally would be hurt. He would not undermine the Marshall Plan and jeopardize the North Atlantic Trade Organization (NATO) military relationship. By the time of the Torquay Round, moreover, the Korean War was raging. Although the round ended in disappointment, Secretary of State Dean Acheson stressed in 1952 that if "we and our partners in the free world are to build the kind of economic and military strength we need for our security, we must all cooperate to reduce and minimize the barriers to trade between us."[21]

On trade, a bipartisan consensus existed. Internationalist Democrats, who enjoyed support on foreign policy issues from like-minded moderate Republicans, regained control of Congress in the 1948 elections. They forged a bipartisan consensus in support of vigorous overseas involvement. Members of Congress from both parties who long gave priority to protecting domestic workers in import-competing industries found themselves unable to block the internationalists. President Truman, a low-tariff Missouri Democrat, championed the reciprocal trade program and trade liberalization, which would boost recovery and prosperity abroad and thereby prove that "the economic system of the free nations is better than the system of communism." Liberal trade policy was an important aspect of the Cold War struggle, with the United States trying to open and integrate markets in order to stimulate world development and undercut the revolutionary claims of the Sino-Soviet bloc.[22]

Despite these government initiatives, private trade recovered slowly from World War II. The years from 1945 to 1950 focused largely on reconstruction and reflected the distortions of trade and payments controls and government aid programs. But in the decade from 1950 to 1960, trading nations began to look outward. World exports rose at a 6.5 percent annual average and then accelerated to 9.2 percent in the following decade (1960–70) and to 20.3 percent from 1970 to 1980. Developing countries generally lagged behind, until the 1970s when Asian exports soared to 30.1 percent growth on an annual average. But for producers of agricultural commodities and raw materials, the post–Korean War slump had devastating consequences for foreign exchange earnings and development plans.[23]

Foreign investment revived slowly after World War II, and thus complicated both postwar recovery and the long-term internationalization process. There were several reasons: the magnitude of destruction in Europe and Japan, the proliferation of national currency and trade restrictions, and investor concerns about political risk and the spread of socialism. Also, high U.S. taxes and a series of Truman era antitrust prosecutions may have discouraged some U.S. overseas investments for a short period after the war. Until the 1970s, government aid, loans, and other transfers surpassed private-sector investment activity, and host governments understandably looked to official sources for aid rather than to private investors. As late as 1970, unilateral transfers from the U.S. government were more than double private-sector transfers. Not until 1954 did American investors display interest in foreign bonds denominated in dollars or European stocks.[24]

However, there was a surge in U.S. direct investments flowing into overseas mining and petroleum during the decade after World War II. It reflected fear that the United States had exhausted its resource base and was running out of oil. By 1948, the United States had become a substantial net importer of petroleum. This was further evidence that America, the world's largest user of petroleum products, was now increasingly dependent on secure access to foreign resources. Hemispheric isolation was no longer a viable national oil strategy. Indeed, U.S. companies sought out new minerals and petroleum supplies in developing countries, a trend that increasingly brought the United States face to face with nationalistic revolutions. The Truman administration eagerly promoted investments in developing countries, grasping an opportunity to acquire strategic materials and to strengthen the Third World against the siren call of communist revolutions. Thus, private capital flowed into mining and petroleum exploration, especially in Canada, Venezuela, and Saudi Arabia. Direct

U.S. foreign investment expanded from the 1946 level of $7.2 billion to $25.26 billion by 1957 (see Table A.8). The largest percentage increase was in foreign petroleum – up 550 percent from $1.4 billion in 1946 to $9.05 billion in 1957. It is important to note that while postwar resource circumstances and national security concerns prompted renewed American interest in developing countries, the private sector was always more interested in high-income markets. In 1950, U.S. foreign direct investment in oil and mining amounted to less than 4 percent of total investments; in 1960, it was still less than 6 percent. In 1950, 45 percent of U.S. investment went to Canada and Europe; ten years later, the figure was 57.5 percent and it reached 65.7 percent in 1980 (Table A.6). In short, as Europe integrated economically and recovered from war, U.S. corporations rushed to establish a presence in the rapidly growing Common Market.[25]

The petroleum issue provides a good example of how resource-supply needs intersected with Cold War security concerns. During World War II, the United States had awakened to the magnitude of Saudi Arabian reserves and to the significance of the Middle East for postwar energy. The Departments of State and Navy concluded that it was in the highest American interest to retain access to Saudi Arabian oil and to develop it rapidly so as to conserve domestic petroleum. A coalition of U.S. government agencies and private companies worked to support ARAMCO and to promote 50–50 profit sharing with the Saudi Arabian government. In Iran, the situation was different. There the British had a long-standing concession but faced pressure from the Soviet Union and indigenous nationalists. To shore up the British position, Washington supported London diplomatically and gained access for U.S. corporations. In 1951, the two allies sought to check nationalization of the petroleum industry by Prime Minister Mohammed Musaddiq. The young Shah of Iran, too weak to handle the experienced Iranian nationalists who railed against British and American imperialism, stood (in American eyes) against the forces of pro-Soviet revolution. Loss of Iran to communism would cut Western Europe off from nearly one-third of its refined oil supplies and curb petroleum to the rest of the Free World.[26]

The popular, erratic Mussadiq was immune to pressure, and the British refused to accept the expropriation of their oil concessions. In September 1951, Iranians seized the major refinery at Abadan; Britain responded with a boycott of Iranian oil, which prevented its distribution. American mediation ensued, the priority being the prevention of Iran slipping into Soviet hands. But a prime consideration – the fear that expropriation might embolden other Third World producers to do the same – worked in the other direction. When the shah replaced Musaddiq in mid 1952, such violence erupted that the new Central Intelligence Agency (CIA) began planning an operation to undermine the nationalists and tap the shah as the key power in Iran, a plan that succeeded in August 1953 and endured until the mid 1970s with substantial American aid. As a result, the United States continued to squeeze the British out of their Persian oil sphere, while expanding America's role in Middle Eastern affairs.[27]

Regional and Economic Integration

American firms had relatively little interest in conquering Asian markets after World War II. War and revolution had devastated the fabled China market. By 1947, Truman decided to cut its losses in China and curb aid to the corrupt regime of Jiang Jeshi, who was defeated in 1949 by communist Mao Zedong and fled to Taiwan. The supposed "loss" of China to communism (Mao Zedong signed a military alliance with Stalin in 1950), as well as Russia's joining the nuclear club in September 1949 and the creation of the North Atlantic Treaty Organization that same year, made Asian bilateral and regional relationships more important to Washington. Indeed in Indochina, America jettisoned its anticolonial stance and funded the French effort to suppress a communist-nationalist rebellion led by Ho Chi Minh. And the Korean War (June 1950 to July 1953) underscored the importance of building up Asian allies to help contain communism. The war quickened plans to rearm the new nation of West Germany within the NATO framework, primed the Japanese economy as well as that of South Korea and Taiwan, and trained American eyes on Southeast Asia as a source of raw materials and markets for nations of the region.[28]

In boosting regional economies, the Korean conflict set the stage for renewed Asian growth. The war was "Toyota's salvation," said its president, for the company's sales and production had been in steep decline until the U.S. military ordered 1,000 trucks a month after the war broke out. "It's the Grace of Heaven," exclaimed Prime Minister Yoshida after hearing news of the North Korean invasion, anxious about the nation's lifeless stock market. With the "divine aid" of procurement orders, Japan rebuilt into a "huge supply depot," the base of regional expansion. A U.S.-Japan Economic Cooperation program began in May 1951 to promote Japanese trade with Southeast Asia. Dollar earnings – the payments from military procurement – were invested in capital improvements for export expansion. American war orders earned Japan over $3 billion by 1954 and stimulated growth in the textile, construction, automotive, metal, communications, and chemical industries. Overall gross national product for the 1950s and 1960s rose by 10 percent.[29] Japan's economy spurred a regional boom and helped integrate area economies into the Free World's global nexus.

By 1952, although fighting in Korea was at a draw, military aid and rearmament had largely replaced economic assistance in American foreign policy, and not just in Asia. Eighty percent of U.S. aid to Western Europe, for instance, consisted of security items. The war forced a rise in commodity prices and European spending on arms, but U.S. aid filled most of the gaps. American trade and investment alleviated dollar shortages after the Marshall Plan officially ended in 1952. In addition, Marshall Planners prepared the ground for permanent capitalist expansion by supervising engineering projects, modernizing plants, and funding business councils that sent European experts to the United States to learn U.S. production techniques. All of these activities readied Europe for regional expansion, and, eventually, global reach.[30]

Western Europeans themselves had begun to organize their own economic bloc. The Organization for European Economic Cooperation administered the sixteen-nation European Recovery Program. By the early 1950s, it oversaw the coordination of Western European and American trade and investment patterns on a multilateral basis, with an eye toward integrating the region into a common market. In addition, European allies overcame the cutoff of coal supplies from the East, as well as historic Franco-German animosity, by establishing the European Coal and Steel Community in 1953. With pragmatic visionaries such as Robert Schuman and the father of European unity, Jean Monnet, at the helm, Western Europe built a regional economic bloc that soon rivaled the industrial, agricultural, and technological output of the United States from the late 1950s onward. It also served as the basis of cooperation between the Atlantic nations and as a symbol of American foreign policy success in the early Cold War.[31]

French Foreign Minister Robert Schuman planted the seeds of the momentous regional integration scheme that today is known as the European Union. In an effort to reconcile the demands of France and Germany, protagonists at the center of two world wars and the foci of the Soviet-American rivalry, Schuman posited a cohesive, supranational arrangement to share the vital resources of coal and steel within and along their borders. This European Coal and Steel Community would provide "the necessary production of coal and steel on the most economical terms without regard for national frontiers or nationality of consumers or producers."

Economic internationalists and European integrationists shared this vision, as did the Americans. Although wary that the community smacked of an international cartel, and departed from multilateral trade principles sponsored by the United States, Dean Acheson endorsed the project as a way to further European unity, harness German power, and ease French fears of a resurgent Germany.[32]

Backed by the creation in 1950 of the European Payments Union, designed to increase the European market and liberalize European trade, the supporters of regional economic integration achieved their ambitions. The Europeans glued together a union of their economies, first in coal and steel and then with the more comprehensive European Economic Community (EEC), or Common Market, in 1957. Great Britain remained aloof from these processes, anxious to protect the position of sterling, its ties to the empire, and its fading power. It succeeded in fashioning a competing economic association of smaller nations – the European Free Trade Association (EFTA) – but EFTA could not arrest the continental drive for economic and political unification.

America supported European integration for various political and economic reasons. Along with Western German membership in NATO (1955), the Common Market further anchored Germany to Western Europe. Also, Washington found appealing the notion that European integration might imitate the American nation-building experience and create a vast market supportive of free enterprise and receptive to American trade and investments. What followed was truly revolutionary. The continental Europeans created a European parliament, an atomic energy authority, and a supranational political authority – the European Commission – in Brussels.[33] Success for the Americans owed much to the Europeans themselves, and particularly to the visionary Frenchman Jean Monnet.

This innovative bureaucrat spent sixty-two years of service in pursuit of one goal – a unified Europe. From the outbreak of World War I, when he helped mobilize British and French supply, to his retirement as president of the Action Committee of the United States of Europe in 1975, Monnet sought to persuade governments and citizens to accept the idea of giving up sovereignty in the name of the greater power of unification. His experience provided solid credentials to promote this vision – he served in the League of Nations between the wars, coordinated U.S. efforts to arm European democracies against fascism, modernized the postwar French economy while working with the difficult Charles de Gaulle, and crusaded for Atlantic unity between Europe and America. The Schuman Plan of pooling coal and steel production among Germany, France, Belgium, and

Holland originated with him. Monnet endorsed the European atomic energy commission and drafted the texts for the union of the six Common
Market nations.

Monnet, who had longed to be a boxer, fought aggressively for European unity. If he could turn Franco-German division into "a common
asset, which will also be European," he and Cold War leaders could meet
their economic, political, and moral responsibilities to manage peace and
prosperity. This was an expansive view that rested on the notion that peace
was impossible if, as he wrote in 1943, the European "States re-establish
themselves on the basis of national sovereignty, with all that this implies
by way of prestige policies and economic protectionism." Monnet recognized that Britain, America, and Russia had their own economic options;
Europe had "a federation or a 'European entity' which will make them a
single economic unit."[34]

Monnet's vigorous expression, promotion, and implementation of the
EEC, Euratom, and other institutions ranked him as the founder of
European unity, but his creations and perspectives were also building
blocks to globalization. His accomplishments helped integrate peoples
and nations of one troubled region into a larger economic, cultural, and
political unit – the European Union. European regionalization thus presaged a new era of overseas expansion in which large European corporations competed for global market share and European champions (Airbus)
battled with American export leaders (Boeing). Had he lived past 1979,
Monnet would have witnessed, with great satisfaction, not only the further integration of Europe but also the expansion of integrative processes
worldwide in the post–Cold War era of globalization.[35]

Ike, Security, and Integration

Dwight D. Eisenhower took office in January 1953 and furthered the
integration process for reasons of security and prosperity. International
developments persuaded Ike and Secretary of State John Foster Dulles to
continue to prosecute the Cold War but look for ways to de-escalate tensions. The superpowers still vied over territory, ideology, and resources,
but Stalin's death in March 1953 provided an opportunity for rethinking
their conflict. Eisenhower and new Soviet leader Nikita Khrushchev welcomed symbolic gestures of sparring by diplomacy rather than the sword
and had some success in easing tensions until the downing of a U.S. spy
plane in 1960 dashed these efforts. Driving the president was his fear of
nuclear war. A direct witness to world war, he understood that nuclear

capabilities had reconfigured world politics; because atomic conflagration could come to every place on the map, a broader security policy was in order. Dulles set out to gird the world with security pacts as part of this policy, while the administration turned to covert actions, nuclear brinkmanship, and the expansive blueprint for prosecuting the Cold War on a global basis called NSC 68 to fight communism. Federal spending on national security primed the economy by benefiting dynamic industries, such as aerospace, communications, and computers. But Ike also fixated on nuclear weapons, and disarmament.[36]

Edward Teller, the father of the hydrogen bomb, had other ideas. He told foreign policy makers in the early 1950s that Soviet testing compelled the United States into a race for nuclear superiority. A Jewish emigre from Germany who had studied with the elite physicists of Europe and then made his way to George Washington University in 1935, Teller understood the broader implications of nuclear weaponry and, indeed, the growing importance of international exchange of scientific knowledge. He created the Lawrence Livermore Laboratory in 1952, from which the research, design, and testing of the "superbomb" emanated once Teller convinced the Atomic Energy Commission (AEC), Congress, the Department of Defense, and President Truman to proceed with its development. Dissenters within the scientific community, such as Robert Oppenheimer (the father of the atomic bomb), and AEC chief David Lilienthal, worried that such a massive weapon could result in war, but they could not stand up to Teller (who they accused of positively "drooling" over the H-bomb) and the Red Scare temper of the times. Various tests proceeded, including the infamous Bravo on Bikini atoll in the Marshall Islands on March 1, 1954, which littered twenty-three unsuspecting Japanese tuna fisherman on the boat *Lucky Dragon* with radioactive fallout. The dangers of nuclear explosions became a worldwide fear. This did not deter Teller, for he welcomed the chance to prove that U.S. possession of nuclear technology would advance the interests of the Free World. With his faith in technology, Teller concluded that "[e]very citizen, whether a politician or a farmer, a businessman or a scientist, has to carry his share of the greater responsibility that comes with greater power over nature."[37]

Yet this tough approach, which Eisenhower adopted along with his disarmament plans, proved to be scary, blustering, or, most ominously, a catalyst to internationalizing the nuclear arms race. In 1955, the People's Republic of China bombarded the offshore islands of Quemoy and Matsu as a possible prelude to invading Taiwan and seizing it for the communists. Dulles warned that America might explode small air bursts of nuclear bombs over the mainland if Mao did not relent. The Chinese backed down, although another offshore island crisis erupted in 1958. And China determined to develop its own nuclear program, which bore fruit in 1964. Atomic bombs were irrelevant in liberating Eastern Europe, most notably when Russia crushed a Hungarian democratic rebellion in 1956.

The Hungarian revolt of October 1956 also showed the difficulties of managing security around the globe in an era of improving communications. Radio Free Europe was enormously popular in Hungary (reaching about 50 percent of the people), and its broadcasting during the revolt provided detailed assistance to the freedom fighters and implied American support would be forthcoming after the U.S. elections.[38] That never happened. And as Soviet tanks moved into Budapest, Eisenhower was dealing with the difficult Suez Crisis. Postwar politics in the Middle East was subject to increasing superpower interest because of oil and the existence of Israel. The latter, created in 1948, had withstood the vengeance of the Arab world only with, at first, Soviet aid and then with American support. Sweeping Arab nationalism, and the withdrawal of British influence in the region, gave Egypt and its vibrant leader Gamel Abdul Nasser a platform to play off both the United States and Soviet Union for economic and military assistance. Nasser did so as the emergent leader of the nonaligned nations, which took neither the communist nor democratic capitalist side in the Cold War. Indeed, Nasser, India's Nehru, and Yugoslavia's Tito originated the term Third World to set themselves apart from the superpowers, but they reaped advantages from both camps.[39]

America and Russia rushed money, technology, and military hardware to Africa and Asia; Nasser, for instance, welcomed a package of American, British, and World Bank loans to build the Aswan Dam to harness the vast power of the Nile River and develop Egypt. At the same time he negotiated a deal with the Americans, he also recognized the People's Republic of China (which the United States refused to do until the 1970s); accepted military planes and tanks from the Soviet bloc; and continued to oppose the state of Israel. This earned the wrath of Congress. The Eisenhower administration rethought its plan of wooing Nasser and withdrew its offer to construct the Aswan Dam. To pay for the dam, enrich Egypt with the canal's revenue ($25 million to $35 million annually), and answer the West, the insulted Nasser promptly nationalized the Suez Canal in July 1956, which was run under a lease set to expire in 1968 by the British Suez Canal Company. This delighted Arab nationalists, angered Britain and France, and terrified the Israelis. The latter three decided to destroy Egyptian power, attacking Nasser in late October and thereby escalating the Suez Crisis. As one historian wrote, the Europeans "resorted to a classic nineteenth-century means of coping with unruly natives"; however, this time around, they ran up against a foe with too much global power to overcome: the United States.[40]

The Americans worried that support of their allies would alienate the Arabs and the entire Third World. Many Asian and African nations had met in 1955 in Bandung, Indonesia, to express the unity of the nonaligned movement – it was Nasser's debut as Third World leader – and the United States feared adding fuel to that fire. Also, America would be supporting imperialism and aggression, and possibly open the door to Soviet support in the Arab world. Acknowledging the financial strain the British had suffered since the war to maintain the position of sterling as a key world currency, the administration applied a type of dollar diplomacy to its closest ally. The Bank of England had limited currency reserves to support sterling convertibility, a key to the city of London's leading role in global finance. The Suez Crisis saw the rapid loss of even more gold and convertible foreign exchange. When Eisenhower refused to bolster the pound with credits and blocked an IMF loan to support sterling until Britain pulled back from Suez, London faced a painful dilemma. It chose to withdraw militarily rather than to devalue the pound or suspend convertibility. The latter might have crippled efforts to reestablish London as a world financial center.

The Suez Crisis ended up in humiliation for the Europeans and the Israelis, who all retreated in the face of U.S. power. British Prime Minister Anthony Eden resigned in disgrace. The strain on NATO was immense, but Ike bailed out Britain with U.S. and IMF credits. Meanwhile, the Europeans hastened the creation of the Common Market, in part as economic self-defense against Washington. For their part, the Americans' role as brokers in the Middle East rose. Suez increased U.S. commitments to yet another part of the world.[41]

Actually, the entire Third World became the battleground for Moscow and Washington. With European colonialism in retreat, and resentment to U.S. neocolonialism on the rise, the dynamic movement of a revolution of rising expectations (if not socialism) swept Africa, Asia, and Latin America. The CIA ensured that the Shah of Iran became America's best friend in the Middle East after his reinstallment in 1953. Eisenhower also used the CIA in 1954 to overthrow a democratic government in Guatemala, which was believed susceptible to leftist infiltration. Many historians think that the country was really only susceptible to the machinations of the dominating United Fruit Company and its allies in

America, including former counsel John Foster Dulles. That year, France exited from Indochina under accords that Eisenhower refused to uphold; in 1955, America began aiding a pro-Western government in South Vietnam. And Dulles did everything possible to discourage nonalignment because neutrality in the Cold War was "obsolete" and even "immoral" in his view.[42]

Bringing morality into play as a weapon against communism abroad and creeping socialism at home typified the administration's public approach to foreign policy. They were helped in this cause by evangelist Billy Graham, who sprang to global fame just before Ike took office and remained a fixture for several decades afterward. This crusader for Christ from North Carolina had impeccable timing – at thirty-one years old in 1949, he had spoken of an America "under judgment" due to the threat of the Soviet atomic bomb and big government at home.

Two sides of Graham made his ministry a good example of the globalized, transnational person-to-person communications that coexisted with government Cold War policy. One was his unflagging belief in free-enterprise capitalism, his "affinity between capitalism and the Protestant ethic" that led him to cast American life in terms of a battle between atheistic communists and those using "God-given" natural resources and talents to build a Christian empire. The other was his status as a religious entrepreneur. In 1950, he began a radio broadcast on ABC over 150 stations in which he held forth on the issues of the day, and earned the highest ratings of any religious program ever. Four years later, his best-selling book, *Peace with God*, sold 125,000 copies in just three months; by 1965, sales reached 1.25 million in English alone. In the years between the broadcast and the book, Graham befriended such kingmakers as Henry Luce and financier Bernard Baruch and members of both political parties, including Senate leader Lyndon B. Johnson and Vice President Richard M. Nixon. He met Truman at the White House and visited the troops in Korea.

Such contacts and marketing helped to explain his worldwide appeal. With money raised from his American Crusades for Christ, he sailed across the Atlantic to tour England and Scotland in 1954. Before disembarking in England, he had made a stir by denouncing the British Labour Party as a socialist evil (he also called France a "pagan" nation). A member of Parliament was so incensed that he introduced a resolution to bar Graham from landing because the evangelist was interfering in British politics. Not to worry, though, Graham apologized and met with the member in the House of Commons, as well as Prime Minister Winston Churchill.

Drawing on new technology, he also hired long-distance phone lines, run through the British post office, to relay his speech to thousands in cities and towns throughout England. The sound was clear and direct, unlike radio. Crowds packed Trafalgar Square to hear him preach.

Graham hopped around the globe in the 1950s. He visited Australia and New Zealand and then went to India in mid decade. There he met Prime Minister Nehru who reacted glumly to the news that only faith in Jesus, not in the United Nations, would bring world peace. Returning to Washington, Graham linked religion with capitalism, advising Eisenhower to send the "pro-Christian" Nehru a state-of-the-art train or a "pure white" Cadillac as a means of winning the Indian leader's adherence to the Free World. Graham remained an international figure. In August 1957, he spoke to the largest crowd ever to gather in Times Square, estimated at 200,000 people. This was impressive, but only a small sample of his total audience that came forward throughout the world to be saved on "the cross of our Lord Jesus Christ."[43]

But the administration had to do something more concrete than preaching to win the hearts, minds, and stomachs of people caught in poverty and revolutionary fervor. Foreign economic policy served as a useful tool. Ike supported trade liberalization and expansion to help other nations. Upon entering office, he appointed a commission led by industrialist Clarence Randall to examine U.S. international economic relationships and to make recommendations for addressing the international shortage of dollars. The commission, which had an internationalist majority, favored renewing the reciprocal trade liberalization program and assisting foreign governments to remove exchange restrictions and make currencies convertible for trade purposes. To support economic development and stability abroad, it urged federal tax cuts to spur corporate investment overseas and steps to increase imports and reduce agricultural protectionism in the United States. Eisenhower adopted these proposals as his "trade not aid" policy, although Congress and the Defense Department constrained his trade program with measures intended to safeguard local production and supply.

Eisenhower feared that a revival of U.S. protectionism would undercut the administration's efforts to respond to the Soviet economic challenge directed at newly independent countries. Russia had not taken much heed of the Third World in Stalin's day, but between 1953 and 1956, aid, trade, and credits flowed more readily to poor nations, and especially nonaligned neutrals. This new offensive was behind the aid to Nasser's Egypt and to India, the largest democracy in the world. The president noted that Russian strategy had "changed into more, apparently, of an economic propaganda plan rather than depending upon force and the threat of force." He responded in alarm when Congress cut $100 million from the 1955 mutual security program. Ike battled members of his own party, who balked at the expense and at sending money to left-leaning nations to restore and expand assistance to the Middle East, Asia, and Africa. In 1957, Congress finally authorized funding but only at a reduced amount.[44] The Third World remained a focus in the Cold War; like the rest of the world, security and economics went hand in hand.

National and International Growth

The Cold War had an impact on the American economy as well. The fiscally conservative Eisenhower reallocated federal spending away from some New Deal-type programs and toward new priorities. While maintaining strong support for defense and foreign assistance, Eisenhower attached significance to improving the nation's road and air transportation infrastructure and to completing the St. Lawrence Seaway.

As it turned out, better transportation facilitated both Cold War military needs and the globalization process. The interstate highway program provided a flexible transportation infrastructure for moving tradable goods and people rapidly through the world's largest high-income market between ports of entry and U.S. producers and consumers. It also expanded individual travel, encouraged consumer-based suburbia, and helped bridge the gap between rural and urban areas. The Eisenhower administration recognized the need to modernize the nation's air traffic control system with new radars and airport expansions to accommodate jet travel. The new passenger jets needed nearly twice as much runway space. The Civil Aeronautics Administration established three transcontinental air corridors, where aircraft would fly on instruments even in clear weather. The revolution in travel became a reality in January 1959 when American Airlines started transcontinental service from New York to Los Angeles. A few months later Pan American launched nonstop flights to Europe.[45]

Improved transportation was one key to post–World War II American growth. During World War II, some had worried that demobilization would bring a renewal of the Depression, but this concern proved unfounded. American consumers had a pent-up demand for consumer goods – especially automobiles, televisions, washing machines, and housing. And, the United States appeared to have the resources to supply those needs. Unlike other major powers, it had huge industrial capacity undamaged from wartime conflict. With a stream of innovations coming out of its universities and scientific research institutes, providing new products for military and civilian use, the United States simultaneously prosecuted the Cold War, restored and energized the Western international economy, and improved living standards at home.

In effect, the bountiful and dynamic American economy gave policy makers considerable flexibility in responding to the Soviet challenge. Unlike the Soviet Union, the United States could produce ample quantities of guns and military materiel without shortages of food and consumer goods. The American standard of living rapidly improved. In the decade from 1947 to 1957, America overcame reconversion jitters and embarked on an era of economic growth, averaging nearly 4.0 percent annually, and creating over nine million jobs for returning veterans and new workers. Average annual earnings of employees rose 39 percent when adjusted for inflation. Rising incomes meant that American consumers could purchase new products. With gasoline cheap and cars in abundance, the number of motor vehicles on U.S. roads rose 77 percent to 67 million. During the decade, 39 million households purchased a television set, and 30 million obtained telephones.

For most ordinary Americans, this was a golden age of progress and prosperity. For the stereotypical GI Joe, the veteran of World War II who had only a high school education or less, the return to civilian life generally meant a secure, good-paying job in industry. The returning veterans married, started families, and soon bought an array of modern consumer products – especially new ranch-style homes, autos, and televisions. In the decade after World War II, millions of ordinary people moved into the ranks of the expanding middle class. For them, the postwar years saw the American dream become a reality. Minorities, including some veterans, did not fare so well, although government data show upward mobility among minorities growing out of the general prosperity. In its campaign to convince the Soviets of the economic advantages in the West, the Voice of America startled listeners with the claim that "nineteen million American Negroes own more cars than the inhabitants of the whole of the Soviet Union."[46] As the good times rolled on, median family income surged – rising in constant dollars from $4,531 in 1947 to $5,888 in 1957 (an increase of 30 percent) and then to $8,473 in 1970 (up 87 percent).[47]

An expanding automobile industry provided jobs in management as well as the factory floor. The auto industry stressed style, comfort, and horsepower in the 1950s. Nobody really listened to prophets of quality control like W. Edwards Deming – his audience was in Japan. GI Joe enjoyed the fruits of what one historian has called the "consumerist embourgeoisement" of labor. Joe reveled in the fact that averages wages in the auto industry nearly doubled between 1947 and 1960, and that in Detroit, Toledo, and Flint, the proportion of owner-occupied homes reached levels of the highest in the nation. He was a product of the success of postwar American economic success (indeed, there was no real competition in the auto industry until the very end of the 1950s, and even that was not too threatening) and a beneficiary of sacrifices made by the militant arm of the labor movement. To be sure, United Auto Worker (UAW) leader Walter Reuther had forced Detroit management to pay higher wages beginning in the early 1950s. Support for UAW-negotiated contracts was near unanimous among the rank and file. In 1955, the AFL (American Federation of Labor) and CIO merged, creating a mainstream organization based on the consensus of productionism and antiradicalism. There was a decline in overt strike violence.

The labor-management accord gave GI Joe a steady paycheck at wages far higher than counterparts in Japan or Germany. But Joe did not realize that his days were numbered. The economy was changing from a manufacturing-led to a service-led economy. In 1956, white-collar workers outnumbered blue-collar labor for the first time in the nation's history. The country was becoming more professionalized, managerial, and clerical – a trend that arose at the beginning of the American Century and accelerated after the U.S. economy converted to peacetime operation in the early 1950s. Factory work and manual labor did not, of course, disappear, but, clearly, the growth of the service sector showed that the country had entered a postindustrial stage that had many negative implications for workers even as they benefited from the transformations in the short run. And most ominous for the GI Joe of Detroit or Pittsburgh, the resurgence of foreign industry with new state-of-the-art plants and the gradual reduction of U.S. tariffs left low-skilled American factory labor increasingly vulnerable to import competition. Except for textiles and a few other labor-intensive industries, however, in 1957, these were problems for the future.[48]

For now, prosperity and peace brought greater individual mobility. Before World War I, an average of 1.5 million people arrived annually on U.S. shores, with about half that many departing. International travel, which declined during the years of the Depression and the Second World War, gradually recovered. Two million people visited the United States in 1956; 10 million, in 1970. Immigration, which fell to a low of 24,000 in 1943 and stagnated during the Depression and World War II, revived slowly after the war, reaching 327,000 in 1957. The largest numbers of immigrants – many of them war refugees – continued to come from Europe, particularly from Germany. Air travel took off. Before the 1940s, the typical traveler from abroad came by sea; after World War II, the traveler arrived by air. On domestic routes, the number of revenue passengers rose rapidly from 6.6 million passengers in 1945, to 48.7 million in 1957, and 153.4 million in 1970. On international routes, the rise was equally dramatic – 476,000 in 1945, 4.5 million in 1957, and 16.3 million in 1970.[49]

One paradox of the decade from 1947 to 1957 was that the U.S. effort to assist defeated and impoverished former adversaries, and exhausted allies, get back on their feet had the long-term effect of strengthening foreign competition for American workers and factories. To be sure, this internationalist, containment policy also benefited U.S. consumers and facilitated the postwar expansion of American cultural, political, and economic influences abroad. Without the Marshall Plan, support for Japan, and containment of the Soviet Union, the history of the Cold War might have turned out quite differently; the same is true for the course of globalization. Soviet-directed expansion would have been far different – far more capricious, authoritarian, and state-managed – than the American-led alternative based on the rule of law, democratic elections, open markets, and the relentless energy of technology and entrepreneurship.

7

Transforming the World, 1958–1973

The last years of the Eisenhower presidency saw enormous changes in world politics and the forces pushing for globalization. Cold War competition intensified around the world – Berlin, Cuba, and Indochina – and expanded into new domains as outer space. Western Europe, having recovered from the devastation of World War II, began to step out from America's shadow and project a distinct regional identity. Meanwhile, a revolution in critical technologies – including trans-Atlantic telephone service, satellite communications, computers, and jet travel – accelerated the globalization process and ushered in a new era of rapid intercontinental travel, instantaneous communications, and economic interdependence.

Fifteen years later, the world was much different. The war in Indochina raised questions about America's purpose. Allies chafed against U.S. dominance. They succeeded in humbling the dollar and forcing its devaluation. In the volatile Middle East, oil producers had new-found cohesion and determination to exploit northern hemisphere vulnerabilities. Youth rebelled against authority and experimented with drugs and countercultural ideas. The war, and the Watergate scandal, also tarnished the presidency and corroded the national-security state. Nonetheless, after years of strong economic growth and scientific advances, many Americans still enjoyed the benefits of unprecedented prosperity. They bought new homes equipped with the latest labor-saving appliances, vacationed and studied abroad, and followed breaking news and sporting events abroad on new color television sets receiving signals transmitted via space satellites. Despite domestic political turmoil, techno-globalization continued to press forward, gradually transforming the world of separate nations into what one prominent academic labeled the "global village."

Technology and the Emerging Global Village

Marshall McLuhan, a Canadian who analyzed the impact of mass media on society, made this metaphor famous in 1962. "The new electronic interdependence recreates the world in the image of a global village." At the time, McLuhan was concerned largely with how noninteractive communications like radio and television were homogenizing the world. Everyone watched the same sporting events, news, and soap operas.[1] He identified a significant trend. The late 1950s was a period of enormous change as technical developments in aviation, transportation, and communications brought cost reductions and improved service. People, goods, and capital began to move across borders, creating interactive bonds among people and between nations. These flows integrated markets, harmonized tastes, and homogenized cultures.

Some of the most significant advances involved air transportation for people and freight. In 1957, Boeing, having gambled 25 percent of its net worth on development of a long-range passenger jet, launched the 707-120, designed as both a tanker for the Air Force and a civilian jet. Equipped with long-range Pratt & Whitney J-57 engines, it halved flying time across the Atlantic and opened the era of cheap air travel. The number of passengers departing internationally on scheduled airliners rose 340 percent (from 4.3 million to 18.9 million) from 1957 to 1973, as airlines introduced tourist-class fares. A round-trip flight, New York to London, fell to $487. The arrival of the wide-bodied Boeing 747 in 1969 further expanded capacity and drove down costs. Originally designed as a cargo carrier, it could accommodate two containers side-by-side that could be transferred to trucks – and soon high-value goods were moving swiftly by jet freighter. It also offered lower operating costs at a time – 45 percent less than the 707 on a per-seat-mile basis – when fuel prices were rising.[2]

Thus, by the early 1970s, improvements in air transport made it possible for business to source suppliers and serve markets globally. From 1957 to 1973, the number of revenue-ton-miles for air cargo on scheduled international flights rose 866 percent from 128.2 billion tons in 1957 to 1.2 trillion tons in 1973. It would be a decade before the full impact of these improvements worked their way through the marketplace. Air service continued to expand rapidly, and airfares fell. Charter service grew rapidly on the trans-Atlantic route, and fares on scheduled airliners fell below $200 (New York to London) by 1970. Millions of college students read Arthur Frommer's bestseller *Europe on $5 a Day* (first published in 1957), put on their backpacks, and set out to see Europe and learn about "foreign affairs." Meanwhile, improved engine design and weight reduction led to longer-range planes. In 1976, Boeing launched the 747 SP, which had the capacity to carry 233 passengers nonstop with full payload between New York and Tokyo. The 747-400, produced in 1989, could carry 412 passengers up to twenty hours at subsonic speeds.[3]

Along with the arrival of reliable, efficient jet freight in the late 1960s, there were other important cost-saving developments in maritime shipping – including containerization. For centuries, gangs of longshoremen had loaded and unloaded freighters. In the 1950s, longshoremen could typically handle ten to fifteen tons of cargo per hour. But as a result of using truck-trailer, standard-size containers, productivity rose to 600 to 700 tons per hour. This meant faster ship turnaround, better coordination, and lower transportation costs. Beginning in April 1956, when Malcolm McLean first moved loaded trailers between two U.S. port cities on an old World War II tanker, containerization took off. The Grace and Matson lines adopted it in 1960, and the rush to containerization accelerated during the Vietnam War. In addition, the international shipping industry developed specially designed ships for automobiles (the first auto carriers could handle 1,000 to 2,000 cars) and liquified natural gas (LNG) tankers after the 1973 Middle East war.[4]

Improvements in communications also boosted the globalization process. Until the mid 1950s, individuals could not communicate quickly and easily across the Atlantic and the Pacific Oceans. Submarine cables, dating to the 1850s, did permit the exchange of coded messages, but ordinary people could not communicate cheaply except by surface mail, which took at least a week to go one way. In 1927, commercial telephone service using high-frequency radio opened between New York and London. But this interactive advance was not designed for mass communications. Radio telephones were noisy, unreliable, and costly – $45 for the first three minutes. September 1956 brought the most significant improvement in communications in over a century when AT&T opened the first Transatlantic Telephone cable (TAT-1), using microwave amplification techniques. The number of trans-Atlantic telephone calls soared – climbing slowly from 10,000 calls in 1927 to 250,000 in 1957 and then jumping in four years to 4.3 million in 1961. Soon large corporations, such as Ford, began using the telephone cable to exchange information and coordinate their overseas operations from the U.S. headquarters. Telephone cables improved business communications among metropolitan centers, but large areas of the world could not take advantage of telephone communications. Even in North America there were remote Eskimo villages with no telephone

6. Container ships like the *President Kennedy* (APL, American President Lines), launched in 1988, are too large to transit the Panama Canal but speed the flow of goods across the Pacific and Atlantic Oceans. The containers are then lifted off the vessel and trucked or shipped by rail to final destinations. (Tylon V. Leung, http://shumsw.tripod.com)

service.⁵ It took satellite communications to end this isolation and make the emerging global village truly interactive.

Without a doubt, the arrival of jet planes and transoceanic telephones facilitated business expansion, but so did American scientific leadership. World War II, and the early Cold War, saw many technological advances, and U.S. firms moved quickly to commercialize products from military research. Between 1945 and 1965, the number of patents granted in the United States more than doubled, rising from 25,695 to 62,857. Five times as many U.S. patents went to U.S. firms as to foreign corporations. As late as 1967, the United States accounted for 69 percent of research and development in major countries. A good illustration was the transformation of International Business Machines (IBM). In 1957, IBM's major products were punch-card accounting machines, time-recording equipment, and electric typewriters. A decade later, the company dominated the world computer market and epitomized multinational business. Initially, IBM was reluctant to enter the computer market; at the time of the Korean War, there was a limited demand for perhaps twenty machines. Thomas J. Watson, Sr., the founder, thought the punch-card era would never end, and he was hostile to computers. But he was also patriotic, and large defense contracts for computers used in B-52 guidance systems and for use in the Semi-Automatic Ground Equipment (SAGE) air defense system against Soviet bomber attack brought a shift in thinking. Thomas J. Watson, Jr., who succeeded his father in 1956, moved the firm rapidly into electronic data processing. Later he said: "It was the Cold War that helped IBM make itself the king of the computer business." Until the late 1950s, the SAGE project accounted for half of IBM's computer sales and enabled it to build automated plants and to train thousands of new workers in electronics.[6]

IBM established computer leadership in the mid 1950s with its 650 series, aimed at large corporate customers. Two thousand units were produced from 1954 to 1962, becoming the most popular computer of the 1950s. The real breakout came in April 1964. IBM announced the System/360, a family of five computers, and some 150 software and related hardware products. The number 360, the number of degrees in a circle, was selected to show that the computer could handle all types of applications. From that point, analysts often referred to the computer industry as Snow White (IBM) and the Seven Dwarfs (Burroughs, Control Data, General Electric, Honeywell, NCR, RCA, and Sperry Rand). In five years, IBM's revenue doubled.

In 1949, IBM established a separate subsidiary IBM World Trade to handle foreign production and sales. It hired down-and-out European aristocrats and used their connections to promote business in Europe. IBM World Trade capitalized on European recovery and grew at double the domestic rate. As a result, foreign sales expanded rapidly, amounting to 20 percent of total IBM revenue in 1960, 35 percent in 1969, and 54 percent by 1979. In 1964, IBM installed 62 percent of the computers in Europe. It had the capacity to deal with nationalistic governments. When the Japanese government in 1957 gave an ultimatum to foreign investors to sell 50 percent of their companies to Japanese investors, IBM refused to capitulate. Technological leadership enabled it to retain 100 percent ownership of its foreign affiliate. Recognizing that its eminence in computers gave it extraordinary opportunities to operate independently, IBM sought to integrate its European operations regionally and promoted intrafirm trade. Its market dominance and perceived ties to the U.S. government presented unique problems, however. Several European nations – including

France, Germany, and Britain – sought to protect their computer industries from "Big Blue" by subsidizing local competition or excluding IBM from bidding on contracts.[7]

Another important reason for the flow of U.S. direct investment into Europe related to large market size, rapid growth, and integration. In March 1957, the European Common Market came into existence, and the British pound and major continental currencies finally became convertible in December 1958. With incomes rising and recovery from World War II largely complete, Europe became a magnet for American direct investment. In 1957, the value of U.S. direct investment abroad was $25.4 billion, of which 35% was in Canada, 29% in Latin America, and 16% in Europe (7% in Common Market countries; 8% in the United Kingdom). By 1973, a new European-directed pattern had emerged. The value of U.S. direct investments abroad was $103.7 billion, of which 25% was in Canada, 37% in Europe (18.3% in the Common Market; 10.6% in the United Kingdom), and 15.9% in Latin America.[8]

One way to evaluate the overall significance of these changes is to look at a standard measure of globalization – trade in goods and services as a share of gross domestic product. In the 1880s, economists estimated that trade was about 20 percent of total U.S. production. It fell sharply during the interwar period to less than 10 percent and remained at this level until the late 1960s. By 1970, trade as a share of gross domestic product approached 11 percent, and it rose sharply to nearly 20.5 percent by 1980.[9] (See Table A.9.)

Technology Gap or Glut?

Paradoxically, at a time in the late 1950s when American technology dominated business markets, many ordinary citizens thought the Soviet Union was winning the Cold War. In October 1957, amateur radio enthusiasts tuned in their ham radios to the chirping sounds of the first man-made satellite passing above them in the atmosphere. This was Russia's *Sputnik* (fellow traveler), which circled the earth at 18,000 miler per hour. It struck Americans with wonderment and fear, and it shook America's image as the world's technological leader, for the Kremlin had launched its satellite with a booster rocket designed to send intercontinental ballistic missiles (ICBMs) 4,000 miles from Russian borders. Soviet science and technology seemed to surge ahead of American know-how. Had the communists progressed while Americans merely consumed? The boastful Nikita Khrushchev welcomed this notion in his propaganda war against the West.

The Eisenhower administration placed strategic air forces on alert and pointed short-range Jupiter missiles toward Moscow from Turkey and Italy.[10]

At home, Americans questioned their public education and scientific capabilities. While a Gallup Poll in December 1955 showed that more Americans thought the United States was winning the Cold War than Russia, a similar poll in January 1958, taken after *Sputnik* was launched, indicated that of respondents in Chicago and Washington, some 67 percent thought Russia was winning. Only 13 percent said that the United States was ahead. Senate Majority Leader Lyndon B. Johnson, who saw *Sputnik* overhead in Texas, began an inquiry that led to the creation of the National Aeronautic and Space Administration (NASA) and the National Defense Education Act of 1958, which increased spending on science, mathematics, and foreign language. The act legitimized federal aid to science just as the GI Bill had done for education. National Science Foundation and Department of Defense contracts spurred basic research throughout the 1960s, and space research particularly spun off growth in intelligence gathering, electronics and engineering, and weaponry. Laboratories hired thousands of corporate engineers to work on missile and aerospace projects, and clusters of companies and labs sprouted up near major academic institutions, such as Route 128 around Boston and Silicon Valley near Palo Alto, California. The space program's budget steadily increased to $1.2 billion by 1962, and steps were taken to orbit a man around the earth (*Mercury*, 1959–60) and eventually send him to the moon (*Apollo*) in 1969. Public officials, like Senator John F. Kennedy, lamented that a growing "missile gap" existed between Russian and American nuclear arms production.

Outer space became a new arena for Cold War competition, and nuclear weaponry, the tools of the trade. In the months before the *Sputnik* launch, the Soviets had tested the world's first ICBM and prepared new models for the future. Ike did not stand idly by. Between 1958 and 1960, the U.S. nuclear stockpile tripled to 18,000 weapons, and America added fourteen *Polaris* submarines to its arsenal. But Eisenhower showed restraint, fending off panicked assessments by his National Security Council and Democrats who demanded a huge expansion in defense spending. His famous farewell address warned of distorting the economy by the collusion of a military-industrial complex in which he warned about "public policy . . . becoming the captive of a scientific-technological elite."[11] Space competition continued, and larger nuclear tests followed. In 1961, the Soviets exploded the biggest atomic device ever and then beat America to the moon by firing a rocket – the first man-made object – on to the lunar surface.

Bragging rights went to the Soviets again in April 1961 when Air Force lieutenant and cosmonaut Yuri Gagarin became the first human to travel to outer space. The emboldened Khrushchev scored psychological points; the premier crowed on the telephone to Gagarin, "let the capitalists countries catch up with our country," and wept before pinning the nation's highest medal – Hero of the Soviet Union – on the cosmonaut. The Russian newspaper *Pravda* lauded the "global superiority of the Soviet Union in all aspects of science and technology," along with the "virtues of socialism." One did not have to endorse communist doctrine to stand in awe; according to experts around the world, Gagarin's mission ranked as the greatest scientific achievement in human history.[12]

Gagarin's feat of circling the earth every eighty-nine minutes in the five-ton *Vostok I*, at an altitude of nearly 188 miles, inspired the Kennedy administration to beat the Soviets to the moon and to best them in satellite communications. A major step had been taken in the Mercury program that sent astronauts Alan Shepard and Virgil Grissom in separate launches into space in 1961.[13]

It was the oldest member of the *Mercury Seven*, forty-year-old John Glenn, who grabbed the limelight by being the first American to orbit the earth. A veteran of air combat in World War II and Korea, this Ohioan became the Charles Lindbergh of his day. He drew on sophisticated technology and communications to rivet the world to his nearly five-hour flight that orbited the planet three times on February 20, 1962. Because of cutting-edge electronic equipment at tracking stations around the globe, Glenn's voyage was projected to millions of Americans on television, including President Kennedy. The astronaut described the night view over Perth, Australia, where residents had turned on their lights for the event, as well as the short passage of days and nights. This was, literally, globalization in travel! Glenn successfully steered to an ocean target and was feted by the nation. He later turned to business, and then another public career as a U.S. senator.[14]

There was another dimension to the space race that had a direct impact on life on earth. It involved satellite communications, one of the keys to the globalization of information, and business, in the late twentieth century. In this race, the Soviets offered no serious competition. At the end of World War II, Arthur C. Clarke, a Royal Air Force (RAF) electronics officer, had written a futuristic article about how satellites in twenty-four-hour orbits high above the world would distribute television programs globally. Twenty years later his vision had become a reality. AT&T's *Telstar*, which was launched in 1962, carried the first live television scenes across the Atlantic, and in 1964 U.S. television viewers watched portions of the Tokyo Olympics. The real triumph for global television came on July 20, 1969, shortly after the launching of *Intelsat III*, which provided coverage to the Indian Ocean. One half billion people watched the *Apollo 11* moon landing, which reestablished American leadership in the space race. Communications satellites facilitated a surge in telephone communications. *Intelsat I (Early Bird)* built by Hughes and launched in 1965 had 240 two-way voice channels or one two-way television channel. But *Intelsat IV* launched in 1971 carried twelve color television channels or 4,000 to 6,000 voice channels and had a capacity greater than all the submarine cables combined. The proliferation of cable and satellite capacity brought a sharp reduction in costs, which benefited business and individual consumers.[15]

The U.S. government and private enterprise were both actively involved in commercial satellite operations, as with the development of wireless radio after World War I. NASA's authorization from Congress limited it to military-related projects and to funding private-sector programs. It was not to be directly involved in commercial satellite operations. But, the Kennedy administration opposed any option that turned over control of space communication to AT&T; consequently, after lengthy negotiations with Congress, the 1962 Communications Satellite Act created COMSAT, a unique public-private partnership. According to President Kennedy, COMSAT (Communications Satellite Corporation) was the "chosen instrument" of U.S. policy with responsibility for constructing and operating a communications satellite system with foreign governments or corporations. Its initial capitalization was $200 million. Established American carriers like AT&T could buy up to half of the stock; the public, the rest; but control stayed in the hands of a board that included government representatives. This was reportedly the first time that officials sat as voting members on the board of a private corporation in which the government was not an investor.[16]

In August 1964, nineteen countries signed agreements establishing the International Telecommunications Satellite Consortium (INTELSAT). COMSAT, the operating arm for the consortium, contracted with Hughes to build a series of satellites placed in synchronous orbit at the equator. From its initial efforts in 1965, INTELSAT grew to a huge consortium of users with the capability of providing hundreds of thousands of circuits. It provided service to the entire globe, not simply the rich countries. In

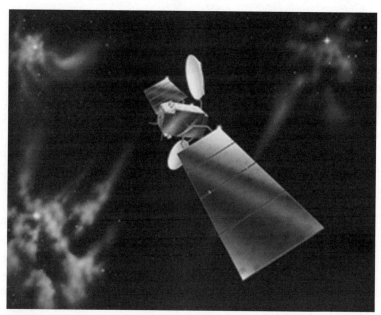

7. Lockheed A2100 communications satellite facilitates flows of information around the globe. (Lockheed Martin Corporation)

1971, when members approved a modification to INTELSAT's arrangements, Arthur C. Clarke, considered the system's father, said, "[Y]ou have just signed far more than yet another intergovernmental agreement. You have just signed the first draft of the articles of the Federation of the United States of the Earth." The Soviets, who refused to participate in INTELSAT, were marginalized on the fringe of space communications. They did not establish the Intersputnik satellite network until 1974. It had fourteen members, most of them members of the Soviet bloc, and the system served primarily television broadcasting. This enabled the Soviet leadership to circulate its own propaganda messages. China did not join INTELSAT; instead it rushed to launch its own satellite network in the 1980s.[17]

Regardless of its comeback in the space and communications races, there was a public perception of American vulnerability in the late 1950s. Russia tested intercontinental missiles, and its annual growth rate apparently surpassed America's. In the United States, there were two brief recessions before a decade of healthy economic expansion. But the Soviets did not enjoy clear sailing in their own spheres of influence. Ideological splits with the People's Republic of China, the independence-minded Yugoslavs, and democrats in Czechoslovakia showed that Moscow wrestled with problems of plurality.

A high-profile debate over the merits of capitalism and communism occurred in July 1959 at the American exhibition in Moscow. The participants were Soviet Premier Khrushchev and Vice President Richard Nixon, and their public debate took place in a model U.S. ranch home with a "gadget-stocked" kitchen. Khrushchev, who told Nixon earlier that "in another seven years we will be on the same level as America," asserted in the kitchen "that all our new houses have this kind of equipment." During the ensuing six weeks of the fair, 2.7 million Soviets toured the exhibition and took in American autos, homes, movies, computers, fashion, and music (including rock 'n' roll and a variety show hosted by Ed Sullivan). The exhibition was a resounding propaganda success. Large Soviet audiences were attracted to American technology as well as consumer goods. One of the most popular exhibits was an IBM Ramac 305 computer programmed to answer 4,000 questions in ten languages spoken in the Soviet Union. Over the longer term, the display of Western consumerism inspired envy and raised expectations within the Soviet bloc. Many wanted to share in the American dream. American consumerism eventually proved to be a powerful weapon for unifying the Free World and ending the Cold War.[18]

Khrushchev also placed the Americans on the defensive in 1958 when he demanded that the Western powers end their occupation of Berlin within six months. Western refusal prompted the Russians to turn over access routes to ally East Germany and thus threatened the NATO powers' rights and West Berlin's lucrative and showy attachment to the capitalist world, which galled the Russians. The crisis abated as Eisenhower and Khrushchev engaged in summitry, including the Soviet leader's visit to the United States in 1959. Economic attainments took center stage. Khrushchev marveled at Iowa corn production and erupted in a temper tantrum for being denied entry into the bastion of American consumer capitalism, Disneyland. Later, while visiting a state-of-the art IBM computer plant in San Jose, Khrushchev revealed the insecurity behind his bluster. "We have plants like this in the Soviet Union," he asserted, and then looking a little puzzled he said half to himself, "we *must* have plants like this in the Soviet Union."[19]

The shooting down of an American U-2 spy plane in 1960 froze superpower relations, but it had even more profound meaning than dooming a summit meeting. In recent years, the CIA have described the U-2 program, begun in 1954, as "one of the CIA's greatest intelligence achievements." At a time in the mid 1950s when the United States was "blind" to Soviet bomber and missile capabilities, the CIA established a partnership with Lockheed Martin, Eastman Kodak, and Raytheon. They developed the U-2 at Lockheed's Burbank, California, "Skunk Works." The plane, which had a prodigious range of 3,500 miles, gave the United States "the eyes to see inside the Iron Box" (the Soviet Union). As a result, Eisenhower "knew for certain – *for certain* – that we had no bomber gap and no missile gap with the Soviet Union, despite all Soviet boasting to the contrary."[20] Five days after the May 1960 episode, Ike authorized the use of satellites to gather electronic intelligence. The first such *GRAB* satellite, launched in June, was a forty-three-pound beach-ball-sized satellite that orbited 500 miles above the Earth and collected Soviet radar signals. It gave the U.S. military a 3,500 mile view into the Soviet Union. Together the U-2 and the reconnaissance satellite had opened the Soviet Union to Western surveillance. As a result, the entire world would soon be open to technologically advanced governments. Engineers and scientists were moving swiftly to access and analyze information.[21]

But reality sometimes looks different to those caught up in daily events. Even though U.S. intelligence had penetrated the Iron Box, the Soviet bluff continued to make the world insecure. Intimidation and showdowns shaped Russo-American relations during the early 1960s. Along with the Berlin Wall crisis, the placement of Soviet missiles in Cuba in 1962 demonstrated that Khrushchev had more in mind that mere economic competition with the United States. Clearly, global modernity had rendered the world more insecure in the name, ironically, of heightened security. In the Berlin crisis, Foreign Minister Andrei Gromyko warned that a Warsaw Pact-NATO confrontation in East Germany "would inevitably spread to the continent of America" through "modern technology."[22] Developments of superbombs, missile technology, and space projects raised tension dramatically in the Cold War. The Cuban Missile Crisis, the nearest miss to superpower conflagration, showed both sides the worldwide dangers of miscalculation.

The understanding that nuclear weapons had created a mutually dangerous standoff led to the signing of the Limited Nuclear Test Ban Treaty of 1963. It prohibited testing anywhere but underground and encouraged detente between the Soviets and Americans. In late 1963, Kennedy agreed to sell wheat to the Russians to prevent a famine, and he installed a "hot-line" between the White House and the Kremlin (a reflection of improved communications technology) to head off future crises. JFK and Khrushchev discussed in secret the joint destruction of China's nuclear testing facility in the Gobi Desert. Soviet disdain for the Chinese was now public, and both superpowers viewed China as a rogue state.[23] A year later, with China having joined the nuclear club, the pace quickened to broaden and globalize arms limits. Thus, in 1966, America and the Soviet Union signed a treaty banning nuclear testing in outer space and, two years afterward, persuaded dozens of nations to sign the Nuclear Non-Proliferation Treaty at the United Nations, in the acknowledgment that atomic capabilities must be diverted into peaceful uses by as many countries as possible.

Part of Kennedy's appeal was his challenging, optimistic, and daring rhetoric of renewal. A vibrant internationalist, committed to Cold War containment and to international engagement, JFK welcomed Third World leaders at the White House in astonishing numbers and launched the Peace Corps that sent American youth around the world to promote development and the Free World. Yet Kennedy could not mask perceptions of America's waning postwar hegemony. Soviet successes in the space-nuclear race symbolized more profound trends of pluralism that indicated changing correlations of power. Even the superpower conflict was subject to global pressures that loosened Cold War structural constraints.

Challenges from Friends

Resistance to the more rigid aspects of America's Cold War strategy erupted within the Western Alliance from the late Eisenhower years onward. The return of Charles de Gaulle to power in 1958 signaled a more independent (and imperious) French approach to U.S. political, military, and economic hegemony in Europe. America also encountered mounting industrial competition from its allies, in key manufacturing such as automobiles and steel in which it had been the undisputed leader for two decades. The Common Market challenged U.S. commercial power by uniting behind a common tariff wall. But it was much more than a trade bloc. The unity of the six nations was an expression of supranational unity that, by the 1990s, encompassed every aspect of life on the continent – from education to atoms to money. The six represented 168 million people in Europe and 63 million in associated (colonial and former colonial) areas, propelled by the agricultural output of France and the industrial strength of West Germany. Common Market purchasing power amounted to half that of America but was expanding rapidly. In 1960, the industrial production of the six bested that of the United States for the first time, as did their total trade volume. But the relative decline of America's share of global production, and Europe's rising share, reflected a more profound development. Europe had largely recovered from the devastation of World War II that destroyed much of its industry.

The United States did not panic at the emergence of a major European competitor. Indeed, Washington took pride in having successfully encouraged European integration, which resulted in a strong, solidified, and stable Cold War ally. Although the Common Market of six members did not speak for all of Europe, its protectionist agricultural policies posed a serious problem for U.S. exports, with dire implications for America's balance of international payments.

Having run huge trade surpluses with Europe and Japan after World War II, the United States found those balances dwindling while it continued to pay out millions of dollars in economic and military assistance. That combination of aid and a dramatically worsening trade balance, starting in 1958, led to big international payments deficits that the United States financed by honoring its pledge to convert dollars into gold upon demand. From 1958 to 1968, the United States lost 47 percent of its monetary gold. This outflow underscored America's unique predicament: the Bretton Woods commitment to redeem dollars was the cornerstone of the world financial system, but it was also the Achilles heel. By the late 1960s, the United States no longer had sufficient gold reserves to sustain this relationship. It was becoming evident that the dollar was overvalued and vulnerable to foreign attacks.[24]

The United States had run a payments deficit every year since 1950, but it climbed precipitously beginning in 1958, as the merchandise trade surplus declined and long-term private capital flows rose. This set off alarm bells in Washington. By 1960, for the first time, foreign dollar holdings exceeded U.S. gold reserves, and America faced a run on the dollar from allies who were converting dollars into gold. The gold reserve had fallen an average of $200 million annually since 1950, but it plummeted $2.5 billion in 1958. Between 1961 and 1963, the payments deficit averaged $2.9 billion. Eisenhower, Kennedy, and their successors Lyndon Johnson and Richard Nixon understood that the worsening payments deficit threatened commitments overseas, exhibiting weaknesses in U.S. leadership. It gave Charles de Gaulle leverage over U.S. foreign policy because he could cash in French dollar holdings for gold, which still served as the foundation of American faith in the dollar. Kennedy feared catastrophe without a solution, for the payments problem could affect the entire capitalist system. As the president noted: "we are the principal banker of the free world and any potential weakness in our dollar spells trouble, not only for us but also for our friends and allies who rely on the dollar to finance a substantial portion of their trade."[25]

These presidents took action to remedy the deficits, but with mixed results. Ike tied foreign loans to purchases of American goods; JFK and Johnson asked allies to share the burden of defense spending; all encouraged the disposal of agricultural surpluses. Eisenhower endorsed, and the rest helped build, a new international economic body with a broad mission to facilitate cooperation among the industrial nations. This Organization for Economic Co-operation and Development (OECD) had twenty members at its first convention in 1960, and it has served an important role as a forum for promoting economic cooperation among nations in the North Atlantic region. The presidents also pushed trade liberalization, seeing it as a vehicle for promoting an economic partnership with the Common Market and for integrating the European bloc into the multilateral trading system. These were the objectives in economic diplomacy toward the core of Europe during the 1960s, particularly regarding Common Market membership and GATT negotiations.[26]

Kennedy succeeded in 1962 in obtaining congressional approval for another major round of multilateral tariff-cutting negotiations. To appease critics of the reciprocal trade program, the administration agreed to remove trade policy from the State Department and to place it with a Special Trade Representative working in the White House. With authority to cut U.S. industrial tariffs as much as 50 percent, the United States helped launch the Kennedy Round of GATT trade negotiations and promoted Britain's application for membership into the EEC, thinking that this long-term ally could point the Common Market in an Atlantic direction rather than in a Gaullist Euro-nationalist way. To be sure, Britain would also add to the economic strength of the six, but the Kennedy administration preferred a stronger, Atlanticist Europe to a stronger, inward-looking entity. De Gaulle, however, viewed Britain as a Trojan horse designed to let American hegemony into Europe by a back door, and he vetoed the British application in a stunning announcement in January 1963. When the general said "Non!" to Britain, he indicated once again the seeping pluralism in the Western camp. His later rejection of NATO ended talk of an Atlantic partnership, which was desired by Kennedy. Western Europeans remained Cold War allies, but they often took independent paths in diplomacy.[27]

It is likely that de Gaulle cared as much about asserting French power as European independence, but he also voiced an alternative to America's vision for an open-world trading system. He chafed at the Monnet vision of a tight European federation, preferring a looser confederation in which each state would keep its own national character. In this he was out of step with the times, for Europe gradually unified under its own government, parliament, and laws. His was a dissonant voice within the Western alliance. On issues of salience to the United States, he set out on a neutralist and distinct course by opposing the Vietnam War, recognizing China, and issuing an embargo of arms to Israel in the Six-Day War. He rejected Britain and, in fact, American grand designs for partnership with the continent. Yet de Gaulle also anticipated the end of the Cold War, and globalization decades hence, when Europe would truly stretch, in his famous expression, "from the Atlantic to the Urals."

Le General did not deter the "Anglo-Saxons," however, for the global advance of American cultural and economic power, known as Americanization by French intellectuals and the Left, side-stepped Gaullism. The French sought strict screening of foreign investment during the mid 1960s, particularly American investments. Even moderates asked the Americans to respect certain limits on the number of dollars flowing into France and Europe, for General Electric's 200,000 products simply overwhelmed domestic producers and General Foods could cut prices a mere 10 percent and bankrupt French candy makers. Disparity in size was a chief reason why de Gaulle had an audience. Chrysler was America's third biggest car company but produced more autos than all French manufacturers put together, General Electric's turnover was 27 billion francs while France's electronic industry in its entirety made less than one-fifth of that, and the New York Stock Exchange was thirty times as large as the Paris Bourse. General Motor's annual sales exceeded the total Dutch gross national product by 10 percent. Others criticized violations of competition policy; Goodyear and Firestone tried to break into the tire market by offering discounts to French automakers. Unions called Remington's layoffs "brutal" and despised rigid contracts at Libby McNeill canneries.

American corporations warned that they would take their business elsewhere, and the French people themselves were rather ambivalent to the American challenge. They drank Coke and tanked up with Mobil gasoline, although they reacted to nationalistic criticism of U.S. investments. Journalist Jean-Jacques Servan-Schreiber addressed the concerns in his popular *The American Challenge* in 1967. He warned that without innovations in research, management, and private-public relations, France and the rest of Europe would become American satellites, overrun by U.S. technology and economic propensity to the point that the region might very well rank as an underdeveloped area. But by this time, the new finance minister, Michel Debre, discarded French restrictions in order to modernize the country and attract dollars into France. It was too late. U.S. investments flowed in more freely than before; however, by 1969 (and de Gaulle's departure), these dollars went increasingly to Germany. American executives noted the French reputation for hostility to Americanization. Still, even a France steeped in Gaullist patriotism welcomed American corporations; the country could not resist U.S. economic power.[28]

In the new era of rapid travel and electronic communications, Europe became a powerful international competitor in popular culture. For example, a "British invasion" hit the rock-and-roll music scene in 1964, fueled by American youth's disenchantment with a sanitized white pop sound and the state of society after the Kennedy assassination of November 1963. Just a few foreign bands endured past the initial import boom, but none could rival the impact of the Beatles. They were a product, in part, of musical globalization. Their earliest influence was black rock 'n' roll brought to Liverpool by American sailors, and their initial fan base came from Hamburg, West Germany, nightclubs. After the 1962 release of "Love Me Do" and the chart-buster "Please Please Me" in January 1963, Beatlemania seized England, grew in popularity in Australia, and emerged on the continent. Yet there was little activity in America because the Beatles were portrayed as the latest in British eccentricity; Capitol Records, the British company EMI's American arm, had turned down their singles and albums. Executives at United Artists recognized the potential sale value of the Beatles, however, and approached them with a short-movie contract. The ground was being prepared for exploitation of the U.S. market, in which the record industry had been stagnating for three years.

In January 1964, "I Want to Hold Your Hand" was issued in the United States, the world's largest record market, with $50,000 publicity from Capitol Records. The song reached number one within weeks, the first song by a British artist to attain that status. The hit also spread to the non-English speaking world, including Scandinavia, West Germany, France, and Japan. The next month, the Fab Four arrived at newly named Kennedy Airport in New York for a three-week visit to the States, wowed the press, and played on the Ed Sullivan show for $2,400. Sullivan, who hosted a Sunday evening variety show, knew the Beatles because he had witnessed screaming fans at London's airport the previous October. A program record 73 million people, about 60 percent of U.S. television viewers, saw the show. Sullivan let them play five songs, not the usual two, recognizing a hit when he saw one.

Film documentaries followed, and the Beatles became world famous. By April 1964, their songs occupied the top five slots on the *Billboard* singles list and their LP, renamed *Meet the Beatles*, became the best-selling record in history. Mass hysteria set in. The Beatles returned to England and then headed out again for Canada, America, and Australia, where hundreds of thousands gathered to catch a glimpse. Between 1963 and 1968, they sold $154 million worth of records worldwide and became the first band to sell out sports stadiums around the globe. In 1965, the Queen honored them for their contribution to the British foreign trade balance. Two years later, they took part in the first live global satellite broadcast, "Our World," a live special originating in eighteen countries on five continents. The Beatles represented the United Kingdom and recorded "All You Need Is Love" for an audience of 500 million, although the program aired to a small U.S. viewership because it was shown on educational television rather than commercial networks.

A new sound, clever lyrics, wit, and aggressive marketing catapulted the Beatles to fame, but they also tapped into the growing cohesion of youth worldwide that attested to the cultural and economic pressures of globalization. Timing the release of their 1967 album *Sgt. Pepper's Lonely Hearts Club Band* for maximum exposure, the Beatles caused a mini-explosion within the Beatles craze itself. "The closest Western civilization has come to unity since the Congress of Vienna in 1815 was the week the *Sgt. Pepper* album was released," wrote one observer. "In every city in Europe and America the stereo systems and the radio played . . . ["Lucy in the Sky with Diamonds"]. For a brief while the irreparably fragmented consciousness of the West was unified, at least in the minds of the young."[29] The affinity the young had for Beatles rock (as well, of course, for other bands) was mimicked in the protest movements against the power structure that swept through the United States, France (in 1968), and even the Soviet bloc (Prague in 1968).

An unceasing flow of cultural and economic exchanges were transforming the Atlantic region and forging closer bonds. American decision makers, such as Undersecretary of State George Ball, who oversaw the JFK-LBJ economic approach to Europe, could only smile in approval. An international corporate lawyer who had backed liberal causes throughout the 1950s, Ball had been a student of Jean Monnet and shared his integrationist ideal. He was representative of a new guard of globalist: the corporate liberal. Ball had a foot in presidential politics (as an active supporter of Adlai Stevenson's two runs for the presidency in the 1950s) and one in international business as a founder of Cleary, Gottlieb

law firm, which he internationalized by representing Venezuelan oil interests, Cuban sugar concerns, and French steel enterprises. He attended
Common Market meetings, commuted to Paris and London, and advocated an English Channel tunnel. This insider built networks joining
business, politics, and diplomacy; typical was the elite Bilderberg Group
of European integrationists, a sort of European Trilateral Commission.
An ardent free-trader, Ball spearheaded administration efforts to insert
Britain into the Common Market and lower tariff barriers. He left politics in protest of Johnson's war in Vietnam, turning down the president's
request to serve as ambassador to the United Nations to work in the
corporate sector.

Ball despised Gaullist nationalism and advanced a distinctive proposal for attacking the "ancient concept of nation-states." This was his
"cosmocorp" theory in which he advocated a treaty of international corporate law administered by a supranational body composed of citizens
from a range of nations. Without such a body, he warned that "conflict
will increase between the world corporation, which is a modern concept
evolved to meet the requirements of the modern age, and the nation-state,
which is still rooted in archaic concepts unsympathetic to the needs of our
complex world." Ball noted the resiliency of nationalism. But he endorsed
the evolution of the European Union as his "global test case" and, especially after the Cold War ended, as a perfect example of balancing business
with political institutions.[30]

Ball's enthusiasm for trade liberalization was tested in the Kennedy
Round of GATT trade negotiations from 1964 to 1967. Conflicts over
Common Market farm protectionism, Japan's unwillingness to open its
market to foreign competition, and squabbles in industrial sectors left a
bad taste in American mouths. When the round limped to a conclusion, it
had essentially reduced tariffs on industrial goods among major trading
countries to insignificance but quotas and other nontariff barriers took on
greater significance. Eager to protect high-cost French and German agriculture, the Common Market successfully blocked efforts to liberalize
world agricultural trade, a topic of intense interest to developing countries and the United States. So disenchanted were U.S. producers with the
results that protectionist sentiment revived in the United States, led by
the American Federation of Labor-Congress of Industrial Organizations
(AFL-CIO), once an advocate of trade liberalization. In a signal of its
displeasure, Congress refused to approve certain agreements on nontariff barriers and delayed renewing the president's trade negotiating authority until 1974 and then on terms that reduced executive discretion.

The resulting fast-track approach enabled Congress to monitor trade negotiations in return for a streamlined approval process that reduced the prospects that the legislative branch would refuse to implement the results of future negotiations. Not since the controversial Smoot-Hawley Tariff of 1930 had trade issues loomed so large in political combat between the White House and Congress.[31]

Japan reaped rewards from the Kennedy Round and, more broadly, from U.S. trade policy during the Cold War. Boosting Japanese economic and political stability by encouraging Japan's exports had been a focus of the Eisenhower administration. Although Ike pushed Japan to limit its textile exports to America on a voluntary basis beginning in 1956, textiles were a special case. Indeed, Kennedy, Johnson, and Nixon all insisted on textile restraints for domestic political reasons, but their overall approach to Japan reflected Cold War concerns. That meant, as one U.S. ambassador proclaimed in the late 1950s, that "Japan must trade or die." He warned that trade restrictions on Japanese exports would bring a "gradual but inevitable shift of Japanese policy away from present close ties with the U.S." Not surprisingly, Tokyo granted only minimal concessions on industrial tariffs at the Kennedy Round. LBJ did not push any harder out of a fear of an "economic cold war where nobody trusts anybody and everybody stagnates."[32]

The Kennedy Round represented a sea-change in America's global economic position. Determined to lead the Cold War alliance against the Sino-Soviet bloc, the United States again tacitly consented to asymmetrical results in trade negotiations that benefited upstart Asian exporters. The United States failed to gain real access to the Japanese markets, protected with a labyrinth of structural and nontariff barriers, but it made concessions that exposed American producers and workers to intense import competition from Japan and emerging low-cost suppliers. Nevertheless, the United States, after abandoning its quest to liberalize agricultural trade, succeeded in keeping the European Community engaged in the multilateral trade negotiating process. This established the basis for a strong trans-Atlantic working relationship in future negotiations. This was a result that pleased national security officials concerned about the future of NATO and cooperation on other political and defense issues. Yet the U.S. payments deficit continued to grow – from –3.6 billion in 1962 to –$11.2 billion ten years later. As Kennedy Round tariff cuts took effect, the merchandise trade surplus gradually disappeared, and in 1971 the U.S. experienced its first trade deficit in the twentieth century.

Third World Challenges

In the developing world, a revolution of rising expectations compelled the United States to modify its Cold War policies. As Britain, France, Belgium, and the Netherlands relinquished colonial empires, dozens of newly in-dependent nations entered the United Nations. Indeed, twenty-eight new members – many from Africa – joined from 1960 to 1963.[33] For Cold War political and economic reasons, as well as humanitarian considerations, the United States sought to integrate the "periphery" into the Western market economy. Some of the newly independent nations had valuable raw materials, and a few such as Indonesia and Nigeria had potentially large markets for export sales if economic development took hold. Except for oil and certain strategic minerals, few had much to attract private investors. With new governments, nationalistic rhetoric, untested legal protections for private property, small markets and low income levels, widespread official corruption, and poorly educated populations, many developing countries in Africa, Asia, and Latin America simply had little prospect for establishing an attractive climate for foreign investors. As it turned out, a few developing countries – Brazil, Taiwan, Hong Kong, Singapore, and South Korea – broke out of the Third World mold to become rapidly growing manufacturing powers during the 1970s. Given the diversity of conditions and opportunities, the Third World proved less a monolith than a mosaic. But its special circumstances challenged U.S. sensitivities and security interests from the late 1950s to the 1970s, during a period when it seemed that the Soviets and Chinese might exploit Third World poverty and discontent and effect a major realignment.[34]

Something of a revolt against the rich industrial countries and their overseas investments in resources and infrastructure did begin in the late 1950s. The alarm bell of Castro's revolution in Cuba in 1958; the prolifer-ation of poor, but newly independent nations in Africa; and the rebellion in Vietnam woke up the Eisenhower administration to the need for augmenting U.S. aid to the "South." America sent billions of dollars in farm products in exchange for local currencies under Public Law 480 (Title One of the Agricultural Trade Development and Assistance Act of 1954), raised lending subscriptions to the Third World in the Ex-Im Bank and World Bank, and supported new credit authorities such as the Inter-national Development Association in 1960. That year, future Kennedy advisor Walt Rostow published *The Stages of Economic Growth*, which argued that massive transfers of public capital to developing nations would enable the middle classes to achieve democratic government and high levels of economic growth. Investment-led growth would push these nations into a "take-off" period leading to industrialization, growth, and political stability. Rostow's analysis, as well as growing instability, helped publicize the development issue during the 1960 presidential campaign.[35]

In Latin America, the threat of Castro's communist revolution in Cuba and the specter of Soviet military influence in the hemisphere (a ghost that materialized in the missile crisis of 1962), pointed Kennedy toward a major aid program for Latin America. This Alliance for Progress, beginning in 1961, enlisted businessmen in a ten-year, $100 billion (America chipped in $20 billion) campaign to end poverty, illiteracy, and disease in Latin America by an annual growth rate of 5 percent. The vast assistance project's goal was economic and social stabilization to promote growth, democracy, and anticommunism.

Except for the last, the alliance came up short. Regional economies grew by a meager 1.5 percent, with agriculture floundering, industrial production stagnating, and unemployment rising; infant mortality rates fell only slightly; and literacy lagged during this so-called Decade of Development. Nine coups during the first five years of the Alliance mocked the democratic ideal. Latin America was not ready for the infusion of private-enterprise ideology, which gave multinational corporations another leg up (in the same way privatization has shaken up economies today). By 1964, business leaders such as David Rockefeller of Chase Manhattan Bank, Walter Wriston of Citibank, and corporate executive J. Peter Grace had convinced the politicians that economic growth by private means must precede social reform, not vice versa. They lamented that private investment had fallen in Latin America. Meanwhile, aid poured into right-wing national police forces and militaries, in the name of fighting communism. The lofty aims of modernizing and energizing the western hemisphere were not attained. They were hard to achieve in light of corruption and political stability in Latin America, as well as differing perspectives on regional security issues (especially Cuba) and the role of private enterprise in economic development.[36]

America's most disastrous endeavor involved military and economic support for South Vietnam. Bringing the new nation into the alliance fold of SEATO in the mid 1950s, the United States set out to build the country into a barrier against communist threats from North Vietnam and, it was believed, China and the Soviet Union. This involved military and economic aid, and established an entangling Cold War commitment, dragging America into its longest, and most frustrating, war.

By 1966, Americans were divided over involvement in Vietnam. Many questioned America's burdensome role in the world and its leadership of the international economy. Businesspeople who were usually patriotic noted the problems of defending a strong dollar and the pledge to convert foreign dollar holdings into gold upon demand. They warned President Johnson that inflation, which doubled in the mid 1960s, and global economic instability would persist as long as the Vietnam War continued. Gold stocks dwindled in the mid 1960s, as foreign central banks continued to cash in dollars for specie. A monetary crisis in Britain in 1967, and soaring U.S. payments deficits, prompted the edgy French to call for a change in the dollar's domination of the global financial system. De Gaulle lashed out that the United States was leveraging its war-inflated dollars to buy out European companies. Meanwhile, the chairman of the Federal Reserve Board cautioned, "I have been trying for the past two years to make the point on 'guns and butter' and the cost of the Vietnam war, economically, without too much success but I think in due course the chickens will come home to roost." Business leaders and foreigners alike feared that attacks on the dollar might lead to devaluation and a subsequent spate of competitive depreciations if the gold drain continued. To buy time, LBJ imposed controls on capital exports, urged foreign governments to build up dollar reserves, and slowed down spending on Vietnam.[37]

The Vietnam War pointed to the pitfalls of global hegemony. Television coverage brought the war home to Europeans and Americans, and protests occurred in many countries. Not only were the French, and many other Europeans, agitated but so were Americans. At home, protesters repeatedly demonstrated. Even before U.S. ground troops arrived, leftist Students for a Democratic Society, led by activist Tom Hayden, had issued a manifesto in 1962 that criticized the centralized national security state and elitist bureaucracies in unions, universities, and government for betraying the people's will. This *Port Huron Statement* demanded participatory democracy and blamed corporations, a corporate ethic, and corporate-liberal politicians of the American Century – from Teddy Roosevelt to John Kennedy – for war, poverty, and social injustice. The document excoriated multinational foreign investment for colonizing people around the world and government-corporate collusion over military contracts. Combined with a growing civil rights campaign, emerging feminism and gay power, and a nascent environmental movement, this 1960s protest began to unravel the consensus politics of the United States, threatening the power elite at home and abroad.[38] These were the early opponents of globalization.

A different type of protest focused on GATT, the international institution responsible for the rules of international trade. High-income members liberalized trade in manufactures, but they also maintained high levels of protection on import-competing agricultural products and textiles. Until the 1960s, most of the poor countries had little interest in the GATT regime or trade expansion. They exported tropical agricultural products and minerals and maintained high duties on manufactured imports, as they sought to spur domestic production. But poor nations saw their share of world exports drop from 31.6 percent in 1950 to 21.4 percent in 1960, while the developed nations enjoyed rising incomes and expanding trade.

Emboldened by their much expanded numbers in the United Nations and the Cold War competition between East and West, Third World nations embarked on a strategy of confrontation in the 1960s. Their frustrations led to the establishment of United Nations Conference on Trade and Development in 1964. UNCTAD organized into a group of seventy-seven nations that demanded improved access for exports of developing countries – particularly agricultural products and textiles. Their confrontational approach reflected the views of UNCTAD's first secretary-general, Argentine economist Raul Prebisch, who issued a report criticizing GATT and asserting that the structure of the international economy destined exporters of raw materials to declining incomes. An economics professor and one of the youngest officials ever to serve the Argentine government, Raul Prebisch made a career of challenging the neoclassical free-trade theories underlying GATT and rallying the Third World. Prebisch's thinking about the need for import substitution and industrialization in developing countries to escape the dependency of reliance on primary products with declining terms of trade became a staple of Third World thought in the United Nations system.

Among economists, the Prebisch dependency thesis sparked wide debate. American and European economists countered that agriculture could not always be associated with poverty and pointed to the successful examples of Denmark, Australia, and New Zealand. Despite the intensity of his rhetoric, Prebisch proved pragmatic. Import substitution could go hand in hand with regional integration, and so he endorsed the Latin American Free Trade Area of eleven nations. As it turned out, this was an idea ahead of the time. Regional free trade made little headway in the 1960s, but it enjoyed a resurgence in the 1990s, under Mercosur and NAFTA. Prebisch was more successful in persuading the developed countries to provide one-way trade preferences for the exports of developing countries.[39]

UNCTAD's impact was mixed under Prebisch's leadership. Although the organization vented frustrations with inequities in the global trading system, it failed to develop the cohesion to press successfully for reforms. The Third World was inherently divided – regionally, culturally, and economically (by income levels). Former European colonies in Africa remained wedded to the Common Market and enjoyed special preferences for their raw material exports, while mineral-exporting nations had interests different from exporters of tropical products and textiles. But UNCTAD's visibility under Prebisch's leadership did give impetus to plans for the Generalized System of Preferences (GSP), a program of one-way concessions provided by Europe and the United States to developing countries. In effect, this program, introduced in the mid 1970s, provided free access to high-income markets for many of the export products of developing countries, without requiring reciprocal openings. During the 1980s, the GSP assisted the export-led growth of many newly industrializing countries, especially Brazil, Mexico, Hong Kong, Singapore, Taiwan, Thailand, Malaysia, and South Korea.[40]

During the 1960s, developing countries also lashed out at multinational corporations. While there was some expropriation of resource properties, developing countries were more successful in preparing the way for an assault on the power of multinational petroleum companies. The so-called Seven Sister companies (five of which were American) ran the extraction and distribution process and had a historical interest in developing the international oil trade. During the late 1950s, independent producers in the Southwest successfully protested the flow of cheap oil from abroad. Thus, Eisenhower imposed restrictions on Venezuelan petroleum, but the quotas also provoked Venezuela, Nigeria, and Middle Eastern countries to form a bloc to protect their exports and grab a larger share of the profits from the multinationals. Established in 1960, this Organization of Petroleum Exporting Countries (OPEC) had little impact at first. By the time of the Six-Day War in 1967, however, it began to challenge the West for control of Middle Eastern oil. The fact that Saudi Arabia, Iran, and smaller nations of the region were exporting one-third of the West's output by the mid 1960s was critical because rising U.S. consumption relied on cheap oil. Three-quarters of Europe's oil needs came from the Persian Gulf, and Japan also met its energy needs with Saudi and Iranian crude. American backing of Israel in the Six-Day War only exacerbated the need for America to become the main broker for peace in the region, for it could not risk a cutoff of oil that would bring global ruin.[41]

Newly independent African countries also tried to use their numbers for political advantage. In 1957, the British colony of Ghana became the first African possession to receive its independence. By 1960, sixteen African colonies became nations and joined the United Nations, thereby transforming voting power in that body. By 1970, fifty African countries had gained independence. Still, the Cold War brought few benefits to black Africans. In 1960, the United States intervened in a bloody civil war in the Belgian Congo that threatened to hand European and American mining interests over to pro-Soviet forces. By 1965, stability eventually derived from support of General Joseph Mobutu, a strongman who gladly took millions of dollars in U.S. aid and CIA help. Mobutu was not America's favorite, but he did limit the influence of the European Common Market, which hoped to perpetuate discriminatory control over such former European territories as the Congo (Zaire). National security needs, namely satellite-tracking stations and access to strategic minerals, also drove America's tepid backing of the apartheid regime in South Africa. Still, Africa remained a backwater of economic development, and largely peripheral to American concerns, regardless of the struggle for African-American civil rights in the United States during the 1960s.[42]

Global Pluralism: 1969–1973

The challenges from abroad and within to American hegemony ended the "heroic phase" of U.S. postwar policy, as one scholar has written. A revolution was not in the offing; rather, the challengers sought a more plural system that lessened their dependency on the United States.[43] By the time of the Nixon administration, they had succeeded in some important respects.

American power entered a period of acknowledged limits after 1969. Richard Nixon and Henry Kissinger, his national security advisor, recognized that the Soviets had attained parity in nuclear arms; thus, they were willing to negotiate the first major disarmament treaty with Moscow under the Strategic Arms Limitation Talks (SALT-I) agreement of 1972. In turn, Moscow put pressure on its North Vietnamese ally to end the American phase of the Vietnam War in 1973, a conflict that had drained the nation of its will for vigorous internationalism and had split the body politic. Reversing twenty-two years of silence toward the People's Republic of China, Nixon traveled to Beijing in 1972, recognizing that the millennia augured a Pacific Century. Overlaying this triangular diplomacy and other developments was the Nixon Doctrine, which proclaimed that the United States would no longer plan for the defense of the Free World wherever a threat existed. Nixon also recognized "five great superpowers" (America, Russia, China, Japan, and the Common Market) that would "determine the economic future" at the end of the century.[44] His was an age of limits, compromise, and maneuvering among the big powers, but much of the adjustment came on America's part.

The first Nixon administration experienced the fallout from expansive economic policies of the 1960s. Presidents Kennedy and Johnson, committed as they were to active state management of the domestic economy, had embraced large expenditures for social and military purposes, and had backed trade liberalization abroad. They sought European regional integration, modernization, openness, and growth. The liberals banked on the multinational corporations to become "a world-historical actor transforming an international arena of mercantilist states into a fragmented pluralistic system of mutual restraint and interdependence." Even culture would be denationalized. But LBJ ultimately halted large-scale outflows of investment dollars to prevent a worsening of the U.S. payments and jeopardy to the dollar. America and Japan – now the third biggest economy in the world – squared off in a textile wrangle that ended in 1971 when Nixon threatened to wield the Trading with the Enemy Act against its own ally unless Tokyo slowed its exports. That year, the nation ran its first merchandise trade deficit since 1893. Illusions of liberalism crashed on the realities of economic hardship.[45]

The most significant shock to the system was the collapse of the Bretton Woods monetary system. It had elevated the dollar as the world's medium of payment in international exchanges, made it the principle reserve currency, and tied it to gold at a price of $35 per ounce. American payments deficits, which were supposed to end after the nation eased heavy aid payments and the Allies returned to currency convertibility, worsened and put pressure on the dollar and gold reserves. The IMF created a new international money – Special Drawing Rights – to maintain sufficient liquidity in the global economy, but pressure on the dollar continued in 1968 with another run on gold. The monetary crisis was contained only by stringent export and currency controls. But the payments deficit persisted. Speculation against the dollar grew rampant. With unemployment and inflation troubling the domestic economy, President Nixon decided the time for action had arrived. In August 1971, he gathered his advisors at Camp David in what was called "the most important weekend in economics" since Franklin Roosevelt closed the banks in March 1933.[46] They decided to slam shut the gold window and suspend convertibility of dollars into gold, thereby destroying the Bretton Woods exchange mechanism.

In taking this action, Nixon signaled to now-powerful competitors in Europe and Japan that the days of their free-riding on U.S. defense, aid, and free-trade commitments had come to an end. Burdened with its overseas obligations, America had grown less competitive as the dollar grew more overvalued. Investments flowed abroad into more attractive markets, while exports had a harder time in international markets. Nixon's shocking economic moves (he also imposed a 10 percent surcharge on imports to reverse the deteriorating trade balance and compel Allies to devalue) were designed to bolster the weak dollar and, therefore, reverse America's sagging economic fortunes worldwide.

The bold gamble appeared to work. The dollar was freed from gold and devalued. In 1973 members of the IMF adopted a system of floating exchange rates among major currencies. The IMF and its sister organization, the World Bank, survived institutionally, but took on different roles. With the shift to floating rates, nations could remove controls, and the IMF no longer needed to supply short-term balance of payments assistance to developed countries. Instead, it increasingly focused on integrating developing countries into the global economy. It trained their officials, urged them to open capital markets and join the GATT system, and provided financial assistance and adjustment plans when emergency assistance was needed. With the Johnson-era controls on direct investment removed, American capital flowed outward once again, and U.S. multinationals resumed their global stretch. Since there was no established alternative to the dollar as a reserve currency, the post–Bretton Woods system marked a return to dollar dominance. European financial leaders, still concerned about the unique privileges of the dollar, could only draw one long-term lesson from the 1971–3 financial crises: a united Europe needed a common currency that might someday rival the dollar. A quarter century later, the European Community launched the Euro, a currency designed to offer the international financial community a respectable substitute for the dollar.

In freeing the dollar from the Bretton Woods straightjacket and preparing the way for U.S. withdrawal from a debilitating struggle in Vietnam, President Nixon abandoned unsustainable positions that threatened U.S. power and prestige. In reopening capital markets and floating the dollar, Nixon laid the keystones for a new era of American economic leadership. America's continued commitment to commercial expansion, open financial markets, and improved global communications would define the last quarter of the twentieth century, help end the Cold War, and fuel the the globalization process.[47]

8

Enduring the Crises, 1973–1986

Access to cheap, abundant energy was one of the critical factors that enabled the United States to manage winning coalitions in two world wars and to provide economic leadership in the half century after World War II. But beginning in the 1970s, dependence on imported oil proved a strategic vulnerability for America and its allies in Western Europe and Japan. The emergence of an Arab-dominated oil cartel determined to drive up oil prices threatened prosperity not simply in the oil-dependent industrial world but also among many developing nations reliant on imported energy. The Organization of Petroleum Exporting Countries succeeded in its effort to fix crude oil prices. The result was both a challenge to U.S. leadership and a period of world economic instability and stagflation (stagnant growth with inflation). The rise of OPEC, which coincided with a gradual decline in Cold War tensions, represented one of the most significant developments of the 1970s, and it further encouraged the ongoing process of world economic and political decentralization begun in the 1950s.

The period from 1973 to 1986 was alive with paradoxes. It opened with OPEC's effort to control the international oil market and ended in a global move toward deregulation and open markets. It began with a Republican, Richard Nixon, espousing Keynesian-style government economic intervention and ended with another Republican, Ronald Reagan, proselytizing for deregulation and free markets. Stagnation in the industrial sectors coincided with dramatic new innovations in computers and telecommunications. For individuals, there were both painful setbacks and exciting new opportunities. Many winners in the early post–World War II job market became losers. Workers discovered the harsh side of life; the 1970s were the end to an era of rising incomes and job security.

Japan, a loser in war, now won in the U.S. market with cheap, high-quality products bearing the labels of Sony, Toyota, and Subaru, among others.

American businesses would weather the energy crises and the final phase of the Cold War in different ways. With U.S. tariff barriers continuing to fall and foreign competition surging in the American market, high-cost domestic industries, such as steel, auto, and machine tools, lost market share to new entrants from abroad. But many big and medium-sized firms did well in a changing, competitive environment. Firms with leading-edge technologies took advantage of new market-opening opportunities to expand abroad. In the era of jet travel and networked business communications, the battle for market share was increasingly fought on a global playing field involving all the world's major high-income markets – Japan, Europe, and North America. Harvard Business School professor Theodore Levitt was one of the first to write insightfully about what was happening. In 1983, he used the term "globalization" in discussing how the powerful force of technology was driving the world toward "converging commonality." Global markets for standardized consumer products had emerged, and transnational companies now sold the same reliable, and low-priced, goods in Brazil as in Biafra. "The globalization of markets is at hand," he predicted, adding that globalization would gradually "break ... down the walls of economic insularity, nationalism and chauvinism."[1]

The World Economy in the Shadow of OPEC

Ironically, the second golden age of globalization emerged from the oil crisis of the mid 1970s. In September 1973, Arab petroleum exporting nations met in Algeria to ponder ways of using oil as a political weapon. They still felt the sting of defeat in the Six-Day War of 1967, when Israel had claimed large chunks of new territory and humiliated their armies. The Algeria meeting was timely, for it came just weeks before another Arab-Israeli conflict, the Yom Kippur War of early October 1973. When the Nixon administration rescued the reeling Israelis, the Arab bloc slapped an oil embargo on America, Holland, and Portugal that lasted until March 18, 1974. President Nixon warned that the country was "heading toward the most acute shortage of energy since World War II."[2] The embargo also curbed the flow of petroleum to Europe and Japan.

The embargo had roots in three years of effective mobilization by the petroleum exporters against Western control of global energy markets.

Throughout most of the 1960s, an oil glut had kept OPEC's power to demand price hikes and higher taxes at a minimum on multinational oil companies, or the majors. But in 1968, Saudi Arabia, Libya, and Kuwait created the Organization of Arab Petroleum Exporting Countries as a complement to OPEC and as a means to use oil for political leverage. The next year, Britain withdrew its military commitments in the Persian Gulf, leaving a power vacuum. Also in 1969, Colonel Muammar Quaddafi, who had long worshiped the Arab nationalist and Egyptian Nasser, took over in Libya. He targeted Occidental Petroleum, which was headed by international businessman Armand Hammer.

Quaddafi forced Hammer, whose company was dependent on Libyan crude, to give him back payments on profits to 1965 and to increase the price of oil. One of the twentieth century's most skilled entrepreneurs, Hammer was a deal maker, an American of Russian descent and of socialist-leaning parents, who had provided medical relief supplies to the new but war-ravaged Soviet Union just after the civil war there in 1921. Soviet leader Vladimir Lenin had allowed him concessions on asbestos, Ford tractors, and pencils; however, when the less capitalist-minded Stalin consolidated power at the end of the 1920s, Hammer picked up his earnings, along with a load of Russian art, and fled the country. By the mid 1950s, the wealthy Hammer had settled in Los Angeles as an art collector. On a whim, he bought the flagging Occidental and turned the company around by discoveries of oil in California in 1961 and by deal making.

Yet "Oxy" became one of the world's largest energy companies by the end of that decade because of the award of key Libyan oil concessions in 1965. The next year, Hammer struck oil in what later became known as the Idris field, named after the king, which Mobil had missed and which became one of the biggest reserves ever. The Six-Day War provided another boon. When Gulf oil was halted through the Suez Canal, Libyan petroleum skyrocketed in price. But Quaddafi then seized power and demanded from the twenty-one oil companies in Libya that they raise prices or face a complete shutdown of production and nationalization. The colonel paid no heed to Nasser, who, under Hammer's urging, warned Quaddafi not to threaten the West.

Quaddafi turned on Oxy. His deputy prime minister began negotiations by unbuckling his .45 pistol and setting it down on the table directly across from Hammer. With terms in hand, Hammer fled the country, fearing for his life. Unable to convince the major oil companies to band together and confront Quadaffi, Hammer agreed to give Libya a 20 percent increase in royalties and taxes. The other companies soon caved in and jacked prices, too. But as experts clearly understood, the agreements had a significance much larger than the price increases. OPEC exporters realized that they could demand greater control over their resources. "Everybody who drives a tractor, truck, or car in the Western world will be affected by this," replied an associate of Hammer.[3]

He was right. Quaddafi went on to sponsor terrorism in the 1980s, but his reach exceeded his grasp as he met the wrath of the Reagan administration, and the dictator faded from the world scene. Hammer survived, too, the only foreign oilman to receive compensation from Quaddafi when the colonel nationalized his oil fields in 1973. But the arena of world energy was forever changed. Hammer's assent to the 30 cents a gallon price hike caused "Middle Eastern dominoes" to fall. Soon, the holdings of several different oil companies in Iran, Iraq, Saudia Arabia, and elsewhere came under pressure.[4]

OPEC Disrupts the World Economy

OPEC's embargo and price hike in 1973 precipitated a world economic crisis. Other commodity exporters in the Third World saw the possibility that similar action could redistribute wealth to their own economies by holding up the industrial nations. The oil boycott also forced individual Americans to awaken to their country's resource dependence and to focus on energy conservation. The United States and its allies had become dangerously reliant on OPEC oil. In 1960, America imported 9.3 percent of its energy supply; this doubled to 19.3 percent in 1973 and peaked at 25.6 percent in 1977. Imports from OPEC, which were 767 million barrels in 1973, nearly tripled to 2.1 billion barrels in 1977. Oil prices quadrupled.[5]

Widespread dependence on oil for energy caused the price surge to ripple through the world economy and depressed economic growth in both rich and poor countries. As Table A.3 suggests, higher energy prices had a severe impact on emerging countries in the Americas and Africa, while developing nations in Asia succeeded in maintaining high rates of real and per-capita growth. They paid for more costly oil imports with expanding exports of manufactures to developed markets. Japan, which was 100 percent dependent on imported oil, undertook a successful conservation program to reduce fuel usage. Americans adapted more slowly.

The effect of the oil embargo and escalation in prices was most telling in world economic power. By 1977, combined earnings of oil exporters rose from $23 billion to $140 billion in five years, thanks to the quadrupling of crude oil prices due to the embargo and OPEC's seizure of control afterward over the setting of prices. Western allies, still reeling from Nixon's monetary shocks, became more open to Arab overtures for arms and consumer goods. Japan shifted to a pro-Arab policy, and to great benefit. Oil flowed to Japan while Nissan rose to the top spot in auto sales in Saudi Arabia. Such spending sent OPEC's 1974 $67 billion surplus into a $2 billion deficit four years later, but these nations still controlled oil. The Shah of Iran, a close U.S. ally, used the revenues from the large oil price hike in December 1973 that he rammed through OPEC to speed his country along toward modernization, as well as line his coffers. A surge in Arab consumption was further evidence of oil's impact on the region.[6]

As Daniel Yergin, a prominent historian of the oil industry related, by the mid 1970s, the oil embargo had the effect of turning the international order "upside down. OPEC's members were courted, flattered, railed against, and denounced" for a simple reason. "Oil prices were at the heart of global commerce, and those who seemed to control oil prices were regarded as the new masters of the global economy." OPEC nations could decide if America fell into recession, bankrolled the global economy with petrodollars, and demanded a new international economic order that redistributed world political power. The Third World would finally attain decisive power. The rulers lived in the Middle East and specifically, Saudi Arabia, which replaced the United States in overseeing the price of world oil.[7] The spotlight swung from Washington to Riyadh, fixing on the master of ceremonies, Saudi oil minister Ahmed Zaki Yamani.

Yamani did not singlehandedly decide oil policy, but he greatly shaped it. A man of great intellect and Muslim piety, he was educated in Cairo and then in the United States in international law. In 1957, he set up Saudi Arabia's first law office and began to advise his and foreign governments on oil policy. Five years later he allied with Prince Faisal, who won a power struggle against his brother for control of Saudi Arabia, and was rewarded with the post of oil minister. After the Six-Day War, he advised Arab nations to cooperate with the major oil companies operating in the region but demanded that oil companies share concessions with OPEC. In 1973, he approved the Arab boycott of oil exports to America and Holland, although he did so only to restore Arab lands from the Israelis and not to maintain oil prices on a permanently high plateau. Yamani prevented the Shah from leading OPEC to jack prices to an unreasonable and dangerously inflationary $20 a barrel in December 1973 and clashed again with the Shah in late 1977 when the latter sought to price petroleum at $100 a barrel.[8]

Yamani became internationally known by the mid 1970s, recognizable with his large eyes and clipped beard. Savvy in using the media, he became the Arab's leading and most visible spokesman on oil, an "oracle for the future of prices in the world's single most important commodity." His face graced the cover of *Newsweek* twice and *Time* once, as well as numerous advertisements and trade journals. He became a cult figure in some quarters, his devotion to astrology was well known. When Faisal died in his arms from an assassin's bullet in 1975, his status rose even further. But it was Yamani's keen negotiating skills – moderating, quiet, logical, his "sweet reasonableness" said an oil executive – that won him influence. That, and the fact that Saudi Arabian subsoil held one-third of the known petroleum reserves of the entire Free World.[9]

Above all, Yamani looked to long-term goals. He knew that his nation would benefit not from the political jousting of the immediate but from a sober and calculated regard of where Saudi Arabia and OPEC should go. This meant that Saudi Arabia would work to moderate world oil prices and cooperate with the consuming West. In the long run, such a policy paid off in terms of good relations with America, military aid, and economic stability. "I can't bear gambling," he remarked. Because of his experience, "Sheikh" Yamani made oil policy, but his prominence also brought him the scorn of the beleaguered West, as well as death threats from extremists. In December 1975, terrorists kidnapped OPEC ministers in Vienna, keeping them hostage before releasing them nearly two days later. Yamani was their prime catch, though they spared his life. Iranian radicals branded him a stooge of Zionists and imperialists. Yamani remained calm and fixated on the interests of Saudi Arabia, as always.[10]

Fixated themselves on the high price of oil, Americans found a friend in Yamani and Saudi Arabia. The Nixon, Ford, and Carter administrations sought to stabilize oil pricing and Middle East politics, because they were fearful that revolutionary forces like Quaddafi might take the mantle of leadership within OPEC. Indeed, the interconnectedness of oil, the global economy, and world politics required delicate diplomacy. Rapid price rises would fuel inflation and thus undermine growth and international trade and exchange. A sudden drop in prices, however, would stifle new exploration and development in the petroleum field as well as Arab consumption of consumer goods. Either scenario could weaken the United States' hand in the Cold War by undercutting military security with economic insecurity. Energy became "the number-one political issue of the mid-1970s" because of the volatile global combination of oil and politics, and Yamani proved he could smooth things out.[11]

The Saudis also used their leverage with the United States and other Western nations. Yamani pronounced a principle that the concession given to ARAMCO – the group of major oil companies controlling Saudi resources since the 1930s – should be turned over in its entirety to Saudi Arabia. Under the new arrangement of spring 1976, the Saudis took over ARAMCO's assets and rights, but the consortium operated the oil fields, marketed most of the petroleum, and received 21 cents a barrel for its efforts. Companies in Saudi Arabia as well as in other exporting nations such as Indonesia shifted from being owners to providing services. Production-sharing contracts became common, and OPEC countries achieved sovereignty over their precious resource. Now bypassing the companies, the state-owned facilities of exporting nations sold directly on world markets, quintupling OPEC's output from 1973 to 1979. The "OPEC Imperium," as Yergin wrote, had, in just over a half decade, moved "beyond production, into the international oil business outside their own borders."[12]

America and the Oil Shortage

Reeling from the Watergate crisis, Americans responded to the oil crisis with expressions of frustration and cynicism. One-quarter surveyed blamed the shortages of oil in 1973–4 on the multinational companies, which had posted higher profits than the year before, and another quarter accused Nixon of mismanagement. But in a way, Americans had only themselves to blame. With only 6 percent of the world's population, the United States consumed 30 percent of the planet's petroleum, much of it in energy-inefficient, heavy, eight-cylinder vehicles. The oil crisis, not surprisingly, ushered in a new era of environmental awareness – and specifically of the depletion of resources – that spread around the globe. Oil was at the core not only of U.S. problems but of those of the world, as concerns over famine, pollution, and conservation mounted.[13]

Successive administrations sought to address the nation's energy problem, but government plans produced few lasting results. The Nixon administration outlasted the first oil crisis but responded with such initiatives as limiting highway speed limits to 55 miles per hour, asking Americans to lower their thermostats and cut back air travel by 10 percent, and initiating Project Independence. It proposed price decontrol as a means of spurring development of new domestic energy resources. In January 1975, President Gerald Ford proposed a massive program to promote independence from oil imports. His plan included building hundreds of nuclear, coal-powered, and synthetic fuel plants as well as funding new coal mines and oil refineries. His vice president, the grandson of John D. Rockefeller, asked for a $100 billion subsidy plan for synthetic fuels and other energy projects. Both the Ford and Nelson Rockefeller ideas lay stillborn when Congress balked at their cost. The Alaskan oil pipeline brought a new source of supply to U.S. markets, and government fuel efficiency standards for automobiles produced both better gas mileage and a boom in sales of energy-efficient Japanese cars.

Increased import competition for domestic auto producers forced plant closings throughout the American Midwest (the center of the car industry) and caused higher rates of unemployment. The country seemed unable to extricate itself from a cycle of stagflation – high rates of joblessness combined with inflationary price spirals. By 1980, interest rates and inflation had climbed into the double digits. President Jimmy Carter and the Federal Reserve responded slowly to the surge in prices, which, by 1980, had climbed to double-digit levels. Carter declared a "moral equivalent of war" on energy crises, but interest groups stymied his efforts to rationalize prices and lower dependence on foreign oil.[14]

Carter's failure was due in part to Americans' perceptions that there was no oil crisis but also to fortuitous circumstances involving Iran. The Shah of Iran faced rebellion in 1978 from Muslim fundamentalists upset by his modernization schemes and identification with the secular West. Although miffed by the shah's efforts to raise oil prices, the United States considered him essential to Middle Eastern stability. Iran bought half of America's total global arms sales. Worried about the insurgents, the strongest of which were led by the Shiite Ayatollah Ruhollah Khomeini, the shah joined with Saudi Arabia in late 1977 to limit oil prices. The Carter administration suspended pressure against the shah for his human rights violations in return for his help within OPEC to moderate prices. That cooperation ended when Khomeini took power in January 1979.[15]

The ensuing Iranian hostage crisis not only devastated Carter's presidency, stalled his global human rights policy, and heightened tensions with the Soviet Union but also precipitated a second oil crisis. The president had achieved a remarkable peace between Israel and Egypt, yet it also provoked Muslim militants to assassinate Egypt's President Sadat. Carter could point to other foreign policy successes, which included a Panama Canal treaty, a strategic arms control agreement with the Soviet Union, and an inspiring human rights campaign. But the Iranian situation dominated news headlines.

Khomeini's victory and the 444-day hostage crisis (lasting until Ronald Reagan was inaugurated on January 20, 1981) shattered Carter's foreign and domestic policies, handicapped his reelection campaign, and brought a second oil crisis. Importation of Iran's six million barrels a day of petroleum ceased when the Ayatollah issued an embargo against the satanic United States. Crude prices rocketed from under $13 a barrel in 1978 to $40 by 1980. To be sure, the oil price surge led to a glut of production, which in turn caused prices to plummet during the mid 1980s, thus ending OPEC's stranglehold on the U.S. economy. But Americans remembered the Carter years as the period when drivers queued at the gas pump, truckers protested fuel shortages, consumer prices climbed 13.5 percent in a single year, and the unemployment rate rose to 7.1 percent. Fed up, Americans disdained the president's calls for lower home temperatures, positive thinking, and increased regulation. Abroad, at the Tokyo Economic Summit of 1979, Carter barely managed a consensus to curb oil imports and stabilize prices. His energy secretary, James Schlesinger, announced that America faced "a world crisis of vaster dimensions than Churchill described half a century ago – made more ominous by the problems of oil." In such circumstances, it was not surprising that 59 percent of the electorate registered their disgust, by not voting for Carter in the 1980 presidential election.[16]

But just as OPEC had risen to power, so it declined. OPEC's triumph with high oil prices disguised the growing fissure within the Arab world. By 1980, Iran and Iraq were at war, splitting the oil cartel and prompting expanded production to finance arms purchases. The demand for oil did not keep pace with supply, and oil prices began to fall by late 1981. The decrease was aided by a buildup of non-OPEC supplies from Mexico, Alaska, and the North Sea, as well as Angola, Egypt, Malaysia, and China. Furthermore, coal and nuclear power began overtaking petroleum as energy sources around the world. Energy efficiency also increased as federal standards required that by model year 1986 domestic new cars average 27.5 miles per gallon, thus saving an estimated 2 million barrels of oil a day. By that year, America was nearly one-third more oil efficient than it had been in 1973.

The results staggered OPEC. Demand fell by 13 million barrels per day by 1983, a 43 percent drop from the second oil crisis levels of 1979. Glut replaced shortages, and analysts soon spoke of a third oil crisis, but this one was the reverse of the first two because producers, not consumers, suffered. Sheikh Yamani convinced OPEC to impose production quotas for the first time in its history in March 1983, but he could not prevent squabbling members from cheating. By 1985, prices slid toward $18; the next year, they dropped to $9 a barrel. President Ronald Reagan and America were the beneficiaries; Yamani was dismissed in 1986 from his post of oil minister, which he had held for nearly a quarter century.[17] OPEC learned the difficulties of sustaining a commodity cartel in a world of geographically dispersed suppliers with differing policy interests.

From Development to Despair – OPEC and the Third World

The United Nations labeled the 1960s a Decade of Development. The 1970s became for many poor countries a Decade of Despair. Debt and food crises accompanied the surge in energy prices. A drought in Africa claimed 10,000 lives a day. High birthrates, combined with a reduction in infant mortality, pushed the world population to over four billion by 1975. Demographers held little hope for over one-quarter of these people because their caloric intake fell below required levels for normal activity. In such circumstances, it was not surprising that a group of seventy-seven UN member states from the Third World became more militant. During the oil crisis, the group focused demands on the creation of a more equitable New International Economic Order (NIEO), favoring commodity cartels, import restrictions to encourage national industrialization, and even nationalization of foreign investments. Not surprisingly, Western Europe and America balked, warning that such proposals to redistribute wealth would disrupt the fragile global market economy, which was adapting to the surge in oil prices and the collapse of the Bretton Woods system. The rich industrial nations warned that the NIEO would discourage private capital flows and promote disrespect for international business law. Nonetheless, the UN General Assembly approved a resolution for a NIEO based on equity, sovereign equality, and the interdependence of the interests of developed and developing countries.[18]

In the UN and affiliate agencies, developing countries pressed several parallel initiatives. One involved a controversial Law of the Sea Treaty, extending the traditional three-mile territorial limit to 200 miles and establishing an international authority to mine and market minerals found in international waters. Led by the militant Algerians, the bloc of seventy-seven wanted profits distributed equitably among all nations. They also pushed a radical proposal for a New World Information and Communication Order. Supporters claimed that a "vertical" flow of information from Europe and America to the world's periphery promoted dependency on Western-based transnational corporations. The result was the establishment of a UN commission, led by Sean McBride of Ireland, that studied communications problems and concluded that "imbalances in national information and communication systems are as disturbing and unacceptable as social, economic, cultural and technological disparities." It held that "rectification of the latter is inconceivable ... without elimination of the former." Critics said the report was biased against private media ownership and private advertising, conflicted with support for the principle of "free flow of information," and offered Third World dictators a pretext to stifle media freedom and impose censorship.[19]

Repeated attacks on multinationals and on high-income countries did little to reassure investors or to sustain a political climate supportive of expanded aid to developing nations. Neoclassical economists, who advised commercial banks and international institutions like the World Bank, had long emphasized that foreign investment could supplement local savings and serve as a vital catalyst in initiating economic growth. Before World War I, British and U.S. investors had constructed railroads, power plants and telephone systems, enabling some poor countries to participate in world markets.[20] During the 1960s and 1970s, nationalistic leaders often rejected this experience, railing against foreign exploitation and blaming multinational corporations for lagging growth. Third World host countries complained about the distribution of profits from mining and resource concessions and voiced concern about the growing political power of multinationals. Indeed, transnational corporations frequently exerted influence over local politics, sometimes paying bribes to chosen leaders or aiding in coups against hostile politicians.

The case of International Telephone and Telegraph's successful pressure on the Nixon administration to rid Chile of socialist Salvador Allende in 1973 was an example that resonated in the Third World. ITT, which owned the Chilean telephone system, feared that Allende would expropriate its properties as Fidel Castro had in Cuba. To oust Allende, the company worked with the CIA, which had Cold War security concerns, as well as Kennecott and Anaconda, two U.S.-owned copper companies, and Chilean newspapers and politicians. The result was a military coup in September 1973. One long-term effect of the episode was an initiative to regulate business conduct. In 1977, Congress passed the Foreign Corrupt Practices Act. It prohibited U.S. firms from paying bribes to foreign officials and required businesses to keep accurate records of their transactions. While well-intentioned, the act could not reach the practices of competing European and Japanese firms, and so U.S. business complained that it left American business at a disadvantage in a world where bribery was widely accepted.[21]

Despite public opposition to multinationals, U.S. business continued to expand abroad in the years 1973 to 1985, investing in many new overseas plants, resources, and services, and thus furthering globalization. But three-quarters of this flow went to developed markets, particularly in Western Europe and Canada. On a historical basis, the value of U.S. direct investments rose from $103.7 billion in 1973 to $230.3 in 1985 (up 122 percent). Of this amount, investments in developed countries climbed faster, up from $72.2 to $172.1 (138 percent), while investment in developing countries rose more slowly from $25.3 billion in 1973 to $52.8 billion (109 percent) in 1985. Much of the latter went into petroleum. Private capital had little interest in such areas of the developing world as sub-Saharan Africa and the Andean region of Latin America, where markets were small and the investment climate unattractive. Meanwhile, bilateral aid flows continued to contract. In 1965, U.S. official development assistance amounted to 0.26 percent of gross national product it fell to 0.03 percent in 1980. The decline reflected domestic pressures to expand the war on poverty and address urban problems, as well as to fund the war in Vietnam.

It also reflected a new political reality. The public and Congress associated foreign aid with wasteful spending. Public opinion seems to have shifted on foreign aid in the mid 1960s. In January 1963, a Gallup survey showed that 59 percent of the public supported foreign aid; in September 1967, another national poll showed that 68 percent wanted to cut foreign aid. The latter pattern continued during the 1970s, with surveys repeatedly revealing that two-third of the public desired to reduce foreign aid.[22]

The 1973–4 oil crisis set in motion events that led to a developing world financial collapse in the early 1980s. Unable to attract outside sufficient aid or investment capital, oil-importing developing countries found it necessary to borrow to finance essential import needs. Indeed, the U.S. Treasury and State Departments encouraged big New York commercial banks, such as Citibank and Chase, to help OPEC countries recycle their petro-earnings, and expand lending. On at least one occasion, the treasury reportedly told the World Bank that the U.S. government did not want the World Bank lending to Colombia. That was the job of commercial banks. The New York banks rapidly expanded their loans, especially to middle-income countries like Mexico and Brazil. Soon the banks were making loans for developing countries to repay previous loans and providing loans that ignored prudent lending standards. Mexico, for instance, borrowed heavily to build steel mills, oil installations, and electrical power plants that depended on imported materials. Much of this investment went to inefficient state-owned agencies and companies, including Pemex, the state oil company. Allegations of corruption at Pemex ran into the billions of dollars. In some instances, it was not so much an issue of poor countries borrowing in excess of their capacity to repay as it was of bankers "pushing" loans on naive borrowers. Mexico and Brazil soon accounted for one-third of developing country debt. In 1981, middle-income countries – mostly in Latin America – had $278 billion in total debt, about half of which was owed to commercial banks. But, low-income countries in Africa frequently could not qualify for private loans, and so they remained debtors to international institutions like the World Bank.[23]

The collapse of oil prices in 1982, and the Falklands War between Argentina and Britain, ignited another virulent phase in the spiraling debt crisis. To tame the overheated U.S. economy, then suffering from double-digit inflation, Federal Reserve Chairman Paul Volcker raised interest rates to 17.4 percent in 1981, about where they remained during the following year. The strong-minded central banker focused on squeezing inflation out of the U.S. economy, and he succeeded. In fact, interest rates stayed relatively high throughout the 1980s, attracting foreign savings to finance America's twin budget and trade deficits. Volcker's successful effort to combat inflation, coupled with President Reagan's stimulative policies to cut taxes and boost military spending, led to the second longest peacetime expansion of the U.S. economy, beginning in 1983. The downside was a growing gap between rich and poor, in addition to steadily mounting trade and budget deficits. Increasing foreign competition also contributed to the general stagnation of average weekly earnings. Peaking at $319 (in constant dollars) in July 1973, that figure fell to $291 in 1975, $272 in 1980, and $262 in 1990.[24]

Volcker's tight money policies helped America out of its recession, but it also helped trigger "an international financial crisis without precedent in modern history." First Mexico, then the rest of Latin America, sought more credits and rescheduling of loans. The International Monetary Fund stepped in, at first issuing new credits and then designing austere structural adjustment programs that required governments to curb budget deficits, devalue their currencies, combat inflation, open markets to international commerce and financial flows, and, in the case of Mexico, join the GATT trading system. From 1982 to 1984, many – led by Mexico and

Brazil – followed IMF dictates, while preparing for a return to private markets. But U.S. banks, which had life-threatening financial exposures, pulled back from international markets, and new private lending dried up. Nervous Latin American elites shifted billions to safe haven in the United States and other rich countries. American officials said that capital flight amounted to $100 billion from Latin America between 1980 and 1985. According to Karin Lissakers, the World Bank estimated that Venezuela's flight of capital exceeded foreign debt by perhaps 40 percent in 1987; Argentina's may have equaled the country's foreign liabilities, and flight from Mexico equaled 50 percent of foreign debt.[25]

Eventually, the Reagan and Bush administrations devised remedies. In 1985, Treasury Secretary James Baker proposed a plan involving concessions by commercial banks, international agencies, and fifteen debtor countries. It succeeded only in buying time, and the problem worsened. While international agencies stepped up lending, commercial banks gradually withdrew. As one historian of the IMF observed, "It is difficult to avoid the conclusion that at least in some cases, commercial banks were being repaid from resources made available by creditor governments and multilateral institutions."[26] A more successful initiative emerged after Nicholas Brady, President George Bush's secretary of the treasury, proposed to negotiate debt reduction, rescheduling, and the conversion of old debt into new Brady bonds collateralized by zero-coupon U.S. Treasury bonds after debtor countries signed accords with the IMF and World Bank. These agreements required, among other things, privatization of state properties and liberalization of trade. Some fifty countries benefited from the Brady plan, and it eliminated the debt overhang and created a more favorable climate for direct investment flows. But to escape the debt crisis, troubled developing countries were forced to abandon years of state intervention, embrace the fundamental tenets of free-market capitalism, and establish a business environment favorable to foreign investors. As a result of this deregulatory philosophy, private investments soared, ending this phase of the debt crisis. Foreign buyers benefited from the privatization, as did billionaires. In 1993, a year when the Mexican economy was stagnant, the number of Mexican billionaires rose from thirteen to twenty-four, one result of the wave of privatization to satisfy international financial markets.[27]

The debt crisis was only one of several factors enhancing the visibility of poorer nations. Others included the militance and voting strength of the group of seventy-seven in the UN and UNCTAD, the twists and turns of the Cold War, and a growing awareness of wretched living conditions and poverty in sub-Saharan Africa. But perhaps television made the most important contribution to world understanding. During the mid 1970s African Americans, and indeed many other ethnic Americans, became interested in their genealogical roots. Alex Haley's bestseller, *Roots*, which explored his own family's abduction in Africa and the difficult Atlantic crossing, followed by three generations of bondage, sold 5.5 million copies and reached a large television audience through an eight-night miniseries on ABC television in January 1977. Along with these cultural and genealogical ties, network sports coverage, such as ABC's "Wide World of Sports," became increasingly international.

Boxer Muhammad Ali renewed interest in Africa. He had captured the heavyweight crown for the first time in 1964 and then had it revoked when he evaded the draft during the Vietnam War. Ali soon became a media star, with his good looks, poetic expressions, and taunts (he had been known as the Louisville Lip). In October 1974, three years after his conviction for draft-dodging had been overturned, he dueled George Foreman in Kinshasa, Zaire, in the first heavyweight bout ever held in Africa. An international audience watched the action live on closed-circuit television, making use of satellites, in movie theaters around the world. Promoter Don King arranged this "rumble in the jungle," having "jive-talked" Ali and Foreman and sweet-talked Zaire's president Mobutu to a grub stake.[28]

For Zaire, this event was the biggest in the nation's short history. Sixty thousand people jammed the stadium. Eagerly looking forward to the bout, Ali had agreed to fight in Africa for the sake of black pride, both at home and abroad. Ironically, Mobutu, who spent $20 million in scarce government funds to sponsor the fight, feared crowds. He stayed in his mansion to watch the match on television with Idi Amin, the mad dictator of Uganda. Not only did Ali win back his title, but he also visited President Gerald Ford at the White House, and *Sports Illustrated* named him Sportsman of the Year. Ali was the most famous man in the world at this point. He retired after a defeat in December 1981, with a record of fifty-six wins (thirty-seven by knockout), five losses, and three heavyweight titles. His global reach lived on, past his boxing career and bout with Parkinson's disease, an individual recognized the world over. In 1996, at the Atlanta Summer Olympic Games, with speculation rampant about who would light the flame to open the competition, Ali appeared. Hands shaking, older, he carried the torch in a moving spectacle. Ali was global sports' most-loved citizen.[29]

Japan Ascendant

Japan, a nation totally dependent on imported oil, enjoyed economic success during the oil crisis. Its exports rose rapidly, and its real growth rate surpassed that in Western Europe and the United States. Among the reasons for Japan's success, along with new state-of-the art industrial plants and an export-or-die mentality, was the open U.S. market. For reasons of economic and political security – both linked to Cold War objectives – the United States had for decades allowed Japan to protect its own industries from foreign competition while it maintained an artificially cheap currency to boost its own exports to America. After the first oil crisis, that approach boosted Japanese trade surpluses with the United States and contributed to the loss of market share for many U.S. industries – especially television, electronics, automobiles, and steel.

A modernized and productive nation, Japan had beaten the United States at its own game of market domination and innovation. Here was a country that produced fewer than 100,000 passenger cars in 1958 but twenty years later became the major foreign auto exporter to the United States. Its success came from lower labor costs, new plants, attention to quality, and sensitivity to consumer tastes, such as fuel-efficient cars. In electronics, office equipment, and steel, the Japanese also prepared to seize market share. By the late 1970s, despite dollar devaluation and political pressure, Japan enjoyed nearly a $10 billion annual trade surplus with the United States. Some critics urged America to adopt an industrial policy that targeted markets, as Japan did. That approach, however, was as foreign to the free-market United States as were the Toyotas that consumers soon snapped up by the boatloads.[30]

In automobiles, the oil price hikes stimulated demand for Japanese imports, which more than doubled between 1975 and 1987. Japan was so successful that pressure grew in Congress for import restraints. Fear of American protectionism and concern that a more expensive yen might hamper export sales prompted Japanese automakers to build green-field assembly plants in Ohio, Tennessee, and Kentucky and avoid protectionist barriers. Japan had made no cars in America in 1978; ten years later, it made 695,000. By 1979, Japan captured 23.5 percent of the U.S. market, a higher share than Ford and Chrysler. One television salesperson for the Japanese auto industry was Susan Ford, the daughter of former President Gerald Ford. She did an advertisement for one Japanese automaker: "Take it from a Ford, Drive Subaru."[31]

The Big Three American car makers tried different strategies to recover market share, but they had difficulty producing small energy-efficient vehicles profitably. One example was GM's ill-fated Vega, introduced in 1970. It bombed due to poor quality at the Lordstown, Ohio, production facility. Responding to the U.S. industry, the Reagan administration negotiated voluntary controls with Japan in 1981. But Japanese exporters used the quantitative limitations to move up the value ladder, introducing the Toyota Camry and Honda Accord, each with attractive styling and superior quality, followed by high-end Infinitis, Lexuses, and Acuras. Thus, the value of Japanese auto exports continued to climb, and they established a strong position in the premium segment of the auto market. As the domestic industry continued to lose market share, it shut plants and laid off workers. Meanwhile the bilateral trade deficit with Japan continued to widen, aggravated by the surge in auto imports. In 1986, the United States experienced an overall global trade deficit of $138 billion. Nearly half of the $58.6 billion deficit with Japan came from motor vehicles, and the percentage changed little for the next half decade.[32]

Trade negotiations yielded few gains in the Japanese market. In multilateral negotiations, Japanese negotiators refused to make significant concessions. In the Tokyo Round, one U.S. official compared bilateral bargaining with "the Chinese water treatment," in which a "great deal of persistence and patience" was necessary to take "tiny steps" toward reaching an agreement.[33] Determined to advance free trade, the U.S. government continued to resist pressure for import protection. Policy makers routinely turned down petitions for relief from U.S. industry, even when the quasi-judicial U.S. International Trade Commission (ITC) recommended temporary relief to facilitate adjustment to increased imports. In thirty escape-clause cases between 1975 and 1985 in which the ITC found serious injury, Presidents Ford, Carter, and Reagan turned down nearly half. Conventional wisdom dictated that the United States avoid protection, for the good of consumers, markets, and partners in the Cold War.

But the Reagan administration did engineer a devaluation of the dollar to provide some relief to U.S. manufacturers. In 1985, the five leading global economic powers met under the prompting of Treasury Secretary James Baker III in New York City, signing the Plaza Accord that called for cooperation to reduce the dollar's value and increase that of other major currencies, particularly the Japanese yen. Subsequently, the yen rose 100 percent against the dollar in the next four years, but contrary to expectations, Japanese trade surpluses continued to increase. Lured by the

Federal Reserve's high-interest-rate policy and the strong yen, Japanese investors turned from buying U.S. securities (between 1981 and 1985, they purchased over one-third of the U.S. Treasury's debt) and began bargain-hunting in American real estate and corporate assets in such an invasive way that they shook American confidence at its core.[34]

Japan was not the only Asian nation to target the U.S. market. In 1979, Washington and Beijing formally recognized each other and a commercial agreement followed a year later. In 1980, exports to China climbed to $4 billion, more than quadruple the total in 1974. China overtook Russia as America's top communist trade partner; in 1981, Coca-Cola opened a bottling plant in China. Once again some American businesses sali-vated about the future of China's huge domestic market, with its nearly one billion potential consumers, and about the prospect for using cheap Chinese labor to assemble goods for the U.S. market. But by 1985, the bilateral trading relationship grew increasingly asymmetrical. Year after year, imports of Chinese apparel, footwear, electronics, and consumer goods swamped U.S. exports to China of technology products. There were annual tensions because Congress had to vote whether to extend temporary most-favored-nation treatment (MFN: the lowest U.S. tariff) to China, which was not a member of GATT and thus not entitled to per-manent MFN status. This meant that issues such as Taiwan, human rights concerns, and national security sensitivities could unsettle the delicate re-lationship and affect the legislative debate. Although America severed for-mal diplomatic relations with Taiwan and withdrew military forces from the island, personal and cultural contacts remained strong, and military aid continued. Early in the Reagan administration, there were tensions when Washington insisted on selling weapons to Taiwan. China threat-ened to retaliate by downgrading relations with America. The two superpowers came to an agreement on arms sales in 1982, however, and the Reagans visited China in 1984, thus smoothing the way for in-creased flows of trade and investment capital and for expanded student exchanges.[35]

Renewed Cold War Crisis

Frosty relations with China were just one element in the Carter-Reagan re-trenchment of the Cold War. This was an era of economic as well as diplo-matic crises, a period that diverted attention from the underlying trend toward globalization. Carter turned away from human rights and hopes of detente with the Soviet Union through arms control when the Russians

invaded Afghanistan in December 1979. He withdrew the SALT-II treaty
from the Senate, halted technology and grain sales to Russia, prevented
the U.S. Olympic team from attending the Summer Games in Moscow in
1980, and issued the Carter Doctrine, warning the Soviets to stay away
from the Persian Gulf region.[36]

Reagan was even more blunt, and had no qualms about raising the
stakes in the Cold War. It was a war he intended to win. In January 1977,
he told his future national security advisor his "idea of American policy
toward the Soviet Union is simple, and some would say simplistic. It is
this: We win and they lose." To this end, Reagan and his aides devised
a program to take advantage of Soviet vulnerabilities. They sought to
deny access to Western technology, exploit its nationality and consumer-
economy problems, weaken Russia in wars of national liberation along
its borders, and exhaust it in an expensive arms competition. Recognizing
that Moscow was about ten years behind in emerging technologies and
dependent on technology transfers from the West, Reagan tightened export controls and did everything possible to reduce Soviet hard currency
earnings from oil and gas sales. The latter provided some 60 percent to
80 percent of Soviet hard currency earnings. Thus, Washington delayed
proposed oil and gas ventures with Western Europe and Japan and persuaded the Saudis to expand oil production from 2 million to 9 million
barrels per day in August 1985, effectively flooding the market. Crude oil
prices plunged from $30 to $12 per barrel and the Soviet Union lost about
half of its hard currency earnings. Naming a tough-minded anticommunist, Jeanne Kirkpatrick, to represent America in the United Nations, he
endorsed her criticism of Third World nations and UN agencies that shied
from fully supporting U.S. foreign policies. Reagan suspended American
support of and participation in UNESCO to show his disdain for UN
globalism.[37]

The administration also used the CIA to support "freedom fighters" –
anticommunist guerillas – in Angola, Mozambique, Afghanistan, and
Central America and went after terrorists worldwide. In arming Afghan
rebels with heat-seeking Stinger missiles, Reagan neutralized Soviet air
dominance and contributed to a bitter Soviet military defeat. In the Middle
East, in particular, the tricky balancing act of backing moderate Arabs and
Israel and of preventing either Iran or Iraq from dominating the Persian
Gulf in their brutal nine-year war tested Reagan interventionism to the
limit. Middle Eastern complexities soon became linked to support of the
Nicaraguan Contras. The administration sold missiles to Iran in return for
that nation's aid in freeing hostages seized by terrorists. The money was

then funneled to the Contras fighting to overthrow the leftist government. When the ploy was discovered, the Democratic Congress held hearings in 1987 and criticized the administration for violations of domestic and international law (as had the World Court before).[38]

Perhaps the Reagan administration's most successful weapon in the Cold War was one former radio announcer "Dutch" Reagan knew best – communications. Reagan understood how information changed lives, attitudes, and wants. "The truth," he said, "is mankind's best hope for a better world," and he thought the Voice of America and Radio Liberty "our primary means of getting truth to the Russian people." He increased spending for Radio Liberty and Radio Free Europe, and on his watch, in 1988, Radio Liberty began to exploit the nationality problem of the "evil empire." National consciousness began spreading among non-Russian peoples; the republics became more assertive in demanding autonomy within the Soviet Union. Reagan also knew the power of pictures. He wanted to show Soviet citizens that in America every home had a car, and often a swimming pool. So, the administration started a satellite television network, Worldnet, to facilitate the spread of information to Eastern Europe. One successful program was an English-language series showing scenes of the American good life – a modern supermarket with electronic checkout facilities and no lines of impatient customers. As it turned out, the increased flows of information fanned internal dissatisfaction in the Soviet Union and desires for change.[39]

Reagan's most controversial move to end the Cold War was his arms buildup. In constant dollars, military spending rose 54 percent during his presidency, from 5 percent to 6.5 percent of the gross national product. The president sent more missiles to Europe and invested heavily in a novel and controversial plan for a Strategic Defense Initiative (SDI) antimissile defense system. Not surprisingly, these actions provoked antinuclear activists around the world to unite against what they said was Reagan's aggressive and dangerous confrontation of the Soviets. However unfeasible at the time, SDI was used as a bargaining chip in disarmament talks with Moscow, and its development promised to benefit future commercial initiatives in robotics, kinetic energy, and optics. As it turned out, SDI was important to ending the Cold War, as were fortuitous events in the Soviet Union.

The death of President Yuri Andropov caused a turnover in the Kremlin and brought to power in 1985 his protege Mikhail Gorbachev, a reformer prepared to push restructuring (*perestroika*) and greater openness (*glasnost*). But in his gamble to save the Soviet Union by reforming it, Gorbachev needed to reduce military spending. At the summit in Reykjavik, Iceland, in October 1986, however, Reagan refused to abandon SDI. According to former British Prime Minister Margaret Thatcher, he "called the Soviets' bluff." They could not hope to match the United States in competition for technological supremacy while pursuing a restructuring that would make more goods available to consumers. Thus, Thatcher credits Reagan for undermining communism. His information offensive, military buildup, and good fortune in restoring noninflationary economic growth all contributed to victory in the Cold War.[40]

Transformation

Away from the media spotlight, several quieter developments lay the foundation for the post–Cold War era – the age of globalization. One was a new international outlook encouraged by better communications, transportation, open borders, deregulation, and revival of neoliberalism. Business leaders began to think globally and to develop global networks that could exert influence over national political leaders through money and ideas. During the energy crisis of 1973, America's corporate elite reached out to foreign business leaders. Under the leadership of Chase Manhattan's David Rockefeller, they formed the multinational Trilateral Commission in 1973, with members from business, politics, law, and academia in America, Western Europe, and Japan. The idea was to facilitate cooperation with resource-rich nations, but outside of government supervision. A precursor to modern-day globalized networks and contacts, the Trilateral Commission "reflected a global orientation among business elites which were more concerned with the survival of multinational corporations than with separate national policies." Among its charter members were Jimmy Carter, Walter Mondale, and George Bush. Similarly, European business leaders began to meet in Davos, Switzerland, in 1982 to develop a common strategy for European business in the international marketplace. This network gradually expanded in the 1980s to include world business and political leaders and to launch the annual World Economic Forum. Held every January in Davos, it brought together the world's movers and shakers to network, deal, and discuss public policy issues. Similarly in America during the Carter and Reagan years, business lobbying expanded, and from initial efforts to contain unions, pursued an active agenda of deregulating markets, cutting taxes, and promoting free trade.[41]

The deregulatory business agenda reflected another important theme, a fundamental shift in the intellectual paradigm of the government-business relationship. From Franklin Roosevelt's New Deal to Lyndon Johnson's Great Society, the Washington consensus stressed an active and expansive role for the federal government. This was a reaction to the perceived mistakes of the laissez-faire 1920s and to the collapse of the Great Depression. According to the tenets of regulatory capitalism, the national government existed not simply to protect the nation's borders, deliver the mail, mint a common currency, and protect property and individual rights. It had more expansive purposes. The federal government should regulate and reform the economy, promote social justice, and ensure full employment. While government favored lower tariff barriers, it wanted to encourage the growth of labor unions and to promote fair labor standards. The rise of government regulation and rule-making was associated with James Landis, a brilliant Harvard-educated lawyer who served on the Federal Trade Commission and the Securities and Exchange Commission. Landis advanced the case for delegating authority to the regulatory branch of government, composed of independent commissions that are disposed to intervene actively in the economy. Another prophet of government activism was British economist John Maynard Keynes. He advanced the case for government deficit spending to promote recovery and to maintain full employment. Until the 1970s, Keynesian economists remained optimistic that they could manage the mixed economy, steering it between the unacceptable extremes of disruptive inflation and high unemployment. Ironically, this cycle of active government peaked during the presidency of Republican Richard Nixon, who surprised his conservative followers with wage and price controls.[42]

In the 1970s, the cycle of respectable economic thought turned again – this time toward a less-regulated marketplace. In part, this reflected frustrations with big government. Murray Weidenbaum, an economist at Washington University in St. Louis, fathered the deregulatory movement. Other evidence that the tide had turned occurred in 1976, when Milton Friedman of the University of Chicago won the Nobel Prize in economics. Emphasizing the importance of monetary policy and free markets, Friedman used his successful publications and public television series, *Freedom to Choose*, to launch a neoclassical attack on Keynesian interventionism. The Washington consensus that emerged during the Reagan years thus emphasized entrepreneurship, reliance on the Federal Reserve and monetary policy to manage the economy, tax relief, labor-market competition, deregulation, fluctuating exchange rates, and free trade in goods. In time, this consensus came to include free trade in money, or capital account convertibility.[43]

As the Cold War wound down in the aftermath of Reykjavik, a new international economic world was taking shape far from the governments' leaders in Washington and Moscow who defined the post–World War II world and the scientists in their remote government laboratories who fashioned nuclear weaponry. The new world was shaped by rapid flows of goods, money, and information (the power of markets), by the enthusiasm of technology nerds, and by the acquisitive instincts of entrepreneurs.

9

Freedom and Free Trade, 1986–1995

Like McKinley, FDR, and Truman, Ronald Reagan proved to be a transformational president, one who left the American presidency much different than he found it and set the agenda for the future.[1] Not only did he push the Cold War to a triumphal end, but Reagan also ambitiously moved to deregulate and privatize government, and his efforts gave impetus to the second age of global business expansion. In pressing internationally for individual freedom and free markets, and in launching the Uruguay Round of trade negotiations, he established policy priorities for his successors – George H. Bush and Bill Clinton – and for the early twenty-first century.

Using the medium he knew best, Reagan initiated a program of Saturday radio messages to expound on the possibilities for freedom under U.S. leadership. He was the first president to push openly for free trade and privatization of government services and one of the first to appreciate how new technologies of communication were transforming the marketplace and weakening the authority of totalitarian regimes. When he spoke of freedom, Reagan usually meant economic and political freedoms; he did not focus on social liberation or issues of family, women, and race. Reagan was especially sympathetic to the plight of political refugees who sought freedom from communist-style oppression, and to ordinary citizens and businesses battling against government regulators. And, he saw the tide turning his way. In his White House farewell speech, Reagan observed that "countries across the globe are turning to free markets and free speech and turning away from the ideologies of the past."

As President Reagan exited from office, the techno-globo revolution was accelerating, bringing major changes to economics and politics, as well as to culture and society. His successors wrestled with the implications of globalization at home and abroad. The freer exchanges of goods, capital, and culture inherent in globalization arose from the Cold War's ashes and took America into a new era in which transnational contacts rivaled state power.[2]

Economic Transformation and Freedom

Reagan entered office with a distinctive, long-term economic agenda: to cut personal income taxes, deregulate and privatize government services, and open foreign markets to trade and investments. America was losing out in international economic competition, he said, because "we have become over-governed, over-regulated and overtaxed." More than any president since Calvin Coolidge, Reagan emphasized the "vitality and magic of the marketplace" and wanted to liberate entrepreneurs and small business owners from government intervention. His emphasis on supply-side tax cuts and privatization was new. The first idea originated with economists like Arthur Laffer. The latter came from Prime Minister Margaret Thatcher's efforts to restructure government in Britain. But deregulation represented an expansion of Ford and Carter administration initiatives popular with the business community, while trade liberalization traced its paternity to Cordell Hull's program.[3]

While the administration pursued these priorities legislatively – winning congressional support for cuts in personal income tax rates in 1981 and 1986 – the Federal Reserve attended to short-run problems. Federal Reserve Chairman Paul Volcker, a Carter appointee, deserved credit for wringing inflation (13.5 percent in 1980) out of the economy with tight money in 1981 and 1982. Fearful that the administration and Congress were cutting income taxes without reducing enough government spending, Volcker engineered a painful recession to extinguish inflation. Yet this bitter medicine provided the foundation for a long boom. Real economic growth, which had been negative in 1979–80, revived and averaged over 4 percent for the period from 1983 to 1989.[4]

Even so, the combination of monetary restraint and economic stimulus had a significant downside. The dollar rose sharply as foreigners bought high-yielding treasury bonds, issued to finance the growing gap between federal spending and tax revenues. A stronger dollar, in turn, made exports more expensive on world markets and foreign goods cheaper for consumers. The trade gap widened sharply to over 2 percent of gross domestic product, and the United States become a debtor country again in 1985. Foreign assets in the country surpassed U.S. assets abroad. The trend continued. Fifteen years later, the U.S. international debt exceeded $2 trillion, making America the world's largest debtor.[5]

On the trade side, America became more reliant on world markets. As late as 1970, U.S. exports plus imports of goods and services amounted to only 10.8 percent of GDP, less than the 11.1 percent reached forty-one years earlier in 1929. But, in the decade 1970 to 1980 America's dependence on trade nearly doubled – rising to 20.5 percent. As the economy increasingly internationalized, imports and exports surged in the 1990s to 26 percent of GDP in 2000.[6] Air freight's share of U.S. merchandise trade rose from 16 percent in 1980 to 28 percent in 1997, reflecting the rising use of air transportation for high-value products. The strong dollar, in conjunction with dramatic improvements in transportation and communications and sharp tariff cuts in multilateral trade negotiations, accelerated the globalization of production and the demise of labor-intensive domestic manufacturing.[7]

A good example was the shoe industry, one of the pillars of the old economy. Despite a sharp drop in shoe tariffs, it still supplied 70 percent of consumption from domestic plants, most of them in small towns in New England and the South. In 1985, it sought import relief, but Reagan refused, saying Americans "must live according to our principles" and ensure that the "world trading system remains open, free, and, above all, fair." The exodus of shoe production to cheap-labor countries continued; by 1999, imports (by quantity) had taken 94 percent of the U.S. nonrubber footwear market, and China supplied 69 percent of U.S. consumption. Over a thirty-year period, the shoe industry lost 178,000 production jobs. Firms like Converse, which began making athletic shoes in New England in 1908 and supplied Larry Bird and the Boston Celtics, attempted for years to resist the import tide. Converse wanted to produce in New England, but it gradually lost market share to cheap imports and finally declared bankruptcy. Among the winners in the new global economy were "hollow corporations," like Nike, which designed and marketed athletic shoes made by low-income workers in developing countries.[8]

The import assault of the 1980s had a severe impact on older mass-production industries – such as autos and steel – forcing firms to restructure and downsize. But some firms succeeded in making the transition by automating and sourcing parts internationally. One famous name, Harley Davidson, the last U.S. maker of heavy motorcycles, used a period of tariff protection to develop new models and become export competitive again.

Others simply closed their doors, or became designers and marketers of imported products. As industrial transformation occurred, job security declined. No longer could workers expect to spend an entire career with a single employer, in large organizations that provided substantial health care and retirement benefits. Pittsburgh, Cleveland, and Detroit – cities that once epitomized American manufacturing – became, for a time, Rust Belt relics. Older industries shed over a million jobs, many of them paying considerably more than the new jobs created in services. For middle-aged workers with little education, the dislocations were often painful. Laid-off industrial workers retrained and took multiple part-time jobs in the expanding, low-end service sector, which added some 15.5 million jobs. Some flipped hamburgers; others became security guards or janitors. Frequently, the new jobs had no health care or retirement benefits. To assist with family expenses, more and more married women entered the work place.[9]

As the old industrial economy based on mass production declined as a share of GDP, a new economy emerged based on information and high-skilled services. In 1986, services amounted to over half of gross national product and accounted for two-thirds of all private sector jobs. Many of the jobs were in low-skilled positions, but others involved highly skilled lawyers, accountants, engineers, business consultants, educators, designers, and information specialists. These Information Age workers produced data and ideas, not goods, and relied on instant communications, computers, and software. Between 1984 and 1993, the percentage of workers using computers doubled, rising from one-fourth to nearly one-half. The information technology sector increased its share of GDP, from 4.9 percent in 1985 to a 8.2 percent in 1998.[10] America's rapid adaptation of the new technology helped give it a competitive advantage in services, and by the mid 1980s, the growing export surplus in services helped offset a rapidly expanding merchandise trade deficit. As government leaders learned about the surge in service-related trade, they supported private sector efforts to gain greater access to foreign markets and to establish internationally accepted rules for business activity.

U.S. antitrust officials made two key decisions that affected the globalization of services. One was to terminate a case filed at the end of the Johnson administration to break up IBM on grounds that it monopolized the market for general-purpose electronic computers. At the time of the suit, IBM held about 70 percent of the market for mainframe computers. The legal proceedings dragged on for twelve years, and in trial the parties largely ignored the revolutionary developments in the personal computer market that transformed competitive conditions in the industry. After the 1980 election, however, the Reagan administration terminated the suit, saying that it had "no merit." This enabled IBM to focus its resources on new products in the emerging personal computer (PC) market. The costly and protracted suit probably undercut IBM's efforts to achieve a dominant position in PCs. But as it turned out, the prospect of further antitrust suits did facilitate competition.

In 1969, when IBM was under pressure from the Justice Department, it decided to unbundle software prices from hardware, thus creating opportunities for a specialized software industry with IBM-compatible programs. To avoid future suits and to enter the surging personal computer market quickly after a late start, IBM chose in the 1980s to partner with Intel for microprocessors and Microsoft for operating software. In effect, the IBM PC represented a new way of doing business for IBM. Rather than relying exclusively on IBM-made parts, the PC used components from outside suppliers. This meant that the IBM system was not proprietary, and it could no longer control the market. Its suppliers soon supplied makers of IBM clones, and in the emerging commodity market for chips, drives, and computer components, suppliers turned to low-labor-cost factories in Singapore, Malaysia, South Korea, Taiwan, and other countries. In the global world in which communications flowed at the speed of light and goods traveled at nearly the speed of sound, labor was becoming a fungible commodity. In computers, but also in many other industries, U.S. manufacturers closed up shop and became marketing organizations for foreign producers. These "hollow corporations" had no production base and relied instead on dynamic networks to take advantage of the cheapest foreign labor and the best technology.[11]

A second decision of great significance involved the breakup of AT&T, the world's largest corporation in 1984, with annual revenues of $70 billion and 1 million employees. During the 1960s, Ma Bell owned 80 percent of all transoceanic cables from America, enjoyed a monopoly over all domestic long-distance service, and controlled 80 percent of the local service markets. But the business community was not satisfied with service – AT&T was slow to authorize new plug-in equipment and its high long-distance fees subsidized local service. In this case, Reagan's Justice Department decided to deregulate and privatize communications. It negotiated a consent decree divesting AT&T of its twenty-two operating companies but permitting AT&T to retain Western Electric, Bell Labs, and its long-distance services. The so-called Baby Bells, regional companies created in this action, were barred from offering long-distance service, telecommunications hardware, and information services.

In effect, the divestiture decision inadvertently opened up the U.S. telecommunications hardware market to foreign suppliers. Japanese and European competitors rushed into the U.S. market and helped turn a $27 billion surplus in high-tech goods into a $2.6 billion deficit by 1986. American industry conceded that this result was justifiable only if foreign telecom markets offered reciprocal access to U.S. providers. Yet, except in the United States, there was a tradition of state monopolies and closed markets. Reagan insisted that telecommunications be included in the up-coming Uruguay Round of multilateral trade negotiations, while using unilateral sanctions (Section 301 of the trade act) to threaten retaliation against foreign restrictive practices. Free trade became the centerpiece of U.S. telecommunications policy.[12]

As a former movie actor and radio announcer, Ronald Reagan was familiar with problems of the entertainment industry. Thus, it is not sur-prising that his administration took the lead in efforts to strengthen inter-national protection for intellectual property (IP) rights. In the late 1970s, the record and film industries became targets of intellectual piracy, as the consumer electronics industry mass produced audio and videocassette players and taping equipment. The problem was that individuals illegally copied cassettes, computer chips, cable and satellite television broadcasts, and books without compensating the holders of patents or copyrights. On the streets of Seoul, Korea, shoppers found authentic-looking Louis Vuitton handbags ($12), Gore-Tex running suits ($45), and Reebok ath-letic shoes ($10). Taiwanese pirates issued their own Chinese version of the *Encyclopedia Britannica* before the authentic version was published. In many Third World countries, video parlors showed foreign movies from unauthorized videocassettes. While pirated goods, tapes, and drugs often suffered in quality – and might endanger health and safety – many were made in the same plants as the authentic items.[13]

How significant was the problem? In 1988, the U.S. International Trade Commission estimated that U.S. firms were losing between $43 billion and $61 billion annually. The study identified Taiwan, Mexico, South Korea, Brazil, China, Canada, and India as culprits of piracy. The Motion Picture Producers Association of America estimated its members lost $1.2 billion a year to foreign pirates, prompting association president Jack Valenti to call this "toxic waste" a "global war [that] we are fighting it on all fronts." The pharmaceutical and software industries expected big losses as the problem spread. Many developing nations tolerated lax efforts to protect patents and copyrights, viewing appropriation of foreign technology as a key to national development, a device to transfer wealth from the industrialized world, and a means of creating jobs.[14]

During the 1980s, Congress and the Reagan administration worked to revise domestic laws to cover computer programs, biotechnology, and satellite signals. In 1988, to persuade other nations that the time had come to enforce patent and copyright laws, the administration unilaterally imposed trade sanctions on Thailand and Brazil. After modifying its own copyright laws to satisfy international standards, the United States joined the Berne Convention, which protected literary and artistic works dating from 1885. President Reagan said expanded copyright protection for U.S.-produced literary and artistic works would undermine "international pirates who make their living by stealing and then selling the creative accomplishments of others."[15]

Signing the copyright convention was also expected to strengthen the hand of U.S. trade negotiators in efforts to persuade developing nations to adhere to international standards. One enforcement problem was that Third World judiciaries often assigned little priority to protecting foreign property rights from local pirates. Officials in Western Europe, Japan, and America considered multilateral protection a more efficient way to promote respect for intellectual property standards throughout the global economy, and so they insisted on addressing this issue in Uruguay Round of trade negotiations (1986–94).[16]

The Global Economy

With the Reagan administration supporting a strong dollar and backing U.S. international business, through unilateral sanctions and international rules, the overseas flow of investment capital expanded rapidly. In 1982, America had $207.8 billion invested abroad, of which $57.8 billion was in petroleum (27.8%); $83.5 billion in manufacturing (40.2%); and $32.9 in banking, finance, real estate, and other services (15.8%). Total foreign direct investment doubled by 1990. Of the $430.5 billion invested abroad, $52.8 billion was in petroleum (12.3%); $170.1 billion in manufacturing (39.5%); and $143.8 billion in banking, finance, real estate, and services (33.4%). By 2000, the total direct investment had grown to $1,293.4 trillion, of which $95.8 billion was in petroleum (7.4%); $353.6 billion in manufacturing (27.3%); and $622.8 billion in banking, finance, real estate, and services (48.2%). The phenomenal growth of American overseas activity by banks, insurance companies, other financial institutions, and a variety of leading-edge service providers was one of the most underreported stories of the era. Yet, the developing world hosted only a small percentage of U.S. direct investment. In 2000, nearly 52.5% of U.S. manufacturing investment was in Europe; 13.6% in Latin America (5.3% in Mexico); 14.4% in Canada; and 18.3% in Asia (4.4% in Japan). For banking, financial, real estate, and other services, Europe was the most important host (55.6%), followed by Latin America (25.7%), and Asia (11.7%). Another 6.3% flowed to Canada.[17] (See Table A.7.)

American manufacturing firms continued to go abroad during this period, but increasingly service firms led the way. On the basis of its success with theme parks in Anaheim and Orlando, Disney entered a joint venture with Japanese investors to build a carbon-copy Disneyland in Tokyo. Visitors ate fried chicken and hamburgers, and shook hands with Mickey Mouse. The park, complete with Cinderella's Castle, was erected on land reclaimed from Tokyo Bay. It attracted 10 million visitors in 1983, its first year of operation, most of whom were already familiar with Disney films, books, and consumer products. Many visitors came from Asia; the son of North Korean dictator Kim Jong Il even tried to enter Japan on a fake passport in 2001 so that his children could visit Disneyland. Enthusiastic about Disney characters, the late Emperor Hirohito occasionally wore a Mickey Mouse watch.[18]

Fast-food retailing giant McDonald's opened its first restaurant in 1955 but did not go abroad until 1967, in neighboring Canada. McDonald's began a big push overseas in the 1970s, seeking to export the unique American life-style based on quick-service food. This initiative was extraordinarily successful at a time when foreign manufacturers had American industry on the defensive in the U.S. market. Opening the first restaurant in Tokyo in 1971, McDonald's Japanese President Den Fujita stated that "the reason Japanese people are so short and have yellow skins is because they have eaten nothing but fish and rice for two thousand years." He added, "If we eat McDonald's hamburgers and potatoes for a thousand years we will become taller, our skin become white and our hair blonde." By 1980, there were 1,000 restaurants abroad and 6,000 in the United States. In 1987, McDonald's announced that it was serving 20 million people a day in forty-seven countries at 10,000 restaurants. Soon the chain had restaurants in Moscow and Beijing. By the turn of the century, McDonald's was selling more burgers and products abroad than in the United States. It had 26,462 restaurants in 119 countries (12,624 in the United States; 5,011 in Europe; 5,704 in Asia; and 1,323 in Latin America).

Critics viewed the popularity of McDonald's outlets as another example of "American economic and cultural imperialism." The more open and successful a country was, the more McDonald's it had. The successful formula, which included an agreement with Disney to use characters like Mickey Mouse, emphasized commitment to the local scene. This involved support for local charities and efforts to design food items for local tastes. Thus, in Japan, McDonald's stressed its Teriyaki McBurger; in Finland the McRye; in Switzerland the Vegi Mac; and in Chile the McNifica. It is arguable that the spread of McDonald's fast-food was a proxy for the impact of America's pop culture.[19]

Another successful service export involved Mary Kay Ash and direct sales of cosmetics. A tireless motivator, she worked to persuade women like herself, who had been passed over in the corporate hierarchy, to sell beauty products. By 1979, Mary Kay's company boasted over $100 million in sales, with consultants and directors numbering 50,000. Driving her trademark pink Cadillacs and combining a faith in God and family with women entrepreneurship, she kept her company in the top ranks in sales, using her gifts as "one of the world's great motivators." By the early 1990s, Mary Kay had moved upscale to compete against the likes of international cosmetic monolith Estee Lauder. And, she pushed into overseas markets, doing $10 million in sales in Russia just after the Cold War ended and pursuing the China market with considerable success through a combination of retail outlets and direct selling. By the twenty-first century, some 600,000 direct sales consultants demonstrated Mary Kay products in the United States and thirty-five other countries, and the privately held firm grossed about $2 billion in sales.[20]

If Disney and McDonald's appealed to the world's youth and Mary Kay to women, VISA's plastic card simplified travel and consumption for everyone. VISA, which boasted a 57 percent world market share in 2001, reflected the dreams of Dee Hock, a former farmhand and loan officer at a Seattle bank. He envisaged a "worldwide consumer payment system," owned by its bank members. In 1968, he led a revolt of licensees against the Bank of America and helped establish a global brand – VISA – and a full-service payments network owned by its 21,000 member financial institutions in the United States and overseas. It was to be "the first truly transnational corporation." A service organization that initially consisted of computer centers and thousands of leased telephone lines, VISA began with 30 million cards in 1970. The cards could be used domestically, and transactions usually needed five minutes to gain authorization. Thirty years later, VISA had one billion cards, which could be used in over 130 countries, and generated annual transactions of $2.1 trillion. It took less than five seconds on average to approve a transaction anywhere in the world.[21]

As the VISA example suggests, U.S. financial services expanded rapidly in the last quarter of the twentieth century. They benefited from a deregulated environment at home, innovation in data processing and communications, and growing internationalization of markets. Financial deregulation began in 1974, when major industrial nations abandoned fixed exchange rates, and Canada, Germany, the Netherlands, Switzerland and the United States removed capital controls. In 1979, Britain and Japan also permitted capital convertibility. The Carter administration and Congress moved forward on domestic financial deregulation, phasing out interest rate ceilings in 1979. Some of the most dramatic developments involved technology. The cost of a three-minute phone call between London and New York dropped nearly 90 percent between 1970 and 1990. The price of computers fell sharply as well, as did the costs of compiling, storing, and analyzing financial data and conducting transactions. The result was a phenomenal expansion in private capital flows among industrial nations and between the industrial and developing world. Cross-border transactions in bonds and equities rose from 9 percent of GDP in 1980 to 89 percent in 1990, and reached 164 percent of American GDP in 1996. The value of U.S. holdings of foreign securities (equities and debt) rose rapidly from $89 billion in 1984 to $314 billion in 1989, and $2,389 billion in 2000. But foreign holdings of U.S. securities also climbed rapidly: $268 billion in 1984, $847 billion in 1989, and $3,650 billion in 2000. Increasingly, U.S. private capital dominated the flow of financial resources to developing countries. In 1980, net flows to the Third World aggregated $13.9 billion ($8.2 billion – 60 percent – from official sources; $4.3 billion on private market terms; $1.3 billion from private voluntary agencies). By 1994, over 78 percent came from the private market, and another 4 percent came from voluntary agencies.[22]

Rising flows of goods, services, and money were not the only factors to benefit from the globalization of improved communications and transportation. The numbers of people crossing borders expanded rapidly as well. Trade association data show that 16.3 million people enplaned on scheduled international flights at domestic airports in 1975, 24.9 million in 1985, and 48.8 million in 1995. In 2000, the figure was 55.5 million – a 240 percent increase over 25 years. (See Table A.11.) Immigration soared, transforming cities and states with foreign cultures, and this despite the tightening of federal law in 1986 to weed out undocumented aliens. Between the mid 1970s and 1990, a half million people a year entered the United States. In 1989, nearly one million people came in, more than any year since the first decade of the American Century. The festive relighting of the Statue of Liberty's torch on July 4, 1986 symbolized Reagan's view that America was a haven of freedom for persecuted refugees. Many others entered to seek better economic opportunities. The Latino population grew 50 percent during the 1980s, and the number of Asian-Americans doubled with the arrival of 3.5 million Filipinos, Vietnamese, Chinese, and Koreans. By 1991, Latinos represented one-fourth of California's population, part of a vast global migration process that changed the U.S. economy and culture.[23]

More and more foreign students came to the United States to learn English and earn graduate degrees. More came from Asia – especially China, India, Japan South Korea, and Taiwan. But far fewer U.S. college students went abroad. In 1985–6, there were only 48,483 studying abroad compared with 343,777 foreign students in the United States. A decade later, the ratio was only slightly more balanced – with 89,242 U.S. students abroad and 453,787 foreign students in the United States. Globalization in education came to America. (See Table A.12.)

Many other ordinary people became "virtual" travelers in the 1990s, visiting distant locations via the Internet, sending e-mail, networking with overseas associates, and transmitting and receiving pictures. In 1997, fewer than 40 million people worldwide were connected, but a year later the number had doubled to more than 100 million. Ironically, the network that liberated people and facilitated cheap global communications grew from U.S. Defense Department research during the 1960s. Fearful of a Soviet strike knocking out a centralized communications system, the Pentagon wanted a "distributed" network. Until the development of the personal computer, the Internet was a tool of the academic elite, but in the 1980s, that changed. Thanks to Apple Computer, IBM, and Bill Gates, ordinary people began using computers. In 1975, when Gates and his friend Paul Allen formed Microsoft, their slogan was "A personal computer on every desk and in every home." Seven years later, *Time Magazine* picked the computer as the "Man of the Year," and everyone wanted one.[24]

Secretary of State George Schultz, a former economist and business school administrator, was one of the first in diplomacy to grasp the importance of the computer and the information revolution. He had monitored the 1982 crisis in Lebanon by satellite telephone and was good friends with Walter B. Wriston, who was using computer technology to convert

Citicorp into a global banking powerhouse. Schultz proclaimed in 1986 that the "industrial age is now ending," supplanted by the Information Age. Power would be determined by who controlled information, rather than by who controlled gold or production. The Soviets faced the choice of embracing new information sources, and thus undermining communist authority, or letting technology pass by, thereby weakening their economy and military.[25] Indeed, it was the information revolution of the 1980s – global networks of news and marketing driven by computer technology that moved power from centralized government bureaucracies and toward individuals and activist groups – that ultimately nailed the coffin shut on communism.

End of the Cold War

One of the ironies of recent history is that Ronald Reagan, the arch anticommunist, and Mikhail Gorbachev, a committed communist, set in motion policies and events that led to the Cold War's end. Both leaders shared a bond of revolutionary fervor. Under *perestroika*, Gorbachev began restructuring the economy toward deregulation and away from heavy-handed central planning and the draining effect of defense sector spending that had permitted the West to surge ahead in production and technology. *Perestroika* had an ambiguous effect, but cultural life and the economy showed signs of opening. In essence, Gorbachev's top-down reforms stimulated bottom-up democratic revolution that led to the demise of the Soviet system itself.[26]

Gorbachev's policy of *glasnost* turned his nation and its empire toward democracy and outwardness. Between 1989 and 1991, the Soviet empire disintegrated as he encouraged the Eastern European satellites to hold free elections. Gorbachev withdrew military forces, giving the green light to democratic mass rebellion. The Berlin Wall fell in November 1989. Revolution then came to the revolutionary leader itself; Moscow granted independence to several republics. In 1991, Gorbachev himself faced rebellion from hardline communists, who were out of touch with the emerging process of globalization. Using new technology of fax machines to communicate and gain support abroad, his defenders resisted the putsch. An outraged Soviet public switched off state-run television and turned to Western broadcasting. Thirty percent listened to Radio Liberty; 18 percent, to the BBC; and 15 percent, to the Voice of America. Cable News Network (CNN), broadcasting in English, telecast pictures of thousands of people gathering around the Russian White House where Gorbachev's successor,

8. President Ronald Reagan and President-Elect George H. W. Bush meet with Soviet General-Secretary Gorbachev on Governor's Island, New York, December 7, 1988. (Ronald Reagan Presidential Library)

Boris Yeltsin, had barricaded himself (fed by truckloads of McDonald's hamburgers).[27] Gorbachev, under house arrest at his dacha in the Crimea, even listened to the BBC and other Western radio stations to find out what was happening. Soviet power disappeared literally in months. The Cold War ended in 1991.[28]

While content about winning the Cold War, President George H. Bush understood that Gorbachev faced tremendous problems. The fall of the Berlin Wall, the subsequent unification of the two Germanies, and the breakup of the Soviet Union could not hide deep economic troubles. Rubles became worthless and were replaced by vodka. Soviet oil exports dried up because of decrepit wells and falling world prices. Bush extended about $4 billion in credit, but it was not enough. One bright light was the inflow of private investment. Pepsico (with its subsidiaries of Pepsi, Frito Lay, and Pizza Hut) invested over $3 billion in Russia, while General Motors spent $1 billion, and Colgate readied plans for a toothpaste factory. McDonald's raised its presence, even opening a restaurant in Red Square in which Gorbachev dined. But Russia was failing; Boris Yeltsin's reforms had sunk one-third of the Russian people below the poverty line.

A Western airlift of food and medicine in the winter of 1991–2 rescued them from starvation.[29]

The collapse of communism and the nearly half century of superpower tension released the ideological, if not the economic, forces of modern-day globalization. In a celebrated article in 1989, scholar Francis Fukuyama proclaimed the "end of history." He meant that the centuries-long era of world conflict had given way to the universal values of liberal democracy once and for all. There would be brushfire wars in spots, but in general, a one-world euphoria of harmony had evolved, with the United States as its leader.[30] While declinism had been fashionable in the late 1980s, due to American economic troubles, the end of the Cold War ushered in a period of American triumphalism within government circles. To be sure, U.S. diplomacy had succeeded against the arch-enemy, but theorists furthered that capitalist democracy had won because of its free-market dogma. The linkage of democracy to economic liberalism and development did not always hold (as, for example, aid to Iraq showed), but it provided a powerful message that the deregulatory, antistatist principles of globalization provided the way to democracy.[31]

Indeed, after Bush dealt with the residue of the Cold War, focused on containing Saddam Hussein in the Persian Gulf, and wrestled with a recession, the Clinton administration veered from the history of the post–World War II era and eagerly adopted the universalist, integrative, and democratic posture of globalization. Economics replaced security in the U.S. policy agenda; globalization became the buzzword of the age. Setting out the administration's strategy in 1993, National Security Council Advisor Anthony Lake tied free markets to democracy: "On one side is protectionism and limited foreign engagement; on the other is active American engagement abroad on behalf of democracy and expanded trade." Sandy Berger, his successor and a trade lawyer, took up this mantra in Clinton's second term. But the president needed no prompting on this score. After the Mexican peso crisis, he placed economic diplomacy at the center of foreign policy. Clinton voiced support for "the consolidation of market democracy" throughout the world, an ideology that put him in stride with global business but at odds with many in his own party who were tied to the traditional big-government, worker-protection liberalism of the past.[32]

Clinton applied his market doctrine to Russia. From its inception in late 1991, Yeltsin's government aimed to reform Russia through free-market capitalism, ridding the new nation of hyperinflation, shortages, and monetary disequilibrium. Bush and Clinton aided the cause by pushing Western aid packages (including over $60 billion in loans from 1992 to 1999) and backed Harvard University economist Jeffrey Sachs's advice to "shock" the former Soviet economy into productivity by strict and oftentimes brutal market reforms. Sachs had built a reputation advising Latin American nations like Bolivia how to reduce inflation and Eastern European countries how to restructure and privatize. He instructed Poland, Yugoslavia, Slovenia, Mongolia, and Russia. In the last situation, Sachs and his Harvard colleagues had their work cut out for them because almost all Soviet industrial enterprise involved state monopolies. They employed 90 percent of workers. Privatizing these entities would force many out on to the street.[33]

Rarely has an academic economist had such a direct effect on actual events. In Russia, Sachs's influence proved disastrous. Massive privatization caused high unemployment, falling production (down one-fifth), and rampant inflation. A Russian mafia ran a lucrative black market and operated in the legal economy as well, even colluding with the old state bureaucracy. When ultranationalists gained ground in 1993 elections by blaming an imagined Jewish international banking conspiracy for humiliating this once-superpower and, the next year, when Russia tried to subdue the breakaway republic of Chechnya, Clinton backed out of plans to integrate Russia into NATO. Crony capitalism corrupted Russia and ruined the banking system. Market processes – the structural basis of globalization – ran aground. The nation simply lacked the preconditions for successful application of Western economic prescriptions. After years of communism, Russia offered few legal protections for private property, lacked an independent judiciary, and suffered from intrusive state intervention.[34]

Elsewhere, communism did not disappear. In China, a growing dissident movement of reformers and students protested against the communist leadership in 1989, provoking the old guard to declare martial law in June and then fire on demonstrators in Tiananmen Square, killing 3,000. Cable television showed the images to an outraged world, including President Bush. Still, hopeful that economic openness and development would encourage democracy, Bush listened to the advice of multinational business and chose to renew most-favored-nation trade status with the People's Republic of China in 1990. In return, China released dissidents. American loans, as well as scientific and technological aid, then flowed to China. During the 1992 presidential campaign, MFN became increasingly partisan, as Democratic candidate Clinton singled out China as a violator of human rights. As president, he first conditioned MFN renewal on

Chinese observation of human rights, but he, too, bowed to the strategic and economic importance of China. Global business, as well as realpolitik, required this reversal. Emphasizing stability in Asia and the need to maintain friendly relations with the next generation of Chinese leaders, Clinton sought engagement with China, claiming that the world's fastest-growing economy also bought over $8 billion of U.S. exports, which supported over 150,000 American jobs.[35]

Middle Eastern Testing Ground

For the process of globalization, a key outcome stood out from the Persian Gulf War, in which UN forces routed Iraqi Saddam Hussein from Kuwait in 1991. Technology triumphed. Pinpoint military technology won the day, and CNN came of age. Sequestered behind the lines in Saudi Arabia, reporters depended on CNN reports for war information. Although the technology itself was not new, its wartime uses were. For the first time, satellite news coverage by the media gave current intelligence to both the United Nations and the Iraqis. Saddam watched his SCUD missiles land in Israel and adjusted targeting accordingly, while the allied forces retargeted their launchers by viewing television. Telephone, photography, computer, facsimile machines, and e-mail combined to bring the war instantly to warriors and viewers alike. This was a revolution in information and communication, as "telediplomacy" and "real-time war" forever changed the roles of governments, militaries, the public, and the media. Beginning with the Gulf War, the media picked up "breaking news of daily events," thus making the world much smaller and more accessible.[36]

Communications tycoon Ted Turner, a flamboyant and outspoken entrepreneur, was the driving force behind this revolution. A former racing sailor and advertiser, and now owner of professional baseball and basketball teams as well as a television station in Atlanta, he had a vision for global news that carried CNN along even when it was a cash drain on his business as late as the mid 1980s. In the 1970s, he turned a small UHF channel into a "Superstation" by, for one, seizing the opportunity presented by satellite technology. He then turned to cable, and the idea of an all-news station. By 1989, ten years after the network was born, CNN accounted for three-quarters of Turner Broadcasting's total profits. Household viewership rocketed from 1.8 million to 58 million in America alone; around the world, satellites fed 140 nations. The CNN *World Report* offered two hours of unedited, uncensored, and oftentimes mundane news from many obscure or ignored nations, through a truly international (rather than national or regional) approach. Local stations could pick up world news, and local citizens could speak directly to the world. Turner hoped that communications would become less Westernized and more global.[37]

CNN enjoyed "international credibility that many diplomats lacked," wrote two students of Turner. World leaders, from Gorbachev and Castro to even the isolationist North Korean Kim Il Sung, were viewers; King Fahd of Saudi Arabia was said to be a junkie, watching breaking news through the night. George Bush later confessed he got more information from CNN than from the CIA. Both Kim and Saddam, enemies of the United States, allowed CNN to cover their countries. Fascinated viewers watched the Chinese government shut down the live feed from Tiananmen Square in 1989; audiences saw government oppression for the first time as tense negotiations between China and CNN continued right up to the moment the communists pulled the plug. "Karl Marx, meet Marshall McLuhan," exclaimed *Newsweek*.

CNN correspondents had power: they were sources of information, and disinformation. A reporter mistakenly announced Gorbachev's resignation in 1989, sending international currency markets into a tailspin. That year was the first of the uplink era. When Bush met Gorbachev off the coast of Malta in December, both let CNN broadcast so they could see how they looked live, and thus initiated a "new age of video self-consciousness, of instant feedback." A day later, when American troops invaded Panama, Moscow did not protest to the U.S. embassy but went directly to CNN's Moscow bureau with a denouncement. "Who needs striped pants and diplomatic pouches," asked *The Wall Street Journal*, when leaders could call CNN? Turner had hoped that his network would be "a positive force in the world, to tie the world together." By the mid 1990s, CNN drew over 75 million viewers. Turner was poised for more globalism. Aided by revenues from CNN, he offered a gift of $1 billion to the United Nations. "I'm an internationalist first and a nationalist second," he noted. CNN was a global network, oftentimes bypassing the state and honing in on person-to-person contacts.[38]

Globalization of television news became the norm, as satellites, video services, regional news exchanges, and international networks such as CNN and the British Sky News connected the world television news system. Nearly a century before, E. H. Harriman had dreamed of a global transportation network; now television truly interconnected across the planet. CNN was pirated by government agencies and private distributors worldwide. Britain's Visnews and Worldwide Television News (WTN) supplied news throughout the world, even to the major U.S. networks. Regional news exchanges, namely the European Broadcasting Union's Eurovision News Exchange, shared national news at the local level. Such services also existed in the former Soviet bloc's Intervision and in Asia through Asiavision. Complex arrangements through national television networks and wire services distributed the news. This massive, interdependent system let viewers receive live images from any point in the world. (There were embarrassing real-life news flashes, too, as when Japanese television inadvertently taped and replayed globally an ill President Bush vomiting on Prime Minister Kiichi Miyazawa in January 1992).[39]

Dynamism in Europe and Asia

In the early 1990s, Bush's proclamation of a New World Order implied a partnership with the European Union, Japan, Arab friends, and others to defend U.S. interests and uphold the rule of law.[40] Furthermore, the dismantling of the Soviet empire and of many of its constituent parts (the Czech Republic, Slovakia, Yugoslavia) compelled Europeans – in both East and West – to formulate ways of reintegrating the "countries in transition" of Eastern Europe into the world economy. In 1993, the European Union pursued these enlargement plans but placed conditions that the East found too discriminatory. American and IMF aid also came with strings attached, in the form of controls and demands for fiscal reform that Eastern Europeans looked on as violations of their sovereignty. Still, the former East bloc became a dynamic area, as private capital stepped in and the region itself evolved increasingly along the model of the European Union.

In 1991, Hungary, Poland, and the Czech and Slovak Federal Republic signed an accord to promote market-based economic cooperation through the free movement of capital and labor. This group established the Central European Free Trade Area (CEFTA) in 1992 with a market of 64 million people, and in 1995, CEFTA decided to admit new members from Eastern Europe who were also members of the World Trade Organization (WTO) and had an association with the European Union. Enjoying the tariff-free zone for industrial goods, Slovenia, Romania, and Bulgaria joined thereafter, and the Baltic states were considering entry. The Central and Eastern European nations were oriented toward the West and the globalization process. They joined the IMF and the World Bank, and eight prepared to enter the European Union (EU) in 2004.

In addition, under the processes of globalization, foreign direct investment skyrocketed to these countries in transition, especially after the

Western recession in 1992. Hungary, the Czech Republic, Poland, and Russia attracted the lion's share. Multinational corporations focused on oil and gas, food processing, machinery, and trade and catering, although they also clashed with nations worried about outside competition. Thus, Volkswagen canceled its investment package with its Czech subsidiary, Skoda, in 1993. The process for enlarging the EU meandered slowly. Sticking points, especially in agricultural protection and emigration issues, bogged down negotiations.[41] Still, globalized market forces and free trade areas promised to integrate the former Soviet empire into the world economy.

Economic revolution was well under way in Western Europe. The EU's $6 trillion gross national product was larger than America's $5.2 trillion, but it planned more than just increasing joint productive capacity of its fifteen members in 1994 (and potentially more, with the accession of Turkey and former Soviet satellites). A customs union had existed since 1968, but this did not mean a single market without borders. During the energy crisis, European growth slowed, inflation soared, and unemployment climbed sharply. During the early 1980s, it appeared that "Eurosclerosis" would thwart further market integration. But with the Single European Act of 1986, the European Union restarted its motor. Europe proposed to harmonize product standards; eliminate all internal trade barriers, including borders; and enhance the opportunities for labor mobility, much like the United States. Under the Maastricht Treaty of 1991 (which renamed the European Economic Community the European Union), these nations agreed to adopt a common currency, the Euro, by 1999, and proceed toward full monetary unification. With only 6.4 percent of the world's population in the mid 1990s, this economic superpower accounted for over one-third of global production and 42 percent of both world imports and exports. Combined national gross domestic products made the European Union the second largest economic bloc in the world, behind NAFTA. Of the world's top one thousand companies, nearly one-quarter were located in the EU (while America had 345 and Japan 310).

The EU's impact on the United States was considerable. America ran trade deficits with the European Union every year since 1983, while it remained a key export destination not only for U.S. commodities but for services like cable television. Two-fifths of U.S. overseas investment, and one-quarter of all U.S. exports, went to the European Union. Imports from these nations amounted to one-fifth of the American total. Foreign direct investment made the United States and the EU interdependent – roughly 55 percent of all foreign direct investment (FDI) in

America, mostly in manufacturing, wholesale trade, and petroleum, was European ($220 billion in 1993), and 40 percent in Europe came from the United States's investments mainly in manufacturing and finance and insurance. Three million people were employed in America by European-owned companies or subsidiaries. Unlike the oftentimes rancorous trade climate, the atmosphere in investment was benign.[42]

One investment, however, turned out to be much more difficult than anticipated. The Disney Company seemed to have a no-lose plan for a theme park in Western Europe, outside of Paris. To excite regional financiers, Disney transported 200 European bankers and their spouses to Orlando in 1989 to see the lucrative Disney marvel for themselves. The company sold its stock offering virtually overnight, as it did for a subsequent bond offering. Communist Party protesters had demonstrated against the French government granting $6 billion in concessions to get the park, but Wall Street was happy, as projections for profits topped $766 million from management fees and royalties, in addition to its dividend payouts, by the new millennium. That was too optimistic; construction costs for the park and the five hotels serving it soon rose above initial estimates. When completed in 1992, Disney's novel idea of nationalizing the attractions (Pinnocchio was narrated in Italian; Snow White in German) failed to lure enough customers. Admission and accommodations were too expensive, especially since the region was suffering through a recession. At one point, local farmers blocked the entrance on opening day, getting the most out of their protests of the government's agricultural policies. Attendance flagged.

Disney hired the esteemed banking house Lazard Freres to restructure part of its $4 billion debt, with a healthy investment offering of $1 billion from European banks. The bankers waived rights to a management fee between 1992 and 1998 and slashed those fees from 6 percent to 1 percent. In return, Disney had to put up over a half million dollars for its 49 percent share of the offering. The prince of Saudi Arabia, a Disney fanatic, also paid $247 million – or one-quarter of the offering – for Disney shares from the American company and the European bankers. In 1995, the park made a small profit, cutting its interest costs by two-thirds. CEO Michael Eisner brought in a Frenchman to run the park and attendance rose by 21 percent. Officials even began looking at new sites near the former communist nations. In 1996, the Walt Disney Company's revenues jumped by 54 percent from the previous year to $18.7 billion. Operating income was up by over one-third, and its net income, of $1.5 billion, had risen by 11 percent. The next year, revenues climbed above $20 billion, and by 1999, it attracted 12.5 million visitors. "Disney touches virtually every human being in America for profit," wrote one analyst, and increasingly did so throughout Western Europe, Asia, and Latin America as well. Grabbing youth first, parents followed. Disney amusement parks, numbering six by the late 1990s, attracted over one billion visitors. The company also branched out into feature films, restaurants, television stations, and even a record label.[43]

Regardless, Eisner and his operatives had gotten a lesson in cultural globalization. Unlike the Tokyo enterprise, Disney's European operation did not, at first, account for local traditions and conditions. In this sense, it pushed a global vision too hard. Intellectuals derided Disneyland as a "cultural Chernobyl." Employees disliked the sanitized dress code and visitors resented the policy of not serving wine or beer (which lost Disney $11 million a year). Some were irritated that Disney equated utopia with America, infusing the park with a U.S. ideology rather than a globalized approach to culture. After the press blasted the company for insensitivity to European consuming habits (even French Premier Jacques Chirac joked with Eisner that a no-alcohol policy smacked of "barbaric American puritanism"), Disney succumbed and served alcoholic beverages. Having been told that Europeans preferred lunch over breakfast, the company lacked adequate space when huge crowds sought out morning meals, and ordered bacon and eggs rather than the plentiful croissants and coffee. Disney solved the problem by sending prepackaged breakfasts to hotel rooms. Cultural critics called Disneyland Paris a threat to French culture; one leftist journal called it "Mousewitz," but the park endured.[44]

In addition to the EU, one of the most dynamic areas in the world economy was the Asian side of the Pacific Rim. Among these, the four "Asian Tigers" – South Korea, Taiwan, Hong Kong, and Singapore – stood out. By the early 1990s, Japan and the nations of Northeast Asia, referred to as newly industrializing countries (NICs), accounted for just under 30 percent of global gross national production; thirty years before, they combined for a paltry 4 percent.[45] The Four Tigers contributed the most to this impressive figure by high savings rates and low population growth rates as well as efficient use of capital. They also drew on substantial foreign direct investment (in the cases of South Korea and Taiwan, this came initially in the form of U.S. military assistance and economic aid) and borrowing to supplement domestic savings, to relax foreign exchange constraints (both of which promoted industrialization), and to integrate their economies into the world economy. Half of the investment came from America and Japan, with U.S. investors focused in the financial and banking sectors and in holding wholly-owned subsidiaries to maintain proprietary rights to advanced technology.

Among the Four Tigers, export-led growth was critical to the economic development miracle. Manufactured goods dominated their exports. From initial exports of textiles and shoes, they moved up the value ladder, selling more and more sophisticated products like consumer electronics and industrial machinery. By the mid 1980s, after just two decades of "take-off," they had tripled their savings rate and increased income per capita by 7 percent annually. Hong Kong and Singapore, the two city-states, enjoyed per capita incomes close to Western European levels. South Korea and Taiwan, with larger populations, also joined the ranks of middle-income nations. Excepts for short periods, they experienced rapid growth, and managed to reduce poverty and inequality steadily. By the mid 1980s, when they burst on the international economic scene, the Four Tigers looked much more like industrial market economies than developing ones.[46]

Japan: Mighty to Mortal

The Four Tigers were part of an Asian economic network that centered on Japan. During the 1980s, the Japanese seemed invincible, defying U.S. market capitalist principles with high-growth government-business partnerships. American automakers continued to complain about unfair trade competition, the transplant strategy (which increased Japanese vehicle sales to nearly 2 million by 1995), and their inability to penetrate Japan's market (even though the Big Three made little effort to adapt cars to Japanese tastes).[47] Japan also entered the emerging semiconductor business, which U.S. producers dominated until Japanese firms began dumping on the open U.S. market. The American market share dropped to a paltry 15 percent by 1988. The U.S. government responded by slapping $300 million in trade sanctions on an array of consumer electronic products, power tools, and computers in 1987 as a warning. But the Pentagon saved the day, mimicking Japan by spending $200 million a year between 1987 and 1992 on Sematech, a research and development consortium that helped regain the U.S. edge. North American chip makers brought new products to market and recovered much of their lost market share. Domestic sales rose to $2.8 billion in 1991, up from $1.2 billion in 1987.[48]

The semiconductor issue pointed to the problem Americans had long had with closed Japanese markets. In telecommunications services and equipment, retailing, construction, and banking, Japan had long limited foreign market access. But the United States was unwilling to push too hard. It needed Japanese military bases, and it relied on Japanese savings to finance the swelling U.S. budget deficit. Thus, upon entering office in 1989, George Bush removed Japan from the target list of unfair trading nations after Tokyo promised to open up its wood products, satellites, and computer market. In 1991, the Americans persuaded Japan to import more beef, oranges, and supercomputers by removing quotas, only to have them replaced by Japanese tariffs. Seven years of talks yielded a commitment to purchase more U.S. supercomputers, but by that time, the Japanese had learned how to make them and soon controlled 95 percent of the public sector market in Japan. Sometimes appeasement was comical. In 1988, Japanese officials persuaded American exporters that Japanese intestines could not digest U.S. beef and pizza. A number of U.S. businesses succeeded in Japan, thus weakening complaints of Japanese unfairness. By 1990, McDonald's had 40 percent of the Japanese hamburger market, IBM had sales of $9.1 billion in Japan, Apple Computer enjoyed growth there, and firms ranging from beverages and movies to electronics and chemicals were gaining market share. Nonetheless, foreign business complained that the Japanese system was rigged to limit foreign investment opportunities. In 1989, for instance, U.S. majority-owned foreign affiliates produced only 0.5 percent of Japan's GDP, compared to 3 percent in Germany, 6.2 percent in the United Kingdom, and 12.4 percent in Ireland.[49]

Meanwhile, Japan, buoyed by its exports, a strong stock market, and a real estate boom, was on an overseas shopping spree, investing in U.S. real estate and building green-field production facilities. Among the prizes were the Westin Hotels in 1987 and Rockefeller Center in 1989, in addition to Sony's purchase of Columbia Pictures (Sony had risen to power after having bought U.S. transistor technology for a scant $25,000). Americans looked at this as the equivalent of "selling the World Series or mom." The Japanese snapped up condominiums, houses, and ranches when the American real estate market weakened; between 1985 and 1990, their real estate purchases totaled $65 billion. During that same period, they bought $170 billion in American securities, at times purchasing upward of 40 percent of treasury bonds at quarterly sales. They dominated art auctions, even buying parts of auction houses themselves, and swept up ski areas and race horses.[50]

Even with the collapse of the Tokyo stock market in 1990, the profits from the trade and business with the United States did not cease. To be sure, purchases stalled, but Japan's pension fund was still tied up in American securities. The next year, Matsushita Electrical Industrial Company paid $6.6 billion for MCA – the entertainment conglomerate – the biggest Japanese buyout ever. The sale included exclusive commercial rights in Yosemite National Park, which so galled Americans that the company eventually sold them to a charity in order to better its image. In the midst of niggling over financing the Gulf War in 1991, Japan bought the premier Pebble Beach Golf Course in Monterey, California, for $1 billion. America was not just selling itself cheap, many thought, but undermining its culture and history.

In 1992 presidential candidate Paul Tsongas said, "the Cold War was over" and Japan won.[51] Economist Pat Choate condemned U.S. trade officials who walked out the revolving door of government to become lobbyists for Japanese corporations. Former Commerce Department official Clyde Prestowitz warned of experienced Japanese negotiators duping their amateur American counterparts who were persuaded to buy the same horse several times in negotiations. These conflicts even entered the fiction best-seller charts with Michael Crichton's *Rising Sun* of 1992, a book and movie that showed Americans helpless in the face of the Japanese economic juggernaut.[52]

As it turned out, this mighty system had an Achilles heel: an inflated stock market and real estate valuations. That bubble broke in 1990. By 1993, the Nikkei stock market stood at 56 percent of its highest level, the residential real estate market was halved, production dropped, and bankruptcies tripled. The estimated losses stood at roughly $7 trillion in assets. What looked like strengths in Japan's long, profitable drive to recover from World War II – a high savings rate, lifetime employment, an industrial system that relied on government guidance, bank loans, and a closed network of suppliers – proved unsuited to an era of deregulation and global competition. The strong yen, slumping export sales, and sluggish domestic demand during the 1990s forced even mighty Toyota and Nissan to close plants at home. Workers, long protected with lifetime employment, were laid off. An aging population, many of whom had purchased homes before prices collapsed, labored under a mountain of debt and refused to splurge on consumer goods. Many banks limped along with nonperforming loans. One government after another sought to prime the pump with deficit spending on public works. As a result, Japan became the most heavily indebted country in the world. For all the Japanese skills at lobbying in Washington and successful government-business cooperation, the Japanese system could not come to grips with catastrophic financial failure and the need for liquidating bad debts.[53]

The Era of Trade Integration

As dramatic improvements in communications and transportation accelerated globalization during the 1980s, business leaders and government officials looked to policy to sustain this growth. They wanted to deregulate and integrate national markets. One especially productive approach during the 1980s involved regional economic cooperation and integration. In Asia, there were several efforts to promote regional economic cooperation, including Asia-Pacific Economic Cooperation (APEC), which included America. Perhaps the most significant was ASEAN, the Association of Southeast Asian Nations, which began inauspiciously in 1967. By the early 1990s, this group expanded to ten low- to middle-income countries in the region with 500 million people. ASEAN advanced a long-term agenda of dismantling economic barriers and promoting regional free trade. Regional free trade also flourished in the Americas. In the mid 1980s, Brazil and Argentina set aside longtime rivalries and established Mercosur, an economic bloc that aspired to become a common market like the European community, with a uniform external tariff, internal free trade, and common institutions. It later added Paraguay and Uruguay.

Meanwhile, in 1987, the Reagan administration negotiated a bilateral free-trade agreement with Canada, America's largest trading partner, at a time when GATT multilateral negotiations seemed deadlocked. Canadian leaders sought the dynamism of assured access to a large market and feared that both the United States and Western Europe might turn inward. The agreement went beyond tariffs to include other border barriers, government procurement, and dispute settlement mechanisms. But it did not fix exchange rates, and afterward the Canadian dollar depreciated, exacerbating the U.S. bilateral trade deficit. A few years later, U.S. leaders turned to Mexico, America's third largest trading partner. Mexico faced difficult economic circumstances in the late 1980s. Heavily in debt after the collapse of oil prices, it had widespread corruption, a rapidly growing population (85 million in 1990), a stagnant economy, and inadequate job opportunities. Millions of Mexican workers flocked illegally to the United States to take low-skilled jobs and to remit earnings to support relatives remaining in Mexico. President Carlos Salinas, a PhD political economist from Harvard, sought to liberalize trade and attract foreign investment to increase exports to high-income markets in the Americas and Europe. With the Cold War winding down and market forces gaining ground, in June 1990, Salinas proposed to President Bush a free-trade agreement with the United States. His action represented a dramatic move to abandon seventy years of Mexican nationalism in order to jump-start the lagging economy.

Bush and Canadian Prime Minister Brian Mulroney leaped at the suggestion and initiated negotiations for a sweeping accord that covered trade in goods, services, investments, and dispute settlement. But the North American Free Trade Agreement (NAFTA) was controversial with domestic constituencies. Organized labor feared that low-skilled manufacturing jobs in the United States and Canada would migrate to Mexico, a process that presidential candidate Ross Perot vividly described as a "great sucking sound." Environmentalists worried that NAFTA would enable dirty industries to escape regulation by shifting operations to Mexico, where enforcement was lax. Yet NAFTA's supporters, generally large business corporations and free-trade enthusiasts, predicted that 170,000 new jobs would be created. American companies would find new export opportunities in Mexico as tariffs fell and consumer incomes rose. Illegal immigration would abate as the Mexican economy generated faster growth. NAFTA, the proponents said, would create opportunities for automobile assembly and parts industries, oil equipment and services, transportation and telecommunications, U.S. banks and insurance companies, and highly mechanized U.S. producers of beef and wheat.[54]

Geopolitics, foreign policy, and investment strategies also shaped the NAFTA debate. During the 1980 presidential campaign, candidates Jerry Brown, John Connally, and Ronald Reagan had all advanced continental visions, distinct from the Carter administration's concern with trilateralism – Europe, Japan, and America. As president, Reagan revived the continental vision in 1983, calling for a "united hemisphere" stretching from the tip of Tierra del Fuego to Alaska. But hemispheric problems became a major concern. As more illegal immigrants crossed the border to find work in the United States, Washington worried about political instability and economic collapse in Mexico compounding the migration problem and producing chaos along the border. American business, while eager to use inexpensive labor, worried about the permanence of Mexico's liberalization program. For business, the core of the so-called free-trade accord was investment. As NAFTA ally William Orme put it: "NAFTA was more an investment agreement than a trade agreement. It was designed to convince investors that Mexico was a safe place to do business." Multinational business wanted to lock in, by treaty, an open investment environment free from restrictions that distorted trade and investment flows. American investors sought national treatment so that they would be treated as favorably as Mexican investors, and they wanted legal protections against restrictions on the transfer of funds and arbitrary nationalization and expropriation. The Bush administration negotiated to address those concerns.[55]

NAFTA remained controversial during the 1992 presidential election. Independent Ross Perot and conservative Pat Buchanan drained votes from Bush with claims that NAFTA would accelerate the outflow of jobs and compromise American sovereignty. The victor, Democrat Bill Clinton, supported the concept of NAFTA but chose to make a few minor side agreements after taking office to appeal to labor and environmental groups. The latter saw Clinton's modifications as fig leafs or as ineffective Band-Aids. To persuade a reluctant Congress – where Democrats enjoyed a thin majority – business, the Mexican government, and the Clinton administration waged an aggressive lobbying campaign. According to one estimate, Mexico spent $6.9 million on Washington lobbyists, and the administration "proceeded to engage in the most aggressive vote-buying operation in recent memory." USA-NAFTA, the lobbying front for the prestigious Business Roundtable, launched a $10 million advertising blitz, featuring former Chrysler executive Lee Iacocca. Clinton even agreed to go duck hunting with an Oklahoma congressman who served on the board of the National Rifle Association.[56]

Congress approved the agreement in November 1994 after Clinton's team made a series of individual deals, relating to sugar, tomatoes, sweet peppers, peanuts, plutonium, broomcorns, and the extradition of a Mexican citizen accused of raping the niece of a congressman's secretary. In victory, Clinton proclaimed that "America has chosen to compete, not retreat." At a signing ceremony, he asserted that NAFTA will "create 200,000 jobs in this country by 1995 alone."[57]

Circumstances soon undermined some of the more extravagant claims. An Indian peasant rebellion, launched on New Year's Day 1994 in the southern state of Chiapas, convulsed Mexico and raised foreign concerns about Mexico's stability. Investors lost confidence in the economy and the overvalued peso, as Salinas turned over the presidency to his hand-picked successor Ernesto Zedillo in December 1994. Suddenly, the peso lost 40 percent of its value, and the stock market collapsed. To protect American holders of Mexican bonds, maintain peso convertibility, avoid financial contagion, and protect the NAFTA program, Treasury Secretary, and former Wall Street banker, Robert Rubin jumped in with a $40 billion loan guarantee program. His bailout stunned Congress and Federal Reserve chief Alan Greenspan, who preferred to let overzealous investors reap the consequences of bad investments. In short order, the Clinton administration had rescued a neighbor, salvaged NAFTA, and pulled Wall Street's bonds out of the fire.[58]

NAFTA was not the path to Utopia for ordinary Mexicans. Low-skilled workers looking for jobs could not legally cross the border without work permits. Instead, NAFTA expanded employment in maquiladoras along the U.S. border – 150,000 jobs annually in the period 1995 to 1997 – and many of these workers assembled electronics, appliances, auto parts, and apparel. American manufacturing continued to move plants south to make use of cheap Mexican labor (who earned less than $1.00 per hour). Mexico increasingly became an export platform serving the U.S. market. Despite this growth, studies show that manufacturing wages lost 21 percent of their purchasing power between 1993 and 1999. Mexico remained poor and socially divided between haves and have nots. With a sharp peso depreciation driving up the price of foreign goods, Mexican imports from the United States fell sharply. As a result, the small U.S. trade surplus with Mexico ($5.4 billion in 1992) turned into another swollen trade deficit. The deficit continued to grow, reaching $24.2 billion in 2000. In the same year, the deficit with Canada amounted to $50.4 billion – a combined NAFTA deficit of $74.6 billion. A major reason for the rising deficit was the continuing transfer of high-cost auto assembly and parts production to Mexico and Canada, neighbors with cheap currencies and lower labor costs. In 2000, the United States ran a deficit on motor vehicles and parts with Mexico of $24 billion and with Canada of $19.3 billion. The $43.3 billion sum was 58 percent of the NAFTA merchandise deficit.[59]

Did NAFTA expand U.S. employment, as big business and President Clinton predicted? Opinions on this point differ. Those who argued that NAFTA created export-dependent jobs frequently ignored the impact of NAFTA imports on employment in import-sensitive industries like apparel. According to Robert Scott, an economist with Economic Policy Institute, a think tank affiliated with organized labor, NAFTA cost America thousands of manufacturing positions. He argued that NAFTA eliminated some 766,000 actual and potential jobs for non-college-educated workers in U.S. manufacturing between 1994 and 2000. Interestingly, of these, more were lost to Canada (398,837) than to Mexico (367,193).[60]

Yet NAFTA also had enormous long-term potential. In 2000, NAFTA comprised a huge market of some 407 million consumers with $10 trillion in gross domestic product. Of course, 90 percent of GDP came from the United States, and about three-quarters of the Mexican population (some 75 million) lived outside the market economy. But if NAFTA achieved the long-term objective of raising Mexican incomes, millions of new middle-class consumers would become a powerful stimulus to the entire NAFTA region. European and Japanese investors recognized this long-term potential. Concerned that NAFTA could become a "fortress North America," they sought free-trade deals with Mexico. The European Union negotiated one in 1999, hoping to gain political influence and easier access through Mexico to the North American market. Japan has similar ambitions. Because Mexico cut preferential deals with six Latin American nations, Europe, the United States, and Canada, it became a magnet for Europeans and Asians looking for ways to obtain cheap labor and to access those markets. Korean electronics giant Samsung built a $100 million television parts plant in Tijuana to benefit from NAFTA tariff cuts, as did some seventy major Japanese firms. The lesson was clear: in the age of globalization, world-class competitors had to produce where labor and other factors of production were cheap and to establish supply chains and marketing networks in each of the world's three major economic regions – Japan and East Asia; North America; and the European Union.[61]

Along with regionalism, transnational business backed multilateral government efforts to open markets and construct a new architecture for conducting global business. Business wanted to end government discrimination against imports of goods, services, and capital; to gain national treatment for foreign investors; to protect intellectual property; and to establish a process for resolving disputes in a timely and impartial manner. During the Latin American debt crisis, the International Monetary Fund did its part to promote this agenda. It linked stabilization assistance to the free convertibility of short-term and portfolio investments – and membership in GATT. To have access to funds in world capital markets, governments were expected to play according to internationally accepted rules. The 1997–8 Asian financial crisis exposed the shortcomings of this approach. In developing markets with weak regulatory institutions, the IMF's insistence on open capital markets encouraged destabilizing hot-capital movements, and speculative attacks. Jagdish Bhagwati, a prominent free-trade economist, accused the IMF of succumbing to the Washington-Wall Street consensus – that free capital movements necessarily stimulated growth.[62]

In the trade arena, North American and European business saw a stronger international trade organization as the most promising way to achieve these goals, particularly improved access to foreign markets for trade in goods and services, protection for intellectual property, and a dispute settlement mechanism.[63] The Tokyo Round of GATT, which ended in 1979, had moved the trade-negotiating agenda beyond tariffs to a variety of border encumbrances, such as product standards, government procurement, and customs valuation issues. Many of the accords reached were imperfect, but they laid the foundation for later efforts in GATT. According to Alonzo McDonald, a businessman and Carter administration deputy trade representative, the Tokyo Round agreements on nontariff barriers "were clearly steps in the right direction and helped to lower the risk level of investments, to expand international commercial business."[64]

The protracted Uruguay Round of GATT lasted from 1986 to 1994 and involved more issues and governments (117) than ever before. It established a new international institution, the World Trade Organization. Also, industrial nations agreed to cut tariffs on manufactures by an average of 38 percent. In addition, textile trade, which previously had been handled by an international Multi-Fibre arrangement, was folded into the WTO's jurisdiction, and quotas were rolled back. Multinational corporations in America and Western Europe succeeded in placing services and intellectual property under the jurisdiction of the WTO, and they established a mandatory dispute-settlement mechanism. In essence, the rich and the less-developed nations struck a bargain: the former rolled back farm subsidies and barriers to importation of agricultural products, raw materials, and textiles in exchange for Third World acceptance of dispute settlement, permanent tariff bindings, harmonization of intellectual property protections, and increased access to emerging markets for service providers. The United States foreswore unilateral sanctions under Section 301 against GATT members in return for mandatory WTO dispute resolution, but retained, like other WTO members, the right to initiate antidumping and countervailing duty actions in accordance with international rules. In essence, the United States prevailed in its primary objectives of protection for international property, access for value-added services, and creation of an adjudicatory approach to resolving disputes. Regarding the last item, one former U.S. negotiator described the result succinctly: "Lawyers triumph over diplomats."[65]

The agreement pertaining to trade-related intellectual property (TRIPS) was significant. It covered the full range of intellectual property rights – patents, copyrights and trademarks, as well as industrial designs, layout designs of integrated circuits, and trade secrets – and set a world standard for IP protection. Relying on the WTO's dispute settlement mechanism for enforcement, the treaty bound parties either to implement rulings, pay fines, or face sanctions. Yet TRIPS had weaknesses. The WTO had a small staff, less than 500 for all functions, and no resources to investigate complaints. Also, only parties to the agreement, that is, governments, could bring grievances to the WTO. Private parties had no standing. As a result, political, policy, and budgetary considerations might shape a member's willingness to file a TRIPS-related complaint.[66]

Some important issues remained unresolved in the Uruguay Round. The Clinton administration did not push labor standards, against objections of poor countries. It did not walk away from the table to gain greater access to foreign markets for Hollywood and entertainment industries, in essence deferring to cultural sensitivities of smaller countries. Nor did it gain a final agreement on telecommunications and financial services. That would come later. In 1997, trade negotiators from sixty-five countries representing the largest telecom markets agreed to regulatory principles consistent with U.S. law. American Special Trade Representative Charlene Barshefsky explained that these WTO members had committed to establishing independent regulatory bodies, had guaranteed that foreign suppliers could interconnect with host country networks at fair prices, had forbid anticompetitive practices such as subsidizing local service with higher fares on international calls, and had accepted transparency of government regulations and licensing. A tradition of closed markets and monopolies, she said, has been "replaced by market opening, deregulation and competition."[67]

In the decade from 1986 to 1995, Ronald Reagan and his successors steered the international community away from a structured bipolar Cold War system, traumatized by nuclear weapons and military alliances, into a volatile and dynamic, market-driven, rapidly integrating environment. In this new age, the imperatives of business and technology often took priority over the concerns of the state and national security. Policy and governance frequently lagged behind the private-sector drivers transforming the world – free markets, free trade, free communications, and greater democracy. The Berlin Wall collapsed. History died. The Internet took off. The World Trade Organization was born. Globalization accelerated. Near the end of the American Century, people everywhere awakened to the potential of life in a global village.

Folding the Flag: Globalization and the New Millennium

The defining theme of the post–Cold War era – and indeed of the entire American century – has been globalization. Even though the concept has long historical roots, the first U.S. president to use the term was George H. W. Bush. His successor, Bill Clinton, made it the mantra of efforts to devise a structure for peace and prosperity in the twenty-first century. Recalling the optimistic words of William McKinley in 1901, Clinton observed that surging optimism about twentieth-century prospects was "not all that much different from the hopes commonly expressed today about the 21st." But he recalled that "rising global trade and communications . . . did not stop the world's wealthiest nations from waging World War I and World War II. . . . It did not stop the Depression, or the Holocaust, or communism." Looking to the future, Clinton urged Americans to "embrace the inexorable logic of globalization, that everything, from the strength of our economy to the safety of our cities to the health of our people, depends on events not only within our borders but half a world away. We must see the opportunities and the dangers of the interdependent world in which we are clearly fated to live." Not surprisingly, his successor, George W. Bush, the forty-third president, a graduate of the Harvard Business School, endorsed the view that America should guide the world toward open markets and economic integration. Globalization, Bush said, is "the triumph of human liberty stretching across national borders . . . it holds the promise of delivering billions of the world's citizens from disease and hunger and want."[1]

The two Bushes and Clinton, the first presidents of the post–Cold War era, perceived that globalization had the potential to harmonize behavior, customs, and politics and to usher in a long-sought period of prosperity, development, and democracy. The United States, as the world's only superpower, had the responsibility to lead and guide this process. Oriented as they were to emerging economic changes, the three U.S. leaders found that they could not avoid the use of military force. Despite some differences in their approaches, each worked with the United Nations, other multilateral institutions, and NATO allies. In 1999, Clinton intervened to defend Kosovar Muslims from Yugoslav aggression. He also took personal interest in attempting to resolve old conflicts involving Northern Ireland, Israeli-Palestinian relations, and North Korea, and in promoting greater respect for human rights in the developing world. After terrorists attacked the New York World Trade Center and the Pentagon in September 2001, killing more than 3,000 people (including 500 foreign citizens, 67 from Britain), Bush organized a coalition against terrorism with British Prime Minister Tony Blair. At the beginning of the twenty-first century, as at the beginning of the twentieth, the special relationship between Uncle Sam and John Bull continued to shape world politics and the globalization process.

Bush, and Blair, embarked on a mission to defend Western civilization and to make free trade and globalization antidotes for terrorism. Free-trade boosterism appealed to business and professional elites – the well educated – who foresaw the opportunities of globalization. But many ordinary Americans had little enthusiasm for either American-style globalization or for world leadership. The residual appeal of isolationism endured. Millions of working people wanted to pay back the terrorists, and they patriotically displayed American flags on their pickups and sports utility vehicles. Yet they also worried about losing jobs and health care benefits, as corporations hollowed out and exported American jobs to cheap-labor countries. Middle-class activists criticized globalization for skewing income distribution, harming the environment, jeopardizing food safety, eroding sovereignty, and homogenizing cultures. This wide-ranging debate suggests that the American people were as unsure about the costs and benefits of globalization at the end of the American Century as they were at its beginning.[2]

The Globalization Craze

Not until the mid 1990s did most ordinary people encounter the benefits and shortcomings of globalization. Widespread use of the Internet (nearly 100 million users in the United States by 2000, an estimated 304 million around the world) facilitated information flows and heightened public interest. When added to the Clinton administration's highly visible efforts to expand American trade and investments overseas, establish NAFTA and the WTO, and facilitate the integration of financial markets, globalization acquired a certain cache among Americans of all political stripes and economic status.[3]

9. "Globalization is revolutionizing the way we work," said President Bill Clinton to the World Economic Forum, Davos, Switzerland, January 29, 2000. (WEF/ swiss-image.ch)

But, surging imports and the growing tendency of corporate America to shift manufacturing to foreign locations with ample quantities of cheap labor aroused blue-collar workers. In Indonesia, even workers in state-of-the art tech plants earned only $60 per month. U.S. professionals also began to question the benefits of globalization when companies began moving engineering, research, and back-room operations to countries like India with large numbers of English-speaking engineers and other college-trained workers in order to cut costs. Engineers in India and other Southeast Asian countries earned less than $20,000 per year, less than one-fourth of an American engineer.[4]

Americans were not the only ones torn between the benefits and dislocations of globalization. In Western Europe and many developing countries, globalization became a dirty word, associated in the public mind with American sneakers, blue jeans, burgers, and videos. The French were most skeptical. In one poll, 65 percent said globalization increased the gap between rich and poor; 56 percent thought it threatened the national identity. Proud of their language and cultural traditions, many French thought globalization a U.S. conspiracy to "dumb down the world " and export its way of life. The French Ministry of Culture sought to rally Europeans and to restrict access for Hollywood films and American television programs. In 1989, France persuaded the European Community to stipulate that domestic programming constitute 40 percent of TV fare. And during the Uruguay Round, it insisted that audiovisual materials be exempt from trade agreements.[5]

Nationalists in many countries worried about the growth of global media empires led by "monsters" of globalization, such as Australian magnate Rupert Murdoch. His News Corporation established a multinational empire based on satellites, wireless communications, television, and prominent newspapers. At first the anticommunist Murdoch embraced the notion that "advances in the technology of telecommunications have proved an unambiguous threat to totalitarian regimes everywhere." This 1993 comment stirred up Chinese communists, who feared Murdoch's Star TV might subvert state authority. To reassure Beijing, Murdoch dropped the BBC from his Chinese satellite television and canceled a publishing contract with the last British governor-general of Hong Kong. Several years later, his son even criticized Western media coverage of China's human rights issues, asserting that "these destabilizing forces today are very, very dangerous for the Chinese government."[6] Murdoch was first and last a businessman, and like William Randolph Hearst of Spanish-American War fame, Murdoch understood that jingoism sold newspapers and attracted television viewers.

Around the world – especially in Muslim countries – defenders of traditional values sought to block the spread of American-style pop culture. Iranian religious fundamentalists raided homes to confiscate videos and satellite dishes, and in neighboring Afghanistan the Taliban closed movie theaters, burned films, denied schooling to women, and halted sports. Try as they might, the fundamentalists could not eradicate the "sway of alien and infidel culture." Their controls benefited contraband smugglers. In both Iran and Afghanistan, the movie *Titanic* proved a blockbuster; underground video stores flourished. Some discreetly hid satellite dishes to access Western television.[7] The failure of Islamic fundamentalists to stamp out Western influences, like the inability of state-controlled societies in Eastern Europe to block the appeal of Western democracy and consumerism, demonstrated the power of mass communications in the era of satellites and video cassettes. It also underscored the global appeal of U.S. values to the young, the well educated, and the affluent, an amorphous yet tangible element of American power in the world.

American pop culture celebrated several universal themes: individualism, consumerism, democracy, materialism, optimism, pragmatism, progress, technology, tolerance, wealth, and youth. Author Salman Rushdie, the target of an Iranian death warrant, defended pop culture and globalization from fundamentalist attacks. "Sneakers, burgers, blue jeans and music videos aren't the enemy," he says. "There are fundamental freedoms to fight for, and it will not do to doom the terrorized women of Afghanistan or the circumcision-happy lands of Africa by calling their oppression their 'culture.'" David Rothkopf, an associate of former Secretary of State Henry Kissinger, carried the point a step beyond to defend American cultural imperialism. "Americans should not deny the fact that of all the nations in the history of the world, theirs is the most just, the most tolerant, the most willing to constantly reassess and improve itself, and the best model for the future." While America tended to glorify the individual at the expense of community interests, its pop culture was more open to foreign influences – such as the Beatles – and more tolerant of diversity. Even Hollywood was not so much an American industry as it was a world-class entertainment business that attracted foreign stars (such as Arnold Schwarzenegger) and foreign capital. Indeed, Joseph Nye, dean of Harvard's Kennedy School described America as a "cultural sponge, a syncretic society that can assimilate influences from all over the world and send them back home." But, high-cost Hollywood could not escape the inexorable logic of globalization and outsourcing. Digital technology meant that movies could be shot anywhere, and in 2002 none of the movies nominated for the 2002 best film Oscar was made in Hollywood. Three were filmed overseas to reduce production costs.[8]

The argument that globalization led inevitably to U.S. cultural dominance ignored the growing appeal of foreign competition. At the time antiglobalization demonstrators were protesting in Seattle against the WTO, *The Economist* observed the ironic fact that "the entire child population of America is enslaved by a Japanese fad...Pokemon." Film industries in India and Hong Kong presented competition to Hollywood, and even MTV discovered the need to vary its formula in the world's various regional markets – providing Chinese music in China and Hindi pop in India.[9]

Among the world's elite – business leaders, government officials, academics, and media types – globalization encouraged a convergence of the cosmopolitans. English became the predominant language of commerce and transnational communications, and business and government leaders wore Western business suits, flew in the same airplanes, stayed in the same hotels, read the same newspapers (the *Wall Street Journal* and the *Financial Times*), and communicated with cellular phones and e-mail. More than the success of U.S. business, the acceptance of American-style globalization reflected the need to play by the rules of the world's largest open market, America's leadership in technological innovation and the information revolution, or the attraction of its universal values. Historical circumstance was also critical to that outcome. Had Germany and Japan prevailed in World War II, or had the Soviet Union won the Cold War, German, Japanese, or Russian might have become the lingua franca of globalization. But the English-speaking powers (John Bull and Uncle Sam) prevailed. They established the UN system, designed the institutions of international economic and financial collaboration, and pressed for acceptance of common standards and the rule of law.[10]

Synergy of Globalization

The post-Cold War era of economic globalization should not be viewed simply as the triumph of Anglo-American internationalism, however. There was a synergistic dimension in which changes in technology, business strategy, and government policies combined to produce effects far more profound than the sum of incremental steps. The changes hinged on the integration of capital markets, the apparent irrelevance of national borders, and technological leveraging of knowledge and talent world-wide. Integration and mobility were keys. Production, capital flows, and workers were increasingly integrated into a global marketplace dictated by transnational corporations. In 1970, there were 7,000 transnational cor-porations; in 2000, there were some 63,000 parents and 690,000 foreign affiliates as well as a large number of interfirm arrangements. Gross prod-uct affiliated with the production of transnationals increased faster than global GDP and global exports. According to UNCTAD, "the world's top 100 (nonfinancial) transnational corporations (TNCs) (with General Elec-tric in first place) . . . are the principal drivers of international production." Their foreign affiliates employed six million persons and had foreign sales of $2 trillion. Their reach in every aspect of the world economy – from production to distribution – grew exponentially. By 2002, Wal-Mart, America's largest retailer, had become the world's largest corporation. It headed the "Fortune 500" list of America's largest corporations and held the dominant retailing position in Mexico, Canada, and the United States. Wal-Mart was expanding rapidly in Asia and Europe. With some 1,200 stores outside the United States, Wal-Mart employed 1.2 million people – more than any other firm in the world. In 2001, foreign sales of $32 billion equaled companywide sales a decade earlier.[11]

As the Internet was empowering ordinary people with information, governance of the global system became more segmented in functional supranational institutions run by specialized elites. The IMF, the World Bank, and the WTO set rules and handed rewards and sanctions. But critics thought these supranational agencies insufficiently transparent and accountable to democratic electorates. A variety of nongovernmental or-ganizations, some of which sought more protection for labor or the envi-ronment or espoused the interests of developing nations or interest groups turned their collective attentions to reforming these global institutions. In-ternational bureaucrats, once held in high esteem, found themselves on the defensive, whipsawed by member governments, activists, and an in-creasingly critical press, at a time when technological and market changes accelerated the growth and volatility of the global economy.

The velocity and variety of the forces driving globalization were stun-ning. International trade expanded rapidly in the period from 1870 to 1913, a period of relatively openness. But the pace accelerated in the last half century. The world economy grew sixfold since 1950, climbing from $6.7 trillion in constant prices to $41.6 trillion in 1998. During the same period, global exports of goods rose seventeenfold, up from $311 billion to $5.4 trillion. Much of the growth occurred among units of transnational corporations and involved services, which now represent one-fifth of total world trade. At the end of the nineteenth century, services and intrafirm transactions were not major factors. Most foreign investment was portfolio investment (in railroads and land), not direct investment in manufacturing. Since 1970, the volume of foreign direct investment rose almost fifteenfold. By 2000, it was twice that of 1990. Dozens of nations had enacted special laws to attract foreign capital.

Financial globalization, reflecting the integration of equity and bond markets, was another powerful factor driving world economic integration and growth. As in late nineteenth-century Britain, the upper and middle classes increasingly invested their savings overseas. The assets of U.S.-based international and global mutual funds climbed from $16 billion in 1986 to $321 billion in late 1996. Forty-four million American households held mutual funds, compared to 4.6 million in 1980. Moreover, the velocity of foreign exchange transactions spiraled. In 1973, average daily turnover in foreign exchange markets was $15 billion; in 1983, $60 billion; in 1993, $880 billion; and in 1998, an estimated $1.5 trillion. Moreover, in a world of electronically integrated financial markets, money flowed into and out of countries in response to changing market conditions. In 1996, foreign investors put $100 billion into Asia; the next year they withdrew $100 billion.[12]

Technology abetted the globalization process: world production of technology multiplied six times between 1975 and 1986; international trade in technology soared nine times. Improvements in communications and transportation brought other changes. In 1956, eighty-nine telephone conversations took place simultaneously through the trans-Atlantic telephone cable. By the end of the millennium, about one million conversations occurred simultaneously by satellite and fiber optics. Add in e-mail and faxes, and the ease, speed, and volume of communications were magnified. Between 1955 and 1998, ship tonnage rose sixfold; the unit cost of carrying freight by sea fell 70 percent between 1920 and 1990. The volume of air freight soared from 730 million to 99 billion ton-kilometers. As with shipping, costs fell sharply. Between 1930 and 1990, the average revenue per mile for air transportation dropped from sixty-eight cents to eleven cents (expressed in constant dollars).[13]

Cheaper airfares also enhanced individual mobility. Between 1950 and 2000, international tourist arrivals rose nearly twenty-eight-fold – from 25 million to 697 million. Two million people crossed a border somewhere in the world every single day. Some of them were political refugees; others were simply seeking economic opportunities. The UN

Commissioner for Refugees estimated that at the end of the twentieth century, some 150 million people lived outside the country of their birth. This amounted to 2.5 percent of the world's population, or one in every forty people. Many of them remitted earnings to families and relatives in native countries. Globally, migrants remit $100 billion annually estimated *The Economist*, an amount far greater than foreign aid from public and private sources. Every year, one million people enter the United States. In fewer than thirty years, the number of immigrants living in America tripled from 9.6 million in 1970 to 26.3 million in 1998. It is estimated that immigrants from Central America remitted $8 billion a year to their home countries. Many of the foreign students who entered the United States for graduate education remain, contributing to the brain drain from developing lands but augmenting the supply of highly trained professionals in America. In 1990, one-third of Silicon Valley's scientists and engineers were foreign born. The International Monetary Fund estimated that one in four Iranians with college degrees was working abroad. One million Iranians settled in the United States.[14]

Many of the less educated who remained in their home lands, moving from countryside to city, have joined the global economy. Low-skilled labor has become part of a global assembly line. Transnationals assemble products in factories throughout the world, wherever labor is cheapest, managing global supply and distribution chains. Many service jobs, particularly those involving data transfers, also flow in and out of countries at great speed, taking advance of commodity labor in a world eager to work. As the new millennium opened, transnationals moved to cut the cost of their back-room operations. In 2002, General Electric promised to slash these costs $10 billion over a three-year period, as it outsourced and hired inexpensive, English-speaking customer-service representatives in India.[15]

The activities of Nike, Inc., offer one controversial example of globalization in action. Interestingly, this famous athletic shoe company manufactures almost nothing. Rather it is a designer, developer, and marketer of imported footwear and accessories manufactured by independent subcontractors in cheap-labor countries like China, Indonesia, and Vietnam. Nike sells its products in 140 countries, and in 2000 non-U.S. sales accounted for 44 percent of its total revenues. Benefiting from the "globalization of sports culture," Nike seeks "to sell a global brand through marketing that appeals to local tastes." According to its vice chairman, the company sought "one management, one theme, one value, one ethic around the world." This was the essence of globalization.[16]

The company profited from the stewardship of Phil Knight, its founder and CEO, and the image of basketball star Michael Jordan. In the mid 1960s, Knight had boldly imported Tiger running shoes from Japan, adapted the soles to the wet weather of the Pacific Northwest by creating a rubber waffle pattern, and, in 1972, launched the Nike line of shoes during the well-publicized Olympic trials. Knight cultivated an outlaw image for Nike, putting his shoes on rogue stars and brats like tennis stars John McEnroe and Andre Agassi and basketball big-mouth Charles Barkley. In the mid 1980s, Knight recruited Chicago Bull's star Michael Jordan.

In one of the most influential advertisements of the century, Jordan was pictured in midflight with a basketball, above the caption "Just Do It!" He became known worldwide as "the man who could fly." The ad rocketed Nike from 18 percent to 43 percent of the sneaker market in the ten years after it aired in 1988. Figures in 1998 showed that his worth to Nike was $5.2 billion, but the "Jordan effect" on commercial culture (professional sports, advertisements, the media, and movies) doubled that amount. Jordan transformed Nike from distributor to marketer, at home and abroad. By the early 1990s, Europe represented one-quarter of the company's sales. In 1995, Japanese teenagers flocked to the Air Max shoe, paying a street price of up to $1,000 a pair. After Jordan retired, Knight turned to golfing phenomenon Tiger Woods to establish a beachhead for Nike in the $200 million a year golf business.[17]

Globalization has enabled Nike to produce its products cheaply, while focusing on adding value through design and marketing. The Nike Air Max Penny basketball shoe consisted of fifty-two material components made in five nations. Nike coordinated "a complex logistical enterprise that weaves together material and non-material [advertising, design, promotion] inputs across national boundaries." Outsourcing to contract suppliers drove production from Japan to South Korea and Taiwan in search of cheap labor. Today, most of Nike's shoes come from China and Southeast Asia, where workers often earn less than $30 per month.

In summer 1996, human rights groups and the media began to target Nike and report on working conditions among its subcontractors. In Indonesia, it was reported that Nike paid workers $1.60 for making a pair of Nike Pegasus that sold for $70. The daily minimum wage in the nation was $2.35. The company hired Andrew Young, former UN ambassador and civil rights leader, to tour its Asian subcontractors, and he reported back that the conditions were acceptable, but he noted that few managers or workers seemed to know Nike's code of conduct. By September 1997, the company had severed ties with four factories for not paying the legal minimum wage or adhering to decent standards, such as hours (some workers were laboring 70- to 80-hour workweeks). Nike's critics suspected that these actions were cosmetic because the attraction of cheap labor drove the footwear and apparel businesses. Indeed, Nike's principal competitors – Reebok, Adidas, and Puma among others – often used the same subcontractors, the same workers, and the same plants.[18]

Whatever the blows to its image, Knight and his high-profile endorsers succeeded in creating worldwide brand recognition for Nike. An American student traveling through a remote region of China in 1997 encountered a group of Tibetans who never strayed far from their isolated village. Nevertheless, they asked the American how Michael Jordan was doing in the NBA that year and inquired into his team, the "Red Oxen" (Chicago Bulls). Globalization made Jordan and Nike buzzwords, showing how an individual within the private sector transcended national consciousness and how a corporation, with shrewd marketing and distribution, reached into every corner of the planet. The empire was not secure, but it never would be in the competitive world of global business.[19]

Along with the globalization of prominent brands, like Nike, McDonald's, Coca Cola, Marlboro, VISA, and others, the process also benefited sports teams. Jordan's star qualities, as well as the global reach of satellite television, established a worldwide following for the Chicago Bulls. Manchester United and the New York Yankees also appealed to extensive audiences. An influx of Eastern European players strengthened the international appeal of the National Hockey League. The National Basketball Association's open-door policy to talent attracted forty-five foreign players from twenty-nine countries; as a result, the NBA broadcast in 210 countries and forty-two languages. Major league baseball, which began opening its season in foreign locations, inaugurated the 2001 season with 854 players – 25 percent of them born outside the United States. As a result of Ichiro Suzuki's success with the Seattle Mariners (most valuable player as a rookie), the team's home games were televised live in Japan. Thousands of Japanese baseball fans even flew to Seattle to attend home games of a club owned by Nintendo president Hiroshi Yamauchi.[20]

Crisis in the Midst of Optimism

Along with rapid growth and increasing integration of markets, the age of globalization produced considerable volatility in the 1990s. Repeatedly, the U.S. Federal Reserve System, chaired by Alan Greenspan, had to demonstrate America's commitment to assisting the global financial system in times of crisis. The Asian contagion of 1997–8 underscored the vulnerabilities of a market-driven system and the importance of the United States's financial leadership in times of crisis. It began in July 1997 with a sharp fall in the Thai currency. Thai investors, who had borrowed in foreign currencies and then invested in red-hot Bangkok stocks and real estate, scrambled to sell baht and buy dollars or yen. The baht lost over 48 percent of its value in days despite government intervention. The financial debacle spread to neighboring nations. Malaysia, South Korea, Indonesia, Singapore, and the Philippines suffered massive outflows of capital, plunges in stock markets from one-third to one-half of values, and major declines in exchange rates. Banks failed (150 Asian financial institutions were closed, nationalized, placed under the control of the IMF, or suspended operations), growth halted, and recession set in. Thailand, Indonesia, and South Korea asked the IMF to for assistance. The crisis hit particularly hard in some of the Four Tigers, as well as in other nations with previously winning strategies for development. Japan was already experiencing banking and stock-market problems. When financial breakdown hit Brazil and Russia shortly after it arrived in Asia, analysts spoke of an Asian flu infecting the rest of the world.

The Asian economic crisis quickly spread to the political arena and aroused concerns about the merits of Western-style free-market globalization. Street protests, stimulated by the economic downturn, forced Indonesia's dictator of thirty-two years from power while politicians jockeyed for control in Thailand, the Philippines, South Korea, and Malaysia. Criminal charges of corruption were brought against some leaders. Faith in the state-directed Asian miracles fell precipitously, replaced by trepidation toward free-market ideology and Western financial advice. Over the preceding decade, Wall Street, Washington, and international financial institutions had encouraged emerging economies to deregulate capital markets and open to foreign banks and financial institutions. The Reagan, Bush, and Clinton administrations badgered countries in Latin America and Asia to end capital controls and let foreign financial institutions become established. "Throughout the 1980s and 1990s," said Jeffrey Frankel, a member of President Clinton's Council of Economic Advisers, "the White House pursued interests of banks and securities dealers in bilateral discussions." Jagdish Bhagwati of Columbia University was blunter, saying that "the U.S. administration really blew it" and that Treasury Secretary Robert Rubin and his deputy Larry Summers "may well have presided over the largest man-made disaster in the world economy since Smoot Hawley." The Clinton administration's mistake, according

to Bhagwati, was its promotion of "imprudent financial liberalization."
He accused the Wall Street-Treasury complex of having hijacked the free-
trade movement and bamboozled it into "celebrating the new world of
trillions of dollars moving about daily in a borderless world, creating
gigantic economic gains, rewarding virtue and punishing profligacy."
Bhagwati claimed there was no necessary correlation between free trade
and economic growth.[21]

But in promoting capital-account convertibility, the IMF proved a willing partner of Wall Street. In September 1997, it approved a charter
amendment giving the IMF authority to require countries to liberalize
the capital as well as current accounts of their balance of payments. With
currency markets permitted to fluctuate since the mid 1980s and capital
flowing in and out of these nations in high volume and with great speed,
markets did not work as smoothly as economic theory suggested.[22]

A different interpretation of the Asian crisis gained favor on Wall Street,
in the Treasury, and among officials at the IMF. Ignoring the catastrophic
consequences of their own imprudent market-opening advice to countries lacking sound regulatory mechanisms and a legal framework, the
bureaucrats sought to shift the blame. Washington and Wall Street attributed the crisis to "crony capitalism," the lack of transparency and
inadequate disclosure of financial data, the absence of independent regulatory authorities, and inadequate accounting standards. These officials
had no doubt that the continued liberalization of financial markets was
mutually beneficial, and they hastened to bail out the troubled economies
and save investors.

Alan Greenspan, Treasury Secretary and Wall Street financier Robert
Rubin, and his deputy, economist Larry Summers, were key players. In
speeches during the crisis, Greenspan warned that the "expectation that
national monetary authorities or international financial institutions will
come to the rescue of failing financial systems and unsound investments
clearly has engendered a significant element of excessive risk-taking."
Having railed against moral-hazard safety nets for investors, Greenspan
insisted that central banks and the IMF had a larger responsibility to
intervene to "quell financial turmoil" and to restore public confidence.
Rubin was accustomed to financial emergencies, having engineered a solution to the Mexican peso crisis a few years before. They all aimed the
IMF at the Asian Crisis in order to stop the run on the banks and refash-
ion Asian economies along market lines in the long run. Greenspan, in
particular, lauded the fact that the Asian Crisis compelled a "worldwide
move toward 'the Western form of free market capitalism.' "[23] He lashed
out against crony capitalism, which he charged created closed personal

networks of trade that smacked of price fixing and other distortions commonly attributed to cartels. The Fed chairman saw the Asian Crisis as a means of ending cronyism by injecting IMF policies that encouraged transparency – disclosures by governments, companies, and financial institutions, competent risk assessment, actual (rather than distorted) price structures, and competition promoted by the rule of law rather than arbitrary state intervention. This plan would promote global prosperity, he believed, in instilling Western-style free-market practices.[24]

That analysis brought Greenspan hearty praise from the market faithful but scorn from critics. Some of the latter, such as Prime Minister Muhamad Mahathir of Malaysia, blamed marauding capitalists (many of them Americans) for destabilizing Third World countries. Others believed that the Asian Crisis stemmed not from national policies but from worldwide transformations in the capitalist structure, namely the vast changes in transnational production, mass consumption, and capital transfers.[25] Greenspan certainly recognized the seriousness of the situation, and not leaving Asia's fate entirely to the whims of the market, he lowered U.S. interest rates six times, beginning in October 1998, as a way of stimulating consumers to buy from the beleaguered region. In effect, the central bank shifted the burden of adjustment to import-competing U.S. industries. As Asian exports to the United States rose to facilitate debt repayments, more and more U.S. apparel plants closed their doors and moved machinery to Mexico, Pakistan, or China, where wages were lower. Regardless, Greenspan's analysis became standard fare in Washington, D.C., and among most economic experts. When he spoke, "the world trembles," wrote European observers; his words were "taken for golden."[26] How many central bankers did it take to screw in a lightbulb, asked a pundit? Just one. Greenspan held the bulb, and the world revolved around him.[27]

A Julliard conservatory dropout, Greenspan began his career as a clarinetist with the Henry Jerome jazz orchestra. Later he attended New York University and Columbia University and then formed a consulting firm in the 1950s, a time when objectivist novelist Ayn Rand befriended him. Her philosophy exalted laissez-faire capitalism as the most moral of economic systems and promoted the notion that people should pursue, above all, their self-interests. Rand persuaded him to advise Richard Nixon in the 1968 presidential campaign; the president appointed him chairman of the Council of Economic Advisors in 1974. He stayed on in the Ford administration, helping to tame inflation but getting blamed for the ensuing recession. In the early 1980s, this clarinetist served on several corporate boards and chaired the National Commission on Social Security Reform until Ronald Reagan appointed him chairman of the Federal

Reserve Board in 1987, in which he succeeded the influential Paul Volcker. Greenspan was renewed for four terms, the last ending in June 2004. He made his mark by advocating banking deregulation and opposing government intervention in the economy, yet opposing tax cuts out of a fear they would add to budget deficits. He preferred to use the Fed to direct the domestic economy to the longest peacetime boom in history, in the 1990s, and he practiced this approach during the Asian Crisis.[28]

Greenspan especially appreciated the power, dangers, and benefits of globalization. The Asian Crisis, he observed, was a conventional slowdown in capital investments and outflows, but it also showed the uncertainty of the new age of globalization. According to Greenspan, both the Mexican and Asian emergencies provided insights into the high-tech international financial system "though there is much we do not yet understand." He warned that at times, "the economic system appears stable" but then suddenly "it behaves as though a dam has been breached, and water (read confidence) evacuates its reservoir." Abrupt "implosions" undermined the "line" of confidence, and when "crossed, prices slip into free fall before markets will stabilize."[29] Still, Greenspan advocated a Darwinian view of the world economy, and he urged Americans to adjust, develop, and deploy new technologies; to educate the population; and to meet international challenges through flexible labor and management policies by heavy investment in ideas and services to put those ideas into effect. There were risks to globalization. But Greenspan insisted that the benefits – competition, reduced service costs, profits for savers and borrowers, efficiency, and rapid spread of innovation – be kept in the fore. Limiting risks to the vulnerable, investors, and others was necessary. But, Chairman Greenspan warned, "[e]fforts to insulate the United States from the inexorable forces of increasing globalization could be very costly to our standard of living."[30]

By the end of the century, Greenspan's robust domestic economy and relatively stable economies overseas (including success in mending vulnerable nations involved in the Asian Crisis) seemed to bear out the benefits of globalization. American unemployment had reached a thirty-year low by 1999, while business creation and stock-market profits soared, until a dramatic drop in technology stocks beginning in Spring 2000 slowed the economy. Mexico's economy revived from the peso crisis and subsequent bailout by 1998; two years later, the nation held its freest presidential election ever, which chased the entrenched Institutional Revolutionary Party from office and brought to power a more conservative businessman Vicente Fox, who pledged economic openness and efforts to crack down on endemic corruption. Supporters and critics of NAFTA continued to differ about its consequences. Labor-intensive factories continued to close and move southward to Mexico. But many of the dislocated workers soon found jobs in the booming American economy. In regard to China, the strong U.S. economy helped to mask criticisms of a rising trade deficit and soaring imports. After years of congressional-executive branch fighting over whether to extend the nation most-favored-nation status in trade, Congress granted China permanent normal trade relations (PNTR) in 2000. Membership in the WTO bound nations to accord other members the lowest tariff treatment accorded any foreign nation. With China bound to implement international rules on trade and investments, private investment capital flowed in to take advantage of new opportunities and low labor costs. In 2000, nearly 75 percent of private investment capital entering Asia went to mainland China or Hong Kong.[31]

In addition, the Clinton administration worked to normalize relations with the Socialist Republic of Vietnam. After restoring diplomatic relations in 1995, Americans cultivated trade and travel with their former enemy. Several American multinationals, including Coca Cola, Chase Manhattan Bank, Citigroup, General Motors, and United Airlines had campaigned against the nineteen-year-old embargo that denied them markets in Southeast Asia. Now they began to invest in the country, even though by 1997, the communist bureaucracy managed to stifle investment with red tape. Still, Clinton's visit to Vietnam in November 2000 brought out enthusiastic crowds and hopes for greater commercial expansion. The president, about to leave office, urged that Vietnamese youth look to the ideals of the global marketplace, of "entrepreneurship, innovation and competition."[32]

Protests Against Globalization

Opposition to the proglobalization agenda emerged among a disparate alliance of activists concerned about the environment, labor standards, and national sovereignty. In 1992, the Bush administration had refused to accept the entire Rio de Janeiro Treaty that protected biodiversity of plant and animal species. An argument also erupted over the existence of global warming, which many scientists and environmental groups blamed on the emission of carbon-based gases into the atmosphere. A total of 150 nations, including the United States, signed the Kyoto Accord of 1997, which pledged to reduce such global emissions to 5.2 percent below the 1990 level. America would cut its release of carbon-based gases by 7 percent. But Clinton faced staunch opposition from powerful business interests such as the Business Roundtable, the Chamber of Commerce, and the National Association of Manufacturers who thought the agreement flawed. The Senate voted 95 to 0 to oppose the protocol if developing countries like China and India did not also cut their emissions. As a result, the administration never sent the agreement to Capitol Hill for ratification. The debate over global warming continued during the 2000 election when Democratic candidate Al Gore insisted that America join the Kyoto pact nations and GOP candidate George Bush countered that additional studies were needed to better understand the problem. As the debate continued, it was increasingly clear that environmental issues, like economic issues, required international cooperation and consensus building.[33]

There were also optimists who saw the free market and meteoric advances in technology as a great boon or as an irreversible phenomenon that could not be halted. Among the most energetic advocates of this view was journalist Thomas Friedman, who announced that the world had entered a period of unity (unlike the divisive forty-five-year Cold War) that rewarded flexibility, high technology, and individualism.[34]

Yet there were others, especially in the labor and environmental movements and within academia, who shunned this new system, calling it a "false dawn" of stability and prosperity that was leading to the disintegration of national economies and cultures. According to this view, workers had become pawns in transnational corporate agendas, the environment had been deregulated by the free-market rules of the WTO, and financial markets had become so decontrolled that the joint efforts of a handful of individuals could destabilize entire nations (as in Indonesia in 1997).[35]

A variety of lobbyists and organizations protested corporate globalization, but few were as spirited as Lori Wallach and her Public Citizen's Global Trade Watch. Founding this national coalition of labor, consumer, environmental, family farm, religious, and civil rights groups, Wallach – a Harvard-educated lawyer dubbed the "trade debate's guerilla warrior" and "Ralph Nader with a sense of humor" – challenged the new status quo of market devotees and their government supporters. Wallach lashed out at supposedly corporate-beholden Washington, which she argued had ceded sovereignty over health and safety standards, resources, and the like in a "slow-motion coup d'etat" to globe-trotting firms and their protectors, such international bodies as the IMF and the WTO. The World Trade Organization, in particular, had moved well beyond traditional tariff and quota matters to limit, in secret meetings in which it was accountable to no nation, a myriad of national laws that might curb the reach of corporations. This move was a direct threat to democratic governance, claimed Wallach, and placed the health and livelihoods of the masses in jeopardy. Besides, trade negotiations had not yielded the projected benefits to the masses, but corporations had surely profited. Wallach, a youthful and vibrant opponent of the WTO, warned against its nineteenth-century free-trade philosophy. She offered instead the bold view that corporate globalization was "not inevitable" but the product of "enormous planning and political work. We still have freedom to oppose the WTO and find real alternatives."[36]

10. Lori Wallach, director of Public Citizen's Global Trade Watch, helped organize the Seattle antiglobalization protests of December 1999. (William Geiger photographer)

Wallach, members of organized labor, environmental activists, and others concerned about globalization took to the streets to voice their objections. The WTO ministerial meetings convened in Seattle in December 1999 to plan a new set of world trade negotiations called the Millennium Round, but huge demonstrations led to such chaos that some delegates representing the 135 WTO member nations found it difficult to leave their hotels. Inspired by the protesters, Third World nations demanded more sensitivity to their needs. The ensuing turmoil prevented the WTO from presenting an agenda for the round. To be sure, many protesters were ill-informed, lashing out in populist fashion against perceived corruption or backing debt relief for the poor without regard to the quality of governance. But Seattle turned out not to be an isolated event; further demonstrations erupted in 2000 at an UNCTAD gathering in Bangkok and at IMF-World Bank meetings in Washington, D.C. The Davos, Switzerland, meeting of the World Economic Forum, a collection of rich, influential, and well-connected elites across professions, experienced the protesters, too. In January 2001, Wallach herself breached the walls by getting an invitation to Davos, where she protested Swiss officials' rough treatment of demonstrators and continued to denounce globalization. Public opinion polls showed Americans divided on such issues as globalization and free trade. In general, those in the middle class and below voiced protectionist sentiments or questioned the fairness of NAFTA and the WTO. Among those warning of the perils of globalization were Pope John Paul II, UN Secretary General Kofi Annan, and former South African President Nelson Mandela.[37]

Toward 2015

As the twenty-first century opened, the globalization revolution continued to roll forward. In a report entitled Global Trends 2015, the Central Intelligence Agency saw globalization as one of the most powerful drivers shaping the world of 2015. The "networked global economy will be driven by rapid and largely unrestricted flows of information, ideas, cultural values, capital, goods and services, and people." Noting that the information technology revolution "represents the most significant global transformation since the Industrial Revolution beginning in the mid-eighteenth century," the report noted that globalization would prove a "net contributor to increased political stability in the world of 2015, . . . its evolution will be rocky, marked by chronic financial volatility and a widening economic divide." The CIA hypothesized two alternative scenarios – one benign, the other pernicious. In the first situation, a "virtuous circle develops among technology, economic growth, demographic factors, and effective governance, which enables a majority of the world's people to benefit from globalization." In the second, "global elites thrive, but the majority of the world's population fails to benefit from globalization." There was rapid population growth, resource scarcities (especially water), and extensive migration out of developing nations. In addition, the new technologies were "exploited by negative and illicit networks and incorporated into destabilizing weapons."[38]

While the global spread of information, the integration of markets, and the erasure of borders had the potential to promote global peace, prosperity, and the convergence of basic values, there was a dark dimension often ignored by corporate boosters. For one, open borders benefited organized criminals and terrorists as well as corporations. The turnover of the criminal economy was estimated at about $1 trillion annually. Narcotics amounted to about half. "Trade in people" was thought to be the "second most lucrative criminal business." Gangs moved four to five million people annually and earned some $7 billion in profits. Annually, organized crime laundered some $500 billion through the world's financial system. According to *Jane's Intelligence Review*, the global "underworld is evolving every bit as rapidly as its legal 'upperworld' counterpart and to a large extent in response to the same pressures and opportunities." Like transnational corporations, gangs formed strategic alliances to maximize efficiency and avoid conflict. Like international business, they, too, became more "inclusive," recruiting people of divergent backgrounds who could operate within the dominant culture. Osama bin Laden's terrorist network also took advantage of globalization in their efforts to thwart it. They transferred funds easily, obtained information about atomic bombs and bioterrorist weapons from the Internet, and moved teams of suicide bombers into the United States, posing as students and travelers, as they prepared for coordinated attacks on commercial and government centers in New York and the Washington, D.C., area. The surprise attack on September 11 exposed American security lapses, and the vulnerabilities of a nation enmeshed in global supply chains. U.S. Customs officials, who had previously concentrated on intercepting drug shipments, suddenly had to contend with 50,000 containers entering U.S. ports daily. Any one might contain nuclear weapons mixed with Nikes, or anthrax-contaminated apparel, that could decimate entire population centers.[39]

In the health area, globalization posed dangerous new challenges. Improvements in transportation, communications, and medical science encouraged trade in body parts. There were reports of kidneys removed from Chinese prisoners before their executions and of a neocannibal couple operating in Uzbekistan (she a surgeon, he a professor) who killed people for body parts. Public health officials worried that increased human mobility enhanced opportunities for microbes. The risks ranged from trade in illegal products and contaminated foodstuffs, divergent safety standards, indiscriminate spread of medical technologies and experimentation, and the sale of prescription drugs without approval of national authorities. With some two million people crossing borders daily, industrialized nations faced threats from emerging infectious diseases, exposure to dangerous substances, and violence such as chemical and bioterrorist attack. Pulitzer Prize winning reporter Laurie Garrett wrote that in the "age of jet travel . . . a person incubating a disease such as Ebola can board a plane, travel 12,000 miles, pass unnoticed through customs and immigration, take a domestic carrier to a remote destination, and still not develop symptoms for several days, infecting many other people." The anthrax attack on congressional offices in late 2001, which killed several postal workers, also illustrates the unpredictable dangers that civilized society faced from rogue states and terrorists.[40]

In the age of instantaneous communication, rapid transport, and volatile markets, it was apparent that complexities of international relationships had moved far beyond the expertise of professional diplomats and foreign ministries. Diplomats and governments no longer served as gatekeepers. In the networked world, individuals, nongovernmental organizations, and officials communicated rapidly and regularly. But even though technological innovation and information had networked millions of individuals in a system without central control, it is worth emphasizing that governments helped fund the networking revolution. The U.S. government had supported basic research in high-speed computers, telecommunications, networking, and aviation, all essential to the interconnected world of globalization. Moreover, Washington's commitment to market-opening, deregulation, and liberalization of trade and finance provided the policy impetus that led to a variety of international agreements and arrangements promoting an open world order. The World Trade Organization, the International Monetary Fund, and World Bank, as well as the leadership of the Federal Reserve System to restore order when instability threatens, all reflected the deep, sustained commitment among members of the American leadership elite to economic internationalism. What is remarkable is how this enthusiasm endured for more than half a century since publisher Henry Luce exhorted Americans to turn their backs on America's isolationist past and provide leadership for the American century.[41]

The tragic events of September 2001 underscored the fragility and asymmetries of the American Century. While billions of people in high-income countries had a stake in globalization, billions did not – more than a billion people, the World Bank estimated, lived on less than $1 per day. In the Middle East, there were millions of angry Muslims who lacked jobs, skills, and opportunities to join the high-consumption world. Resentful of life at the margin, some of them found appealing the fundamentalist rantings of radical and charismatic religious leaders who rejected modern values and exhorted *jihad* (Holy Wars). Accepting martyrdom, in exchange for the promise of eternal life in Paradise, they launched suicide missions against symbols of the American empire.

It was unclear as this book went to press whether the War Against Terrorism marked a significant turning point in the evolution of globalization, as World War I had. In 1914, nations turned inward and erected barriers to flows of goods, capital, and individuals. Over time, this led to competitive trade and preferential blocs. It was also possible that the September suicide missions represented only a temporary setback to globalization, one that even had a silver lining: it punctured the myth of the nation-state as a dinosaur waiting to die. Before September 11, it was assumed that politics and centralized authority were withering in the face of a postnational globalized commercial future. In the aftermath of September 11, nervous corporate and business elites turned not to Wal-Mart and General Electric but to government and the nation-state for safe homelands and secure borders. It had become evident that a peaceful and prosperous future depended on more than privatization, free trade, and cowboy capitalism. It required intergovernmental cooperation to suppress terrorism and to establish a global economic system that provided order, opportunity, and justice. The challenge for statesmen was to channel the aggressive instincts of militants everywhere into peaceful competition rather than constant jihads. If they failed, regionalism might supplant globalism, and clashing cultures and religious strife might jeopardize world stability and prosperity. Whatever happened, the new millennium promised to be as dynamic and unpredictable as the American Century.[42]

Appendix: Statistical Tables

TABLE A.I. *The Great Powers, 1913*[a]

Country	Population (million)	GDP ($ billion)	GDP/per capita ($)	Exports ($ billion)
United States	97.6	518.0	5,307	2.380
Great Britain	42.6	214.5	5,032	2.555
Germany	37.8	145.1	3,833	2.454
	64.6			
France	41.5	143.1	3,452	1.328
Japan	51.7	68.9	1,334	0.315
Russia/USSR	156.2	232.4	1,488	0.783

[a] Data from Angus Maddison, *Monitoring the World Economy 1820–1992* (Paris: OECD, 1995). See also, Paul Bairoch, "European Trade Policy, 1815–1941" in *Cambridge Economic History of Europe*, vol. VIII, eds. Peter Mathias and Sidney Pollard (Cambridge: Cambridge University Press, 1989), 3. Maddison's data treats Russia as the USSR, and Germany as the Federal Republic. Periodic shifts in boundaries present unusual problems for measuring economic performance over time. In 1913, Maddison's Germany (essentially the area that was to become the Federal Republic) had a population of 37.8 million, but the Germany of 1913 had about 64.6 million. In light of these data problems, readers will want to view the tables with caution. Gross domestic product for 1913 expressed in 1990 dollars (180–2). Per capita domestic product for 1913 expressed in 1990 dollars (194–6). Exports in dollars at current prices at 1913 exchange rate (Maddison, *Monitoring the World Economy*, 234).

TABLE A.2. *Growth of GDP and GDP per Capita, 1870–1913/1913–50*[a]

Country	GDP growth (%)	Population growth (%)	Per capita GDP growth (%)
United States	3.94/2.84	2.09/1.21	1.81/1.61
Great Britain	1.9/1.19	0.87/0.27	1.01/0.92
Japan	2.34/2.24	0.95/1.31	1.38/0.92

[a] Estimates in Maddison, *Monitoring the World Economy 1820–1992* (Paris: OECD, 1995), 255.

TABLE A.3. *Real Growth/Per Capita Real Growth*[a]

Country or region	1960–70	1970–80	1980–90	1990–98
Developed countries	5.1/4.0	3.1/2.2	3.2/2.5	2.0/1.4
United States	4.4/3.1	2.8/1.7	3.4/2.4	2.8/1.8
Europe	4.7/3.8	2.9/2.4	2.5/2.2	1.8/1.5
Japan	10.3/9.1	4.3/3.1	4.1/3.5	1.2/1.0
Developing countries	6.0/3.4	5.6/3.1	3.0/0.6	4.9/3.1
Americas	5.5/2.7	5.8/3.2	1.6/−0.6	3.6/1.9
Africa	5.7/2.9	4.6/1.7	1.8/−1.2	2.5/−0.2
Asia	6.4/3.8	5.9/3.4	4.5/2.1	5.9/4.3
South and SE Asia	5.1/2.6	6.0/3.6	6.2/3.9	7.1/5.6

[a] UNCTAD, *Handbook of International Trade Statistics, 1991* (Geneva: United Nations, 1992), 438–43; UNCTAD, *Handbook of International Trade Statistics, 2000* (Geneva: United Nations, 2000), 296–302.

TABLE A.4. *Comparative Strength of the Warring Powers in World War II (1990 prices)*[a]

Bloc/Country	Population 1938	GDP/per capita (1938)	Armed forces (1943)
Allies			
United Kingdom	47.5 million	$284.2 billion/$5,983	4,761,000
France	42.0 million	$185.6 billion/$4,424	–
USSR	167.0 million	$359.0 billion/$2,150	11,858,000
USA	130.5 million	$800.3 billion/$6,134	9,020,000
Axis			
Germany	68.6 million	$351.4 billion/$5,126	9,480,000
Italy	43.4 million	$140.8 billion/$3,244	3,815,000
Japan	71.9 million	$169.4 billion/$2,356	3,700,000
Comparisons	Allies/Axis 1942 great powers only: 2.1/1.0	Allies/Axis GDP: 2.5/1.0	Allies/Axis: Eastern front 1.4/1 Western and Pacific 1.9/1

[a] Data from Mark Harrison, ed., *The Economics of World War II: Six Great Powers in International Comparison* (Cambridge: Cambridge University Press, 1998), 3, 7, 10, 14.

TABLE A.5. *U.S. Trade Patterns, 1900–2000[a]*

Country	1900 Exports	1990 Imports	1913 Exports	1913 Imports
TOTAL	$1,394 million	$850 million	$2,466 million	$1,813 million
Europe	74.6%	51.9%	60.0%	49.3%
United Kingdom	38.3%	18.8%	24.2%	16.3%
France	06.0%	8.6%	5.9%	7.6%
Germany	13.4%	11.4%	13.5%	10.4%
Canada	6.8%	4.6%	16.8%	6.7%
Latin America	9.5%	21.8%	14.1%	25.3%
Asia	4.9%	17.2%	5.7%	16.4%
Japan	2.1%	3.9%	2.4%	5.1%
China	1.0%	3.2%	0.9%	2.2%

	1929 Exports	1929 Imports	1938 Exports	1938 Imports
TOTAL	$5,241 million	$4,399 million	$3,094 million	$1,960 million
Europe	44.7%	30.3%	42.9%	28.9%
United Kingdom	16.2%	7.5%	16.8%	06.0%
France	5.1%	3.9%	4.3%	02.8%
Germany	7.8%	5.8%	3.5%	03.3%
Canada	18.1%	11.4%	15.1%	13.3%
Latin America	18.8%	25.4%	18.5%	25.2%
Mexico	2.6%	2.7%	2.0%	2.5%
Asia	12.3%	29.1%	16.7%	29.1%
China	2.4%	3.8%	1.1%	2.4%
Japan	4.9%	9.8%	7.8%	6.5%

	1950 Exports	1950 Imports	1960 Exports	1960 Imports
TOTAL	$10,275 million	$8,852 million	$20,575 million	$14,654 million
Europe	32.2%	16.4%	36.0%	29.1%
United Kingdom	05.3%	03.8%	7.2%	06.8%
France	04.6%	01.5%	03.4%	02.7%
Germany	04.3%	01.2%	06.2%	06.1%
Canada	19.8%	22.1%	18.5%	19.8%
Latin America	27.9%	35.1%	18.8%	27.0%
Mexico	5.1%	3.6%	4.0%	3.0%
Asia	15.0%	18.5%	20.3%	18.6%
Japan	4.1%	02.1%	7.0%	7.8%

(continued)

TABLE A.5 *(continued)*

	1970 Exports	1970 Imports	1980 Exports	1980 Imports
TOTAL	$43,224 million	$39,952 million	$220,783 million	$244,871 million
Europe	34.3%	28.5%	32.3%	19.6%
United Kingdom	5.9%	5.5%	5.8%	4.0%
France	3.4%	2.4%	3.4%	2.2%
Germany	6.3%	7.8%	5.0%	4.8%
Canada	21.0%	27.8%	16.0%	16.9%
Latin America	15.1%	14.6%	16.3%	12.2%
Mexico	3.9%	3.1%	6.9%	5.1%
Asia	23.2%	24.1%	27.3%	32.8%
Japan	10.8%	14.7%	9.4%	12.5%

	1990 Exports	1990 Imports	2000 Exports	2000 Imports
TOTAL	$393,592 million	$495,310 million	$782,429 million	$1,222,772 million
Europe	28.7%	22.5%	23.2%	19.7%
United Kingdom	6.0%	4.1%	5.3%	3.6%
France	3.5%	2.7%	3.7%	2.4%
Germany	4.8%	5.7%	2.6%	4.8%
Canada	21.3%	18.4%	22.9%	18.7%
Latin America-Mexico	4.8%	5.8%	7.6%	6.0%
Mexico	7.2%	6.1%	14.3%	11.1%
Asia/Pacific Rim	30.6%	41.9%	26.3%	34.2%
Japan	12.3%	19.0%	8.3%	12.0%
China	1.2%	3.2%	2.1%	8.2%

[a] Data from U.S. Bureau of the Census, *Statistical Abstract of the United States* (Washington, D.C.: GPO, various issues).

TABLE A.6. *U.S. Foreign Direct Investment, 1914–2000*[a]

	1914	1929	1950	1963
TOTAL	$2652.0 million	$7,477.7 million	$11,804 million	$40,686 million
Europe	21.6%	18.1%	15.0%	25.4%
United Kingdom	–	6.5%	7.1%	10.3%
France	–	1.9%	2.4%	3.1%
Germany	–	2.9%	1.7%	4.4%
Canada	23.3%	26.2%	30.2%	32.1%
Latin America	–	33.0%	39.6%	21.3%
Mexico	–	9.1%	3.4%	2.2%
Cuba	–	12.3%	5.4%	NA
Asia and Oceania	5.2%	5.3%	8.5%	6.9%
China	–	1.5%	NA	NA
Japan	–	0.8%	0.2%	1.2%

	1970	1980	1990	2000
TOTAL	$78,178 million	$215,578 million	$424,086 million	$1,293,431 million
Europe	31.4%	44.8%	49.8%	52.5%
United Kingdom	10.3%	13.3%	16.1%	18.7%
France	3.3%	4.3%	4.5%	3.0%
Germany	5.9%	7.2%	6.4%	3.9%
Netherlands	1.9%	3.8%	5.3%	9.1%
Canada	29.2%	20.9%	15.8%	10.0%
Latin America	15.7%	12.3%	9.8%	19.5%
Brazil	2.4%	3.6%	3.5%	3.0%
Mexico	2.3%	2.8%	2.2%	2.9%
Asia–Pacific	10.6%	11.8%	14.8%	15.9%
Australia	4.23%	3.6%	3.5%	2.7%
China	–	NA	0.07%	0.8%
Japan	1.9%	2.9%	5.0%	4.6%

[a] Mira Wilkins, *The Emergence of Multinational Enterprise: American Business Abroad from the Colonial Era to 1914* (Cambridge, Mass.: Harvard University Press, 1970), 110; Cleona Lewis, *America's Stake in International Investments* (Washington, D.C.: Brookings, 1938), 606; U.S. Department of Commerce, *American Direct Investments in Foreign Countries* (Trade Information Bulletin No. 731) (Washington, D.C.: GPO, 1930); *Survey of Current Business* 30:12 (December 1952):8; *Survey of Current Business* 43:9 (September 1965):24; *Survey of Current Business* 50:11 (November 1972):30; *Survey of Current Business* 60:8 (August 1982):21; *Survey of Current Business* 72:6 (June 1992):55, 57; *Survey of Current Business* 81:7 (July 2001):27.

TABLE A.7. *U.S. Foreign Direct Investment by Sector*[a]

Area	1982	1990	2000
Total FDI	$207.8 billion (100%)	$430.5 billion (100%)	$1,293.4 billion (100%)
Asia	$28.3 billion (13.6%)	$67.7 billion (15.7%)	$205.3 billion (15.9%)
Canada	$43.5 billion (20.9%)	$69.5 billion (16.1%)	$128.8 billion (10.0%)
Europe	$92.4 billion (44.5%)	$214.7 billion (49.8%)	$679.5 billion (52.5%)
Latin America	$28.2 billion (13.6%)	$71.4 billion (16.6%)	$251.9 billion (19.5%)
Manufacturing FDI	$83.5 billion (100%)	$170.16 billion (100%)	$353.6 billion (100%)
Asia	$9.2 billion (11.0%)	$26.4 billion (15.5%)	$65.0 billion (18.3%)
Canada	$18.8 billion (22.5%)	$33.3 billion (19.6%)	$50.8 billion (14.4%)
Europe	$37.8 billion (45.2%)	$85.0 billion (50%)	$185.7 billion (52.5%)
Latin America	$15.8 billion (18.9%)	$23.7 billion (13.9%)	$48.0 billion (13.6%)
Banking, finance, real estate, and services	$32.9 billion (100%)	$143.8 billion (100%)	$622.8 billion (100%)
Asia	$4.7 billion (14.3%)	$11.3 billion (7.9%)	$73.0 billion (11.7%)
Canada	$6.9 billion (20.8%)	$15.0 billion (10.6%)	$39.1 billion (6.3%)
Europe	$20.9 billion (63%)	$78.4 billion (54.5%)	$346.1 billion (55.6%)
Latin America	$0.0 billion (0%)	$37.4 billion (26%)	$159.8 billion (25.7%)

[a] U.S. Bureau of Economic Analysis, web site at http://www.bea.doc.gov/bea/di/dilusdbal. htm; Maria Borga and Daniel R. Yorgason, "Direct Investment Positions for 2001: Country and Industry Detail," *Survey of Current Business*, 82:7 (July 2002): 28.

TABLE A.8. *Foreign Direct Investment in the United States*[a]

	1914	1937	1950	1960
TOTAL	$7,100 million	$1,882 million	$3,391 million	$6,910 million
Europe	95.2%	71.0%	66%	68.1%
United Kingdom	59.9%	44.3%	34%	32.5%
France	6.8%	–	–	2.4%
Germany	15.5%	–	–	1.5%
Netherlands	9.2%	9.5%	9.8%	13.7%
Switzerland		3.9%	10.3%	11.2%
Canada	3.9%	24.6%	30.3%	28.0%
Latin America	NA	–	–	–
Mexico	NA	–	–	–
Japan	0.4%	–	–	1.3%

	1970	1980	1990	2000
TOTAL	$13,270 million	$68,351 million	$396,702 million	$1,214,254 million
Europe	72.0%	66.9%	63.3%	68.8%
United Kingdom	31.1%	17.9%	25.9%	17.6%
France	2.2%	4.3%	4.7%	10.8%
Germany	5.1%	7.1%	7.1%	10.3%
Netherlands	16.2%	24.7%	16.1%	12.1%
Switzerland	11.6%	17.9%	4.5%	5.7%
Canada	23.5%	14.7%	7.6%	9.4%
Latin America	NA	1.4%	1.5%	4.5%
Mexico	NA	NA	0.1%	0.6%
Asia–Pacific	NA	NA	23.0%	16.6%
Japan	1.7%	6.2%	20.6%	13.5%

[a] Mira Wilkins, *The History of Foreign Investment in the United States to 1914* (Cambridge, Mass.: Harvard University Press, 1989), 159. The figures for 1914 are Wilkins's estimates and include both direct and portfolio investment. Data for 1937 to 1970 from U.S. Census Bureau, *Historical Statistics of the United States: Bicentennial Edition* (Washington, D.C.: GPO, 1975), 2:871–2; *Survey of Current Business* 51:8 (August 1973):50; *Survey of Current Business* 60:8 (August 1982):36; *Survey of Current Business* 82:7 (July 2002):21–8.

TABLE A.9. *U.S. Trade in Goods and Services as a Share of Gross Domestic Product*[a]

Year	GDP	Exports (goods & services)	Imports (goods & services)	Trade/GDP
1929	$103.7 billion	$5.9 billion	$5.6 billion	11.1%
1938	$86.1 billion	$3.8 billion	$2.8 billion	7.7%
1950	$294.3 billion	$12.3 billion	$11.6 billion	8.1%
1957	$461.5 billion	$23.9 billion	$19.9 billion	9.5%
1960	$527.4 billion	$25.3 billion	$22.8 billion	9.1%
1965	$720.1 billion	$35.4 billion	$31.5 billion	9.2%
1970	$1,039.7 billion	$57.0 billion	$55.8 billion	10.8%
1975	$1,635.2 billion	$136.3 billion	$122.7 billion	15.8%
1980	$2,795.6 billion	$278.9 billion	$293.8 billion	20.5%
1990	$5,803.2 billion	$557.2 billion	$628.6 billion	20.4%
1995	$7,400.5 billion	$818.6 billion	$902.8 billion	23.3%
2000	$9,872.9 billion	$1,102.9 billion	$1,466.9 billion	26.0%

[a] Table computed from Brent R. Moulton, "Improved Estimates of the National Income and Product Accounts for 1929–99: Results of the Comprehensive Revision," *Survey of Current Business* 80:4 (April 2000):14; "BEA Current and Historical Data," *Survey of Current Business* 82:7 (July 2002): D-3, D-12.

TABLE A.10. *Merchant Ships Registered thousand tons of steam and motor ships*[a]

Year	United Kingdom	Germany	France	United States	Japan
1913	10,992	2,832	980	5,333	1,500
1918	9,497	–	850	7,471	–
1920	10,777	–	1,085	13,823	2,996
1929	11,889	2,312	1,775	14,162	4,187
1938	10,300	2,364	1,486	12,007	5,007
1942	9,000	–	1,583	11,072	5,367
1945	10,341	–	1,546	30,247	1,344
1960	11,797	3,729	4,809	23,553	6,931
1970	14,700	7,040	5,921	18,463	27,004
1980	25,769	5,027	11,239	18,464	40,960
1988	6,603	3,399	4,129	20,832	32,074

[a] B. R. Mitchell, *International Historical Statistics* (3 vols., New York: Stockton Press, 1992–95).

TABLE A.11. *Passengers/Cargo on U.S. Scheduled Airlines*[a]

	Passengers enplaned (millions)		Cargo Freight & Express (million ton miles)	
Year	Domestic	International	Domestic	International
1930	–	0.033,000	0.101	–
1940	2.5	0.163,000	3.5	–
1950	17.3	1.675	152.2	60.6
1960	52.4	5.5	386.9	191.6
1965	84.5	10.2	943.1	597.3
1970	153.7	16.3	2,215	1,299
1975	188.7	16.3	2,747	2,048
1980	272.8	24.1	3,277	2,465
1985	357.1	24.9	3,144	2,887
1990	423.6	42.0	5,075	5,471
1995	499.0	48.8	6,397	8,181
2000	610.0	55.5	7,943	13,200

[a] For early years to 1960, U.S. Bureau of the Census, *Historical Statistics*, 769–770; for later years Air Transport Association of America, "Traffic Summary 1960–2000: U.S. Scheduled Airlines," http://www.air-transport.org/public/industry/display1.asp?id=9

TABLE A.12. *Foreign Students Studying at U.S. Colleges and Universities*[a]

	1954–5	1975–6	1985–6	2000–1
Total students	34,232	179,344	343,777	547,867
Africa	3.6%	14.1%	9.9%	6.2%
Europe	15.2%	8.1%	10.0%	14.7%
Latin America	24.7%	16.6%	13.2%	11.6%
Middle East	11.9%	18.2%	15.3%	6.7%
North America	13.8%	5.4%	4.7%	4.7%
Asia	29.7%	36.0%	45.6%	55.1%

[a] http://opendoors.iienetwork.org

Notes

Introduction

1. Theodore Levitt, "The Globalization of Markets," *Harvard Business Review* 61:3 (May–June 1983):92–102.
2. U.S. Central Intelligence Agency, *Global Trends 2015: A Dialogue about the Future with Nongovernment Experts* (Washington, D.C.: National Intelligence Council, 2000), 8–13.
3. Thomas W. Zeiler, "Just Do it! Globalization for Diplomatic Historians," *Diplomatic History* 25 (Fall 2001): 531. The Wisconsin school had roots in the thinking of Charles A. Beard and William Appleman Williams, who revived interest in the economic aspects of foreign relations. While accurately appreciating that business was a powerful force for domestic and global expansion, this interpretation often discounted strategic, humanitarian, and idealistic considerations. Antiestablishment in the tradition of Midwestern populism, members of the group sometimes pressed a simplistic view of capitalism's contradictions, while neglecting terminology and analysis familiar to business analysts and neoclassical international economists. See Lloyd C. Gardner, Walter F. LaFeber, and Thomas J. McCormick, *Creation of the American Empire: U.S. Diplomatic History* (Chicago: Rand McNally, 1973).
4. David M. Pletcher, *The Diplomacy of Trade and Investment: American Economic Expansion in the Hemisphere, 1865–1900* (Columbia: University of Missouri Press, 1998), 1.
5. Fareed Zakaria, "The New American Consensus: Our Hollow Hegemony," *New York Times Magazine*, November 1, 1998, 44.
6. "Insider Trading," *Economist*, June 24, 1995, S6; Larry Reynolds, "Has Globalization Hurt America?" *AMA Management Review* 78:9 (1989):16.
7. The terms "multinational" and "transnational" corporations are often used interchangeably in the literature despite some differences. In this book, we have followed standard usage, while recognizing subtle differences. Succinctly stated, a multinational firm is an international business that operates differently in various national markets, whereas a transnational corporation looks at the global economy as a single unit in

which it can source, produce, and market its products. Transnational corporations tend to think of themselves as citizens of the world; multinationals, as corporate citizens operating in a variety of nations.

8. Kenichi Ohmae, *The End of the Nation State: The Rise of Regional Economies* (New York: Free Press, 1995), jacket. For a discussion of the battle between markets and the state, see Daniel Yergin and Joseph Stanislaw, *The Commanding Heights* (New York: Simon and Schuster, 1998).

9. Historian Daniel Boorstin wrote that "the supreme law of the Republic of Technology is convergence, the tendency for everything to become more like everything else." Daniel J. Boorstin, *The Republic of Technology: Reflections on our Future Community* (New York: Harper & Row, 1978), 5.

10. Alfred D. Chandler, Jr., and James W. Cortada, eds., *A Nation Transformed by Information: How Information Has Shaped the Untied States from Colonial Times to the Present* (New York: Oxford University Press, 2000).

11. Karl Marx and Frederick Engels, "Manifesto of the Communist Party" (1848), see http://www.anu.edu/au/polsci/marx/classics/manifesto.html.

Chapter 1

1. Alan M. Kraut, *The Huddled Masses: The Immigrant in American Society, 1880–1921* (Arlington Heights, Ill.: Harlan Davidson, 1982), 102–109; Lizabeth Cohen, *Making a New Deal: Industrial Workers in Chicago, 1919–1939* (Cambridge: Cambridge University Press, 1990), 173, note 12.

2. See Robert W. Rydell, *All the World's a Fair* (Chicago: University of Chicago Press, 1984).

3. William Becker, *The Dynamics of Business-Government Relations: Industry and Exports, 1893–1921* (Chicago: University of Chicago Press, 1982), 69–112.

4. Mahan quoted in Robert Wiebe, *The Search for Order, 1877–1920* (New York: Hill and Wang, 1967), 233. See also Walter LaFeber, *The American Search for Opportunity, 1865–1913* (Cambridge: Cambridge University Press, 1993), 116.

5. George Baer, *One Hundred Years of Sea Power, 1890–1990* (Stanford, Calif.: Stanford University Press, 1994), 12.

6. Thomas G. Paterson, J. Garry Clifford, and Kenneth J. Hagan, *American Foreign Relations: A History to 1920, Vol. I*, 4th ed. (Lexington, Mass.: D.C. Heath and Company, 1995), 179–80; Baer, *Sea Power*, 30, 33.

7. LaFeber, *Search for Opportunity*, 148, also 164. See also, Baer, *Sea Power*, 25–7; Walter Millis, *Arms and Men: A Study in American Military History* (New York: G. P. Putnam's Sons, 1956), 168–9.

8. LaFeber, *Search for Opportunity*, 170; Charles I. Bevans, comp., *Treaties and Other International Agreements of the United States of America, 1776–1949* (Department of State Pub. 8549) (Washington, D.C.: GPO, 1971), 6:695–708. On key principles of WTO, see Christopher Arup, *The New World Trade Organization Agreements: Globalizing Law Through Services and Intellectual Property* (Cambridge: Cambridge University Press, 2000), 10–12.

9. John Whiteclay Chambers II, *The Tyranny of Change: America in the Progressive Era, 1890–1920*, 2nd ed. (New York: St. Martin's Press, 1992), 58; Kristin L.

Hoganson, *Fighting for American Manhood: How Gender Politics Provoked the Spanish-American and Philippine-American Wars* (New Haven, Conn.: Yale University Press, 1998), 38, 67.

10. Chambers, *Tyranny of Change*, 77. See also Alfred D. Chandler, Jr., *Scale and Scope: The Dynamics of Industrial Capitalism* (Cambridge, Mass.: Harvard University Press, 1990); Naomi R. Lamoreaux, *The Great Merger Movement in American Business, 1895–1904* (Cambridge: Cambridge University Press, 1985).

11. James D. Richardson, comp., *Compilation of the Messages and Papers of the Presidents* (New York: Bureau of National Literature, 1911), XIV, 6618–22. On the revolution in information brought by the telegraph, see Tom Standage, *The Victorian Internet* (New York: Berkley Books, 1999).

12. On the legalist approach to international dispute settlement, see Francis Anthony Boyle, *Foundations of World Order: The Legalist Approach to International Relations (1898–1922)* (Durham, N.C.: Duke University Press, 1999). On the development of international economic law, see David Kennedy, "Interdisciplinary Approaches to International Economic Law: The International Style in Postwar Law and Policy: John Jackson and the Field of International Economic Law," *American University Journal of International Law & Policy* 10 (Winter 1995): 671.

13. U.S. Department of State, *Commercial Relations of the United States 1900* (Washington, D.C.: GPO, 1901), 16.

14. Angus Maddison, *Monitoring the World Economy 1820–1992* (Paris: OECD, 1995), 38.

15. U.S. Bureau of the Census, *Historical Statistics, of the United States (Bicentennial Edition)* (Washington, D.C.: GPO, 1975), 2:887; William Lovett, Alfred Eckes, and Richard Brinkman, *U.S. Trade Policy: History, Theory and the WTO* (Armonk, N.Y.: M. E. Sharpe, 1999), 52–4.

16. U.S. Department of State, *Commercial Relations 1900*, 16, 27–8.

17. Benjamin H. Thwaite, *The American Invasion; or England's Commercial Danger* (Wilmington, N.C.: Hugh MacRae & Co., 1902), 21–9.

18. William Stead, *The Americanization of the World* (New York: Garland, 1972, reprint of 1902 ed.), 141; John K. Brown, *The Baldwin Locomotive Works 1831–1915* (Baltimore: Johns Hopkins University Press, 1995).

19. Fred MacKenzie cited in Stead, *Americanization of the World*, 138, 139. See also Albert K. Steigerwalt, *The National Association of Manufacturers 1895–1914* (Ann Arbor: University of Michigan, 1964), 59–63.

20. Thwaite, *American Invasion*, 5, 20–2. See also Charles H. Duell, "The American Patent System," *Scientific American Supplement* (February 16, 1901): 21008–9.

21. Chauncey Smith, "A Century of Patent Law," *Quarterly Journal of Economics* 5(1) (October 1890): 44–69.

22. Mira Wilkins, *The Emergence of Multinational Enterprise: American Business Abroad from the Colonial Era to 1914* (Cambridge, Mass.: Harvard University Press, 1970), 214.

23. U.S. Department of Commerce, *Patents: Spur to American Progress* (Washington, D.C.: GPO, 1969 rev.); David J. Jeremy, *A Business History*

of Britain, 1900–1990s (New York: Oxford University Press, 1998), 113–14; Chandler, *Scale and Scope*, 214; Harold C. Passer, *The Electrical Manufacturers, 1875–1900* (Cambridge, Mass.: Harvard University Press, 1953); William Becker, *Business-Government Relations*, 32–33, 52–4.

24. Alfred Chandler, "The Beginnings of 'Big Business' in American Industry," *Business History Review* 33 (Spring 1959): 1–31; John F. Wilson, *British Business History, 1720–1994* (Manchester, U.K.: Manchester University Press, 1995), 86–132; P. J. Cain and A. G. Hopkins, *British Imperialism: Innovation and Expansion, 1688–1914* (New York: Longman, 1993), 125–34.

25. On Singer, see Robert B. Davies, *Peacefully Working to Conquer the World: Singer Sewing Machines in Foreign Markets, 1854–1920* (New York: Arno, 1976).

26. Wilkins, *Emergence*, 110; John H. Dunning, *Explaining International Production* (New York: Harper, 1988), 72–7.

27. Rene De La Pedraja, *The Rise and Decline of U.S. Merchant Shipping in the Twentieth Century* (New York: Twayne, 1992), 47.

28. William Lovett, ed., *United States Shipping Policies and the World Market* (Westport, Conn.: Quorum, 1996), 6–7; Paul Zeis, *American Shipping Policy* (Princeton, N.J.: Princeton University Press, 1938); David Pletcher, *The Diplomacy of Trade and Investment: American Economic Expansion in the Hemisphere, 1865–1900* (Columbia: University of Missouri Press, 1998): 275, 380–1.

29. Data from U.S. Bureau of the Census, *Historical Statistics*, 2:782, 791; Daniel Headrick, *The Invisible Weapon: Telecommunications and International Politics, 1851–1945* (New York: Oxford University Press, 1991), 4, 28, 32, 36–9. Quotes on pages 28, 36.

30. See generally, George P. Oslin, *The Story of Telecommunications* (Macon, Ga.: Mercer University Press, 1992).

31. P. L. Cottrell, "Great Britain" in *International Banking 1870–1914*, eds. Rondo Cameron and V. I. Bovykin (New York: Oxford University Press, 1991), 25–6.

32. Wilkins, *Emergence*, 141–63, especially 147, 151, 159. See also, Lance Davis and Robert J. Cull, *International Capital Markets and American Economic Growth, 1820–1914* (Cambridge: Cambridge University Press, 1994), 17–19; William G. Robbins, *Colony and Empire: The Capitalist Transformation of the American West* (Lawrence: University of Kansas Press, 1994), 63, 91.

33. Wilkins, *Emergence*, 199–217.

34. Steigerwalt, *NAM*, 24, 81–2, 169; Headrick, *Invisible Weapon*, 4, 28, 32.

35. Baer, *Sea Power*, 47; LaFeber, *Search for Opportunity*, 117.

36. Quoted in Headrick, *Invisible Weapon*, 3.

37. Chambers, *Tyranny of Change*, 75. See also James R. Reckner, *Teddy Roosevelt's Great White Fleet* (Annapolis, Md.: Naval Institute Press, 1988), 16–17.

38. William H. Becker, "1899–1920: America Adjusts to World Power" in *Economics and World Power: An Assessment of American Diplomacy Since 1789*, eds. William H. Becker and Samuel F. Wells, Jr. (New York: Columbia University Press, 1984), 186–8.

39. LaFeber, *Search for Opportunity*, 191.

40. Emily Rosenberg, *Financial Missionaries to the World: The Politics and Culture of Dollar Diplomacy, 1900–1930* (Cambridge, Mass.: Harvard University Press, 1999), 31–60; LaFeber, *Search for Opportunity*, 192–201; David McCullough, *The Path Between the Seas: The Creation of the Panama Canal, 1870–1914* (New York: Simon & Schuster, 1977), 543–54. On Central American intervention, see also articles in Paul W. Drake, ed., *Money Doctors, Foreign Debts, and Economic Reforms in Latin America from the 1890s to the Present* (Wilmington, Del.: Scholarly Resources, 1994).

41. Raymond A. Esthus, *Theodore Roosevelt and the International Rivalries* (Claremont, Calif.: Regina Books, 1970); Bradford Perkins, *The Great Rapprochement: England and the United States, 1895–1914* (New York: Atheneum, 1968), 53.

42. Quoted in Frank Ninkovich, *Modernity and Power: A History of the Domino Theory in the Twentieth Century* (Chicago: University of Chicago Press, 1994), 32, 35. See also Rosenberg, *Financial Missionaries*, 61–79.

43. Gabriel Kolko, *The Triumph of Conservatism: A Reinterpretation of American History, 1900–1916* (New York: The Free Press, 1963). 165–77.

44. Lester D. Langley and Thomas Schoonover, *The Banana Men: American Mercenaries and Entrepreneurs in Central America, 1880–1930* (Lexington: University of Kentucky Press, 1995), 33–41; Stacy May and Galo Plaza, *United Fruit Company in Latin America* (New York: National Planning Association, 1958), 18–19.

45. George Kennan, *E. H. Harriman: A Biography, Vol. II* (Boston: Houghton Mifflin Company, 1922), 1, also 2–26; Maury Klein, *The Life and Legend of E. H. Harriman* (Chapel Hill: University of North Carolina Press, 2000), 283–5.

46. Klein, *E. H. Harriman*, 287, also 290.

47. Becker, "America Adjusts to World Power," 199–200; LaFeber, *Search for Opportunity*, 214–33; Wiebe, *Search for Order*, 252–3.

48. Ninkovich, *Modernity and Power*, 31.

49. Kennan, *E. H. Harriman*, 28–9; Rosenberg, *Financial Missionaries*, 79–96.

50. *Congressional Record*, 57th Cong., 1st sess., (February 27, 1902), p. 2201.

51. See Michael Hunt, *The Making of a Special Relationship: The United States and China to 1914* (New York: Columbia University Press, 1983), 293. Also, Jon Thares Davidann, *A World of Crisis and Progress: The American YMCA in Japan, 1890–1930* (Bethlehem, Pa.: Lehigh University Press, 1998); John Tomlinson, *Cultural Imperialism: A Critical Interpretation* (Baltimore, Md.: Johns Hopkins University Press, 1991); William R. Hutchison, *Errand to the World: American Protestant Thought and Foreign Missions* (Chicago: University of Chicago Press, 1987).

52. David Healy, *US Expansionism: The Imperialist Urge in the 1890s* (Madison: University of Wisconsin Press, 1970), 130–6.

53. Ian R. Tyrrel, *Woman's World/Women's Empire: The Woman's Christian Temperance Union in International Perspective, 1880–1930* (Chapel Hill: University of North Carolina Press, 1991), 61, 76, 147.

54. Kathy Peiss, *Hope in a Jar: The Making of America's Beauty Culture* (New York: Henry Holt and Company, 1998), 63–6.

55. Richard Heathcote Heindel, *The American Impact on Great Britain 1898–1914: A Study of the United States in World History* (New York: Octagon Books, 1968 rep. of 1940 ed.), 335; Perkins, *Great Rapprochement*, 137.

56. Generally, Emily S. Rosenberg, *Spreading the American Dream: American Economic and Cultural Expansion, 1890–1945* (New York: Hill & Wang, 1982); Heindel, *The American Impact on Great Britain*; Perkins, *Great Rapprochement*, 149.

57. Ralph G. Martin, *Jennie: The Life of Lady Randolph Churchill: The Romantic Years, 1854–95* (Englewood Cliffs, N.J.: Prentice Hall, 1969); Perkins, *Great Rapprochement*, 151.

58. Steigerwalt, *NAM*, 45–6.

59. Perkins, *Great Rapprochement*, 152.

60. Raymond B. Fosdick, *The Story of the Rockefeller Foundation* (New York: Harper, 1952); Carnegie quote, 5. See also John Ensor Harr and Peter J. Johnson, *The Rockefeller Conscience: An American Family in Public and in Private* (New York: Scribner, 1991); Ron Chernow, *The Titan: The Life of John D. Rockefeller, Sr.* (New York: Random House, 1998); and Merle Curti, *American Philanthropy Abroad: A History* (New Brunswick: Rutgers University Press, 1963), 223.

61. David Wallechinsky, *The Complete Book of the Summer Olympics* (Boston: Little, Brown, 1996), xi. See generally, John E. Findling and Kimberley D. Pelle, eds., *Historical Dictionary of the Modern Olympic Movement* (Westport, Conn.: Greenwood Press, 1996). On British cheating, see Perkins, *Great Rapprochement*, 119–20. British officials allowed their tug-o-war team to wear hobnailed boots for better traction, a violation of Olympic rules. They also stopped the 400-meter final on a dubious interference call when an American was clearly going to win. And they dragged a prostrate Italian marathoner across the finish line, ahead of a charging American. A U.S. protest found its way to Teddy Roosevelt's desk, and the president then complained. Such were the still powerful currents of nationalism in an age of globalization.

62. Richard Cobden, *Speeches on Questions of Public Policy* (London: Macmillan, 1880), 187; Frank Vanderlip, *The American "Commercial Invasion" of Europe* (New York: Arno, 1976, reprint of 1902 ed.), 12; Norman Angell, *The Great Illusion* (New York: Garland, 1972, reprint of 1911 ed.), vii.

63. H. G. Wells, *The Future in America: A Search After Realities* (New York: Harper and Brothers, Publishers, 1906), 257.

Chapter 2

1. Ernest L. Bogart, *Direct and Indirect Costs of the Great World War* (New York: Oxford University Press, 1920), 266–7. Historian Niall Ferguson speculated about the counterfactual situation in which Britain opted not to join the European war. See his *The Pity of War* (London: Penguin, 1998), 460–1.

2. Avren Offer, *The First World War: An Agrarian Interpretation* (Oxford: Clarendon Press, 1989), 15–16; Paul Kennedy, *The Rise of the Anglo-German Antagonism* (London: Allen & Unwin, 1980), 464, 470.

3. Offer, *First World War*, 219–20.

4. Offer, *First World War*, 25, 321–2; Alfred Eckes, *The United States and the Global Struggle for Minerals* (Austin: University of Texas Press, 1979), 11–14; Daniel Yergin, *The Prize: The Epic Quest for Oil, Money & Power* (New York: Simon and Schuster, 1991), 179–83.

5. Data from U.S. Department of Commerce, *Trade of the United States with the World 1912–1913*, Miscellaneous Series No. 15 (Washington, D.C.: GPO, 1914); Vincent P. Carosso and Richard Sylla, "U.S. Banks in International Finance," in *International Banking 1870–1914*, eds. Rondo Cameron and V. I. Bovykin, (New York: Oxford University Press, 1991), 48; League of Nations, Economic, Financial, and Transit Department, *Industrialization and Foreign Trade* (Geneva: League of Nations, 1945), 13; B. R. Mitchell, *International Historical Statistics: Europe 1750–1988* (New York: Stockton Press, 1992), 592–652.

6. Offer, *First World War*, 81–92, 217–32, 402–3.

7. Daniel Headrick, *The Invisible Weapon: Telecommunications and International Politics, 1851–1945* (New York: Oxford University Press, 1991), 4, 28, 32, quote on page 28. M. L. Sanders and Philip M. Taylor, *British Propaganda during the First World War, 1914–18* (London: Macmillan, 1982), 167–207.

8. Reinhard R. Doerries, *Imperial Challenge: Ambassador Count Bernstorff and German-American Relations 1907–1917* (Chapel Hill: University of North Carolina Press, 1989); Count Bernstorff, *My Three Years in America* (New York: Scribner, 1920); C. Paul Vincent, *The Politics of Hunger: The Allied Blockade of Germany, 1915–19* (Athens: Ohio University Press, 1985).

9. Thomas G. Paterson, J. Garry Clifford, and Kenneth J. Hagan, *American Foreign Relations, A History: Since 1895, Vol II*, 5th ed. (Boston: Houghton Mifflin, 2000), 286–94.

10. William H. Becker, "America Adjusts to World Power" in *Economics and World Power: An Assessment of American Diplomacy Since 1789*, eds. William H. Becker and Samuel F. Wells, Jr. (New York: Columbia University Press, 1984), 207–9. See also Arno Mayer, *Political Origins of the New Diplomacy, 1917–1918* (New Haven: Yale University Press, 1959).

11. Arthur Link, ed., *Papers of Woodrow Wilson* (Princeton, N.J.: Princeton University Press, 1991), 66: 619 (August 20, 1919); Kathleen Burk, *Britain, America and the Sinews of War, 1914–1918* (Boston: George Allen & Unwin, 1985), 5, 9; Offer, *First World War*, 376.

12. Merle Curti, *American Philanthropy Abroad: A History* (New Brunswick, N.J.: Rutgers University Press, 1963), 224–58.

13. George W. Baer, *One Hundred Years of Sea Power: The U.S. Navy, 1890–1990* (Stanford, Calif.: Stanford University Press, 1993), 64–82. On oil transportation problems, see George Sweet Gibb and Evelyn H. Knowlton, *History of Standard Oil Company (New Jersey): The Resurgent Years, 1911–1927*, 222–6. See also, J. A. Salter, *Allied Shipping Control: An Experiment in International Administration* (Oxford: Clarendon Press, 1921), 3–4. Control of the seas was only one dimension of England's shipping problems. Delays from inefficient port facilities also cost supplies.

14. Edward M. Lamont, *The Ambassador from Wall Street: The Story of Thomas W. Lamont, J. P. Morgan's Chief Executive* (Lanham, Md.: Madison Books, 1994), 69, 102–3. See Burk, *Sinews of War.*

15. Mira Wilkins, *The Maturing of Multinational Enterprise* (Cambridge, Mass.: Harvard University Press, 1974); U.S. Bureau of the Census, *Historical Statistics of the United States: Colonial Times to 1957* (Washington, D.C.: GPO, 1960); Burk, *Sinews of War*, 223.

16. Ron Chernow, *The Warburgs: A Family Saga* (London: Pimlico, 1995), 162–9, 180–1.

17. Wilkins, *Maturing of Multinational Enterprise*, 4, 30. She seems to rely on Bureau of the Census, *Historical Statistics of the United States*, 565.

18. Barry Eichengreen, *Globalizing Capital: A History of the International Monetary System* (Princeton, N.J.: Princeton University Press, 1996), 46–7.

19. Benjamin H. Williams, *Economic Foreign Policy of the United States* (New York: Howard Fertig, 1967 reprint of 1929 edition), 342–3; U.S. Bureau of the Census, *Statistical Abstract of the United States 1929* (Washington, D.C.: GPO, 1929), 457–8. See generally William Becker, *The Dynamics of Business-Government Relations: Industry and Exports, 1893–1921* (Chicago: University of Chicago, 1982), 131–56. Jeffrey J. Safford, "The American Merchant Marine as an Expression of Foreign Policy: Woodrow Wilson and the Genesis of Modern Maritime Diplomacy," in *The Atlantic World of Robert G. Albion*, ed. Benjamin W. Labaree (Middletown, Conn.: Wesleyan University Press, 1975), 144–68, quote on page 145. See also J. R. Richardson, comp., *Messages and Papers of the Presidents* (New York: Bureau of National Literature, 1917), 8151–2.

20. Safford, "The American Merchant Marine," 154; Rene De La Pedraja, *The Rise and Decline of U.S. Merchant Shipping in the Twentieth Century* (New York: Twayne Publishers, 1992), 62. On British suspicions of the American merchant fleet program, see David French, " 'Had We Known How Bad Things Were in Germany, We Might Have Got Stiffer Terms': Great Britain and the German Armistice," in *The Treaty of Versailles: A Reassessment after 75 Years*, eds. Manfred F. Boemeke, Gerald D. Feldman, and Elisabeth Glaser (Cambridge: Cambridge University Press, 1998), 78.

21. William A. Lovett, ed., *United States Shipping Policies and the World Market* (Westport, Conn: Quorum Books, 1996), 49–54; Williams, *Economic Foreign Policy*, 333.

22. Wilkins, *Maturing of Multinational Enterprise*, 31.

23. Wilkins, *Maturing of Multinational Enterprise*, 20–2; Paul P. Abrahams, *The Foreign Expansion of American Finance and Its Relationship to the Foreign Economic Policies of the United States, 1907–1921* (New York: Arno Press, 1976).

24. Becker, *Business-Government Relations*, 136–7.

25. Harold van B. Cleveland and Thomas F. Huertas, *Citibank, 1812–1970* (Cambridge, Mass: Harvard University Press, 1985), 300–1.

26. Kristin Thompson, *Exporting Entertainment: America in the World Film Market 1907–34* (London: British Film Institute, 1985), quote on page 95; Kristin Thompson, "The Rise and Fall of Film Europe," in *"Film Europe" and "Film*

America": Cinema, Commerce and Cultural Exchange 1920–1939, eds. Andrew Higson and Richard Maltby (Exeter, England: University of Exeter Press, 1999), 56–81. On Creel, see Thomas C. Sorensen, *The Word War: The Story of American Propaganda* (New York: Harper & Row, 1968), 6.

27. Paul A. C. Koistinen, *Mobilizing for Modern War: The Political Economy of American Warfare, 1865–1919* (Lawrence: University of Kansas Press, 1997), 101, 113–32.

28. John Whitclay Chambers, To *Raise an Army: The Draft Comes to Modern America* (New York: The Free Press, 1987), 126. See also Kenneth J. Hagan, *The People's Navy: The Making of American Sea Power* (New York: The Free Press, 1991), 249, 256.

29. Walter Millis, *Arms and Men: A Study in American Military History* (New York: G. P. Putnam's Sons, 1956), 213–40; Koistinen, *Mobilizing for Modern War*, 253, 295.

30. F. David Cronon, ed., *The Cabinet Diaries of Josephus Daniels 1913–21* (Lincoln: University of Nebraska Press, 1963); Wilkins, *Maturing of Multinational Enterprise*, 37; Gibb and Knowlton, *Resurgent Years*, Chapter 4.

31. Business historian Ron Chernow observes the irony that Woodrow Wilson, the one-time critic of big business, became by 1916 a reluctant promoter of business and financial expansion. "[N]obody was more emboldened by the new financial power than President Wilson who was eager to undertake liberal dreams with Wall Street money ... the House of Morgan ... would evolve into a shadow government and move in tandem with official policy." Chernow, *The House of Morgan: American Banking Dynasty and the Rise of Modern Finance* (New York: Simon & Schuster, 1990), 206. See also Robert Sobel, *RCA* (New York: Stein and Day, 1986), 26–7. On business-government cooperation during the Wilson administration, see also Burton I. Kaufman, *Efficiency and Expansion: Foreign Trade Organization in the Wilson Administration 1913–1921* (Westport, Conn.: Greenwood Press, 1974). On internationalists, see Thomas J. Knock, *To End All Wars: Woodrow Wilson and the Quest for a New World Order* (New York: Oxford University Press, 1992), 48–57.

32. Becker, *Business-Government Relations*, 137–43; Link, *Papers of Woodrow Wilson*, Wilson quote on pages 43–4 in Wilson to Frank L. Polk (March 4, 1920).

33. Abrahams, *Foreign Expansion of American Finance*, 139–41.

34. De La Pedraja, *U.S. Merchant Shipping*, 59–60; Cronon, *Cabinet Diaries*, 536.

35. Michael Hogan, *Informal Entente: The Private Structure of Cooperation in Anglo-American Economic Diplomacy, 1918–1928* (Columbia: University of Missouri Press, 1977), 105–58. For documentation, U.S. Department of State, *Foreign Relations of the United States* (1920), (Washington, D.C.: GPO, 1936), II: 700–4. Young quote cited in Frank Costigliola, *Awkward Dominion: American Political, Economic, and Cultural Relations with Europe, 1919–1933* (Ithaca, N.Y.: Cornell University Press, 1984), 63; Eugene Lyons, *David Sarnoff: A Biography* (New York: Harper & Row, 1966), 74–84. See also, Sobel, *RCA*, 17–35.

36. Headrick, *Invisible Weapon*, 206.

37. Yergin, *The Prize*, 176–7, 194.

38. Cronon, *Cabinet Diaries*, 502. See also John A. DeNovo, "The Movement for an Aggressive American Oil Policy Abroad, 1918–1920," *American Historical Review* LXI: 4 (July 1956): 854–76; Stephen J. Randall, *United States Foreign Oil Policy, 1919–1948: For Profits and Security* (Kingston, Ont.: McGill-Queen's University Press, 1985), 18–24; William Stivers, *Supremacy and Oil: Iraq, Turkey and the Anglo-American World Order, 1918–1930* (Ithaca, N.Y.: Cornell University Press, 1982), 112–13; Herbert Feis, *Petroleum and American Foreign Policy* (Stanford, Calif.: Food Research Institute, Stanford University, 1944); Gibb and Knowlton, *Resurgent Years*, 287–8.
39. Kenneth Bourne and D. Cameron Watt, *British Documents on Foreign Affairs, Part II. Series C, North America, 1919–39* (Frederick, Md.: University Publications of America, 1993), 10:27, and 13:24.
40. Antoine Fleury, "The League of Nations: Toward a New Appreciation of its History," eds. Boemeke et al., *Treaty of Versailles*, 507–22.
41. Arthur S. Link, *Woodrow Wilson: Revolution, War, and Peace* (Arlington Heights, Ill.: Harlan Davidson, 1979), 24.
42. Frank Ninkovich, *The Wilsonian Century: U.S. Foreign Policy Since 1900* (Chicago: University of Chicago Press, 1999), 45. See also Link, *Woodrow Wilson*, 98–9.
43. Frank A. Ninkovich, *Modernity and Power: A History of the Domino Theory in the Twentieth Century* (Chicago: University of Chicago Press, 1994).
44. Ninkovich, *Wilsonian Century*, 72–3.
45. Knock, *To End All Wars*, 27–30, 48–69, 227–70.
46. Knock, *To End All Wars*, 273–4.
47. Lloyd C. Gardner, *Safe for Democracy: The Anglo-American Response to Revolution, 1913–1923* (New York: Oxford University Press, 1987); Wilkins, *Maturing of Multinational Enterprise*, p. 40.

Chapter 3

1. Thomas A. Bailey, *A Diplomatic History of the American People*, 9th ed. (Englewood Cliffs, N.J.: Prentice Hall, 1970). One of Bailey's chapters on the interwar period is entitled "The Retreat to Isolationism 1919–1935."
2. William H. Becker, "1899–1920: America Adjusts to World Power" in *Economics and World Power: An Assessment of American Diplomacy Since 1789*, eds. William H. Becker and Samuel F. Wells, Jr. (New York: Columbia University Press, 1984), 212–19; Melvyn P. Leffler, "1921–1932: Expansionist Impulses and Domestic Constraints," in *Economics and World Power*, 227–30, 233–9; Roger Dingman, *Power in the Pacific: The Origins of Naval Arms Limitation, 1914–1922* (Chicago: University of Chicago Press, 1976), 89–90, 216–17; Akira Iriye, *The Globalizing of America, 1913–1945* (New York: Cambridge University Press, 1993), 75–9.
3. Iriye, *Globalizing of America*, 83; Leffler, "1921–1932," 234.
4. Lester Chandler, *Benjamin Strong, Central Banker* (Washington, D.C.: Brookings, 1958), 291–331; Barry Eichengreen, *Globalizing Capital: A History of the International Monetary System* (Princeton, N.J.: Princeton University Press, 1996), 57–60.

5. Barry Eichengreen, *Golden Fetters: The Gold Standard and the Great Depression, 1931–1939* (New York: Oxford, 1992), 161–7. For a critique of Federal Reserve policies, see Herbert Hoover, *The Memoirs of Herbert Hoover, Vol. III The Great Depression, 1929–1941* (New York: Macmillan, 1952), 6–14. For a critical discussion of Britain's return to gold, see P. J. Cain and A. G. Hopkins, *British Imperialism: Crisis and Deconstruction 1914–1990* (London: Longman, 1993), 63–70.

6. Edward Lamont, *The Ambassador from Wall Street: The Story of Thomas W. Lamont, J. P. Morgan's Chief Executive* (Lanham, Md.: Madison Books, 1994), 89; Chandler, *Benjamin Strong*.

7. Kathleen Burk says "it is probable that the success of British foreign policy during the 1920s owes more to the support of the House of Morgan than has ever been acknowledged." See her *Britain, America and the Sinews of War, 1914–1918* (London: G. Allen & Unwin, 1985), 224; Ron Chernow, *The House of Morgan: An American Banking Dynasty and the Rise of Modern Finance* (New York: Simon & Schuster, 1990), 279–83.

8. Frank Costigliola, *Awkward Dominion: American Political, Economic and Cultural Relations with Europe, 1919–1933* (Ithaca, N.Y.: Cornell University Press, 1984), 133–5, 147–8.

9. John T. Madden, Marcus Nadler, and Harry C. Sauvain, *America's Experience as a Creditor Nation* (New York: Prentice Hall, 1937), 76–9; Eichengreen, *Globalizing Capital*, 69–72. On Austria, see Reinhold Wagnleitner, *Coca-Colonization and the Cold War: The Cultural Mission of the United States in Austria After the Second World War* (Chapel Hill: University of North Carolina Press, 1994), 42–3.

10. Iriye, *Globalizing of America*, 80, also 105–111; generally, Robert F. Byrnes, *Awakening American Education to the World: The Role of Archibald Carey Coolidge 1866–1928* (Notre Dame, Ind.: Notre Dame University Press, 1982).

11. Iriye, *Globalizing of America*, 80, also 105–11.

12. Jeffrey A. Charles, *Service Clubs in American Society: Rotary, Kiwanis, and Lions* (Urbana, Ill.: University of Illinois Press, 1993), 124–40. On Tokyo earthquake, online at http://www. tokyo-rc.gr.jp/ehis/eho2.htm.

13. Quotes, Lamont, *Ambassador from Wall Street*, 171; Costigliola, *Awkward Dominion*, 140; Henry Ford, *My Philosophy of Industry* (New York: Coward-McCann, 1929), 45. Generally, James Warren Prothro, *The Dollar Decade: Business Ideas in the 1920's* (Baton Rouge: Louisiana State University Press, 1954); George L. Ridgeway, *Merchants of Peace: Twenty Years of Business Diplomacy through the International Chamber of Commerce, 1919–1938* (New York: Columbia University Press, 1938); Akira Iriye, *Cultural Internationalism and World Order* (Baltimore: Johns Hopkins University Press, 1997). Young had similar enthusiasm for America's moral leadership. Josephine Young Case and Everett Needham Case, *Owen D. Young and American Enterprise* (Boston: Godine, 1982), 265–6, 316.

14. William G. Robbins, *Colony and Empire: The Capitalist Transformation of the American West* (Lawrence: University of Kansas Press, 1994), 4, also 3. See also Ellis W. Hawley, *The Great War and the Search for a Modern Order*, 2nd ed. (New York: St. Martin's, 1993), 48–50, 83–4, 96; David Burner, *Herbert*

Hoover: A Public Life (New York: Atheneum, 1984), 184–5; Joan Hoff Wilson, *Herbert Hoover: Forgotten Progressive* (Boston: Little, Brown, 1975), 12–23.

15. Mira Wilkins, *The Maturing of Multinational Enterprise* (Cambridge, Mass.: Harvard University Press, 1974), 129; David Sarnoff, *Looking Ahead: The Papers of David Sarnoff* (New York: McGraw-Hill, 1968), 19–20. See also, Robert Sobel, *RCA* (New York: Stein & Day, 1986), 17–35.

16. Wilkins, *Maturing of Multinational Enterprise*, 130–1; Chernow, *House of Morgan*, 308. See also Robert Sobel, *ITT: The Management of Opportunity* (New York: Times Books, 1982), 35–65.

17. George P. Oslin, *The Story of Telecommunications* (Macon, Ga.: Mercer University Press, 1992), 294; Wagnleitner, *Coca-Colonization*, 49.

18. Lawrence A. Clayton, *Grace: W. R. Grace and Co., the Formative Years, 1850–1930* (Ottawa, Ill.: Jameson Books, 1985).

19. Marylin Bender and Selig Altschul, *The Chosen Instrument: Juan Trippe, PanAm* (New York: Simon & Schuster, 1982), 87–8.

20. Wilkins, *Maturing of Multinational Enterprise*, 135. See also, Matthew Josephson, *Empire of the Air, Juan Trippe and the Struggle for World Airways* (New York: Harcourt Brace, 1943); Robert Daley, *Juan Trippe and His Pan Am Empire: An American Saga* (New York: Random House, 1980), 12–17, 27–34, 59–92; T. A. Heppenheimer, *Turbulent Skies: The History of Commercial Aviation* (New York: John Wiley, 1995), 46–74; Oliver James Lissitzyn, *International Air Transport and National Policy* (New York: Council on Foreign Relations, 1942). See also, Eric Paul Roorda, "The Cult of the Airplane among U.S. Military Men and Dominicans during the U.S. Occupation and the Trujillo Regime" in *Close Encounters of Empire: Writing the Cultural History of U.S.-Latin American Relations*, eds. Gilbert M. Joseph, Catherine LeGrand, and Ricardo D. Salvatore (Durham, N.C.: Duke University Press, 1998), 271.

21. Wilkins, *Maturing of Multinational Enterprise*, 118–22; Edward Peter Fitzgerald, "Business Diplomacy: Walter Teagle, Jersey Standard, and the Anglo-French Pipeline Conflict in the Middle East, 1930–1931," *Business History Review* 67:2 (June 22, 1993):207.

22. Chernow, *House of Morgan*, 292, 296; Lamont, *Ambassador from Wall Street*, 280–8.

23. Robert Freeman Smith, *The United States and Revolutionary Nationalism in Mexico, 1916–1932* (Chicago: University of Chicago Press, 1972), 257, also 242–58. See also W. Dirk Raat, *Mexico and the United States: Ambivalent Vistas*, 2nd ed. (London: University of Georgia Press, 1996), 123.

24. Costigliola, *Awkward Dominion*, 157–63; Christine A. White, *British and American Commercial Relations with Soviet Russia, 1918–1924* (Chapel Hill: University of North Carolina Press, 1992).

25. Quoted in John B. Rae, ed., *Henry Ford* (Englewood Cliffs, N.J.: Prentice-Hall, 1969), 54–5. See also H. W. Brands, *Masters of Enterprise: Giants of American Business From John Jacob Astor and J. P. Morgan to Bill Gates and Oprah Winfrey* (New York: The Free Press, 1999), 105; Allan Nevins and Frank Ernest Hill, *Ford: Expansion and Challenge, 1915–1933* (New York: Charles Scribner's Sons, 1957), 80, 244–6, 356–78; Mira Wilkins and Frank Ernest Hill, *American Business Abroad: Ford on Six Continents* (Detroit,

Mich.: Wayne State University Press, 1964), 80. Generally, James J. Flink, *The Automobile Age* (Cambridge, Mass.: MIT Press, 1988).

26. William Victor Strauss, "Foreign Distribution of American Motion Pictures," *Harvard Business Review* 8:3 (April 1930):307–15; Frank A. Southard, *American Industry in Europe* (Boston: Houghton-Mifflin, 1931), 94–9; Robert Sklar, *Movie-Made America: A Cultural History of American Movies* (New York: Random House, rev. 1994), 215–27. See also Iriye, *Globalizing of America*, 113.

27. Eileen Whitfield, *Pickford: The Woman Who Made Hollywood* (Lexington: University of Kentucky Press, 1997), 208. See also Charles J. Maland, *Chaplin and American Culture: The Evolution of a Star Image* (Princeton, N.J.: Princeton University Press, 1989), 64–8.

28. Costigliola, *Awkward Dominion*, 177; Whitfield, *Pickford*, 253; Maland, *Chaplin and American Culture*, 111; Roger Manvell, *Chaplin* (Boston: Little, Brown and Company, 1974), 136.

29. Kerry Segrave, *American Films Abroad: Hollywood's Domination of the World's Movie Screens from the 1890s to the Present* (Jefferson, N.C.: McFarland, 1997), 53–4; David Strauss, *Menace in the West: The Rise of French Anti-Americanism in Modern Times* (Westport, Conn.: Greenwood Press, 1978), 141–5; Andrew Higson and Richard Maltby, eds., *"Film Europe" and "Film America": Cinema, Commerce and Cultural Exchange 1920–1939* (Exeter, U.K.: University of Exeter Press, 1999). For Robert Aron and A. Dandieu, *Le cancer americaine* [*The American Cancer*], see Iriye, *Globalizing of America*, 114.

30. Hoover in Leffler, "1921–1932," 232. See also U.S. Department of Commerce, Bureau of Foreign and Domestic Commerce, *Commerce Yearbook 1930* (Washington, D.C.: GPO, 1930), 1: 102, 426.

31. Iriye, *Globalizing of America*, 95–6; Leffler, "1921–1932," 244–6.

32. Leffler, "1921–1932," 244.

33. Leffler, "1921–1932," 248, also 250–1.

34. Jonathan Brown, "Why Foreign Oil Companies Shifted Their Production from Mexico to Venezuela during the 1920s," *American Historical Review* 90 (2) (April 1985): 362–85.

35. Wilkins, *Maturing of Multinational Enterprise*, 101. For a sympathetic discussion of United Fruit, see Samuel Crowther, *The Romance and Rise of the American Tropics* (New York: Doubleday, Doran and Company, 1929).

36. Iriye, *Globalizing of America*, 93.

37. Wilkins, *Maturing of Multinational Enterprise*, 67–8. Josephine Y. Case, *Owen D. Young and American Enterprise: A Biography* (Boston: D. R. Godine, 1982); Wyatt Wells, *Antitrust & The Formation of the Postwar World* (New York: Columbia University Press, 2002), 19–23. Also, Michael J. Hogan, *Informal Entente: The Private Structure of Cooperation in Anglo-American Economic Diplomacy, 1918–1928* (Columbia: University of Missouri Press, 1977), 136–51.

38. Wilkins, *Maturing of Multinational Enterprise*, 52–3.

39. Wilkins, *Maturing of Multinational Enterprise*, 52–3.

40. U.S. Bureau of the Census, *Historical Statistics of the United States: Bicentennial Edition* (Washington, D.C.: GPO, 1975), 1: 404–6. See also, F. W. Ogilvie,

The Tourist Movement: An Economic Study (London: P. S. King, 1933), 37, 53, 210. Other data computed from B. R. Mitchell, *International Historical Statistics: Europe, 1750–1988* (London: Macmillan, 1992), 124.

41. Edgar Ansel Mowrer, *This American World* (London: Faber & Gwyer, 1928), 221, 246.

42. Leonard Mosley, *Lindbergh: A Biography* (Garden City, N.Y.: Doubleday and Company, 1976), 85, 104–16, 161; Costigliola, *Awkward Dominion*, 181; Charles Vale, ed., *The Spirit of St. Louis: One Hundred Poems* (New York: George H. Doran Company, 1927).

43. Leffler, "1921–1932," 250–6; Costigliola, *Awkward Dominion*.

44. In the Senate, Smoot, who was respected by his colleagues, took a number of positions that reflected the teachings and interests of the Mormon Church. While defending Utah sugar and the Church's business interests, he condemned pornography and sought to have the Food and Drug Administration regulate tobacco. He found tobacco advertising, which featured young women, offensive. Milton R. Merrill, *Reed Smoot: Apostle in Politics* (Logan: Utah State University Press, 1990), 163–4.

Chapter 4

1. W. Arthur Lewis, *Economic Survey 1919–1932* (London: Unwin University Books, 1949), 12. See also Michael D. Bordo, Claudia Goldin, and Eugene N. White, *The Defining Moment: The Great Depression and the American Economy in the Twentieth Century* (Chicago: University of Chicago Press, 1998); Harold James, *The End of Globalization: Lessons from the Great Depression* (Cambridge, Mass.: Harvard University Press, 2001).

2. Robert Skidelsky, *John Maynard Keynes: The Economist as Savior* (New York: Penguin, 1994), 477; Arnold Moggridge, ed., *The Collected Writings of John Maynard Keynes: Activities 1931–1939* (New York: Macmillan, 1982), XXI:236–7. On American economic thinking, see Joseph Dorfman, *The Economic Mind in American Civilization* (New York: Viking, 1946–59), IV: 582–8; V: 658–70.

3. "Transition," *Newsweek*, November 22, 1937, 5.

4. For good summaries of the Depression's effects, see Akira Iriye, *The Globalizing of America, 1913–1945* (Cambridge: Cambridge University Press, 1993), 116–20. For a discussion of equity and bond markets, Barrie A. Wigmore, *The Crash and Its Aftermath: A History of Securities Markets in the United States, 1929–1933* (Westport, Conn.: Greenwood Press, 1985).

5. Computed from data in B. R. Mitchell, *International Historical Statistics: Europe, 1750–1988* (London: Macmillan, 1992), 124. U.S. Bureau of the Census, *Historical Statistics of the United States Bicentennial Edition* (Washington, D.C.: GPO, 1975), 1: 404.

6. U.S. Bureau of the Census, *Historical Statistics*, 2:891–3; League of Nations, *Monthly Bulletin of Statistics*, February 1934, 51, as cited in Charles P. Kindleberger, *The World in Depression 1929–1939* (Berkeley: University of California Press, 1973), 172. With adjustments for changing price levels, the flow of U.S. direct investment capital did not return to 1929 levels until 1956,

and the inflow of foreign direct investment did not reach the 1928 level until 1966. The classic on interwar currency conditions is Ragnar Nurkse, *International Currency Experience: Lessons of the Inter-War Period* (Geneva: League of Nations, 1944). For a more recent interpretation, Barry Eichengreen, *Globalizing Capital: A History of the International Monetary System* (Princeton, N.J.: Princeton University Press, 1996).

7. Melvyn P. Leffler, "1921–1932: Expansionist Impulses and Domestic Constraints" in *Economics and World Power: An Assessment of American Diplomacy Since 1789*, eds. William H. Becker and Samuel F. Wells, Jr. (New York: Columbia University Press, 1984), 258–9.

8. On the stock-market crash, see Wigmore, *The Crash and Its Aftermath*. On the international dimensions of the collapse, see Kindleberger, *World in Depression*; John Kenneth Galbraith, *The Great Crash, 1929* (Boston: Houghton Mifflin Company, 1988), 100. A revisionist interpretation critical of government and the New Deal is Larry Schweikart, *The Entrepreneurial Adventure: A History of Business in the United States* (New York: Harcourt, 2000), particularly Chapter 9, 317–70. On the role of Smoot-Hawley, see Alfred E. Eckes, "Smoot-Hawley and the Stock Market Crash, 1929–1930," *International Trade Journal* 12:1 (Spring 1998):65–82. See also Maury Klein, *At Rainbow's End: The Crash of 1929* (New York: Oxford University Press, 2001); James, *The End of Globalization*.

9. William E. Leuchtenburg, *The Perils of Prosperity, 1914–32* (Chicago: University of Chicago Press, 1958), 256–7.

10. Alan Brinkley, *Voices of Protest: Huey Long, Father Coughlin, and the Great Depression* (New York: Vintage Books, 1983), 151–2. See also Studs Terkel, *Hard Times: An Oral History of the Great Depression* (New York: Pantheon Books, 1986), 316–27.

11. David M. Kennedy, *Freedom From Fear: The American People in Depression and War, 1929–1945* (New York: Oxford University Press, 1999), 241.

12. Brinkley, *Voices of Protest*, 151–2; Kennedy, *Freedom From Fear*, 241; Wayne S. Cole, *Senator Gerald P. Nye and American Foreign Relations* (Minneapolis: University of Minnesota Press, 1962), 61–4.

13. Iriye, *Globalizing of America*, 127–38.

14. David Burner, *Herbert Hoover: A Public Life* (New York: Knopf, 1979); Robert S. McElvaine, *The Great Depression: America, 1929–1941* (New York: Times Books, 1984), 55; U.S. Bureau of the Census, *Historical Statistics*, 1:135, 166, 228.

15. He was the official who requested that General Electric confer with the Navy before selling Alexanderson alternators to the British-related Marconi companies. See Robert Sobel, *RCA* (New York: Stein and Day, 1986), 23–9.

16. Robert Dallek, *Franklin D. Roosevelt and American Foreign Policy, 1932–1945* (Oxford: Oxford University Press, 1979), 19–20; Robert M. Hathaway, "1933–1945: Economic Diplomacy in a Time of Crisis" in *Economics and World Power: An Assessment of American Diplomacy Since 1789*, eds. William H. Becker and Samuel F. Wells, Jr. (New York: Columbia University Press, 1984), 280; Raymond Moley, *After Seven Years* (New York: Harper Brothers, 1939), 46–51; Dorfman, *The Economic Mind*, Vol. 5, 654–57. William

J. Barber, *Designs within Disorder: Franklin D. Roosevelt, the Economists, and the Shaping of American Economic Policy, 1933–1945* (New York: Cambridge University Press, 1996).

17. Edgar B. Nixon, ed., *Franklin D. Roosevelt and Foreign Affairs* (Cambridge, Mass.: Harvard University Press, 1969), I: 19.

18. Michael A. Butler, *Cautious Visionary: Cordell Hull and Trade Reform, 1933–1937* (Kent, Ohio: Kent State University Press, 1998), 51. See also Lloyd Gardner, *Economic Aspects of New Deal Diplomacy* (Madison: University of Wisconsin, 1964), 29.

19. Barry Eichengreen, *Golden Fetters: The Gold Standard and the Great Depression, 1919–1939* (New York: Oxford University Press, 1995), 343–4; Kindleberger, *World in Depression*, 199–231.

20. On Roosevelt's decision to devalue the dollar, see Eichengreen, *Golden Fetters*, 323–47; Eichengreen, *Globalizing Capital*; Kindleberger, *World in Depression*, 199–231. For another critique of the gold-purchase program, see Milton Friedman and Ann Jacobson Schwartz, *A Monetary History of the United States, 1867–1960* (Princeton, N.J.: Princeton University Press, 1969). Gold data calculated from Eichengreen, *Golden Fetters*, 352–3.

21. Kindleberger, *World in Depression*, 235; Friedman and Schwartz, *Monetary History of the United States*, 483–91.

22. See generally, Bordo, Goldin, and White, *Defining Moment*; Eichengreen, *Golden Fetters*, 344. For a new interpretation of the New Deal period, see Colin Gordon, *New Deals, Business, Labor, and Politics in America, 1920–1935* (Cambridge: Cambridge University Press, 1994). Gordon appreciates the contradiction that existed between the New Deal approach to domestic regulation and economic internationalism. "High tariffs made costly regulatory experimentation possible; the possibility of future tariff revision (let alone full-blown free trade) made it risky." Quote on page 293.

23. Eric Hobsbawm, *Industry and Empire: The Making of Modern English Society* (New York: Pantheon Books, 1968), II:205–6; John F. Wilson, *British Business History, 1720–1914* (Manchester, U.K.: Manchester University Press, 1995), 168–73.

24. B. W. E. Alford, *Britain in the World Economy since 1880* (London: Longman, 1996), 136–68; Peter Dewey, *War and Progress: Britain 1914–1945* (New York: Longman, 1997) offers a good review of the latest literature.

25. Ronald Dore and Radha Sinha, *Japan and World Depression Then and Now: Essays in Memory of E. F. Penrose* (New York: St. Martin's, 1987); William Miles Fletcher, III, *The Japanese Business Community and National Trade Policy 1920–1942* (Chapel Hill: University of North Carolina Press, 1989).

26. Gardner, *Economic Aspects*, 73.

27. Quoted in Walter LaFeber, *The Clash: A History of U.S.–Japan Relations* (New York: W. W. Norton, 1997), 176. See also Michael A. Barnhart, *Japan Prepares for Total War: The Search for Economic Security, 1919–1941* (Ithaca, N.Y.: Cornell University Press, 1987), 115–35.

28. Hathaway, "1933–1945," 302–7.

29. Adolph Hitler, *Hitler's Second Book* (New York: Grove Press, 1961), 22.

30. Quotes in Hitler, *Hitler's Second Book*, 99. Also, R. J. Overy, *War and Economy in the Third Reich* (Oxford: Clarendon Press, 1994), 4.
31. Iriye, *Globalizing of America*, 146; Gardner, *Economic Aspects*, 36; Hathaway, "1933–1945," 291.
32. Iriye, *Globalizing of America*, 147–8.
33. Irwin F. Gellman, *Good Neighbor Diplomacy: United States Policies in Latin America, 1933–1945* (Baltimore: The Johns Hopkins University Press, 1979), 17–73.
34. Butler, *Cautious Visionary*, 7, 10; Gardner, *Economic Aspects*, 29.
35. Quote in Gardner, *Economic Aspects*, 93. For one critique of the reciprocal trade program, as administered by the State Department, see Alfred E. Eckes, Jr., *Opening America's Market: U.S. Foreign Trade Policy since 1776* (Chapel Hill: University of North Carolina Press, 1995). See also Thomas Ferguson, "Industrial Conflict and the Coming of the New Deal: The Triumph of Multinational Liberalism in America" in *The Rise and Fall of the New Deal Order, 1930–1980*, eds. Steve Fraser and Gary Gerstle (Princeton, N.J.: Princeton University Press, 1989), 18–24.
36. Cited in Alfred Eckes, *A Search for Solvency: Bretton Woods and the International Monetary System, 1941–1971* (Austin: University of Texas Press, 1975), 162.
37. Hathaway, "1933–1945," 286.
38. A. S. Young, *Negro Firsts in Sports* (Chicago: Johnson Publishing Company, 1963), 103–5; Kennedy, *Freedom From Fear*, 411, 414–18; James A. Page, *Black Olympian Medalists* (Englewood, Colo.: Libraries Unlimited, 1991), 91.
39. William J. Baker, *Jesse Owens: An American Life* (New York: The Free Press, 1986), 75–109, quote on page 87; Edwin B. Henderson and Editors of *Sport* Magazine, *International Library of Negro Life and History: The Black Athlete: Emergence and Arrival* (New York: Publishers Company, 1968), 15–16, 32–3.
40. Kennedy, *Freedom From Fear*, 423–4.
41. Minister quoted in Cole, *Gerald P. Nye*, 74, also 87. See also C. H. Grattan, *Why We Fought* (New York: The Vanguard Press, 1929); Walter Millis, *The Road to War* (New York: Houghton Mifflin, 1935); Charles Beard, *The Devil Theory of War* (New York: Vanguard, 1936). See generally Wayne S. Cole, *Roosevelt and the Isolationists 1932–1945* (Lincoln: University of Nebraska Press, 1983). For discussion of the Nye Committee, see Paul A. C. Koistinen, *Planning War Pursuing Peace: The Political Economy of American Warfare 1920–1939* (Lawrence: University of Kansas Press, 1998), 253–304; Brinkley, *Voices of Protest*, 151; Cole, *Gerald P. Nye*, 65–96.
42. Mira Wilkins, *Maturing of Multinational Enterprise* (Cambridge, Mass.: Harvard University Press, 1974), 181–3; U.S. Bureau of the Census, *Historical Statistics of the United States* (Washington: GPO, 1970), 2: 866–7.
43. It is difficult from this distance to evaluate the contradictory claims fully. For a defense of Standard Oil's position, see Henrietta M. Larson, Evelyn H. Knowlton, and Charles S. Popple, *History of Standard Oil Company (New Jersey): New Horizons 1927–1950* (New York: Harper & Row, 1971), 432–443. For a vigorous critique of U.S. business, see Gabriel Kolko, "American

Business and Germany, 1930–1941," *Western Political Quarterly, 1930–1941* XV (4) (December 1962): 712–27.

44. Renault quote in Allan Nevins and Frank Ernest Hill, *Ford: Expansion and Challenge 1915–1938*, (New York: Scribner's, 1957), 556; Nevins and Hill, *Ford: Decline and Rebirth, 1933–1962* (New York: Scribner's, 1963), 95–101.

45. Wilkins, *Maturing of Multinational Enterprise*, 187–9; Robert Sobel, *ITT: The Management of Opportunity* (New York: Times Books, 1982), 88; John Weitz, *Hitler's Banker: Hmalmar Horace Greeley Schacht* (Boston: Little Brown, 1997), 215; "Thomas J. Watson Is Decorated by Hitler for Work in Bettering Economic Relations," *New York Times*, July 2, 1937, 8; William Rogers, *Think: A Biography of the Watsons and IBM* (New York: Stein and Day, 1969), 107–49; Thomas J. Watson, Jr., *Father, Son and Co.: My Life at IBM and Beyond* (New York: Bantam Books, 1990), 55.

46. Roland N. Stromberg, "American Business and the Approach of War 1935–1941," *Journal of Economic History* XIII:1 (Winter 1953):65; Edward M. Lamont, *The Ambassador from Wall Street: The Story of Thomas W. Lamont J. P. Morgan's Chief Executive* (Lanham, Md.: Madison Books, 1994), 410–16.

47. Mira Wilkins, "American-Japanese Direct Foreign Investment Relationships, 1930–1952," reprinted in *The Growth of Multinationals*, ed. Mira Wilkins (Brookfield, Vt.: Edward Elgar Publishing, 1991), 428–49, quote on page 435. Masaru Udagawa, "The Prewar Japanese Automobile Industry and American Manufacturers," 576–94. See also, Mira Wilkins, "The Role of U.S. Business," in *Pearl Harbor as History: Japanese-American Relations 1931–1941* eds. Dorothy Borg and Shumpei Okamoto (New York: Columbia University Press, 1973), 352–76, quote on page 370; Lamont, *The Ambassador from Wall Street*, 416.

48. LaFeber, *The Clash*, 162.

49. LaFeber, *The Clash*, 188–90.

50. Matthew Josephson, *Empire of the Air: Juan Trippe and the Struggle for World Airways* (New York: Harcourt, Brace and Company, 1944), 208. See also Jack E. Robinson, *American Icarus: The Majestic Rise and Tragic Fall of Pan Am* (Baltimore: Noble House, 1994), 90; T. A. Heppenheimer, *Turbulent Skies: The History of Commercial Aviation* (New York: Wiley, 1995); William Leary, ed., *The Airline Industry (Encyclopedia of American Business History and Biography)* (New York: Facts on File, 1992).

51. U.S. Bureau of the Census, *Historical Statistics*, 762, 770, 790–1; George P. Oslin, *The Story of Telecommunications* (Macon, Ga.: Mercer University Press, 1992), 321–3.

52. Jerome S. Berg, *On the Short Waves, 1923–1945: Broadcast Listening in the Pioneer Days of Radio* (Jefferson, N.C.: McFarland, 1999), 59; James Wood, *History of International Broadcasting* (London: Peter Peregrinus, 1992).

53. Kerry Segrave, *American Films Abroad: Hollywood's Domination of the World's Movie Screens from the 1890s to the Present* (Jefferson, N.C.: McFarland, 1997); Denis Morrison, "Pix Aim to Please 'Em All: Hollywood Finds Film Purity Pays," *Variety*, 127:7 (July 28, 1937):1, 34; Raymond Moley,

Hays Office (Indianapolis, Ind.: Bobbs-Merrill, 1945), 169–86; Motion Picture Producers and Distributors of America, *Report of the President* (March 28, 1936), 25–6.

54. See particularly, Richard Schickel, *The Disney Version: The Life, Times, Art & Commerce of Walt Disney* (New York: Simon and Schuster, 1968); Bob Thomas, *Walt Disney: An American Original* (New York: Simon and Schuster, 1976), 106 (for Hitler quote); Steven Watts, *The Magic Kingdom: Walt Disney and the American Way of Life* (Boston: Houghton Mifflin, 1997).

55. Hathaway, "1933–1945," 313, also 308–12. See also Butler, *Cautious Visionary*, 114–62; David Reynolds, *The Creation of the Anglo-American Alliance, 1937–1941: A Study in Competitive Co-Operation* (Chapel Hill: University of North Carolina Press, 1982), 51–3.

Chapter 5

1. Sally Bedell Smith, *In All His Glory: The Life of William S. Paley* (New York: Simon and Schuster, 1990), 166, 176. See also Joseph E. Persico, *Edward R. Murrow: An American Original* (New York: McGraw Hill, 1988).

2. For a good general introduction, see I. C. B. Dear, ed., *The Oxford Companion to World War II* (New York: Oxford University Press, 1995). Under the Axis scheme, London and Washington might also have dominated their own regional or imperial trading blocs. On German frustrations with the treaty of Versailles, see Fritz Klein, "Between Compiegne and Versailles: The Germans on the Way from a Misunderstood Defeat to an Unwanted Peace," in *The Treaty of Versailles: A Reassessment after 75 Years*, eds. Manfred F. Boemeke, Gerald D. Feldman, and Elisabeth Glaser (Cambridge: Cambridge University Press, 1998), 203–20. For Italy's grievances, see H. James Burgwyn, *Italian Foreign Policy in the Interwar Period 1918–1940* (Westport, Conn.: Praeger, 1997); Denis Mack Smith, *Mussolini's Roman Empire* (New York: Viking, 1976). On Japan's dissatisfaction, see especially Frederick R. Dickinson, *War and National Reinvention: Japan in the Great War, 1914–1919* (Cambridge, Mass.: Harvard University Press, 1999); Naoko Shimazu, *Japan, Race and Equality: The Racial Equality Proposal of 1919* (London: Routledge, 1998). On the quest for resources, see Alfred Eckes, *The United States and the Global Struggle for Minerals* (Austin: University of Texas, 1979), 57–87.

3. Mark Harrison, ed., *The Economics of World War II: Six Great Powers in International Comparison* (New York: Cambridge University Press, 1998), 5; Daniel Yergin, *The Prize: The Epic Quest for Oil, Money & Power* (New York: Simon and Schuster, 1990), 337.

4. Yergin, *The Prize*, 337. See also Robert Goralski and Russell W. Freeburg, *Oil and War; How the Deadly Struggle for Fuel in World War II Meant Victory or Defeat* (New York: Morrow, 1987); Milward, *War, Economy and Society* (Berkeley, Calif.: University of California Press, 1977), 317–21; Richard Overy, "Raw and Synthetic Materials" in *Oxford Companion to*

World War II, ed. I. C. B. Dear (New York: Oxford University Press, 1995), 930–4.

5. As cited in Thomas E. Mahl, *Desperate Deception: British Covert Operations in the United States, 1939–44* (Washington, D.C.: Brassey's, 1998), 1. See also John Gooch, "Churchill as War Leader" in *The Oxford Companion to World War II*, ed. I. C. B. Dear (New York: Oxford University Press, 1995), 235–42.

6. Rene De La Pedraja, *The Rise and Decline of U.S. Merchant Shipping in the Twentieth Century* (New York: Twayne Publishers, 1992), 134–5; Dear, *Oxford Companion to World War II*, 677–83, 1285.

7. Mahl, *Desperate Deception*, 1–8; Robert A. Divine, *Second Chance: The Triumph of Internationalism in America during World War II* (New York: Atheneum, 1967); Edward Lamont, *The Ambassador from Wall Street: The Story of Thomas W. Lamont, J. P. Morgan's Chief Executive* (Lanham, Md.: Madison Books, 1994), 444–6, 450–7; Ron Chernow, *The House of Morgan: An American Banking Dynasty and the Rise of Modern Finance* (New York: Simon and Schuster, 1990), 446–68. For the involvement of business in war mobilization, see Paul A. C. Koistinen, *Planning War Pursuing Peace: The Political Economy of American Warfare 1920–1939* (Lawrence: University of Kansas Press, 1998), 305–10.

8. Theodore A. Wilson, *The First Summit: Roosevelt and Churchill at Placentia Bay, 1941*, rev. ed. (Lawrence: University of Kansas Press, 1991), 155–6; David Reynolds, *The Creation of the Anglo-American Alliance, 1937–1941* (Chapel Hill: University of North Carolina Press, 1981), 269–82; Warren F. Kimball, *The Juggler: Franklin Roosevelt as Wartime Statesman* (Princeton, N.J.: Princeton University Press, 1991), 46; Randall B. Woods, *A Changing of the Guard: Anglo-American Relations, 1941–1946* (Chapel Hill: University of North Carolina Press, 1990).

9. Richard M. Leighton, *U.S. Merchant Shipping and the British Import Crisis* (Washington, D.C.: U.S. Army Center of Military History, 1990), 201–3; Mancur Olson, Jr., *The Economics of Wartime Shortage: The History of British Food Supplies in the Napoleonic War and in World Wars I and II* (Durham, N.C.: Duke University Press, 1963), 119; Milward, *War, Economy and Society*, 245–55. On submarine warfare, see Michael Gannon, *Operation Drumbeat* (New York: Harper, 1990); on merchant shipping, see Andrew Gibson and Arthur Donovan, *The Abandoned Ocean: A History of United States Maritime Policy* (Columbia: University of South Carolina Press, 2000). Henrietta Larson, Evelyn H. Knowlton, and Charles S. Popple, *History of Standard Oil Company (New Jersey): New Horizons, 1927–1950* (New York: Harper & Row, 1971), 392–8, 526.

10. Robert M. Hathaway, "1933–1945: Economic Diplomacy in a Time of Crisis" in *Economics and World Power: An Assessment of American Diplomacy Since 1789*, eds. William H. Becker and Samuel F. Wells, Jr. (New York: Columbia University Press, 1984), 313–14.

11. William Lovett, ed., *United States Shipping Policies and the World Market* (Westport, Conn.: Quorum Books, 1996), 15–16, 56; Gibson and Donovan, *The Abandoned Ocean*, 155–68; Harrison, ed., *Economics of World War II*, 94,

101; Thomas H. McCraw, *American Business, 1920–2000: How It Worked* (Wheeling, Ill.: Harlan Davidson, 2000), 67–102.

12. David M. Kennedy, *Freedom from Want: The American People in Depression and War, 1929–1945* (New York: Oxford University Press, 1999), 665, 814; Nathan Miller, *War at Sea: A Naval History of World War II* (New York: Oxford University Press, 1995), 391–410.

13. Michael Riordan and Lillian Hoddeson, *Crystal Fire: The Invention of the Transistor and the Birth of the Information Age* (New York: Norton, 1997), quote 9, 123–5; Martin Campbell-Kelly and William Aspray, *Computer: History of the Information Machine* (New York: Basic Books, 1996); Robert Buderi, *The Invention That Changed the World* (New York: Simon and Schuster, 1996); G. Pascal Zachary, *Endless Frontier: Vannevar Bush, Engineer of the American Century* (New York: Free Press, 1997). On government involvement in the computer, see Kenneth Flamm, *Creating the Computer: Government, Industry, and High Technology* (Washington, D.C.: Brookings, 1988); for background on war mobilization, see Koistinen, *Planning War, Pursuing Peace*.

14. See generally T. A. Heppenheimer, *Turbulent Skies: The History of Commercial Aviation* (New York: Wiley, 1995). On Boeing, see McCraw, *American Business*.

15. For further discussion of this issue, see Eckes, *Global Struggle for Minerals*, 121–3; Alan Bateman, "Wartime Dependence on Foreign Minerals, "*Economic Geology* 41 (June–July 1946): 308–27.

16. Eckes, *Global Struggle for Minerals*, 89–119. For efforts to obtain uranium from the Belgian Congo, see Jonathan E. Helmreich, *Gathering Rare Ores: The Diplomacy of Uranium Acquisition, 1943–1954* (Princeton, N.J.: Princeton University Press, 1986). On rubber, see Vernon Herbert and Attilio Bisio, *Synthetic Rubber: A Project That Had to Succeed* (Westport, Conn: Greenwood Press, 1985).

17. Mira Wilkins, *The Maturing of Multinational Enterprise* (Cambridge, Mass.: Harvard University Press, 1974), 269.

18. Yergin, *The Prize*, 395.

19. Larson et al., *New Horizons*, 426–7; Edward W. Chester, *United States Oil Policy and Diplomacy: A Twentieth-Century Overview* (Westport, Conn: Greenwood Press, 1983), 123–32. British ambassador quoted in Fiona Venn, *Oil Diplomacy in the Twentieth Century* (New York: St. Martin's Press, 1986), 95. Samuel Flagg Bemis, an eminent diplomatic historian, described the Mexican settlement as an example of the "new dollar diplomacy," in which the U.S. government substituted public funds for private capital, while leaving "private creditors to fend for themselves." *The Latin American Policy of the United States* (New York: Harcourt Brace, 1943), 351.

20. Stephen G. Rabe, *The Road to OPEC: United States Relations with Venezuela, 1919–76* (Austin: University of Texas Press, 1982), 66–93.

21. Larson et al., *New Horizons*, 474–88, quote, 484; Yergin, *The Prize*, 433–7.

22. Wilkins, *Maturing of Multinational Enterprise*, 249–50; see generally Aaron David Miller, *Search for Security: Saudi Arabian Oil and American Foreign Policy, 1939–1949* (Chapel Hill: University of North Carolina Press, 1980); Chester, *United States Oil Policy and Diplomacy*; Goralski and Freeburg, *Oil and War*;

Stephen J. Randall, *United States Foreign Oil Policy 1919–1948: For Profits and Security* (Kingston, Ontario: McGill-Queen's University Press, 1985); Venn, *Oil Diplomacy in the Twentieth Century.*

23. Yergin, *The Prize*, 395–403; Ickes quote, 395.

24. Wilkins, *Maturing of Multinational Enterprise*, 277–80.

25. On ITT see Robert Sobel, *ITT: The Management of Opportunity* (New York: Truman Talley, 1982); on wartime telecommunications conflicts, see Daniel R. Headrick, *The Invisible Weapon: Telecommunications and International Politics 1851–1945* (New York: Oxford, 1991), 260–71. Also, see Wilkins, *Maturing of Multinational Enterprise.* On Pan Am, see Jack E. Robinson, *American Icarus: The Majestic Rise and Tragic Fall of Pan Am* (Baltimore, Md: Noble House, 1994), 104–41; Marilyn Bender and Selig Altschul, *The Chosen Instrument: Pan Am, Juan Trippe, The Rise and Fall of an American Entrepreneur* (New York: Simon & Schuster, 1982). For postwar U.S. aviation policy, see Alan P. Dobson, *Peaceful Air Warfare* (Oxford: Clarendon Press, 1991), 138–51. On shipping, see Andrew Gibson and Arthur Donovan, *The Abandoned Ocean: A History of United States Maritime Policy* (Columbia: University of South Carolina Press, 2000).

26. Kerry Segrave, *American Films Abroad: Hollywood's Domination of the World's Movie Screens from the 1890s to the Present* (Jefferson, N.C.: McFarland, 1997); Michael S. Schull and David Edward Wilt, *Hollywood War Films, 1937–1945* (Jefferson, N.C.: McFarland, 1996), 139, 201–2.

27. Segrave, *American Films Abroad*, 135; Ian Jarvie, *Hollywood's Overseas Campaign: The North Atlantic Movie Trade, 1920–1950* (Cambridge: Cambridge University Press, 1992), 379–81, 384.

28. Mark S. Foster, *Henry J. Kaiser: Builder in the Modern American West* (Austin: University of Texas Press, 1989), 165, also 169–78; H. W. Brands, *Masters of Enterprise: Giants of American Business from John Jacob Astor and J. P. Morgan to Bill Gates and Oprah Winfrey* (New York: The Free Press, 1999), 150–1; Elizabeth A. Cobbs, *The Rich Neighbor Policy: Rockefeller and Kaiser in Brazil* (New Haven, Conn.: Yale University Press, 1992), 231–3. See also Stephen B. Adams, *Mr. Kaiser Goes to Washington: The Rise of a Government Entrepreneur* (Chapel Hill: University of North Carolina Press, 1997).

29. Robert A. Divine, *Second Chance: The Triumph of Internationalism in American during World War II* (New York: Athenenum, 1967), 104–7.

30. Mark Pendergast, *For God, Country, and Coca-Cola: The Unauthorized History of the Great American Soft Drink and the Company That Makes It* (New York: Charles Scribner's Sons, 1993), 216, also 213–27. See also Brands, *Masters of Enterprise*, 204–6.

31. Henry Luce "The American Century," *Life*, 10, February 17, 1941, 61–5, and generally, Robert E. Herzstein, *Henry R. Luce: A Political Portrait of the Man Who Created the American Century* (New York: Charles Scribner's Sons, 1994).

32. John Kobler, *Luce: His Time, Life, and Fortune* (Garden City, N.Y.: Doubleday and Company, 1968), 2, 6.

33. John K. Jessup, ed., *The Ideas of Henry Luce* (New York: Atheneum, 1969), 242, 245, also 21. See also W. A. Swanburg, *Luce and His Empire*

(New York: Charles Scribner's Sons, 1972); Herzstein, *Henry R. Luce*, 181–2.

34. Wendell Willkie, *One World* (New York: Simon and Schuster, 1943), 202–3; Henry A. Wallace, *Century of the Common Man* (New York: Reynal and Hitchcock, 1943).

35. Zachary, *Endless Frontier*, 3, 218–39, 391–8.

36. Townsend Hoopes and Douglas Brinkley, *FDR and the Creation of the U.N.* (New Haven, Conn.: Yale University Press, 1997), 204; Robert C. Hilderbrand, *Dumbarton Oaks: The Origins of the United Nations and the Search for Postwar Security* (Chapel Hill: University of North Carolina Press, 1990). For speech of Gunnar Jahn, chairman of Nobel Committee (1945), see http://www.nobel.se/peace/laureates/1945/press.html.

37. Douglas Williams, *The Specialized Agencies and the United Nations: The System in Crisis* (New York: St. Martin's Press, 1987), 29–30, 36–9. In 1986, the Big Four became the Big Five with the addition of the UN Industrial Development Organization (UNIDO).

38. WHO, *The First Ten Years of the World Health Organization* (Geneva: WHO, 1958), 38, also 15–29, 37, 44, 79–81. See also Murray Morgan, *Doctors to the World* (New York: Viking Press, 1958), 251; Gerhard L. Weinberg, *A World at Arms: A Global History of World War II* (Cambridge: Cambridge University Press, 1994), 585; Moshe Y. Sachs, ed., *Worldmark Encyclopedia of the Nations: United Nations* (New York: John Wiley & Sons, Inc., 1984), 158–9; "A Triumph of Experience Over Hope," *The Economist*, May 26, 2001, 79–80.

39. G. A. Johnston, *The International Labor Organization: Its Work for Social and Economic Progress* (London: Europa Publications, 1970), 11–24, 37–43, 277–81; David A. Morse, *The Origin and Evolution of the I.L.O. and Its Role in the World Community* (Ithaca, N.Y.: Cornell University Press, 1969), 28–33; Edward C. Lorenz, *Defining Global Justice: The History of U.S. International Labor Standards Policy* (Notre Dame, Ind.: University of Notre Dame Press, 2001), 66–217; Williams, *The Specialized Agencies*, 35–6; David Trubek, "Book Review and Note," *American Journal International Law* 91 (April 1997): 398; Virginia A. Leary, "Book Review and Note," *American Journal International Law* 91 (April 1997): 402.

40. Thomas Buergenthal, *Law-Making in the International Civil Aviation Organization* (Syracuse, N.Y.: Syracuse University Press, 1969), 3–12, 117–19, 123–5, 229–30; Jack Vivian, "ICAO Assistance to Civil Aviation in the Developing World," *Impact of Science on Society* 31 (1981): 305–13; Williams, *The Specialized Agencies*, 38; "Come Fly with Me," *The Economist*, June 20, 1998, 69; "Opening Wider," *The Economist*, March 10, 2001, special section, p. 7. On the Chicago conference, see Bender and Altschul, *The Chosen Instrument*, 382–98.

41. Harold G. Vatter, *The U.S. Economy in World War II* (New York: Columbia University Press, 1985), 159.

42. James Boughton, "Harry Dexter White and the International Monetary Fund," *Finance and Development* 35 (3) (September 1998). See http://www.imf.org/external/pubs/ft/fandd/1998/09/boughton.htm. Barry Eichengreen,

Globalizing Capital: A History of the International Monetary System (Princeton, N.J.: Princeton University Press), 93–106.

43. Harold James, *International Monetary Cooperation Since Bretton Woods* (New York: Oxford University Press, 1996), 58–66; Alfred E. Eckes, Jr., *A Search for Solvency: Bretton Woods and the International Monetary System, 1941–1971* (Austin: University of Texas Press, 1975), 99–100.

44. Woods, *A Changing of the Guard*, 73–5; Richard N. Gardner, *Sterling-Dollar Diplomacy: The Origins and Prospects of Our International Economic Order*, 2nd ed. (New York: McGraw-Hill Book Company, 1969), 111–12; Margaret Garritsen de Vries, "The Bretton Woods Conference and the Birth of the International Monetary Fund" in *The Bretton Woods-GATT System: Retrospect and Prospect After Fifty Years*, ed. Orin Kirshner (Armonk, N.Y.: M. E. Sharpe, 1996), 31–17.

45. David Rees, *Harry Dexter White: A Study in Paradox* (New York: Coward, McCann and Geoghegan, 1973), 11; John Earl Haynes and Harvey Klehr, *Venona: Decoding Soviet Espionage in America* (New Haven, Conn.: Yale University Press, 1999), 138–45; Bruce Craig, "Treasonable Doubt: The Harry Dexter White Case, 1948–1953" (Ph.D. dissertation, American University, 1999).

46. Quoted in Georg Schild, *Bretton Woods and Dumbarton Oaks: American Economic and Political Planning in the Summer of 1944* (New York: St. Martin's Press, 1995), 92. See also Armand Van Dormael, *Bretton Woods: Birth of a Monetary System* (New York: Holmes and Meier Publishers, Inc., 1978).

47. Devesh Kapur, John P. Lewis, and Richard Webb, *The World Bank: Its First Half Century* (Washington, D.C.: Brookings, 1997), 76–82.

48. Milward, *War, Economy, and Society*, 364. See also Gardner, *Sterling-Dollar Diplomacy*, 71–95; Vatter, *The U.S. Economy*, 159–63; Kapur, Lewis, and Webb, *World Bank*, 5–6.

49. Joan Edelman Spero, *The Politics of International Economic Relations*, 3rd ed. (New York: St. Martin's Press, 1985), 36–42.

50. Gardner, *Sterling-Dollar Diplomacy*, 145–380; Thomas W. Zeiler, *Free Trade, Free World: The Advent of GATT* (Chapel Hill: University of North Carolina Press, 1999); Alfred E. Eckes, Jr., ed., *Revisiting U.S. Trade Policy: Decisions in Perspective* (Athens: Ohio University Press, 2000), 2–3, 37–8.

51. Russell D. Buhite, *Decisions at Yalta: An Appraisal of Summit Diplomacy* (Wilmington, Del.: Scholarly Resources), 1986; Lloyd C. Gardner, *Economic Aspects of New Deal Diplomacy* (Madison: University of Wisconsin Press, 1964), 302–25; John Lewis Gaddis, *The United States and the Origins of the Cold War, 1941–1947* (New York: Columbia University Press, 1972), 282–346; Melvyn P. Leffler, *A Preponderance of Power: National Security, the Truman Administration, and the Cold War* (Stanford, Calif.: Stanford University Press, 1992), 63–140; Walter L. Hixson, *George F. Kennan: Cold War Iconoclast* (New York: Columbia University Press, 1989), 26–45; Fraser J. Harbutt, *The Iron Curtain: Churchill, America, and the Origins of the Cold War* (New York: Oxford University Press, 1986).

52. On this point, which addresses the ideals of modernization theorists, see Nick Cullather, "Research Note: Development? It's History," *Diplomatic History* 24 (Fall 2000):653.

Chapter 6

1. B. R. Mitchell, *International Historical Statistics: Africa, Asia & Oceania 1750–1988*, 2nd rev. ed. (New York: Stockton Press, 1995), 345; B. R. Mitchell, *International Historical Statistics: Europe, 1750–1988*, 3rd ed. (New York: Stockton Press, 1993), 411.

2. See John Lewis Gaddis, *The United States and the Origins of the Cold War, 1941–1947* (New York: Columbia University Press, 1972), 316–52. On Stalin's decision to shun the Bretton Woods international monetary system, see Harold James, *International Monetary Cooperation since Bretton Woods* (New York: Oxford, 1996), 68–71.

3. Melvyn P. Leffler, *A Preponderance of Power: National Security, the Truman Administration, and the Cold War* (Stanford, Calif.: Stanford University Press, 1992), 176. See also Daniel Yergin, *Shattered Peace: the Origins of the Cold War* (New York: Penguin Books, 1977), 5–6; Michael J. Hogan, *A Cross of Iron: Harry S. Truman and the Origins of the National Security State, 1945–1954* (Cambridge: Cambridge University Press, 1998); Michael Sherry, *In the Shadow of War: The United States Since the 1930s* (New Haven, Conn.: Yale University Press, 1995), 123–87.

4. Arch Puddington emphasizes the NSC 68 mandate in *Broadcasting Freedom: The Cold War Triumph of Radio Free Europe and Radio Liberty* (Lexington: University of Kentucky Press, 2000), 11. On U.S. plans to foment insurrection in satellite countries, see Peter Grose, *Operation Rollback: America's Secret War Behind the Iron Curtain* (Boston: Houghton Mifflin, 2000). Also see Gregory Mitrovich, *Undermining the Kremlin: America's Strategy to Subvert the Soviet Bloc, 1947–1956* (Ithaca, N.Y.: Cornell University Press, 2000). On CIA efforts to shape elite opinion, see Frances Stonor Saunders, *The Cultural Cold War: The CIA and the World of Arts and Letters* (New York: New Press, 1999).

5. On the VOA's promulgation of Luce's American Century, see Maureen J. Nemecek, "Speaking of America: The Voice of America, Its Mission and Message, 1942–1982" (Ph.D. dissertation, University of Maryland, 1984), 54–5. Another excellent book on Western broadcasting during the Cold War is Michael Nelson, *War of the Black Heavens: The Battles of Western Broadcasting in the Cold War* (Syracuse, N.Y.: Syracuse University Press, 1997).

6. Nelson, *War of the Black Heavens*, 18–20; Puddington, *Broadcasting Freedom*, 153–5.

7. Data on exchange programs from Institute of International Education, *Open Doors* (1994–1995) (New York: Institute of International Education, 1996), 6, online at http://www.opendoors.iienetwork.org. On the beginnings of U.S. cultural diplomacy, see Charles A. Thomson and Walter H. C. Laves, *Cultural Relations and U.S. Foreign Policy* (Bloomington: Indiana University Press, 1963); Frank Ninkovich, *The Diplomacy of Ideas: U.S. Foreign Policy and Cultural Relations, 1938–1950* (Cambridge: Cambridge University Press, 1981);

Philip H. Coombs, "The Past and Future in Perspective" in *Cultural Affairs and Foreign Relations*, ed. Robert Blum (Englewood Cliffs, N.J.: Prentice-Hall, 1963), 139–42. On the early Cold War, see in particular Walter Hixson, *Parting the Curtain: Propaganda, Culture and the Cold War, 1945–1961* (New York: St. Martin's, 1997).

8. On business attitudes, see Kim McQuaid, *Big Business and Presidential Power: From FDR to Reagan* (New York: William Morrow, 1982), 122–68; Kim McQuaid, *Uneasy Partners: Big Business in American Politics 1945–1990* (Baltimore: Johns Hopkins University Press, 1994), 36–47; Karl Shriftgiesser, *Business Comes of Age: The Story of the Committee for Economic Development and Its Impact Upon the Economic Policies of the United States, 1942–60* (New York: Harper, 1960). On Reuther, see Nelson Lichtenstein, *The Most Dangerous Man in Detroit: Walter Reuther and the Future of American Labor* (New York: Basic Books, 1995), 329–39; Denis Macshane, *International Labor and the Origins of the Cold War* (Oxford: Clarendon Press, 1992), 119–43.

9. Michael J. Hogan, *The Marshall Plan: America, Britain, and the Reconstruction of Western Europe, 1947–1952* (Cambridge: Cambridge University Press, 1987), 97–9; Paul G. Hoffman, *Peace Can Be Won* (Garden City, N.Y.: Doubleday & Company, 1951), 90–111. Ironically, with Hoffman engaged in public policy between 1948 and 1953, the Studebaker Company failed to adapt to market trends and allowed higher labor costs and lax productivity to endanger its future. Hoffman returned to negotiate what proved to be an unsuccessful merger with Packard in 1954. See Alan R. Raucher, "Paul Gray Hoffman" in *The American Automobile Industry, 1920–1980* (Encyclopedia of American Business History and Biography), ed. George S. May (New York: Facts on File, 1989), 192–5.

10. Leffler, *A Preponderance of Power*, 145.

11. Robert A. Pollard and Samuel F. Wells, Jr., "1945–1960: The Era of American Hegemony" in *Economics and World Power: An Assessment of American Diplomacy Since 1789*, eds. William H. Becker and Samuel F. Wells, Jr. (New York: Columbia University Press, 1984), 343.

12. Diane B. Kunz, *Butter and Guns: America's Cold War Economic Diplomacy* (New York: The Free Press, 1997), 31–5, 48.

13. Leffler, *A Preponderance of Power*, 158–62; Pollard and Wells, "1945–1960," 355–7; Philip J. Funigiello, *American-Soviet Trade in the Cold War* (Chapel Hill: University of North Carolina Press, 1988), 76–96, quote 77. See also Ian Jackson, *The Economic Cold War: America, Britain, and East-West Trade, 1948–63* (Houndsmills, England: Palgrave, 2001), 11–110; Michael Mastanduno, *Economic Containment: CoCom and the Politics of East-West Trade* (Ithaca, N.Y.: Cornell University Press, 1992), 69, 82–3.

14. Walter LaFeber, *The Clash: U.S.-Japanese Relations Throughout History* (New York: W. W. Norton & Company, 1997), 269, also 264–8.

15. LaFeber, *The Clash*, 274.

16. Michael Schaller, *The American Occupation of Japan: The Origins of the Cold War in Asia* (New York: Oxford University Press, 1985), 141–2, also 157–8.

17. Quoted in William S. Borden, *The Pacific Alliance: United States Foreign Economic Policy and Japanese Trade Recovery, 1947–1955* (Madison: University

of Wisconsin Press, 1984), 166. See also Aaron Forsberg, *America and the Japanese Miracle: The Cold War Context of Japan's Postwar Economic Revival, 1950–1960* (Chapel Hill: University of North Carolina Press, 2000); Michael Schaller, *Altered States: The United States and Japan Since the Occupation* (New York: Oxford University Press, 1997), 50, 60–1.

18. Lloyd Dobyns and Clare Crawford-Mason, *Quality or Else: The Revolution in World Business* (Boston: Houghton Mifflin, 1991), 10; Margaret Graham, "The Threshold of the Information Age: Radio, Television, and Motion Pictures Mobilize the Nation," in *A Nation Transformed by Information*, eds. Alfred D. Chandler, Jr., and James W. Cortada (New York: Oxford University Press, 2000), 172; Kenneth Bilby, *The General: David Sarnoff and the Rise of the Communications Industry* (New York: Harper, 1986), 222.

19. Stephen B. Adams and Orville R. Butler, *Manufacturing the Future: A History of Western Electric* (New York: Cambridge University Press, 1999), 152–3, 207; James C. Abegglen and George Stalk, Jr., *Kaisha: The Japanese Corporation* (Rutland, Vt.: Charles E. Tuttle, 1985), 126–8. Akio Morita discusses his efforts to obtain a license for the transistor in *Made in Japan: Akio Morita and SONY* (New York: Dutton, 1986), 63–9. See Michael Riordan and Lillian Hoddeson, *Crystal Fire: The Invention of the Transistor and the Birth of the Information Age* (New York: Norton, 1997), 214–17. On the rebuilding of Japanese science, see Hideo Yoshikawa and Joanne Kauffman, *Science Has No Natural Borders: Harry C. Kelly and the Reconstruction of Science and Technology in Postwar Japan* (Cambridge, Mass.: MIT Press, 1994); Bowen C. Dees, *The Allied Occupation and Japan's Economic Miracle: Building the Foundations of Japanese Science and Technology 1945–1952* (Tokyo: Japan Library, 1997); Kyoko Hirano, *Mr. Smith Goes to Tokyo under the American Occupation, 1945–1952* (Washington, D.C.: Smithsonian, 1992), 175–6.

20. Thomas W. Zeiler, *Free Trade, Free World: The Advent of GATT* (Chapel Hill: University of North Carolina Press, 1999), 110. See also Leffler, *A Preponderance of Power*, 189–92.

21. Zeiler, *Free Trade, Free World*, 190, also 170–88.

22. Zeiler, *Free Trade, Free World*, 167.

23. United Nations Conference on Trade and Development (UNCTAD), *Handbook of International Trade and Development Statistics (1993)* (New York: United Nations, 1993), 22.

24. U.S. Bureau of the Census, *Historical Statistics of the United States: Bicentennial Edition* (Washington, D.C.: GPO, 1975), 2: 866, 869; Joseph A. Zettler and Frederick Cutler, "U.S. Direct Investments in Foreign Countries," *Survey of Current Business* (December 1952): 8; Mira Wilkins, *The Maturing of Multinational Enterprise: American Business Abroad from 1914 to 1970* (Cambridge, Mass.: Harvard University Press, 1970), 285–324; Paul Meek, "United States Investment in Foreign Securities," in *U.S. Private and Government Investment Abroad*, ed. Raymond F. Mikesell (Eugene: University of Oregon, 1962), 241.

25. Pollard and Wells, "1945–1960," 352–4. See also Alfred E. Eckes, Jr., *The United States and the Global Struggle for Minerals* (Austin: University of Texas, 1979), 123. Data on direct investments from Wilkins, *Maturing of Multinational Enterprise*, 328–31.

26. An excellent study by a historian with first-hand experience in the oil industry is Irvine H. Anderson, *ARAMCO, The United States and Saudi Arabia: A Study of the Dynamics of Foreign Oil Policy 1933–1950* (Princeton, N.J.: Princeton University Press, 1981). On uranium, see Jonathan E. Helmreich, *United States Relations with Belgium and the Congo, 1940–1960* (Newark: University of Delaware Press, 1998) and Jonathan E. Helmreich, *Gathering Rare Ores: The Diplomacy of Uranium Acquisition, 1943–1954* (Princeton, N.J.: Princeton University Press, 1986). The CIA and the military were concerned about the security of Congo supplies, 221–4. See also Eckes, *Global Struggle for Minerals*, 170–3.

27. Leffler, *A Preponderance*, 422–4, 478–80, 482–4; Daniel Yergin, *The Prize: The Epic Quest for Oil, Money & Power* (London: Simon & Schuster, 1991), 409–79. For British Petroleum's view of the situation, see James Bamberg, *The History of the British Petroleum Company: The Anglo-Iranian Years, 1928–1954* (Cambridge: Cambridge University Press, 1994).

28. William Stueck, *The Korean War: An International History* (Princeton, N.J.: Princeton University Press, 1995), 367–70; Leffler, *A Preponderance*, 403.

29. Schaller, *Altered States*, 47–9.

30. Kunz, *Butter and Guns*, 48–9.

31. Hogan, *The Marshall Plan*, 403–26; Pollard and Wells, "1945–1960," 346, 356–7.

32. Leffler, *A Preponderance*, 233, 349; Kunz, *Butter and Guns*, 50–1; John Gillingham, *Coal, Steel, and the Rebirth of Europe, 1945–1955: The Germans and French from Ruhr Conflict to Economic Community* (New York: Cambridge University Press, 1991); Pascaline Winand, *Eisenhower, Kennedy, and the United States of Europe* (New York: St. Martin's Press, 1993), 21–2.

33. Winand, *Eisenhower*, 25–111.

34. W. W. Rostow, "Jean Monnet: The Innovator as Diplomat" in *The Diplomats, 1939–1979*, eds. Gordon A. Craig and Francis L. Loewenheim (Princeton, N.J.: Princeton University Press, 1994), 260, 269–70. See also Merry Bromberger and Serge Bromberger, *Jean Monnet and the United States of Europe* (New York: Coward-McCann, 1969), 95–156; Jean Monnet, *Memoirs* (Garden City, N.Y.: Doubleday & Company, 1978), 417–30.

35. Monnet, *Memoirs*, 12.

36. John Lewis Gaddis, *Strategies of Containment: A Critical Reappraisal of Postwar American National Security Policy* (Oxford: Oxford University Press, 1982), 90–109, 127–63; Kunz, *Butter and Guns*, 63.

37. Paul Boyer, *By the Bomb's Early Light: American Thought and Culture at the Dawn of the Atomic Age* (Chapel Hill: University of North Carolina Press, 1994), 337; Edward Teller, *Better a Shield Than a Sword: Perspectives on Defense and Technology* (New York: The Free Press, 1987), 84. See also Herbert York, *Arms and the Physicist* (New York: AIP Press, 1995), 113–38; Stanley A. Blumberg and Louis G. Panos, *Edward Teller: Giant of the Golden Age of Physics* (New York: Charles Scribner's Sons, 1990), 28–34; Stanley Blumberg and Gwinn Owens, *Energy and Conflict: The Life and Times of Edward Teller* (New York: G. P. Putnam's Sons, 1976), 379–414; Leffler, *A Preponderance*, 327–8.

38. Puddington, *Broadcasting Freedom*, 89–114; Nelson, *Black Heavens*, 69–82.

39. Thomas J. McCormick, *America's Half-Century: United States Foreign Policy in the Cold War and After*, 2nd ed. (Baltimore: Johns Hopkins University Press, 1995), 118.

40. Warren I. Cohen, *America in the Age of Soviet Power, 1945–1991* (Cambridge: Cambridge University Press, 1993), 113, also 111–14.

41. Kunz, *Butter and Guns*, 69–87; Diane B. Kunz, *The Economic Diplomacy of the Suez Crisis* (Chapel Hill: University of North Carolina Press, 1991).

42. Gaddis, *Strategies of Containment*, 154.

43. William G. McLoughlin, Jr., *Billy Graham: Revivalist in a Secular Age* (New York: Ronald Press Company, 1960), 97, 99; John Pollock, *Billy Graham: The Authorized Biography* (New York: McGraw-Hill Book Company, 1966), 70, also 62, 77, 85–96, 102, 111–212; Marshall Frady, *Billy Graham: A Parable of American Righteousness* (Boston: Little, Brown and Company, 1979), 338.

44. Burton I. Kaufman, *Trade and Aid: Eisenhower's Foreign Economic Policy, 1953–1961* (Baltimore: Johns Hopkins University Press, 1982), 73, also 34–71.

45. On developments in aviation, see T. A. Heppenheimer, *Turbulent Skies: The History of Commercial Aviation* (New York: Wiley, 1995), 178–85. Nick A. Komons, "Civil Aeronautics Administration" in *The Airline Industry*, ed. William M. Leary (New York: Facts on File, 1992), 101–4; Michael H. Gorn, "Elwood R. Quesada" in *The Airline Industry*, ed. William M. Leary (New York: Facts on File, 1992), 387–93.

46. On inflation-adjusted family incomes, see U.S. Bureau of the Census, *Historical Statistics of United States*, 1: 290–1; Kunz, *Butter and Guns*, 64–6; Nelson, *Black Heavens*, 97.

47. U.S. Bureau of the Census, *Historical Statistics of United States*, 1: 131, 164, 226–7, 297; 2: 716, 783, 796. See also Angus Maddison, *Monitoring the World Economy 1820–1992* (Paris: OECD, 1995), 197.

48. Nelson Lichtenstein, *The Most Dangerous Man In Detroit: Walter Reuther and the Fate of American Labor* (New York: Basic Books, 1995), 287–8; Bruce Levin, Stephen Brier, David Brundage, Edward Countryman, Dorothy Fennell, Marcus Rediker, and Joshua Freeman, American Social History Project, *Who Built America? Working People and the Nation's Economy, Politics, Culture and Society, Volume II: From the Gilded Age to the Present* (New York: American Social History Productions, 1992), 503–30.

49. U.S. Bureau of the Census, *Historical Statistics of United States*, 1: 119, 2: 769.

Chapter 7

1. Marshall McLuhan, *The Gutenberg Galaxy* (New York: Mentor, 1962), 43; Paul Levinson, *Digital McLuhan: A Guide to the Information Millennium* (London: Routledge, 1999), 65.

2. Eugene Rodgers, *Flying High: The Story of Boeing and the Rise of the Jetliner Industry* (New York: Atlantic Monthly, 1996).

3. Peter Hugill, *World Trade since 1431* (Baltimore: Johns Hopkins University Press, 1993), 283, 297, 304; Marylin Bender and Selig Altschul, *The Chosen*

Instrument: Juan Trippe, Pan Am (New York: Simon and Schuster, 1982), 469–75, 502–3; T. A. Heppenheimer, *Turbulent Skies: A History of Commercial Aviation* (New York: John Wiley, 1995), 192–3, 203–6. Data from U.S. Department of Transportation, *FAA Statistical Handbook of Aviation* (Washington, D.C.: GPO, various issues 1968–80). But government efforts to develop supersonic commercial jets were less successful. Impressed with the prestige of Soviet and American scientific achievements, French President Charles DeGaulle proposed Anglo-French cooperation to develop a supersonic transport (SST), named the *Concorde*. He hoped the Europeans could use binational collaboration to challenge "America's colonization of the skies." The *Concorde* became available in 1969 and in 1976 even inaugurated flights to the United States from Paris and London, but the plane's technology proved unsuited for a time of energy austerity and concern about noise pollution. In America, President Kennedy proposed a government partnership with private industry to develop an SST, but after much work Congress chose to shut off funding for the project in 1971. Environmentalists aroused public concern about sonic booms and ozone depletion.

4. Andrew Gibson and Arthur Donovan, *The Abandoned Ocean: A History of United States Maritime Policy* (Columbia, S.C.: University of South Carolina Press, 2000), 209–11; Rene De La Pedraja, *The Rise and Decline of U.S. Merchant shipping* (New York: Twayne Publishers, 1993).

5. John Brooks, *Telephone: The First Hundred Years* (New York: Harper, 1975), 245–7; Brian Winston, *Media, Technology and Society: History: From the Telegraph to the Internet* (London: Routledge, 1998), 293–4.

6. On America's leader in patents and research, see John Dunning, "Changes in the Level and Structure of International Production: the Last One Hundred Years" in *The Growth of Multinationals*, ed. Mira Wilkins (Brookfield, Vt.: Edward Elgar Publishing Company, 1991), 116–17. Also, U.S. Bureau of the Census, *Historical Statistics of the United States: Bicentennial Edition* (Washington, D.C.: GPO, 1975), 2: 957–8; Emerson W. Pugh, *Building IBM: Shaping an Industry and Its Technology* (Cambridge, Mass.: MIT Press, 1995), xi; Thomas J. Watson, Jr., and Peter Petre, *Father Son & Co.: My Life at IBM and Beyond* (New York: Bantam Books, 1990), 230–3.

7. Kenneth Flamm, *Creating the Computer: Government, Industry, and High Technology* (Washington, D.C.: Brookings, 1988), 86–7, 101; Paul E. Ceruzzi, *A History of Modern Computing* (Cambridge, Mass.: MIT Press, 1998), 143–5; Pugh, *Building IBM*, 182, 296. On foreign criticisms of Big Blue, see Nancy Foy, *The Sun Never Sets on IBM* (New York: William Morrow, 1975), 153–4; Watson and Petre, *Father Son & Co.*, 175–6, 344–5; "Why IBM Split Its World Operations," *Business Week*, March 24, 1975, 122; "Reshaping IBM," *The Economist*, October 29, 1977, 92.

8. Samuel Pizer and Frederick Cutler, "United States Assets and Investments Abroad," *Survey of Current Business*, August 1961, 23; Julius N. Freidlin and Leonard A. Lupo, "U.S. Direct Investment Abroad in 1973," *Survey of Current Business*, August 1974, 52; Mira Wilkins, *The Maturing of Multinational Enterprise: American Business Abroad from 1914 to 1970* (Cambridge, Mass.: Harvard University Press, 1974), 342–3.

9. Robert M. Dunn, Jr., "Has the U.S. Economy Really Been Globalized?" *Washington Quarterly* 24:1 (Winter 2001):53.

10. Richard Rhodes, *Visions of Technology* (New York: Simon & Schuster, 1999), 206.

11. Walter LaFeber, *America, Russia, and the Cold War, 1945–1992*, 7th ed. (New York: McGraw-Hill, 1993), 195–200; Richard Rhodes, ed., *Visions of Technology: A Century of Vital Debate About Machines, Systems and the Human World* (New York: Simon & Schuster, 1999), 228–9; Stuart W. Leslie, *The Cold War and American Science: The Military-Industrial-Academic Comples and MIT and Stanford* (New York: Columbia University Press, 1993), 88–132; David Baker, *The History of Manned Space Flight* (New York: Crown Publishers, 1981), 29–51; Walter A. McDougall, *The Heavens and the Earth: A Political History of the Space Age* (New York: Basic Books, 1985), 160; James R. Killian, Jr., *Sputnik, Scientists, and Eisenhower: A Memoir of the First Special Assistant to the President for Science and Technology* (Cambridge, Mass.: MIT Press, 1977). Gallup data from George H. Gallup, *The Gallup Poll: Public Opinion, 1935–71* (New York: Random House, 1972), 1393, 1521, 1534. An October 27, 1957, poll after Sputnik showed Americans thinking by a 49 to 32 margin that Russia was ahead in missile development. The January 1958 poll surveyed citizens of seven nations about who was ahead in the Cold War. The consensus was that Russia was by a 48–22 margin.

12. William B. Breuer, *Race to the Moon: America's Duel with the Soviets* (Westport, Conn.: Praeger, 1993), 163. See also Shirley Thomas, *Men of Space: Profiles of the Leaders in Space Research, Development, and Exploration* (Philadelphia: Chilton Company, 1961), 97–116.

13. Breuer, *Race to the Moon*, 160–3.

14. Peter Bond, *Heroes in Space: From Gagarin to Challenger* (Oxford: Basil Blackwell, 1987), 26–47; Breuer, *Race to the Moon*, 166–8.

15. David J. Whalen, "Communications Satellites: Making the Global Village Possible," online at http://www.hq.nasa.gov/office/pao/History/satcomhistory.html; Winston, *Media, Technology and Society*, 292–3.

16. Edward Comor, *Communication, Commerce, and Power: The Political Economy of America and the Direct Broadcast Satellite, 1960–2000* (New York: St. Martin's Press, 1998), 43. Heather E. Hudson, *Communication Satellites: Their Development and Impact* (New York: Free Press, 1990), 25–6; Winston, *Media, Technology and Society*, 290.

17. Winston, *Media, Technology and Society*, 290–2; Whalen, "Communications Satellites"; Hudson, *Communication Satellites*, 37–8, 129–33.

18. Walter Hixson, *Parting the Curtain: Propaganda, Culture, and the Cold War, 1945–1961* (New York: St. Martin's Press, 1998), 179, 203–13, 229–31. Reinhold Wagnleitner, *Coca-Colonization and the Cold War: The Cultural Mission of the United States in Austria After the Second World War* (Chapel Hill: University of North Carolina Press, 1994), 280, 284–5.

19. Watson and Petre, *Father Son & Co*, 330.

20. George J. Tenet, "The U-2 Program: The DCI's Perspective," see http://www.cia.gov/csi/studies/winter98-99/art01.html.

21. George Leopold, "Government Declassifies Engineering Details of First U.S. Reconnaissance Satellite," *Electronic Engineering Times*, June 29, 1998 [General News: Magazines and Journals. Online, Lexis-Nexis Academic Universe. August 29, 2002]. Walter J. Boyne, *Beyond the Horizons: The Lockheed Story* (New York: St. Martin's, 1998), 200–8.

22. Quoted in John Lewis Gaddis, *Russia, the Soviet Union, and the United States: An Interpretive History*, 2nd ed. (New York: McGraw-Hill, 1990), 237, also 232–42.

23. Gordon H. Chang, *Friends and Enemies: The United States, China, and the Soviet Union, 1948–1972* (Stanford, Calif.: Stanford University Press, 1990), 249.

24. U.S. Bureau of the Census, *Historical Statistics*, 2: 995.

25. Quoted in Thomas W. Zeiler, *American Trade and Power in the 1960s* (New York: Columbia University Press, 1992), 49, also 24–9. See also Thomas W. Zeiler, *Dean Rusk: Defending the American Mission Abroad* (Wilmington, Del.: Scholarly Resources, 2000), 54–6; Philip J. Funigiello, *American-Soviet Trade in the Cold War* (Chapel Hill: University of North Carolina Press, 1988), 147–76; Pascaline Winand, *Eisenhower, Kennedy, and the United States of Europe* (New York: St. Martin's Press, 1993).

26. Burton I. Kaufman, *Trade and Aid: Eisenhower's Foreign Economic Policy, 1953–1961* (Baltimore: Johns Hopkins University Press, 1982), 152–96; Winand, *Eisenhower*, 128–36.

27. Zeiler, *American Trade*, 160, also 56–9. See also Steve Dryden, *Trade Warriors: USTR and the American Crusade for Free Trade* (New York: Oxford University Press, 1995), 52–59; Winand, *Eisenhower*, 328, 336–66; Oliver Bange, *The EEC Crisis of 1963: Kennedy, Macmillan, de Gaulle, and Adenauer in Crisis* (Houndmills, U.K.: Macmillan Press, 2000), 106–15.

28. Charles G. Cogan, *Charles de Gaulle: A Brief Biography with Documents* (Boston: Bedford Books, 1996), 111–53; Harold van B. Cleveland, *The Atlantic Idea and Its European Rivals* (New York: McGraw-Hill, 1966), 145–7; Richard F. Kuisel, "The American Economic Challenge: De Gaulle and the French" in *De Gaulle and the United States: A Centennial Reappraisal*, eds. Robert O. Paxton and Nicholas Wahl (Oxford: Berg, 1994), 196–211; Daniel J. Mahoney, *De Gaulle: Statesmanship, Grandeur, and Modern Democracy* (Westport, Conn.: Praeger, 1996), 131–49. By 1963, total U.S. investment in the Common Market broke down in the following way: 40 percent went to West Germany, 25 percent to France, and 15 percent to Italy. By the end of 1967, France took $1.9 billion, slightly more than Italy but much less than Britain's $6.1 billion and West Germany's $3.5 billion. In 1958, France and West Germany received roughly the same amount dollars, but by 1965, American capital flowed to the latter at a level of $349 million while France got only $163 million.

29. Greil Marcus, "The Beatles" in *The Rolling Stone Illustrated History of Rock & Roll* (New York: Random House, 1980), 183, also 177–82; Allan Kozinn, *The Beatles* (London: Phaidon Press, 1995), 76–92, 103, 106, 127; Steve Chapple and Reebee Garofalo, *Rock 'n' Roll Is Here to Pay: The History and Politics of the Music Industry* (Chicago: Nelson-Hall, 1977), 69–71. It should be noted that the Beatles side-stepped globalization in one

respect: they were among the last rock bands to open a web site (in November 2000).

30. James A. Bill, *George Ball: Behind the Scenes in U.S. Foreign Policy* (New Haven, Conn.: Yale University Press, 1997), 130–1, 135, also 40–54, 75–6, 110–29.

31. Zeiler, *American Trade*, 218–58; Dryden, *Trade Warriors*, 115–27.

32. Alfred E. Eckes, Jr., *Opening America's Market: U.S. Foreign Trade Policy since 1776* (Chapel Hill: University of North Carolina Press, 1995), 239, also 200; Francis Bator to the president, March 16, 1967, box 1, Name Files: Francis Bator, National Security Files, Lyndon B. Johnson Library.

33. Zeiler, *Dean Rusk*, 85.

34. Thomas J. McCormick, *America's Half Century: United States Foreign Policy in the Cold War and After*, 2nd ed. (Baltimore: Johns Hopkins University Press, 1995), 135–7.

35. Robert A. Pollard and Samuel F. Wells, Jr., "1945–1960: The Era of American Economic Hegemony" in *Economics and World Power: An Assessment of American Diplomacy Since 1789*, eds. William H. Becker and Samuel F. Wells, Jr. (New York: Columbia University Press, 1984), 372–3, 378–9; W. W. Rostow, *The Stages of Economic Growth: A Non-Communist Manifesto* (New York: Cambridge Unversity Press, 1960). For a recent critique of Rostow's theory, see David Landes, *The Wealth and Poverty of Nations: Why Some Are So Rich and Some So Poor* (New York: W. W. Norton, 1998).

36. Stephen G. Rabe, "Controlling Revolutions: Latin America, the Alliance for Progress, and Cold War Anti-Communism" in *Kennedy's Quest for Victory: American Foreign Policy, 1961–1963*, ed. Thomas G. Paterson (New York: Oxford University Press, 1989), 110–13; Zeiler, *Dean Rusk*, 66–8; Diane B. Kunz, *Butter and Guns: America's Cold War Economic Diplomacy* (New York: The Free Press, 1997), 130–48.

37. William McChesney Martin quoted in Robert Buzzanco, *Vietnam and the Transformation of American Life* (Oxford: Blackwell Publishers, 1999), 99, also 98, 175–6. See also Robert D. Schulzinger, *A Time for War: The United States and Vietnam, 1941–1975* (New York: Oxford University Press, 1997), 243.

38. Allen J. Matusow, *The Unraveling of America: A History of Liberalism in the 1960s* (New York: Harper & Row, 1984), 312–15; James Miller, *Democracy Is in the Streets: From Port Huron to the Siege of Chicago* (Cambridge, Mass.: Harvard University Press, 1994), Appendix, *The Port Huron Statement*, 340, 344, 348–9, 359, 363.

39. L. E. Chasanovitch memorandum, June 25, 1964, Board of Trade 241: 1348, British Public Record Office. Luis Eugenio Di Marco, ed., *International Economics and Development: Essays in Honor of Raul Prebisch* (New York: Academic Press, 1972), xvii–xix, 3–12; Raul Prebisch, "The Latin American Periphery in the Global System of Capitalism" in *Paradigms in Economic Development: Classic Perspectives, Critiques, and Reflections*, ed. Rajani Kanth (Armonk, N.Y.: M. E. Sharpe, 1994), 165–75; Robert J. Alexander, "Import Substitution in Latin America in Retrospect" in *Progress Toward Development in Latin America: From Prebisch to Technological Autonomy*, eds. James L. Dietz and Dilmus D. James (Boulder: Lynne Rienner Publishers, 1990),

15–21. Besides the Latin American Free Trade Association (LAFTA), nations also created the Central American Common Market, the Andean Pact, and the Caribbean Common Market.

40. Joan Spero, *The Politics of International Economic Relations*, 3rd ed. (New York: St. Martin's Press, 1985), 223–39; Zeiler, *American Trade*, 190–216.

41. Douglas Little, "A Fool's Errand: America and the Middle East, 1961–1969" in *The Diplomacy of the Crucial Decade: American Foreign Relations During the 1960s*, ed. Diane B. Kunz (New York: Columbia University Press, 1994), 294, 310.

42. Thomas Noer, "New Frontiers and Old Priorities in Africa" in *Kennedy's Quest for Victory: American Foreign Policy, 1961–1963*, ed. Thomas G. Paterson (New York: Oxford University Press, 1989), 261–8, 275; Gerald E. Thomas, "The Black Revolt: The United States and Africa in the 1960s" in *The Diplomacy of the Crucial Decade: American Foreign Relations During the 1960s*, ed. Diane B. Kunz (New York: Columbia University Press, 1994), 320–55.

43. David P. Calleo, "Since 1961: American Power in a New World Economy" in *Economics and World Power: An Assessment of American Diplomacy Since 1789*, eds. William H. Becker and Samuel F. Wells, Jr. (New York: Columbia University Press, 1984), 396.

44. Kunz, *Butter and Guns*, 216.

45. Calleo, "Since 1961," 398–409. See also Michael Schaller, *Altered States: The United States and Japan Since the Occupation* (New York: Oxford University Press, 1997), 220–5, 231–40.

46. Quote of economic aide Herbert Stein in Schaller, *Altered States*, 234.

47. Calleo, "Since 1961," 412–24; McCormick, *America's Half Century*, 162–5.

Chapter 8

1. Theodore Levitt, "The Globalization of Markets," *Harvard Business Review* 61:3 (May–June 1983): 92–102.

2. Peter N. Carroll, *It Seemed Like Nothing Happened: The Tragedy and Promise of American in the 1970s* (New York: Holt, Rinehart and Winston, 1982), 118. See also Frank B. Wyant, *The United States, OPEC, and Multinational Oil* (Lexington, Mass.: Lexington Books, 1977), 74–83.

3. Daniel Yergin, *The Prize: The Epic Quest for Oil, Money, and Power* (New York: Simon & Schuster, 1991), 580, also 574–9; Armand Hammer, *Hammer* (New York: Perigree Books, 1987), 333–55; Edward Jay Epstein, *Dossier: The Secret History of Armand Hammer* (New York: Random House, 1996), 233–44.

4. Steve Weinberg, *Armand Hammer: The Untold Story* (Boston: Little, Brown and Company, 1989), 263–360; Epstein, *Dossier*, 245–6.

5. U.S. Bureau of the Census, *Statistical Abstract of the United States, 1986* (Washington, D.C.: GPO, 1987), 557, 562, 564; C. Fred Bergsten, "The Threat from the Third World," *Foreign Policy* 11 (Summer 1973): 78.

6. Yergin, *The Prize*, 634–8.

7. Yergin, *The Prize*, 633, also 634. See also Warren I. Cohen, *America in the Age of Soviet Power, 1945–1991* (Cambridge: Cambridge University Press, 1993), 200–1, 205–7.

8. Jeffrey Robinson, *Yamani: The Inside Story* (New York: The Atlantic Monthly Press, 1989), 59–71, 94–104; Abdulaziz Al Sowayegh, *Arab Petro-Politics* (London: Croom Helm, 1984), 113–14.

9. Robinson, *Yamani*, 12, 74, also 110–13, 186–92.

10. Yergin, *The Prize*, 639–42.

11. Yergin, *The Prize*, 643–4.

12. Robinson, *Yamani*, 135–8; Yergin, *The Prize*, 651–2.

13. Carroll, *It Seemed Like Nothing Happened*, 118–19, 123–6, 252–96, 317–29.

14. Carroll, *It Seemed Like Nothing Happened*, 118; Yergin, *The Prize*, 660–70; Diane B. Kunz, *Butter and Guns: America's Cold War Economic Diplomacy* (New York: Free Press, 1997), 240; Barry Bluestone and Bennett Harrison, *The Deindustrialization of America: Plant Closings, Community Abandonment, and the Dismantling of Basic Industry* (New York: Basic Books, 1982).

15. Yergin, *The Prize*, 642–6.

16. Quoted in Yergin, *The Prize*, 698, also 694; Robinson, *Yamani*, 211–16; Jimmy Carter, *Keeping Faith: Memoirs of a President* (New York: Bantam Books, 1982), 112–14.

17. Yergin, *The Prize*, 714–22, 746–52; Robinson, *Yamani*, 253–82; Shukri Ghanem, *OPEC: The Rise and Fall of an Exclusive Club* (London: KPI, 1986), 165–84.

18. See generally, Marc Williams, *Third World Cooperation: The Group of 77 in UNCTAD* (London: St. Martins Press, 1991). For text of key UN declarations on NIEO, see Karl P. Sauvant and Joachim W. Muller, eds., *The Collected Documents of the Group of 77* (New York: Oceana Publications, 1995), 680–709.

19. Daya Kishan Thussu, *International Communication: Continuity and Change* (New York: Oxford, 2000), 44–8. William Preston, Jr., Edward S. Herman, and Herbert I. Schiller, *Hope & Folly: The United States and UNESCO, 1945–1985* (Minneapolis: University of Minnesota Press, 1989). International Commission for the Study of Communications Problems (Sean MacBride, chairman), *Many Voices, One World* (New York: UNESCO, 1980).

20. See for instance, Raymond Vernon, *Sovereignty at Bay: The Multinational Spread of U.S. Enterprises* (New York: Basic Books, 1971); Mira Wilkins, *The History of Foreign Investment in the United States to 1914* (Cambridge, Mass.: Harvard University Press, 1989). See also, David Pletcher, *The Diplomacy of Trade and Investment: American Economic Expansion in the Hemisphere, 1865–1900* (Columbia: University of Missouri Press, 1998).

21. The reasons for U.S. involvement in Chile are more fully discussed in Robert Sobel, *ITT: The Management of Opportunity* (New York: Truman Talley, 1982), 302–35; Paul E. Sigmund, *The U.S. and Democracy in Chile* (Baltimore: Johns Hopkins University Press, 1993), 58–63. On the Foreign Corrupt Practices Act, see Carolyn Hotchkiss, "The Sleeping Dog Stirs: New Signs of Life in Efforts to End Corruption in International Business," *Journal of Public Policy and Marketing* 17:1 (Spring 1998): 108. It would be wrong to think that multinationals were solely responsible for corrupting developing nations. In many developing nations, it was widely expected that business (domestic and foreign) should supply politicians with campaign

contributions, jobs, and other financial aid in exchange for favors. The annual "corruption indexes" of Transparency International show that bribery is well established in most developing economies, and some industrial ones. See http://www.transparency.de/documents/cpi/index.html.

22. World Bank, *World Development Report, 1980* (New York: Oxford University Press, 1980), 141; World Bank, *World Development Report, 1987* (New York: Oxford University Press, 1987), 243; Devesh Kapur, John P. Lewis, and Richard Webb, *The World Bank: Its First Half Century* (Washington, D.C.: Brookings, 1997), I: 210. Gallup poll of 1,525 respondents on January 11, 1963, and Opinion Research Corporation poll of 1,086 participants on August 28, 1967, http://web.lexis-nexis.com.

23. Kapur, Lewis, and Webb, *The World Bank*, I:596. On Citibank's efforts to recycle petrodollars, see Phillip L. Zweig, *Wriston: Walter Wriston, Citibank, and the Rise and Fall of American Financial Supremacy* (New York: Crown, 1995), 384–439; 567–81. On Colombia, see Zweig, *Wriston*, 575. On Mexico, see Steve Frazier, "Oils Lure Led Mexico and Banks into Payment Woes," *Wall Street Journal*, May 15, 1984, 32; William Darity, Jr., and Bobbie L. Horn, *The Loan Pushers: The Role of Commercial Banks in the International Debt Crisis* (Cambridge, Mass.: Ballinger, 1988); Karin Lissakers, *Banks, Borrowers, and the Establishment: A Revisionist Account of the International Debt Crisis* (New York: Basic Books, 1991); Harold James, *International Monetary Cooperation since Bretton Woods* (New York: Oxford, 1996), 347–408.

24. U.S. Department of Labor, *Employment, Hours, and Earnings United States, 1909–94*, Bulletin 2445 (Washington, D.C.: GPO, September 1994), 2:1202. Median income of households actually rose during the period as more women entered the workforce and as family members took multiple jobs. See U.S. Bureau of the Census, *Statistical Abstract of the United States 2000* (Washington, D.C.: GPO, 2001), 466. Constant prices in 1992 dollars.

25. James, *International Monetary Cooperation*, 357–8; Lissakers, *Banks, Borrowers, and the Establishment*, 137–42; Bill Orr, "After a Decade, Bankers say 'Adios' to Latin Debt Crisis," *ABA Banking Journal* 84:7 (July 1992):36.

26. James, *International Monetary Cooperation*, 398.

27. Kunz, *Butter and Guns*, 270–86. See also Michael G. Hadjimichalakis, *The Federal Reserve, Money, and Interest Rates: The Volcker Years and Beyond* (New York: Praeger Publishers, 1984), 23–55; David P. Calleo, "Since 1961: American Power in a New World Economy" in *Economics and World Power: An Assessment of American Diplomacy Since 1789*, eds. William H. Becker and Samuel F. Wells, Jr. (New York: Columbia University Press, 1984), 438. On Mexican billionaires, see Carlos M. Urzua, "Five Decades of Relations between the World Bank and Mexico," in Kapur, Lewis, and Webb, *The World Bank*, II: 93–4.

28. Bert Randolph Sugar, *"The Thrill of Victory": The Inside Story of ABC Sports* (New York: Hawthorn, 1978).

29. Donald Spivey, *Sport in America: New Historical Perspectives* (Westport, Conn.: Greenwood Press, 1985), 167–9, 172–8; Howard Bingham and Max Wallace, *Muhammad Ali's Greatest Fight: Cassius Clay vs. the United States of America* (New York: M. Evans and Company, 2000), 74, 211–15; Michael Oriard,

"Muhammad Ali: The Hero in the Age of Mass Media" in *Major Problems in American Sport History*, ed. Steven A. Riess (Boston: Houghton Mifflin Company, 1997), 391–2; Gerald Early, ed., *The Muhammad Ali Reader* (Hopewell, N.J.: The Ecco Press, 1998), 139–40, 217; Jack Newfield, *Only in America: The Life and Crimes of Don King* (New York: William Morrow, 1995), 61–84.

30. Ezra F. Vogel, *Japan as Number One: Lessons for America* (Cambridge, Mass.: Harvard University Press, 1979), viii–ix, 11–16, 226–36.

31. Tom Zito, "Goodbyes, Hellos, and Billy Speaks," *Washington Post*, January 3, 1979, B-1.

32. Maryann Keller, *Rude Awakening: The Rise, Fall, and Struggle for Recovery of General Motors* (New York: William Morrow, 1989), 22; William T. Ziemba and Sandra L. Schwartz, *Power Japan: How and Why the Japanese Economy Works* (Chicago: Probus, 1992), 88; Jeffrey A. Hart, *Rival Capitalists: International Competitiveness in the United States, Japan, and Western Europe* (Ithaca, N.Y.: Cornell University Press, 1992), 238–48.

33. Alfred E. Eckes, Jr., ed., *Revisiting U.S. Trade Policy: Decisions in Perspective* (Athens: Ohio University Press, 2000), 139–41. See also Steve Dryden, *Trade Warriors: USTR and the American Crusade for Free Trade* (New York: Oxford University Press, 1995), 207–78.

34. Kunz, *Butter and Guns*, 307–12; Walter LaFeber, *The Clash: U.S.-Japanese Relations Throughout History* (New York: W. W. Norton and Company, 1997), 363–76; Michael Schaller, *Altered States: The United States and Japan Since the Occupation* (New York: Oxford University Press, 1997), 254–5.

35. Carroll, *It Seemed Like Nothing Happened*, 128, 226–7; Thomas G. Paterson, J. Garry Clifford, and Kenneth J. Hagan, *American Foreign Relations, A History: Since 1895, Vol. II*, 5th ed. (Boston: Houghton-Mifflin, 2000), 428; Michael Schaller, *Reckoning with Reagan: America and Its President in the 1980s* (New York: Oxford University Press, 1992), 126.

36. Gaddis Smith, *Morality, Reason and Power: American Diplomacy in the Carter Years* (New York: Hill and Wang, 1986).

37. Reagan quote in Richard V. Allen, "Ronald Reagan: An Extraordinary Man in Extraordinary Times" in *The Fall of the Berlin Wall: Reassessing the Causes and Consequences of the End of the Cold War*, ed. Peter Schweizer (Stanford, Calif.: Hoover Institution Press, 2000), 52. See generally, Peter Schweizer, *Victory: The Reagan Administration's Secret Strategy that Hastened the Collapse of the Soviet Union* (New York: Atlantic Monthly Press, 1994), 217–19. The fall of oil prices also brought havoc to U.S. independent producers in Texas and Oklahoma, and left U.S. producers bitter. Arthur Gottschalk, "Book Alleging Reagan Oil Plot Stuns Independent Producers," *Journal of Commerce*, December 1, 1994, 5B; Larry Nation, "10 Years Ago, That Sinking Feeling Came Over all 'Oilies,' " *Houston Chronicle*, January 21, 1996, 4; Bill Mintz, "Old Policy Haunts White House; Oilmen Concerned Reagan-era Deal with Saudis Still Stands," *Houston Chronicle*, October 25, 1994, 1.

38. Peter Schweizer, "The Fall of the Berlin Wall after Ten Years – an Essay," in *The Fall of the Berlin Wall*, ed. Peter Schweizer, 1–47; Philip J. Funigiello, *America-Soviet Trade in the Cold War* (Chapel Hill: University of North Carolina Press, 1988), 190–207; Schaller, *Reckoning with Reagan*, 122–70.

39. Arch Puddington, *Broadcasting Freedom* (Lexington: University of Kentucky Press, 2000), 292–3; Michael Nelson, *War of the Black Heavens* (Syracuse, N.Y.: Syracuse University Press, 1997), 173–8; Alvin A. Snyder, *Warriors of Disinformation: American Propaganda, Soviet Lies, and the Winning of the Cold War, An Insider's Account* (New York: Arcade, 1995), 32–3, 74, 184.

40. Margaret Thatcher, *The Downing Street Years* (New York: Harper Collins, 1993), 471, 813. For an alternative view, see David Greenberg, "The Empire Strikes Out; Why Star Wars Did Not End the Cold War," *Foreign Affairs* 79:2 (March/April 2000): 136, a review of Frances Fitzgerald's *Way Out There in the Blue: Reagan, Star Wars and the End of the Cold War* (New York: Simon & Schuster, 2000). Journalist Lou Cannon, who covered Reagan extensively in California and in national politics, noted that Star Wars may have hastened the demise of the Soviet Union and cited Vladimir Lukhim, a former high-ranking Soviet official, as saying: "It's clear that SDI accelerated our catastrophe by at least five years." Lou Cannon, "Reagan's Big Ideas; How the Gipper Conceived Star Wars," *National Review* LI: 3 (February 22, 1999):40–2. See also Schweizer, *The Fall of the Berlin Wall*, 32–4; Schweizer, *Victory*, 3. Steward Nozette and Robert Lawrence Kuhn, *Commercializing SDI Technologies* (New York: Praeger Publishers, 1987).

41. Carroll, *It Seemed Like Nothing Happened*, 134. On the World Economic Forum, see http://www.weforum.org. On lobbying in the United States, Kim McQuaid, *Uneasy Partners: Big Business in American Politics 1945–1990* (Baltimore: Johns Hopkins University Press, 1994), 172–94.

42. Daniel Yergin and Joseph Stanislaw, *The Commanding Heights: The Battle Between Government and the Marketplace That Is Remaking the Modern World* (New York: Simon & Schuster, 1998).

43. Yergin and Stanislaw, *The Commanding Heights*, 9–17, 325–63.

Chapter 9

1. In acquiring the Philippines, William McKinley made the United States a Pacific power and placed America on a collision course with Japan. To cope with the problems of the Great Depression, Franklin D. Roosevelt expanded the size and scope of the federal government, setting the domestic agenda for the next half century. Internationally, he made the fateful decisions to abandon American isolation, to enter World War II, and to commit America to the postwar international economic and security structure. Harry Truman, who succeeded Roosevelt in April 1945, inaugurated the age of nuclear diplomacy with his decision to use the atomic bomb and committed America to the long-term strategy of containing the Soviet Union.

2. For an introduction to Reagan's personal thoughts, see in particular Kiron K. Skinner, Annelise Anderson, and Martin Anderson, *Reagan, In His Own Hand* (New York: Free Press, 2001), 221–3, 228–9, 311–17. They point out that Reagan's pre-presidential radio addresses focused on foreign and defense policy (27 percent) and economics (25 percent). In a total of 1,044 essays for radio, only one was written on abortion. Less than 1 percent considered the family, women, and race.

3. Skinner, Anderson, and Anderson, *Reagan, In His Own Hand*, 473. First quotation from March 13, 1980, "State of the Union" Speech delivered to Chicago Council on Foreign Relations. Second quotation cited in James Freeman, "Reagan's Second Greatest Achievement," *USA Today*, December 10, 1999, online at http://www.usatoday.com/news/comment/columnists/freeman/ncjf45.htm. On the Thatcher interest in privatization, see Daniel Yergin and Joseph Stanislaw, *The Commanding Heights: The Battle Between Government and the Marketplace That Is Remaking the Modern World* (New York: Simon and Schuster, 1998), 92–125.

4. Murray Weidenbaum, who served as chairman of President Reagan's Council of Economic Advisors, gave credit to the Federal Reserve in his *Rendezvous with Reality: The American Economy after Reagan* (New York: Basic Books, 1988), 11–13. Data from U.S. Bureau of Census, *Statistical Abstract of the United States 1987*, (Washington, D.C.: GPO, 1988), 417, 463. Brent R. Moulton, "Improved Estimates of the National Income and Product Accounts for 1929–99: Results of the Comprehensive Revision," *Survey of Current Business* 80:4 (April 2000):15.

5. U.S. Bureau of the Census, *Statistical Abstract of the United States 1990* (Washington, D.C.: GPO 1997), 793; Barry Eichengreen, "U.S. Foreign Financial Relations in the Twentieth Century," in *The Cambridge Economic History of the United States*, eds. Stanley L. Engerman and Robert E. Gallman (New York: Cambridge University Press, 2000), III: 502–3; U.S. Trade Deficit Review Commission, *The U.S. Trade Deficit: Causes, Consequences and Recommendations for Action* (Washington, D.C.: GPO, November 14, 2000), A28–9.

6. "GDP and Other Major NIPA Series, 1929–99," *Survey of Current Business* 80:4 (April 2000): 131; "BEA Current and Historical Data," *Survey of Current Business* 82:7 (July 2002):D-3, D-12; U.S. Trade Deficit Review Commission, *The U.S. Trade Deficit: Causes, Consequences and Recommendations for Action* (Washington, D.C.: GPO, November 14, 2000), A25–6.

7. U.S. Department of Transportation, *Transportation Statistics Annual Report 1999* (Washington, D.C.: GPO, 1999), 51.

8. Alfred E. Eckes, *Opening the American Market: U.S. Foreign Trade Policy since 1776* (Chapel Hill: University of North Carolina Press, 1995), 245–8; Meg Vaillancourt, "Converse Files for Chapter 11," *Boston Globe*, January 23, 2001, D1. Recent data from U.S. International Trade Commission, *Nonrubber Footwear Statistical Report 1999*, Publication 3289 (Washington, D.C.: USITC, March 2000), 7.

9. U.S. Department of Labor, *Handbook of Labor Statistics*, Bulletin 2340 (Washington, D.C.: GPO, August 1989), 290–1, 320–2; Alvin Toffler, "Beyond the Age of Glitz," *Industry Week*, November 19, 1990, 12.

10. Dan Schiller, *Digital Capitalism: Networking the Global Market System* (Cambridge, Mass.: MIT Press, 1999), 15–16; U.S. Department of Commerce, Secretariat on Electronic Commerce, *The Emerging Digital Economy* (Washington, D.C.: GPO, 1998), 4; U.S. Bureau of the Census, *Statistical Abstract 1990*, 400, 427.

11. Paul Ceruzzi, *A History of Modern Computing* (Cambridge, Mass.: MIT Press, 1999), 106, 168–71, 248–50; Thomas J. Watson, Jr., and Peter Petre, *Father*

Son & Co.: My Life at IBM and Beyond (New York: Bantam Books, 1990), 377; Alfred Chandler and James W. Cortada, "The Information Age: Continuities and Differences," in *A Nation Transformed by Information*, eds. Alfred D. Chandler, Jr., and James W. Cortada (New York: Oxford University Press, 2000), 295; Thomas McCraw, *American Business 2000: How It Worked* (Wheeling, Ill.: Harland Davidson, 2000), 196–7. Charles H. Ferguson and Charles R. Morris, *Computer Wars: How the West Can Win in a Post-IBM World* (New York: Times Book, 1993), 10–11, 23–5; John W. Wilson, "And Now, the Post-Industrial Corporation," *Business Week*, March 3, 1986, 64; Norman Jonas, "The Hollow Corporation," *Business Week*, March 3, 1986, 57.

12. Edward A. Comor, *Communication, Commerce and Power: The Political Economy of America and the Direct Broadcast Satellite, 1960–2000* (New York: St. Martin's, 1998), 45, 132–3, 138, 141–2, 153.

13. "How Pirates Are Plundering the Studios," *Business Week*, February 21, 1983, 81; "Global Product Piracy May Be Costing Firms Billions," *Washington Post*, February 27, 1988, B2.

14. Harvey J. Winter, "Endnote: The Role of the United States Government in Improving International Intellectual Property Protection," *Journal of Law and Technology* 2 (Fall 1987): 325; Calvin Sims, "Wounded by Patent Piracy," *New York Times*, May 13, 1987, 1. The Software and Information Industry Association said in May 2000 that global software piracy topped $59 billion during the preceding five years. The study estimated that eight in ten business software applications are pirated in nineteen countries, among them Vietnam, China, and Russia. See http://www.siia.net/sharedcontent/press/2000/5-24-00.html. The International Intellectual Property Alliance also monitors national enforcement activities and pressures U.S. Trade Representative (USTR) to focus on trade-related intellectual properties implementation, optical media piracy, piracy by organized crime, Internet copyright piracy, and similar activities. See http://www.iipa.com. The Business Software Alliance said worldwide dollar losses due to software piracy amounted to $11.75 billion in the year 2000. "Software Piracy on the Rise in Asia, Study Says." *The Industry Standard.com* (May 22, 2001) [General News: Magazines and Journals. Online. Lexis-Nexis Academic Universe. August 30, 2002].

15. "Legal Affairs," *Business Week*, May 22, 1989, 78; Lionel S. Sobel, "U.S. Enters New Era in International Copyright Relations," *Entertainment Law Reporter* 10:6 (November 1988) [Legal News. Online. Lexis-Nexis Academic Universe. August 30, 2002]. On U.S. use of unilateral sanctions to enforce intellectual property rights, see Thomas O. Bayard and Kimberly Ann Elliott, *Reciprocity and Retaliation in U.S. Trade Policy* (Washington, D.C.: Institute for International Economics, September 1994).

16. Andrea Adelson, "Entertainment Industry Adds Anti-Piracy Tricks," *New York Times*, November 21, 1988, 8.

17. U.S. Bureau of Economic Analysis, web site, http://www.bea.gov.

18. Larry Armstrong, "Disneyland Abroad: Today Tokyo, Tomorrow the World," *Business Week*, March 9, 1987, 68.

19. http://www.mcspotlight.org/company/company history.html; http://www.mcdonalds.com/corporate/press/financial/2001/04192001/04192001.html;

John F. Love, *McDonald's: Behind the Arches*, 2d ed. (New York: Bantam, 1995), 410–48, Fujita quote on page 423; Adam Sage, "McDonald's Rebrands Itself as 100 Per Cent Pure French," *London Times*, March 31, 2001, 18. For the "Golden Arches theory of conflict prevention," see Thomas Friedman, *The Lexus and the Olive Tree: Understanding Globalization* (New York: Farrar, Straus, Giroux, 1999), 195–205.

20. Mary Kay Ash, *Mary Kay* (New York: Harper and Row Publishers, 1981), 174. See also H. W. Brands, *Masters of Enterprise: Giants of American Business from John Jacob Astor and J. P. Morgan to Bill Gates and Oprah Winfrey* (New York: The Free Press, 1999), 228–33, 250–4; Hoover's Company Profile Database (2001), Lexis-Nexis.

21. "Lydia Chavez, "Dee Hock's Cosmic Vista for VISA International," *New York Times*, June 7, 1981, III: 4; "Buying Up the World with Plastic," *The Economist*, June 13, 1981, 65; "Electronic Banking," *The Economist*, September 18, 1982, 94; http://corporate.visa.com/mc/stats/main.shtml.

22. Richard J. Herring and Robert E. Litan, *Financial Regulation in the Global Economy* (Washington, D.C.: Brookings, 1995), 21, 35; Robert Solomon, *Money on the Move: The Revolution in International Finance since 1980* (Princeton, N.J.: Princeton University Press, 1999), 110; U.S. Treasury, *Report on U.S. Holdings of Foreign Long-Term Securities* (April 2000), 10, online at http://www.treas.gov/fpis/flts.html. Elena L. Nguyen, "The International Investment Position of the United States at year end 2001," *Survey of Current Business* 82:7 (July 2002): 10–19.

23. Air Transport Association of America, "Traffic Summary 1960–2000: U.S. Scheduled Airlines," online at http://www.air-transport.org/public/industry/display1.asp?id=9; Michael Schaller, *Reckoning with Reagan: America and Its President in the 1980s* (New York: Oxford University Press, 1992), 96–8.

24. Stephen Segaller, *Nerds 2.0.1: A Brief History of the Internet* (New York: TV Books, 1998), 14; "Engineer of the Electronic Era: Bill Gates," *Financial Times*, December 31, 1994, 6; "Time Picks Computer as 'Man of the Year'," *Christian Science Monitor*, December 28, 1982, 2.

25. Walter LaFeber, "Technology and U.S. Foreign Relations," *Diplomatic History* 24 (Winter 2000): 13–14.

26. Fred Coleman, *The Decline and Fall of the Soviet Empire: Forty Years That Shook the World, From Stalin to Yeltsin* (New York: St. Martin's Press, 1996), 217–96; Andrzej Brzeski, "The End of Communist Economies" in *The Collapse of Communism*, ed. Lee Edwards (Stanford, Calif.: Hoover Institution Press, 2000), 129–37.

27. Coleman, *The Decline and Fall of the Soviet Empire*, 346; Walter LaFeber, *America, Russia, and the Cold War, 1945–1992*, 7th ed (New York: McGraw-Hill, 1993), 345.

28. Michael Nelson, *War of the Black Heavens: The Battles of Western Broadcasting in the Cold War* (Syracuse, N.Y.: Syracuse University Press, 1997), 193–6.

29. LaFeber, *America, Russia*, 343–5.

30. Francis Fukuyama, "The End of History," *The National Interest* 16 (Summer 1989): 4.

31. R. J. Johnson, "The United States, the 'Triumph of Democracy' and the 'End of History'" in *The American Century: Consensus and Coercion in the Projection of American Power*, eds. David Slater and Peter J. Taylor (Oxford: Blackwell Publishers, 1999), 149–65; Peter G. Boyle, *American-Soviet Relations: From the Russian Revolution to the Fall of Communism* (London: Routledge, 1993), 227–48.

32. Alvin Z. Rubinstein, Albina Shayevich, and Boris Slotnikov, *The Clinton Foreign Policy Reader: Presidential Speeches with Commentary*, 16, Lake quoted on page 26. See also David E. Sanger, "Economic Engine for Foreign Policy," *The New York Times*, December 28, 2000, A1, A12.

33. Jeffrey Sachs, *The Economic Transformation of Eastern Europe: The Case of Poland* (Memphis, Tenn.: P. K. Seidman Foundation, 1991), iii–iv, xi–xii, 108; Stanley Fischer, "Russia and the Soviet Union Then and Now" in *The Transition in Eastern Europe, Volume I: Country Studies*, eds. Olivier Jean Blanchard, Kenneth A. Froot, and Jeffrey D. Sachs (Chicago: University of Chicago Press, 1994), 240–1.

34. Thomas G. Paterson, J. Garry Clifford, and Kenneth J. Hagan, *American Foreign Relations: A History, Since 1895*, 5th ed. (Boston: Houghton Mifflin Company, 2000), 469, 472; Juliet Johnson, *A Fistful of Rubles: The Rise and Fall of the Russian Banking System* (Ithaca, N.Y.: Cornell University Press, 2000); Janine R. Wedel, "Tainted Transactions: Harvard, the Chubais Clan, and Russia's Ruin," *The National Interest*, 59 (Spring 2000): 24–34.

35. John Robert Greene, *The Presidency of George Bush* (Lawrence: University of Kansas Press, 2000), 93–7; Andrew Rosenthal, "Bush Called Ready to Renew China Trade Status for a Year," *New York Times*, May 23, 1990, A1; William G. Hyland, *Clinton's World: Remaking American Foreign Policy* (Westport, Conn.: Praeger Publishers, 1999), 110–15; Rubenstein, Shayevich, and Slotnikov, *The Clinton Foreign Policy Reader*, 112. Clinton and other administration spokespersons liked to stress the jobs created by exports, not the positions lost to imports. But, some industries – especially apparel – lost hundreds of thousands of jobs as imports from China soared.

36. Linda Jo Calloway, "High Tech Comes to War Coverage: Uses of Information and Communications Technology for Television Coverage in the Gulf War" in *The 1,000 Hour War: Communication in the Gulf*, eds. Thomas A. McCain and Leonard Shyles (Westport, Conn.: Greenwood Press, 1994), 56. See also Greene, *The Presidency of George Bush*, 109–39.

37. Ingrid Volkmer, *News in the Global Sphere: A Study of CNN and Its Impact on Global Communication* (Luton, U.K.: University of Luton, 1999).

38. Robert Goldberg and Gerald Jay Goldberg, *Citizen Turner: The Wild Rise of an American Tycoon* (New York: Harcourt Brace and Company, 1998), 399, 400, also 398; Brands, *Masters of Enterprise*, 275, also 276–91; Don M. Flournoy, *CNN World Report: Ted Turner's International News Coup* (London: John Libbey & Company 1992), 1–2, 5–14; Royce J. Ammon, *Global Television and the Shaping of World Politics: CNN, Telediplomacy, and Foreign Policy* (Jefferson, N.C.: McFarland and Company, 2001).

39. David L. Swanson and Rebecca A. Carrier, "Global Pictures, Local Stories: The Beginning of Desert Storm as Constructed by Television News Around

the World" in *The 1,000 Hour War: Communications in the Gulf*, eds. Thomas A. McCain and Leonard Shyles (Westport, Conn.: Greenwood Press; 1994), 129–32; Greene, *The Presidency of George Bush*, 175.

40. Yasumasa Kuroda, "Bush's New World Order: A Structural Analysis of Instability and Conflict in the Gulf" in *The Gulf War and the New World Order*, eds. Tareq Y. Ismael and Jacqueline S. Ismael (Gainesville: University of Florida Press, 1994), 53–4; Malcolm Hayward, "The Making of the New World Order: The Role of the Media" in *The Gulf War and the New World Order*, eds. Tareg Y. Ismael (Gainesville: University of Florida Press, 1994), 236.

41. Marie Lavigne, *The Economics of Transition: From Socialist Economy to Market Economy*, 2nd ed. (New York: St. Martin's Press, 1999), 203–63; Roger Manser, *Failed Transitions: The Eastern European Economy and Environment Since the Fall of Communism* (New York: The New Press, 1993), 39–69.

42. John McCormick, *The European Union: Politics and Policies* (Boulder, Colo.: Westview Press, 1999), 285; William Molle, *The Economics of European Integration: Theory, Practice, Policy*, 3rd ed. (Aldershot, U.K.: Ashgate, 1997), 48–9; Mike Artis and Norman Lee, *The Economics of the European Union*, 2nd ed. (New York: Oxford University Press, 1997), 21; David Wood and Birol A. Yesilada, *The Emerging European Union* (White Plains, N.Y.: Longman, 2001), 184–7; Michael J. Baun, *An Imperfect Union: The Maastricht Treaty and the New Politics of European Integration* (Boulder, Colo: Westview Press, 1996); Christopher Piening, *Global Europe: The European Union in World Affairs* (Boulder, Colo.: Lynne Rienner Publishers, 1997), 103; LaFeber, *America, Russia*, 347; Dianne Kunz, *Butter and Guns: America's Cold War Economic Diplomacy* (New York: The Free Press, 1997), 317; Edward S. Kaplan, *American Trade Policy, 1923–1995* (Westport, Conn.: Greenwood Press, 1996), 56–60.

43. Carl Hiaasen, *Team Rodent: How Disney Devours the World* (New York: The Ballantine Publishing Group, 1998), 10; Robin Allan, *Walt Disney and Europe: European Influences on the Animated Feature Films of Walt Disney* (Bloomington: Indiana University Press, 1999), 257–9; Joe Flower, *Prince of the Magic Kingdom: Michael Eisner and the Remaking of Disney* (New York: John Wiley and Sons, 1991), 243; Michael D. Eisner, *Work in Progress* (New York: Random House, 1998), 228, 262–3, 265, 284–8; Timothy Belknap, "Europe's Struggling Travel Mecca Heads Straight for Tomorrowland," *Business Week*, September 18, 2000, 4.

44. Eisner, *Work in Progress*, 283, also 271–4. See also Hiaasen, *Team Rodent*, 20; Ron Grover, *The Disney Touch: Disney, ABC & the Quest for the World's Greatest Media Empire*, rev. ed. (Chicago: Irwin Professional Publishing, 1997), 236–47, 302; Alan Bryman, "Global Disney" in *The American Century: Consensus and Coercion in the Projection of American Power*, eds. David Slater, and Peter J. Taylor (Oxford: Blackwell, 1999), 261–70. Disney was careful to cultivate a clean image abroad, as well as incorporate European culture into the park. Eisner changed the initial design to include art nouveau detail on buildings, Paris Metro signs on streets, and gardens and fountains. Disney thus returned to its European roots, with castles, formal gardens, and a Jules Verne spaceship. Moreover, when taking French lessons in Paris, he learned

how inaccurate translations were in film. He thus ordered Disney the world over to review any voice used on a company program as well as to dub in legitimate colloquial expressions.

45. T. J. Pempel, "Introduction" in *The Politics of the Asian Economic Crisis*, ed. T. J. Pempel (Ithaca, N.Y.: Cornell University Press, 1999), 5.

46. Anis Chowdhury and Iyanatul Islam, *The Newly Industrializing Economies of East Asia* (London: Routledge, 1993), 7–17, 72–86, 108–13; World Bank, *The East Asian Miracle: Economic Growth and Public Policy* (New York: Oxford University Press, 1993).

47. Jeffrey A. Hart, *Rival Capitalists: International Competitiveness in the United States, Japan, and Western Europe* (Ithaca, N.Y.: Cornell University Press, 1992), 238, 248; Maryann Keller, *Rude Awakening: The Rise, Fall, and Struggle for Recovery of General Motors* (New York: Morrow, 1989), 257. See also William S. Dietrich, *In the Shadow of the Rising Sun: the Political Roots of American Economic Decline* (University Park, Pa: Pennsylvania State University Press, 1991), 222.

48. Sympathetic to Sematech is Martin and Susan Tolchin, *Selling Our Security: The Erosion of America's Assets* (New York: Knopf, 1992), 195–200. However, Richard K. Lester concluded that Sematech "played a modest role in the semi-conductor industry's turnaround (though probably a larger one in the recovery in the equipment industry." Lester, *Productive Edge: How U.S. Industries Are Pointing the Way to a New Era of Economic Growth* (New York: Norton, 1998), 130.

49. Anthony DiFilippo, *Cracks in the Alliance: Science, Technology, and the Evolution of U.S.-Japan Relations* (Aldershot, U.K.: Ashgate, 1997); data from Raymond J. Mataloni, Jr., "U.S. Multinational Companies Operations in 1998," *Survey of Current Business* 80 (7) (July 2000): 34.

50. William T. Ziemba and Sandra L. Schwartz, *Power Japan: How and Why the Japanese Economy Works* (Chicago: Probus, 1992), 179, 180.

51. Michael Schaller, *Altered States: The United States and Japan Since the Occupation* (New York: Oxford University Press, 1997), 255.

52. Kunz, *Butter and Guns*, 315; Pat Choate, *Agents of Influence: How Japan's Lobbyists in the United States Manipulate America's Political and Economic System* (New York: Knopf, 1990); Michael Crichton, *Rising Sun* (New York: Knopf, 1992).

53. Walter LaFeber, *The Clash: U.S.-Japanese Relations Throughout History* (New York: W. W. Norton & Company, 1997), 393–4. See also Ryuzo Sato, Rama V. Ramachandran, and Myra Aaronson, eds., *Trade and Investment in the 1990s: Experts Debate on Japan-U.S. Issues* (New York: New York University Press, 1996); Leonard J. Schoppa, *Bargaining with Japan: What American Pressure Can and Cannot Do* (New York: Columbia University Press, 1997); "Eyeing the Debt Mountain," *The Economist*, May 12, 2001, 46.

54. Alan S. Lederman and Bobbe Hirsh, *The NAFTA Guide: How NAFTA Will Affect You and Your Business* (San Diego: Harcourt Brace Professional Publishing, 1995), 1–3, 6–8.

55. Jeremiah Novak, "The Trilateral Controversy," *Christian Science Monitor*, April 17, 1980, 12; Clayton Jones, "Reagan's 'North American Accord'

Has Support . . . ," *Christian Science Monitor*, December 26, 1980, 4; Stephen Lande, "Foreign Investment in NAFTA," *Business Mexico* [General News: Magazines and Journals. Online. Lexis–Nexis Academic Universe. August 30, 2002]; Marc Levinson, "Let's Have No More Free-Trade Deals, Please," *Newsweek* 70:4, August 17, 1992, 40; M. Delal Baer, "North American Free Trade," *Foreign Affairs* 70:4 (Fall 1991): 132; John R. MacArthur, *The Selling of "Free Trade": NAFTA, Washington, and the Subversion of American Democracy* (New York: Hill & Wang, 2000), 133–7, 276.

56. MacArthur, *Selling of "Free Trade,"* 256–7, also 223, 264–6, 306. See also Susan Aaronson, *Taking Trade to the Streets: The Lost History of Public Efforts to Shape Globalization* (Ann Arbor: University of Michigan Press, 2001), 137.

57. Kaplan, *American Trade Policy*, 151, also 139–53. See also Kunz, *Butter and Guns*, 317; Greene, *The Presidency of George Bush*, 170–1; Hyland, *Clinton's World*, 68–71, 73–4; MacArthur, *Selling of "Free Trade,"* 277.

58. As it turned out, Clinton scaled back Rubin's plan, and both the International Monetary Fund and the Bank for International Settlements joined.

59. Carlos Salas, "The Impact of NAFTA on Wages and Incomes in Mexico," EPI Briefing Paper (April 2001), see http://www.epinet.org/briefingpapers/nafta01/mx.html. U.S. earnings on services and investments probably reduced the impact of the NAFTA merchandise deficit in 2000. In 1999, these earnings offset about half of the merchandise deficit. U.S. Department of Commerce, *Survey of Current Business* 80 (7) (July 2000): 118–19.

60. Hyland, *Clinton's World*, 71–2. Trade data from http://www.census.gov/foreign-trade/Press-Release/2000pr/12; Farhan Haq, "Mexico: U.S. Bank Urged Action Against Zapatistas," Inter Press Service (February 13, 1995) [World News. North/South America News Sources, Online, Lexis-Nexis Academic Universe. August 30, 2002]. For Robert E. Scott, "NAFTA's Hidden Costs," (April 2001), see http://www.epinet.org/briefingpapers/nafta01/us.html.

61. Lederman and Hirsh, *The NAFTA Guide*, 7–8; Tony Emerson, "The Great Walls," *Newsweek*, April 23, 2001, 40; Patricia Kranz, "A Novel Trade Deal," *Business Week*, December 13, 1999, 68.

62. Jagdish Bhagwati, "The Capital Myth: The Difference between Trade in Widgets and Dollars," *Foreign Affairs* 77:3 (May–June 1998):6. On the power of markets and the "electronic herd," see Friedman, *The Lexus and the Olive Tree*, 107–10.

63. Khosrow Fatemi, "New Realities in the Global Trading Arena" in *The North American Free Trade Agreement*, eds. Khosrow Fatemi and Dominick Salvatore (New York: Pergamon, 1994), 9; Dominick Salvatore, "NAFTA and the EC: Similarities and Differences," op. cit., 28–30; Robert C. Shelburne, "The Effects of NAFTA and the ATPA on the Caribbean Basin Countries," op. cit., 42–3; M. Hosein Abghari, "NAFTA and the Single European Act: Economic Impact and Implications for U.S. Banks," op. cit., 220–8; Shahid S. Hamid, Roswell E. Mathis, III, and Krishnan Dandapani, "The Impact of NAFTA on the North American Equity Markets," op. cit., 167–8; Pochara Theerathorn and Carlos Alcerreca-Joaquin, "Linkages in the North American Stock Markets: A Test of Cointegration and a Modeling of Error-correction

Mechanisms," op. cit., 181–2; Patricia H. Hall, "The Effect of the Announcement of NAFTA on a Cross-section of U.S. Security Prices", op. cit., 190–2.

64. McDonald quoted in Alfred E. Eckes, ed., *Revisiting U.S. Trade Policy* (Athens: Ohio University Press, 2000), 164; see also 170–2 and comments of Jules Katz, 169. On the Tokyo Round, see Eckes, *Opening the American Market*, 257–77; Kaplan, *American Trade Policy*, 89–108; Steve Dryden, *Trade Warriors: USTR and the American Crusade for Free Trade* (New York: Oxford University Press, 1995), 167–206, 231–53.

65. Michael K. Young, "Dispute Resolution in the Uruguay Round: Lawyers Triumph over Diplomats," *International Lawyer* 29 (Summer 1995):389.

66. Christopher Arup, *The New World Trade Organization and Agreements: Globalizing Law Through Services and Intellectual Property* (Cambridge: Cambridge University Press, 2000), 178–83; Ulick Bourke, "WTO and WIPO Agree to Joint Management of World's IP Rights," *IP Worldwide* (July/August 1996) [Legal News, Online, Lexis-Nexis Academic Universe, August 30, 2002]. For an Argentine perspective on these issues, see Carlos M. Correa, *Intellectual Property Rights, the WTO and Developing Countries: The TRIPS Agreement and Policy Options* (New York: Zed Books, 2000).

67. Bruce Stokes, "The Big Deal," *National Journal* 26:7 (February 12, 1994): 353; Keith M. Rockwell, "Uruguay Accord Leaves Many Issues Up in Air," *Journal of Commerce*, May 23, 1994, 8A. Regarding the WTO, see WTO, *Trading into the Future: WTO, The World Trade Organization* (Geneva: WTO Information and Media Relations Division, 1995); statement of Ambassador Charlene Barshefsky regarding Basic Telecom Negotiations, February 15, 1997, online at http://www.ustr.gov/html/barshefsky.html.

Chapter 10

1. George H. W. Bush, "Remarks at Signing for Paper Market Access Agreement with Japan," April 23, 1992, online at http://bushlibrary.tamu.edu/papers/1992/92042301.html; *Public Papers of the Presidents*, 1999 (Washington, D.C.: GPO, 1999), 272. Clinton quoted from McKinley's last public speech on September 5, 1901. See James D. Richardson, comp., *A Compilation of the Messages and Papers of the Presidents* (New York: Bureau of National Literature, 1917), 6619–20. George W. Bush "Remarks by President to the World Bank," July 17, 2001, online at http://www.whitehouse.gov/news/releases/2001/07/text/20010717-1.html.

2. *Business Week* concluded in April 2000 that "Americans are deeply divided about globalization and free-trade pacts. In the abstract, they like both concepts; 64 percent of those polled think globalization benefits the U.S. economy, and 68 percent think U.S. consumers gain. But the public is split about whether the advancing global economy hurts the environment and jobs. And 69 percent believe that trade agreements with low-wage countries drive down U.S. wages." "BW/Harris Poll: Globalization: What Americans Are Worried About," *Businessweek online*, April 24, 2000.

3. According to the U.S. Internet Council, use of the Internet grew from 90,000 in 1993 to 304 million in 2000. Lori Martin, "State of Internet 2000,"

Boardwatch Magazine XIV:11 (November 2000):174–5. In November 2001, the Internet Council claimed a half billion users worldwide with native English speakers representing only 45 percent of all Internet users. Press Release, November 12, 2001, online at http://www.usic.org/.

4. Jane Perlez, "U.S. Envoy Campaigns for Trade Pacts on Asian Trip," *New York Times*, April 7, 2002, I:4; Evelyn Iritani, "Highest Paid Jobs Latest U.S. Export," *Los Angeles Times*, April 2, 2002, A-1; Malou A. Buenconsejo, "Asian Relocation – Engineers Follow the Money," *Electronic Engineering Times*, October 29, 2001, 40. See also Daniel H. Pink, *Free Agent Nation: How America's New Independent Workers Are Transforming the Way We Live* (New York: Warner Books, 2001).

5. "French Say Globalized Economy Worsens Social Divide," Agence France Press, October 6, 1999, Lexis-Nexis; "Culture Wars," *The Economist*, September 12, 1998, 97; John Micklethwait and Adrian Wooldridge, *A Future Perfect: The Challenge and Hidden Promise of Globalization* (New York: Crown, 2000), 186–91. For a Canadian perspective, see "Disney's Dark Side: The Pervasive Empire Is Corrupting our Cultural Heritage," *Canadian Business and Current Affairs* 7:48 (July 29, 1996):32–5.

6. William Shawcross, "Rupert Murdoch," *Time*, October 25, 1999, 116; Rupert Murdoch, "Dawn of the Convergent, Interactive Era," *Business Times*, (Singapore), September 17, 1993, 24; Tunku Varadarajan, "Bowing Low to China," *Wall Street Journal*, March 27, 2001, A-22.

7. Rory McCarthy, "Taliban: No Subversive Gateaux; As Titanic Fever Grips Kabul, Harline Militia Proves No Match for ... Iced Cakes," *The Guardian* (London), November 24, 2000, 20; Scott Peterson "Hollywood Delivered at Iranian Doorsteps," *Christian Science Monitor*, July 18, 2000, 9; Peter Goodspeed, "Bold Youth Defy Iran's Rigid Rules," *Chicago Sun Times*, June 3, 2001, 27; Neil Strauss, "The Pop Life: Iran's Shadowy Tape Man, Spreading What's Forbidden," *New York Times*, October 5, 2000, E-1; Barry Bearak, "Kandahar Journal; This Job Is Truly Scary: The Taliban Are Watching," *New York Times*, June 1, 2001, A-4.

8. Paul Farhi, "American Pop Penetrates Worldwide," *Washington Post*, October 25, 1998, A-1; "Salman Rushdie Defends American Culture, Globalization," Agence France Press, March 5, 1999 [News Wires, Online, Lexis-Nexis Academic Universe, August 30, 2002]; David Rothkopf, "In Praise of Cultural Imperialism? Effects of Globalization on Culture," *Foreign Policy*, 107, June 22, 1997, 38–53; Derek N. Shearer, "Hollywood Belongs to the World," *Los Angeles Times*, May 13, 1998, 9-B; Michael Elliott, "A Target Too Good to Resist," *Newsweek*, January 31, 2000, 20; Christopher Parkes, "Farewell My Lovely: Hollywood Is Hollowing Out," *Financial Times*, April 4, 2002, 25; online at http://www.globalpolicy.org/globaliz/cultural/globcult.htm.

9. "Pokemon, Teletubbies and the 'Evils' of Globalization," *San Diego Union-Tribune*, December 1, 1999, B-7; "American Pop Penetrates Worldwide," *Washington Post*, October 25, 1998, A-1.

10. Rothkopf, "In Praise of Cultural Imperialism?" 38–53.

11. UNCTAD, *World Investment Report 2000* (Geneva: UNCTAD, 2001), 1; "A Future As Momentous as Its Past," *MMR* 19:4 (February 25, 2002):11.

12. Hilary French, *Vanishing Borders – Protecting the Planet in the Age of Globalization* (New York: Norton, 2000). We used chapter available on the web site.]; [http://www.worldwatch.org/pubs/ea/van1.html]; Matthew Miller, "Who Lost Capitalism?" *U.S. News and World Report* , October 12, 1998, 46.

13. French, *Vanishing Borders*.

14. World Tourism Organization, "World Tourism Stalls in 2001," press release January 29, 2002, online at http://www.world-tourism.org; UN High Commissioner on Refugees, online at http://www.unhcr.ch/cgi-bin/texis/vtx/home?page=publ; James Lardner, "Give Us Your Wired Elite!," *U.S. News & World Report*, July 10, 2000, 34; "The Uses of Strangers," *The Economist*, March 31, 2001, 26–9; Harry Maurer, "The Educated Can't Wait to Leave," *Business Week*, February 28, 2000, 4; Gabriel Escobar, "Immigrants Ranks Tripled in 29 Years," *Washington Post*, January 9, 1999, A-1.

15. Robert Went, *Globalization: Neoliberal Challenge, Radical Responses* (London: Pluto Press, 2000), 7–22; Jane Fraser and Jeremy Oppenheim, "What's New About Globalization?" *The McKinsey Quarterly* 2 (1997):169–79; General Electric, *GE Annual Report 2001* (Fairfield, Conn.: GE, 2002), 4.

16. Standard & Poor's Corporate Descriptions, online at http://web.lexis-nexis.com/universe/document?; Robert Goldman and Stephen Papson, *Nike Culture: The Sign of the Swoosh* (London: SAGE Publications, 1998), 4, also 5.

17. James B. Twitchell, *20 Ads That Shook the World: The Century's Most Ground-breaking Advertising and How It Changed Us All* (New York: Crown Publishers, 2000), 207, 215; H. W. Brand, *Masters of Enterprise: Giants of American Business From John Jacob Astor and J. P. Morgan to Bill Gates and Oprah Winfrey* (New York: The Free Press, 1999), 264, also 256–63.

18. "Hitting the Wall: Nike and International Labor Practices," Harvard Business School (Case 9-700-047, Rev. September 15, 2000); Goldman and Papson, *Nike Culture*, 6–13; Brands, *Masters of Enterprise*, 264–5.

19. Walter LaFeber, *Michael Jordan and the New Capitalism* (New York: W. W. Norton & Company, 1999), 14–15, 49–67, 102–9, 144–51.

20. Ross Newhan, "Japanese Success Points Up World of Possibilities," *Los Angeles Times*, April 8, 2001, D-10; Mark Elliott, "Globalization's Got No Game; In Professional Sport, the Big Teams Think International But Act Local," *Time*, June 4, 2001, 30. See also Alexander Wolff, *Big Game, Small World: A Basketball Adventure* (New York: Warner Books, 2002).

21. Jeffrey Frankel, "The Crusade for Free Trade: Evaluating Clinton's International Economic Policy," *Foreign Affairs* 80:2 (March–April 2001):255; Jagdish Bhagwati, "The Capital Myth; The Difference between Trade in Widgets and Dollars," *Foreign Affairs* 77:3 (May–June 1998):7.

22. T. J. Pempel, "Introduction" in *The Politics of the Asian Economic Crisis*, ed. T. J. Pempel (Ithaca, N.Y.: Cornell University Press, 1999), 1–9. For the debate on capital account convertibility, see "Capital Controversies," *The Economist*, May 23, 1998, 72. Also critical of open capital markets for developing countries was former World Bank chief economist Joseph E. Stiglitz, *Globalization and its Discontents* (New York: Norton, 2002), 53–88.

23. Joseph J. Norton, "A 'New' International Financial Architecture," *International Lawyer* 33 (Winter 1999): 891; Joseph Stiglitz, "What I Learned at the World Economic Crisis," *New Republic*, April 17–24, 2000, 56; Bruce Cumings, "The Asian Crisis, Democracy, and the End of 'Late' Development' " in *The Politics of the Asian Economic Crisis*, ed. T. J. Pempel (Ithaca, N.Y.: Cornell University Press, 1999), 29; Greenspan testimony to House Committee on Banking and Financial Services, Jan. 30, 1998, online at http://www.federalreserve.gov/boarddocs/testimony/1998/19980130.htm.

24. Gary Hamilton, "Asian Business Networks in Transition: or, What Alan Greenspan Does Not Know about the Asian Business Crisis" in *The Politics of the Asian Crisis*, ed. T. J. Pempel (Ithaca, N.Y.: Cornell University Press, 1999), 47–9. See in particular Greenspan's paper, "The Globalization of Finance," presented October 14, 1997, to the Cato Institute and published in the *Cato Journal*. See http://www.cato.org/pubs/journal/cj17n3-1.html. Also, see Greenspan speech remarks on May 7, 1998, online at http://www.federalreserve.gov/boarddocs/speeches/19980507.htm.

25. Hamilton, "Asian Business," 49–59.

26. David B. Sicilia and Jeffrey L. Cruikshank, *The Greenspan Effect: Words That Move the World's Markets* (New York: McGraw-Hill, 2000), ix.

27. Justin Martin, *Greenspan: The Man Behind the Money* (Cambridge, Mass.: Perseus Publishing, 2000), 221.

28. Martin, *Greenspan*, pp. 10–15; Federal Reserve Board, "Alan Greenspan," online at http://www.federalreserve.gov/bios/Greenspan/htm; Steven K. Beckner, *Back From the Brink: The Greenspan Years* (New York: John Wiley & Sons, 1996), 9–20; *Encarta Encyclopedia*, "Greenspan, Alan," http://encarta.msn.com/find/Concise.asp?ti=04B6B000.

29. Sicilia and Cruikshank, *The Greenspan Effect*, 112.

30. Sicilia and Cruikshank, *The Greenspan Effect*, 138, also 131–3, 137. See also Bob Woodward, *Maestro: Greenspan's Fed and the American Boom* (New York: Simon and Schuster, 2000), 189–90, 196.

31. UNCTAD, *World Investment Report 2001* (Geneva: UNCTAD, 2001), 23–5. Generally accepted international corruption rankings, prepared by Transparency International, placed Mexico in fifty-first place among some ninety nations, tied with Panama, but behind Bulgaria and Colombia. Canada was in seventh place; the United States was in sixteenth. See http://www.transparency.org/documents/cpi/2001/cpi2001.html#cpi. On the significance of NAFTA, *Business Week* was generally optimistic, but the Economic Policy Institute and Citizen Trade Watch continued to advance negative critiques. "NAFTA's Scorecard: So Far, So Good," *Business Week*, July 9, 2001, 54.

32. Quoted in Robert D. Schulzinger, *American Diplomacy in the Twentieth Century* (New York: Oxford University Press, 2001), 19.

33. William H. Miller, "The Split over Global Warming," *Industry Week*, June 8, 1998, 10; Patrick Crow, "Buenos Aires Climate Change Meet Unlikely to Achieve Breakthroughs," *Oil & Gas Journal*, November 2, 1998, 27.

34. Thomas L. Friedman, *The Lexus and the Olive Tree: Understanding Globalization* (New York: Farrar Straus Giroux, 1999).

35. John Gray, *False Dawn: The Delusions of Global Capitalism* (New York: The New Press, 1998); William Greider, *One World, Ready or Not: The Manic Logic of Global Capitalism* (New York: Simon & Schuster, 1997).

36. Lori Wallach and Michell Sforza, *The WTO: Five Years of Reasons to Resist Corporate Globalization* (New York: Seven Stories Press, 1999), 79, 13, 14, 15.

37. Alfred E. Eckes, Jr., "Backlash Against Globalization?" *Global Economic Quarterly* 1 (June 2000): 117–22. See also Susan Ariel Aaronson, *Taking Trade to the Streets: The Lost History of Public Efforts to Shape Globalization* (Ann Arbor: University of Michigan, 2000). The debate over globalization did not subside. In February 2001, NAFTA readied to implement its decision to allow Mexican trucks, most of which were deemed unsafe by U.S. standards, to roll freely into America along American highways. The new president, George W. Bush, had backed NAFTA's decision during the election campaign as a way of bolstering the reformist Mexican government of Vicente Fox. Wallach, meanwhile, had supported Clinton's delay of the agreement. She had never liked NAFTA. The side agreements on labor and environment were a sham because they offered weak enforcement mechanisms, she held. Free-trade agreements of this sort, between two nations of such unequal economic status, meant sacrifices on the part of the United States and gains for global capital operating in Mexico. But like the many issues touching on globalization, the trucking episode also addressed the limits of sovereignty, economic opportunity, common standards, and distribution of wealth.

38. U.S. Central Intelligence Agency, *Global Trends 2015: A Dialogue About the Future with Nongovernment Experts*, NIC 2000–02 (Washington, D.C.: CIA, December 2000), 8–15, 83–4.

39. Mark Galeotti, "Crimes of the New Millennium," *Jane's Intelligence Review* 12:8 (August 1, 2000); Mark Galeotti, "The New World of Organized Crime," *Jane's Intelligence Review* 12:9 (September 1, 2000), online at http://www.Janes.com. See also, Stephen Flynn, "Protecting the Homeland," *Foreign Affairs* 81:1 (January/February 2002), 60–74; John Kerry, *The New War: The Web of Crime that Threatens America's Security* (New York: Simon & Schuster, 1997).

40. CIA, *Global Trends 2015*, 41–2; Gill Walt, "Globalization of International Health," *Lancet* 351 (February 7, 1998): 434–7; Christopher P. Howson, Harvey V. Fineberg, and Barry R. Bloom, "The Pursuit of Global Health," *Lancet* 351 (February 21, 1998): 586–90; Laurie Garrett, "The Return of Infectious Disease," *Foreign Affairs* (January–February 1996):66. See also "When a Body Can Be Worth $220,000," *Irish Times*, March 15, 2001, 15.

41. For a discussion of how globalization had changed diplomacy, see Center for Strategic and International Studies (CSIS), *Reinventing Diplomacy in the Information Age*, October 9, 1998, online at http://www.csis.org/.

42. For a vision of clashing futures, see Shell International, *People and Connections: Global Scenarios to 2020*, Public Summary (London: Shell International, 2002), see http://www.shell.com/scenarios. See also David Brooks, "Looking Back Tomorrow," *The Atlantic Monthly*, April 2002, 22.

Index